The Forty Sieges
of Constantinople

The Forty Sieges of Constantinople

The Great City's Enemies and Its Survival

John D Grainger

Pen & Sword
MILITARY

First published in Great Britain in 2022 by
Pen & Sword Military
An imprint of
Pen & Sword Books Ltd
Yorkshire – Philadelphia

Typeset by Mac Style
Printed and bound in the UK by CPI Group (UK) Ltd,
Croydon, CR0 4YY.

Pen & Sword Books Limited incorporates the imprints of Atlas,
Archaeology, Aviation, Discovery, Family History, Fiction, History,
Maritime, Military, Military Classics, Politics, Select, Transport,
True Crime, Air World, Frontline Publishing, Leo Cooper, Remember
When, Seaforth Publishing, The Praetorian Press, Wharncliffe
Local History, Wharncliffe Transport, Wharncliffe True Crime
and White Owl.

For a complete list of Pen & Sword titles please contact

PEN & SWORD BOOKS LIMITED
47 Church Street, Barnsley, South Yorkshire, S70 2AS, England
E-mail: enquiries@pen-and-sword.co.uk
Website: www.pen-and-sword.co.uk

Or

PEN AND SWORD BOOKS
1950 Lawrence Rd, Havertown, PA 19083, USA
E-mail: Uspen-and-sword@casematepublishers.com
Website: www.penandswordbooks.com

Contents

Introduction: The City   viii

Part I: Byzantion   1

Chapter 1   Enemy from the East – The Persians   3

Chapter 2   Enemies from the South – the Greeks   11

Chapter 3   Enemy from the West – the Macedonians   24

Chapter 4   Enemies from the North-West and the East –
                  The Galatians and the Seleukids   39

Chapter 5   Enemy from the East – Antiochos II   49

Interlude I: Polybios on Byzantion   51

Chapter 6   Destruction from the West – The Romans   55

Chapter 7   Enemies from the North – Goths and Heruli   65

Chapter 8   Conqueror from the West –
                  Constantine the Great   71

Interlude II: The Five Walls of the City   82

Part II: Constantinople   89

Chapter 9   Enemy from the North-West – the Goths   91

Chapter 10   An Enemy from Within – Vitalian   95

Chapter 11   Enemy from the North – the Kutrighur Huns   100

Chapter 12   Enemies from the Northwest, the East, and from
                  Within – Avars, Persians and Greeks   103

Chapter 13   Enemies from the East – Muslim Arabs   115

Chapter 14   Two Civil Wars: Artabasdas versus Constantine V,
                Thomas the Slav versus Michael II   126

Interlude III: Conversions   131

Chapter 15   Enemy from the Northwest – The Bulgars   135

Chapter 16   Enemy from the North – the Rus   142

Chapter 17   Enemies from the West – the First Crusade   147

Chapter 18   Enemies from the West – the Fourth Crusade   155

Interlude IV: The Latin Empire   173

Chapter 19   Recovery from the East –
                The Empire of Nikaia   178

Chapter 20   Enemies within – Civil Wars   188

Chapter 21   An Encircling Enemy – The Ottoman Turks   194

Chapter 22   Success for the Ottoman Turks   207

Interlude V: Islamization of the City   224

Chapter 23   Enemy from the Balkans – the Bulgarians   229

Chapter 24   Enemies from the Sea –
                The Great War Allies   239

Bibliography   249
Notes   253
Index   268

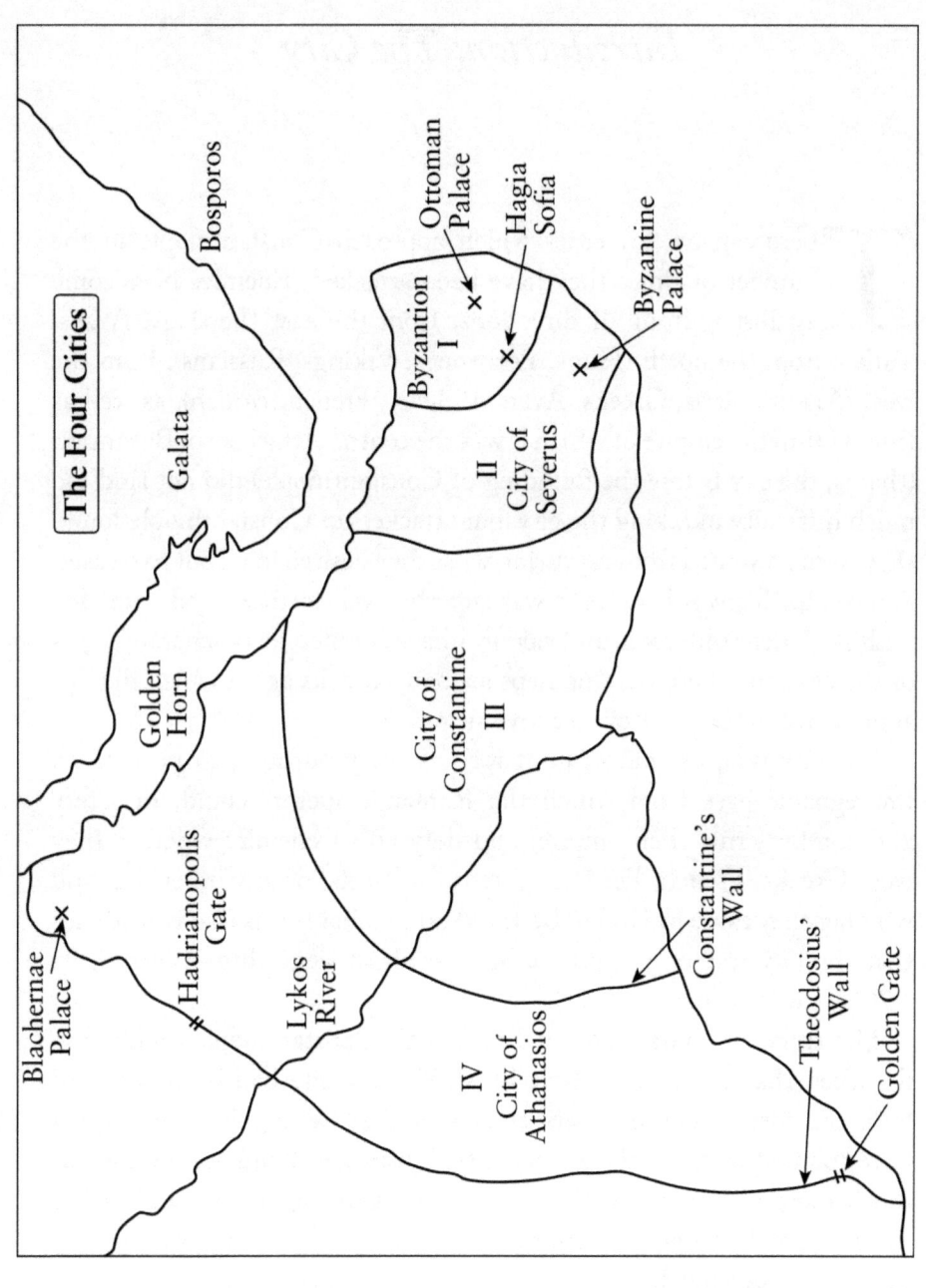

The Four Cities

Bosporos

Byzantion
I

Ottoman
Palace
×

Hagia
Sofia
×

Byzantine
Palace
×

City of
Severus
II

Galata

Golden
Horn

City of
Constantine
III

Constantine's
Wall

Blachernae
Palace
×

Hadrianopolis
Gate

Lykos
River

City of
Athanasios
IV

Theodosius'
Wall

Golden Gate

Introduction: The City

There can be few cities which approach Constantinople in the number of times they have been attacked. Enemies have come against it from all directions, from the east (Persians, Arabs, Turks), from the north (Huns, Pechenegs, Vikings, Russians), from the west (Macedonians, Greeks, Avars, Bulgars, French, British), as well as from within the empire of which it was the centre. Attackers of Byzantion (that is, the city before the founding of Constantinople) did not find too much difficulty in taking the city, but attackers of Constantinople found they were prevented from capturing what they desired in all but two cases. Above all, this was because it was superbly well fortified and defended with skill, determination, and valour. I have counted forty separate sieges of the city, and there were perhaps as many attacks again which did not actually reach the stage of an active siege.

The city was, of course, built for that very purpose, to provide an impregnable base from which the Roman emperors could, in safety and comfort, rule their empire, and defy all its enemies whether they were Greeks, French, Persians, Arabs, or Turks, or any other foe, and whether they came by land or by sea. And so reliable was that confidence that the city was only captured as a result of siege three times in its 1,700-year existence.

The story, of course, cannot begin with Constantinople's founding, for when that event took place, in AD 324, the site had been occupied by a city for a thousand years already, and some of the forty sieges I have counted were attacks on that city, Byzantion. Being smaller, it was much more vulnerable, with a less determined population, and facing much more formidable enemies, this version of the city was not so successfully defended.

Byzantion had been founded as a colony of Greek settlers organized by, and sent out from, Megara in central Greece at some uncertain date in the seventh century BC.[1] They took control of the headland between the Sea of Marmara to the south and the inlet called the Golden Horn to the north, with the Bosporos flowing past on the third, eastern, side. The headland is relatively high, connected with the mainland by lower land, and thus provided a naturally fortifiable place which was rapidly improved by a wall enclosing the new city on the land side.

This was necessary from the start because the site had already been occupied by a group of Thracians (and by others before them back to the Neolithic Age). Thracians were the people who occupied the European land on the west of the Straits and had spread across the Strait to the Asian coast. Indeed, the Greeks later claimed that the city was called after the king of that place, a Thracian called Byzas – certainly a Thracian name – unless he was a Megarian, or the offspring of the gods; the Greek imagination was clearly busy at obscuring the city's Thracian past.[2] It may be assumed that, in common with several other Greek colonies around the Sea of Marmara, this theft of Thracian land was resented, and continued to be resented for decades afterwards, and it may be further assumed that hostilities followed. We have, however, no details, but it is quite likely that attacks took place on the walled city, possibly even brief sieges, though the Thracians did not have the capability to mount lengthy attacks. It may even have been by a siege that the first Greek settlers secured the site. (Thus there were probably more than forty sieges of the city, but only those recorded can be discussed.)

This was the city which was occasionally besieged and captured, occupied and sacked, from the time of its foundation as a Greek colony until it fell foul of one of the more brutal Roman emperors, Septimius Severus, in AD 193. His siege lasted two years and ended with the physical and legal destruction of the city; he then followed this by the subsequent re-foundation of the city, but on the lower land between the original city and the inland, giving a different name, which no-one remembers, nor ever used, so far as can be seen. This new situation made it impossible to defend the new city with any success. This was the place which, over a century later, Constantine chose as his new imperial capital, but only after considering any number of other possible sites.

He had used a long series of cities, spread from York to Thessalonica, as his capitals during his slow, twenty-year-long conquest of the Empire. After eliminating Licinius, his last rival, he considered several places in the area around the Straits as possible sites for a city which would replace

Rome as the imperial capital. It was to be a Christian city, rather than pagan like Rome, which had a heavy weight of pre-Christian history and an obdurately pagan aristocracy to deter him. He had used Licinius' and Diocletian's capital at Nikomedia for a time, and where Constantine had lived as a youth. He considered Thessalonica and Troy and others in the region, but eventually, as the least bad site, he concluded that Byzantion would have to do. No other possible site was apparently perfect, for there was always some serious objection, geographical, territorial, a shortage of water or food resources, or a strong pagan presence. Byzantion, wrecked and humbled and scarcely recovered from Severus' siege even then, did not suffer from too many such objections.[3]

Constantine's city was large, certainly compared with the previous Byzantions. It included the size of the wrecked first colonial city; the weak, new, Severan city; and as much again of the land inland to the west.[4] A wall was a priority, and it was built in a curved line from the Golden Horn to the Marmara shore, but the precise line is not now certainly known. (No doubt it will be found eventually, but archaeology in the city is very difficult, and a discontinued wall which lasted less than a century is not a priority.) The city was always known from then on by his name – Constantinopolis, 'the city of Constantine' – though its official name, at least for some centuries, was 'New Rome'. (The Turks called it 'the city', as did the Byzantine Greeks, and so made it 'Istanbul'; I use that name from 1453, when the Turks captured it.)

Constantine equipped it with the public buildings considered necessary for a Greco-Roman city: the Senate House, a hippodrome, theatre, temples (though he built these as Christian churches), docks, warehouses, and so on – and a palace for himself and his administrators, built on part of the site of the original city, which was still littered with debris when this new city was being built. Private housing was assisted with imperial subsidies in order to attract a wealthy population, people whose needs and purchases could provide employment for the poor and customers for the shopkeepers. A food dole was organized, at the expense of that which had been allocated for many centuries to old Rome, for an expected recruited citizen population of 80,000. This was never fully taken up and was reduced to 40,000 later, whether because the population did not reach the planned figure, or the ration was reduced. The source of the food was always Egypt, and eventually, when Egypt fell to the Persians, the dole ended altogether. (The alternative supply, from Africa, had already become intermittent, and was at first directed at Rome.)

The city was decorated, as old Rome had been, by collecting trophies from the provinces of the Empire, including items from Delphi and Egypt, plus statues of the emperors, of course. The building of these things took decades to produce a really livable city – the church of Hagia Sofia, for example, took three or four decades to finish – and it was not until the 370s that an adequate water supply, by way of a new aqueduct instituted in the time of the Emperor Valens, was constructed.

Fairly soon the wall of Constantine's city was seen to be inadequate and badly sited. It was in the lower level and was overlooked by hills which were not too far away. In the early years of the fifth century the Emperor Theodosios II's praetorian prefect, Anthemius, arranged the building of the present walls, sited along those hills 1,500 metres to the west, further forward, of the existing wall. This was a project, to design and build the wall, which employed men whose expertise was the cumulation of several centuries of experience of building city walls and cities. Well-sited, high, with towers and walkways, the walls could be manned by a relatively small garrison, even though they were 7 kilometres long. It was a masterpiece of construction, and for eight centuries that wall was never breached, and only twice in its existence was it overwhelmed. The complex of walls even successfully defended the city into the twentieth century. (There was one main wall, but also others, including the sea wall, and an advanced wall, not to mention the naval defence.) It is to be noted that it was military requirements which forced the building of these new walls, not that the original city was crowded and needed more space. The land inside the walls was never fully occupied until the nineteenth century.[5]

The city was not just the place on land. With the sea on three sides it was inevitably a trading centre and a centre of naval power. This had been clear by 513 BC, when the Persian commander Megabazos remarked that its twin city on the east shore of the Bosporos, Kalchedon, must have been founded by blind settlers if they could ignore the better site across the water.[6] By then, a century and more after the foundation of the two cities, only seventeen years apart, Byzantion had far outstripped Kalchedon in wealth, and this was the basis of Megabazos' comment. But Kalchedon had been chosen by the first Greek settlers because it had a good supply of agricultural land, which was what the settlers wanted, whereas Byzantion was hilly and dry. Both were already occupied by Thracians when the Greeks arrived, and Thracian Kalchedon was more populous than 'Byzas' city' – the result of possessing that extensive agricultural land. In order to flourish Byzantion had to attract trade, and trade guaranteed wealth – it was Megabazos who was blind, at least to the purposes of the original Greek inhabitants.

The wall of Theodosios defined the city until the late nineteenth century. It was not sensible until then to build outside the walls, given the number of attacks the city had suffered, but in fact it was also not until late in that century that the land inside the walls was fully occupied. (The Turkish census did not include the extra-mural population of any size until after the 1850s.)[7] The population, as discovered by census in 1927 was 200,000 in the area within the walls. This gives the maximum possible population of the inter-vallum space, and it was clearly less than that for much of the city's history. Since the 1850s the city has expanded continually, so that 'Metropolitan Istanbul' (a bit of an oxymoron, but it will serve) now extends as far as Selymbria along the Marmara coast, includes the suburbs along the Bosporos to the north, and has engulfed the land east of the Strait, including Kalchedon and other places. Its gross population is now about 12,000,000 – a monster city, and so still one of the greatest in the world).

One of the purposes for extending the city's area by building the new walls, apart from the new walls being a better and stronger line of defence, was to enclose land which could be used to pasture animals and grow food – the real threat to the city in war was possible starvation through the extinction of food supplies. (The water supply was ensured by constructing large cisterns and Valens' aqueduct, though this latter would be the first target of besiegers.) Some extension took place northwards across the Golden Horn in the Middle Ages into the suburb of Galata, later Pera; similarly across the Bosporos, where Kalchedon became the Uskudar suburb, but the main city was always within Theodosios' walls, and indeed for much of the time the population was enclosed even within the line of Constantine's walls.

There was another element in the site and siting of the city, since supply by sea was almost always possible even in the tightest siege. Most enemies who attacked by land had no sea capability, and those who came by sea usually had no land forces with them of sufficient size to enforce a land siege – the sheer length of the Theodosian Wall was a defence in itself since an attacker would need a huge army to enforce a proper siege, and, as in Napoleonic Spain, in Thrace large armies starved. The only cases where the city fell were those in which the enemies were strong enough to field both an army and a navy, at least until wall-smashing cannon were developed, and in the final siege by the Turks in 1453, they had all three – a large army, dominating navy, and a powerful cannon force. Even so, its defendants – only about 7,000 of them – held out for weeks. This constraint for attackers had been evident even in the time of Byzantion. In most sieges supplies could be brought into the city by boat, hence the need for an attacker's navy, and in the fourth century BC Byzantion extended its city territory outside the walls to include lands on both shores of the Marmara, presumably for that very reason.

In fact, there was always another ready source of food supply even without access to food supplies from overseas. The Bosporos was a passageway for migratory tuna, who came through in such numbers that the Byzantines could catch them by the dozen with little effort. The fish, salted and processed, were a staple of the city's food supply at all times and were one of its major export products. The city did not produce much otherwise, at least until it was wealthy enough to support manufacturing, but its situation enabled it to develop as an entrepot, and when strong or desperate enough, it was able to enforce taxes on the passing shipping, though it took a couple of centuries for the taxation system to be applied, and then it was first done not by the Byzantines. In turn, this required the city to have a fleet of warships. The necessity for a navy was understood from the beginning, and it had sufficient ships to transport an army to attack a new Greek settlement at Perinthos along the north Marmara coast as early as 600 BC, no more than a generation or so after its own foundation. Together with an ally, the Byzantines fought the fleet from Samos which had come to rescue the besieged Perinthians. The Byzantines lost to the more professional Samians, but they had shown that they had a fleet and were prepared to use it. This remained the case all through until the city fell under Roman control.

It is frequently claimed that Constantinople occupies a natural site for an imperial city, that its geographical site determined in some way its imperial history. Yet Byzantion was never an imperial city in its first millennium, from the seventh century BC to the fourth century AD. It was never even a city of any outstanding political importance during that millennium, and it had a population of only about 20,000 at the very most, and usually less than that; it was regularly either beaten in its wars or caved in to an enemy at the first sign of hostility – a common reaction by other cities in the region; in the third century BC for sixty years it succumbed to regular blackmail by a Galatian kingdom established in Thrace. It was only when it was converted into Constantinople that the imperial importance of the city was registered by anyone. The one ancient historian who grasped the power of Byzantion's situation, Polybios, only drew attention to the value of the site as an economic asset, not its political power.[8]

That is to say, Constantinople, as a city of power, was the creation of a series of Roman emperors over the century between Constantine's selection of the city to be developed and the completion of the new walls of Theodosios. Only when the peninsula was fortified did it become a powerful imperial city. As an imperial power it was a human construct. There is no such thing as a 'natural' site for a powerful city.

Part I

Byzantion

Chapter 1

Enemy from the East – The Persians

The Sieges of 478 and 470 BC

In 517 BC the Persian Great King Dareios I advanced with a massive army into the western borderlands of his empire. He had seized the kingship in a civil war in which the legitimate king and his challenger had both died, leaving Dareios the last claimant standing. He was, or so he claimed, a member of a branch of the royal house, but he had to fight to convince everyone of his right to the throne, which in formal terms was minimal. He established that right by defeating every competitor, in the centre of the empire, in the eastern regions, and now it was the west which was to feel the benefits of his not-so-benign attention.[1] Extending the lands of the empire, as he did particularly in both the east in India, and in the west, was also a claim to legitimacy.

One of the matters he felt merited his attention was the problem of the nomads north of the Black Sea, the Skythians. They were related, by blood and lifestyle, to other nomads in Central Asia whom he had already fought, and these in the west had shown that they were similarly hostile. To deter them from further hostility he intended to move into their homelands and damage their homes, herds, and resources. He was not intent on seizing their land, for he knew enough about the nomads to understand that they would simply fade away into the distance at the approach of his army, and would then evade him until he went home. So the campaign would be a raid rather than a conquest. If he could inflict sufficient damage on them in some way, he would feel that they would understand that, if he could do it once, he could repeat the lesson.

On the way he could deal with problems in the western part of Asia Minor, the coastal cities, and the Aegean islands, which had been conquered by King Kyros (aka Cyrus the Great, founder of the Persian Empire), but had hardly been thoroughly attended to so far. The islands of Samos and Lesbos were secured without difficulty. The Persian preference had become that the cities should be ruled by tyrants, natives of the cities they ruled, but installed by the Persians, and Byzantion was one such city, controlled, it appears, by a tyrant called Ariston.[2] These men were now called on to help with the campaign in Skythia, but since their people were mainly foot soldiers, hoplites, they were not expected to campaign deep into the Ukraine. Instead it was primarily the cities' sailors who were required, and it was Greek ships which were used to transport the army, while Greek engineers and presumably Greek workmen built the bridges across the Bosporos and the Danube River.

It is probable that an underlying main object of this 'Skythian' campaign was to conquer Thrace, which had to be traversed first. There are indications that the army's march went some way inland, and at least one tribe, the Getai, fought against the Persian advance.[3] The king of Macedon was summoned to submit, and did so, and Persian strongpoints, notably at Doriskos on the north Aegean coast, were founded.

The route to the Skythians' homeland, therefore, lay through the lands to the west of the Straits and the Black Sea, through Thrace. To get to Thrace he had to transport his army over the Bosporos, the strait through which water from the Black Sea flowed into the Sea of Marmara, and then through the Hellespont and into the Aegean Sea and the Mediterranean. Before he arrived, the tyrants of Kalchedon and Byzantion had, like Macedon and the other Greek cities, already been summoned and had submitted. And before the Persian army reached the region a specially constructed bridge across the Bosporos to the north of the two Greek cities was built by a Samian architect called Mandrokles. Ariston at Byzantion was taken to the Danube crossing along with other Greek rulers, suggesting that Dareios was confident that the city was under control. The lord of Kalchedon was not taken with the army, and it has been supposed that he was left to guard the bridge.[4] Mandrokles went on to build another bridge over the Danube, using ships sent from the Greek cities of the Aegean, which were there marshalled into a pontoon bridge. Dareios had collected the ships from the cities, partly to provide raw materials for the bridges, and partly to transport men and supplies for the army, though most of the army marched by land to subdue Thrace.[5] Herodotos claims that the assembled tyrants at the Danube bridge debated whether to destroy the bridge and strand the Persian army north of the river. This is widely doubted, since its supposed originator,

Miltiades, lord of the Chersonese, probably later used the story to defend himself against the charge of tyranny when on trial at Athens.[6] On the other hand, it is surely likely that the idea occurred to them. But the tyrants needed Persian support to sustain their own positions at home, and Dareios also needed their support to control the cities.

The Danube bridge survived for the Persians to use, but the fate of the Bosporos bridge is not recorded. Both will have been dismantled after the campaign, if they had survived as long as that. One of the pillars Dareios set up, inscribed with 'his' achievement in crossing the Bosporos, was eventually taken to Byzantion and built into an altar to Artemis;[7] this, of course, does not mean that the bridge was destroyed. It probably was, in fact, though dismantled might be the best description, for the ships composing it would not be abandoned.

Dareios crossed back to Asia by the Hellespont crossing at Sestos/Abydos. This may be because there was trouble at the Bosporos.[8] Dareios had appointed Otanes as a new governor 'of the coast', meaning the coast of Hellespontine Phrygia. He faced enmity from Byzantion and Kalchedon, and swiftly took control of both cities, as well as Antandros and the islands of Imbros and Lemnos; only the last of these made any serious resistance.[9] However, since Dareios was heading for Sardis the Hellespont crossing was the shortest route, which is the best explanation for this particular journey rather than any minor trouble at the Bosporos.

The tyrants of Byzantion and Kalchedon no doubt returned to their cities, once authority had been returned to them by the Persians – unless they had been the source of the anti-Persian agitation. No doubt the leading opponents of the Persians were punished and the rule of the Persians bore down much harder on the inhabitants than under the preceding tyrants. But from the Persians' point of view, whatever had been involved, matters had been sorted out successfully, and the cities were now quiet. The Persian commander Megabazos, with an army, remained to rule in Thrace. His comment that Kalchedon was founded by unseeing settlers who should have chosen Byzantion as the better site implies that Byzantion was doing unexpectedly well.

This peacefulness lasted for a little over a decade. In 499 BC revolt broke out in Ionia, and by capturing and burning Sardis the rebels enraged the Persians. The Ionians were defeated in the subsequent fighting, and yet the revolt still spread. A fleet was collected, from the same cities which had contributed to the Persian fleet in the Skythian campaign, and it was used to further the revolt in areas so far unaffected. One of these was the Propontis, where Byzantion was persuaded to join in the rebellion. This may have been a difficult decision; geographically the Byzantines were on the very fringe of the rebellion, and had unpleasant memories of recent Persian conquest and rule. Nevertheless, the city joined in; the fate of Ariston the tyrant, if he still ruled, is unknown.[10]

The city soon became the base for Histiaios, an expelled Milesian tyrant who had joined the revolt. He collected eight triremes from Lesbos, and established himself at Byzantion to intercept the merchantmen sailing from the Black Sea, from which he exacted tolls. Attempting to define Histiaios' role is almost impossible – was he a pirate, a privateer, a patriot, a legitimate agent of taxation? – but here the main point of interest is his position in Byzantion.[11]

Eight triremes implies a total crew of a few hundred men, a force easily small enough to be expelled by the Byzantines if Histiaios' activities were obnoxious. One must therefore assume that Histiaios' presence was welcome in the city, or at least tolerated, presumably in return for a cut of the take, and certainly his men would be welcome to spend their wages in the city. The Byzantines were therefore at least complicit in his activities. There is no sign of any Byzantine ships being involved in this Histiaion adventure, and it may be that the city had not recently directed any of its resources into developing a navy; it was perhaps prevented from doing so by the Persians while they were in control, or by Ariston, who would no doubt understand the democratic temper of sailors, and that they would be a threat to him if organized.

Histiaios' activities were the Byzantines' undoing. The Persians recovered control of Ionia, and the Persian forces spread out to extinguish the last embers of the revolt. Histiaios showed his true priorities by sailing back into the Aegean to continue the fight against the Persian reconquest, and was defeated and executed.[12] The Persian forces arrived to attack the two Bosporos cities, and they in turn displayed their true feelings, and their understanding of Persian anger, by evacuating the cities and fleeing to Mesambria on the Black Sea coast to the north.[13] This place is described as a new colony of the Byzantines, but excavations have shown that it was a long-established Thracian town which had already received a Greek population.[14] The Persians therefore captured cities which had become more or less deserted, and, given their strategic importance, they presumably installed garrisons.

In a book such as this on the sieges of Byzantion-Constantinople, there are bound to be doubtful cases, and the events of 513 and 493 BC are such. In neither case was the city laid under siege, so far as we know, but in both cases it was captured. In 513 BC Otanes certainly attacked the city, and captured both it and Kalchedon, but given Herodotos' emphasis on the resistance made by the Lemnians, neither Byzantion nor Kalchedon can have resisted for very long, if at all, certainly not long enough for a formal siege to be required. In 493 BC they did not resist at all, but, knowing what was coming, the inhabitants deserted both cities. Do these count as sieges? Perhaps Otanes' attack might, if we had more information, but that of 493 BC cannot.

There can be no doubt, however, about the recapture of Byzantion in 478 BC. The city had been burnt by the Phoenician ships' crews who had taken the site when the inhabitants fled fifteen years before, but probably enough of the city remained, or was rebuilt, for the Persians to use the site as a fort. Nothing is known of the place subsequently, until the retreat of the Persian forces under Artabazos after the Battle of Plataia in 479 BC. He had taken an ambiguous part in the battle, and now he took a surviving part of the army north while the rest had been beaten and massacred by the vengeful Greeks in Boiotia. Meanwhile, a Greek naval force had gained control of the Hellespont while Artabazos was marching through Thessaly and Thrace, so he crossed at the Bosporos, from Byzantion to (presumably) Kalchedon.[15] It is possible that he left an enhanced garrison in Byzantion as he crossed. He will have known that the Persians had no intention of accepting their defeat in Greece as final. The Greek ships from the Hellespont sailed to Byzantion later, quite possibly carefully late to avoid colliding with Artabazos' army, which by now was no doubt feeling as vengeful as the Greeks had been. (A small Persian force certainly defended itself with some success in Sestos for some time, and another at Doriskos.) A Persian garrison therefore remained in Byzantion, and was a standing threat to the trade, in particular the food supplies directed at the rest of Greece, which came through the Bosporos – a leaf taken from Histiaios' book, therefore. The ruined city was besieged by the ships' crews, Greeks this time, under the command of the Spartan Pausanias. This siege lasted for an unknown period of time, and finally captured the city.[16] This therefore is the first siege of which we know anything, though even that is not much.

The commander of the Greek forces, Pausanias, was the victor of the decisive battle at Plataia, and half of his ships were Athenian, and half from Sparta and other cities. The political result of his new success was hardly what Pausanias expected. His overbearing command style had annoyed several of the contingents from the islands, and they attempted to persuade the Athenian Aristeides to take over the command. He demurred, so they organized what was in effect a coup by threatening Pausanias' ship; it is claimed in one source that they actually rammed it.[17] This further threatened to cause the rest of the fleet to disintegrate. Pausanias was recalled to Sparta and probably all the Peloponnesian ships returned home with him.[18] This recall was less to do with Pausanias' arrogance, though that probably had something to do with it, and more because the Spartans felt that they, as the premier warrior-state in Greece, were entitled to exercise the command, whereas it was clear that few of the allies felt that way; Pausanias was thus recalled, and Athens, much keener on continuing the fight, succeeded to the command. One might suggest that Aristeides had a good deal to do with this.[19] As Pausanias left, a meeting of the disaffected Greek captains and Aristeides was held on board Aristeides' flagship, still at Byzantion, and this laid out the basis for the continuation of the wartime alliance, at first under Aristeides' leadership. This developed into the Delian League and later the Athenian Empire.[20]

For Byzantion the result was a return to autonomy. Those refugees at Mesambria who wished to return did so, and the rebuilding began, or at least we may so assume. Into this situation Pausanias now returned, alone.[21] He quietly left Sparta and returned to the scene of his triumph and humiliation, and was welcomed by the Byzantines. The position he occupied in the city is not clear, but 'tyrant' does not fit. He was diplomatically active in negotiating with the Persian governor at Daskyleion, and with the Thracians. This activity later was regarded as 'Medizing' (sympathizing with the 'Medes' or Persians), but many of the details are not known, nor possibly were they ever fully known to anyone but Pausanias himself. Enough information got out, however, to cast suspicion on his deeds and motives. It is possible that the Byzantines welcomed and tolerated him in part because they did not wish to be part of the Delian League; they certainly abstained from it for some time, and later were only intermittent members.

What does seem clear is that Pausanias remained in the city, Medizer or not, for seven years, which would be about 477 or 476 to 471 or 470 BC.[22] No accusation of tyranny is made against him, so he clearly was comfortable in the city, and was able to pursue his private diplomacy in peace. One must assume, however, that his intrigues with, or diplomacy with, or friendship with, the Persian authorities became known, no doubt in a distorted and/or exaggerated form, and became regarded as suspicious, if not by the Byzantines, who possibly knew what he was doing, and accepted it, but by the Athenians, and the Delian League they controlled. The league was still fighting the Persians, and the knowledge that Pausanias in Byzantion was in contact with their enemy eventually brought Kimon, the current Athenian commander of the Delian League's forces, to the Propontis to expel him.

It took a siege of the city to persuade Pausanias to leave, which indicated clearly enough that he had plenty of support from the city government, which was probably an oligarchy, and from the citizens. How long the siege lasted is not known, but it was clearly of sufficient length to require more than the expulsion of a single individual. (Pausanias took refuge at Kolonai, a town in the Troad, where he stayed for some time, but continued 'intriguing'.)[23]

This episode suggests that Byzantion was never very content to be part of the League – the city did not join until after the siege and the departure of Pausanias – though for some time it gave no trouble. One would suppose that the city's energies were directed for some time mainly at rebuilding. It had to re-establish the city as a trading entrepot, and develop its own trading systems; a local naval force was clearly now required. But it had twice had to be captured by siege by a mainly Athenian force, and this may well have rankled as badly as the memory of the Persian occupation, which also originated by force. It is relevant that, as a Megarian colony, it was Dorian in speech and 'race'; the Athenians were Ionian and there was always a certain tension between these two sets of Greeks. The Byzantines had no reason to welcome the Athenians or to like the thought of being part of their league.

The city had been captured twice and besieged twice in three decades, and destroyed and evacuated as well. One of those sieges had resulted in its capture, the other in forcing it to expel a guest. All four attacks had come by water – the Persians across the Bosporos, the Athenians through the Propontis. Damage had been serious as a result of the Persian attacks, minimal from the Athenians. The whole sequence was actually a set of actions and conflicts which had resulted from the arrival of the Persian Empire on the Byzantines' doorstep. Even the final attack, which seems on the surface to be an inter-Greek dispute, was actually the result of Pausanias' contacts with the Persians, from the Great King downwards.

The city was in all this a pawn in the contest between greater powers, though that condition was less obvious in the fourth case. In the first two captures the Byzantines had simply given up without a fight, even to the extent of abandoning their city. In the third the Persians were at last the victims, and were defeated. In the fourth the Byzantines were defeated, but only in the sense that they did as their attackers required. It is unlikely that they liked it. It did, however, set the pattern of the city's international relations for the next five centuries; it was a small city amid greater powers; its diplomacy was necessarily nimble if it was to avoid further captures and sacks.

Chapter 2

Enemies from the South – the Greeks

The Sieges of 407 and 400

The successful siege by the forces of the Delian league in 470 BC resulted in the expulsion of Pausanias from Byzantion, but it also had wider effects, both internally and in the city's external relations. Whatever governing system existed in the 470s while Pausanias was in the city will have been dismantled by the result of the siege and the defeat of the city. It seems likely that it was an oligarchy, given Pausanias' Spartan origins, but once the Athenians had secured control, in 470 BC, it will probably have become a democracy, in accordance with general Athenian policy. In external matters the city was enrolled in the Delian League. No source attests to this, but it is likely that Athens, whose main purpose in having a fleet in the Propontis was to ensure the uninterrupted passage of ships through from the Black Sea to the Aegean, will have insisted on this also.[1] This will have meant Byzantine participation in the Asian war, which had been avoided while Pausanias was in the city.

The institution of an oligarchic regime in the city is traceable to Pausanias, who arrived in the city at the beginning of its physical rebuilding, and would soon be influential. He was later venerated as a *ktistes*, a city founder, whose task was to regenerate the city; by organizing the rebuilding, this was what Pausanias was doing, at least at first. As a Spartan he seems to have favoured oligarchy – this was the choice before the Persian War, and later in the Spartan Empire – but the institutions of the city were the usual set common to any Greek city – assembly, *boule*, a board of executives, and a head of state, appointed annually, with no power; in Byzantion this was an *hieromnemon*.

This is to a degree speculative, but may be acceptable as a starting point. At later stages of the city's history, it is known that an oligarchy had power, and possibly on occasion a tyrant seized power, but that only reinforces the impression that Byzantion was in many ways a typical Greek city, most of which alternated in their governmental regimes between democracy, oligarchy, and tyranny; Athens as always is the exemplar.

The city's geographical location imposed some adaptations to the basic Greek pattern. It was sited, possibly even deliberately, with a view to controlling the exit from the Bosporos – that is, imposing its own rules on the passing traffic. The pattern may have been, for those who came after, that of Histiaios, but it seems probable that the Persians may have already imposed a toll system earlier, from their base at the significantly named post of Chrysopolis, on the Asian side, next door to Kalchedon.[2] Histiaios may therefore have been only taking over the Persian practice, and perhaps Pausanias did the same in Byzantion's name, giving the excuse no doubt that the city needed the cash to help it rebuild and repair the damage caused by the Persians. But once the city was in the Delian League, it would be Athens which administered the tolls, or perhaps permitted Byzantion to do so; this was certainly the case later, after Thrasyboulos' visit in 389 BC.

There seems to be no record of these tolls, and it is possible that Athens did not impose them at first, relying on collecting the league tribute from the city instead. Alkibiades imposed a ten per cent duty, the *dekate*, which was collected at Chrysopolis, in 410 BC. However, it seems unlikely that a city-empire such as that of Athens would fail to collect that which the Persians and Histiaios, and perhaps Pausanias and Byzantion, had collected. By the time Athens took over, in 470 BC, the toll had existed for more than a generation, perhaps for much longer. And yet at the same time, if it was levied, the lack of complaints about such a toll is even more surprising. It seems that Alkibiades had no difficulty in organizing his collection system, and it may be that the preceding Spartan system had abolished them as a means towards gaining support.

Byzantion's membership of the Delian League was thus enforced by Athens, and probably resented all along. While the league remained a loose collection of cities devoted to the fight against the still-threatening Persian Empire, this was no doubt bearable, but once a sort of peace was achieved (the Peace of Kallias, 449 BC) Athens proceeded to turn the league into its own empire, so the situation changed, and resentment amongst the larger cities grew. There was some trouble close to Byzantion in the early 440s, in which over fifty Athenians died.[3] This was probably a war against the city's Thracian neighbours, stimulated by Athens' anti-

Thracian activities in the Chersonese. This might be construed in Athens as a defence of Byzantion but in Byzantion it could have been seen as a provocation which raised Thracian hostility.

In 440 BC a civil war broke out on the island of Samos. This was one of the few Aegean communities which counted as independent allies of Athens, having insisted on retaining its own naval force as its contribution to the alliance. The Athenians, under Perikles, intervened in the fighting, partly to prevent the Samians enlisting Persian help, partly to restore the island as, or turn it into, a 'normal' demilitarized member of the league/empire. The city of Byzantion joined the Samians.

Why it did this is not known. Conjecture suggests a link with the city's mother city, Megara, which was itself annoyed with Athens at the time; it seems unlikely that the Byzantines had any obvious sympathy with Samos. The best interpretation may be that Byzantion's long resentment at its subordination to Athens had allowed it to take advantage of Athens' difficulties. It had been a resentful member of the league, and its assessed tribute was already one of the highest, at fifteen talents annually. There may have been difficulties in finding enough money for payment, for it appears to have been paid in instalments.

The Byzantine 'revolt' was brief. Once Samos had been subdued there was no point in continuing; on the other hand, Athens spent 128 talents on the anti-Byzantine campaign (contrasted with 1,400 for the Samian campaign).[4] Soon afterwards, and certainly by 433 BC, the city's tribute assessment rose to eighteen talents, and by 429 it was twenty-one.[5] This is one of the three highest assessments in the empire.

The source of this wealth is clearly the passing trade through the Bosporos, the wealth generated by trade in the city, and the collection of a toll on shipping. The agency for the collection of the toll was therefore, in the 440s, partly Byzantion itself, which paid over its tribute to Athens out of the proceeds. (The amount of tribute before 450 BC is not known, since it was only from 454 BC, when Athens moved the treasury of the league from Delos to Athens, that detailed inscribed records began, and some of these are fragmentary). At the same time, the cities around the Propontis were all paying larger than average tributes – Kyzikos, Lampsakos, Perinthos, even Selymbria, were all paying between six and ten talents. Trade may be seen as the source of this civic wealth, except for Lampsakos, which had gold mines. The voyage of the Athenian fleet to the Black Sea under Perikles in 437 BC was no doubt partly intended to remind these wealthy cities of their political dependence on Athens.[6]

Whatever resentment the Byzantines felt – if they did – they did not take advantage of Athens' preoccupation with the war which began in 433 BC against the Peloponnesian League headed by Sparta. There is no reference to the city in Thucydides during the first section of that war (433–421 BC), nor during the Athenian agony in Sicily in 415–413 BC. But all Athens' enemies (Persia, Sparta, members of the Peloponnesian league), saw that the Athenian losses at Syracuse had decisively weakened the city. In the Spartan war, which was resumed in 412 BC, one of the earliest events was the rebellion of Byzantion, or rather, probably the other way about, the rebellion preceded the war. This was partly organized internally, and the message went to the Spartan fleet which was at Miletos asking for assistance. A detachment of ten ships under a Megarian commander, Helixos – a clever choice – reached Byzantion from the Aegean, having forced its way through the Hellespont, and that was enough to bring the city to the point of active rebellion.[7]

The involvement of the Megarian Helixos was significant. Byzantion was a Megarian colony and the ties were still clearly potent. Selymbria was also Megarian in origin, and it followed Byzantion into revolt. Even more significant was the spread of the revolt to Kalchedon and Kyzikos, neither of which was Megarian in origin. This collection of enemies in a strategic region constituted a clear threat to Athens' supplies of food and its trade from the Black Sea and quickly brought reinforcements of both Spartan and Athenian ships into the Propontis. The two fleets met in battle at Kyzikos; the Athenians won, driving the Spartan fleet underwater or out of the region.[8]

This left the way clear for the Athenian forces to regain control of the cities which had broken away from the empire. Kyzikos was taken at once, and provided a large quantity of booty. The Athenians crossed to the north coast and at once took over Perinthos and Selymbria.[9] The speed of this suggests that the rebellion in these cities had always been half-hearted – both Perinthos and Kyzikos were capable of standing a siege.

These defeats persuaded the Spartans to offer terms of peace, but one of the terms they suggested was that those places held by Sparta which had formerly been in the Athenian Empire should continue to be Spartan, and that the cities which had broken away should continue to be independent. This was unacceptable to Athens, and indeed, if accepted, would probably have led fairly quickly to a resumption of warfare. The cities in question included Abydos at the Hellespont Narrows, and both Kalchedon and Byzantion. The recalled Athenian commander Alkibiades had set up a version of the Persian customs post at Chrysopolis to tax the passing shipping,[10] but the security of the Bosporos demanded control of the two cities as well. The Spartan peace offer failed.

There was no further follow-up on the victory at Kyzikos, apart from the capture of the three cities. The Athenians did not, it seems, feel strong enough to move against the other rebellious cities. The Kyzikos victory was essentially a naval affair, and the submission of the three cities was due to the threat from the sea, and in at least one case was incomplete. But the other cities were less vulnerable and more determined. The Athenians therefore needed foot soldiers to pursue attempts to gain control of the cities, and cavalry to defeat both the hoplites on the other side and to defend against the Persian cavalry. They had left garrisons in Perinthos and Kyzikos, and this further reduced their effective numbers.

Meanwhile, as Athens gathered its strength and tried to work out its priorities, Sparta set to work to revive its navy, building ships at Antandros from timber cut on Mount Ida, just outside the Hellespont.[11] An Athenian force commanded by Thrasyllos, including both ships and hoplites, intercepted a Syracusan squadron before it could reach the Hellespont, sank several of the ships, and drove the rest away.[12] Thrasyllos' force then headed for the Propontis. The Spartans did the same, sending fifteen ships, commanded by Klearchos and manned by Megarians and other allies, through the Hellespont in the face of the Athenian ships. Klearchos lost three ships, but the rest got through to Byzantion.[13]

The delay, which was largely caused by uncertainty about Spartan intentions, had focussed Athenian considerations on its priorities in the north. The junction of Alkibiades' and Thrasyllos' forces gave them much greater effectiveness and the strength to deal with the cities in the north one at a time, but the main priority was to prevent more Spartans reaching the Propontis, where they would be welcomed by Byzantion and Kalchedon. This meant mounting an attack on Abydos on the Hellespont, held by a Spartan garrison, which in turn helped to keep the Hellespont available for Spartan ships. The attack failed, largely because the Persian cavalry of the satrap Pharnabazos managed to intervene to assist the garrison. The Persians were driven off but the Athenian attack which had been intended to be a surprise, had alerted the Spartan garrison and there was no chance of a new attack succeeding.[14]

Athenian attention turned back to the Bosporos cities. From Chrysopolis, the Athenians under Theramenes had been raiding into Kalchedonian territory, causing damage and developing a great enough threat so that the city handed over its treasure to the Bithynians for safekeeping. Alkibiades marched his troops along the coast, paced by the ships at sea, and into Bithynia. The Bithynians decided that the threat was too great, and surrendered the Kalchedonian treasures.

Kalchedon was then besieged. This is an example of Greek limitations in siege warfare, and at the same time of their initiative. The first stage was to build a wooden wall to enclose the whole city, stretching from the Bosporos round to the Propontis. Any Persian intervention was thereby blocked, though they had brought up a large army of infantry and cavalry. The Spartan garrison came out from the city to dispute the Athenian siege, fighting a battle in the space between the city's wall and the Athenian palisade. A last-minute intervention by Alkibiades commanding the Athenian cavalry and some extra hoplites, produced a victory of sorts, but the Spartans avoided any pursuit and got back into the city, though their commander Hippokrates had been killed.

The Athenians did not want to have to sit down to blockade the city, which would have immobilized them for months; still less did they wish to launch attacks on the walls. The Kalchedonians, and no doubt the Spartans in the garrison, were as unwilling to contemplate the prospect of gradual debilitation which would result from the blockade. The Athenian wall and the Athenian fleet effectively isolated the city on all sides. So both sides faced a possible lengthy period of delay and increasing misery.

Then there was Pharnabazos the satrap, whose territory had suffered from Athenian ravaging, and whose army had been defeated at Abydos. Yet he was the key to the situation. Alkibiades was away collecting money, loot, and troops, but the other Athenian generals, Theramenes and Thrasyllos, contacted Pharnabazos; after negotiations, they came to an agreement that the city would pay over its arrears of tribute, to which Pharnabazos would add twenty talents. In return the Athenians would not attack either the city or Pharnabazos, and would send envoys to the Great King at Sousa, seeking peace. There was, it seems, no mention of the Spartans. Their commander and a considerable number of the troops had died in the fight, so perhaps they were so much reduced that they were negligible – or perhaps they were allowed to leave before the agreement was concluded, going possibly to Byzantion; their absence would make the agreement easier to reach. Certainly the Kalchedonians would not betray them. The various commanders, including the returned Alkibiades, swore oaths to observe the terms, which were to last until the Athenian envoys returned from their journey to Sousa, which would take at least six months.[15]

Kalchedon and Pharnabazos having thus been skilfully neutralized, the Athenians turned to deal with Byzantion. Theramenes and Thrasyllos took their forces across the Bosporos to begin developing a new siege. Alkibiades had gone off again to gather reinforcements (which the Athenians, who had collected Kalchedon's treasure, its tribute arrears, and Pharnabazos' twenty talents, could now afford). He found some mercenaries, perhaps more Athenians, and hired a force of Thracian soldiers. He went as far as the Chersonese in this recruiting exercise. On his way back he stopped at Selymbria, which had paid up on his previous visit after the Kyzikos battle, but had not permitted the Athenians to enter the city. With his new force, Alkibiades contacted Athens' supporters inside the city, who opened a gate one night. But he then made generous terms with the city as a whole, ensuring that his soldiers – Thracians were traditional enemies of all the north Propontis cities – behaved correctly. He collected more money (arrears of tribute, no doubt), left a garrison in the city, and quickly marched on to Byzantion. He had recovered a city for Athens at no cost, collected money to pay his troops, and by moving out quickly from Selymbria he had ensured that no obvious enmity developed – though he no doubt left his supporters in control of the city government.

The Athenian forces, ships and soldiers, under the three generals, laid siege to Byzantion. They had a large fleet, almost 200 ships, manned by perhaps 30,000 men, and an army of sufficient size to control all access to the city. And, thanks to the tribute, the loot, and Pharnabazos' contribution, the generals had money enough to pay their soldiers and secure them some supplies – though that would not last long with all the men they commanded. They were thus under time pressure, as always.

The Byzantines were commanded by Klearchos, tough and ruthless, a man disdainful of all but other Spartiates (full Spartan citizens). He had a mixed force of Byzantines, Megarians under Hexilos, non-Spartiates and some freed Helots from Lakedaimon, Boiotians commanded by Koiratadas, and a force of mercenaries. With such a mixture he would need to be tough. They were, however, quite enough to defeat the initial Athenian attempts to take the city by assault. The Athenian fleet enforced a fairly strict blockade, and they had built one of their enclosing walls to make their land blockade easier to enforce.[16] Like the Athenians, the city was under time pressure.

The siege had therefore quickly sunk into a stalemate. To break it each side had a ploy available. Alkibiades could contact the Athenian party in the city, as he had at Selymbria, and perhaps persuade them to open a gate one dark night. Klearchos, however, began operating his own ploy first, though it was a rather long-range one. Having seen the early Athenian assaults fail, he assumed that the population and the garrison were loyal, or at least were under strict control and supervision. He slipped out of the city (so much for the tightness of the Athenian blockade). His aim was to meet Pharnabazos, but the satrap had left on the journey to Sousa with the Athenian envoys. Klearchos also had a second, and probably more hopeful, purpose, which was to collect all the Spartan ships he could find. There were some left in the Propontis here and there, above all at Abydos, some at Antandros where the building had continued, and some on the Thracian coast under a subordinate commander. Even all together they would not be enough to defeat the Athenian fleet in open battle, but he could make life in the Propontis difficult, cutting supplies, harassing detachments, and could draw off Athenian ships from the city. The smaller cities along the Hellespont would be vulnerable, as might the larger cities which had fallen to the Athenians after the Battle of Kyzikos earlier.[17]

But Klearchos' work would take longer to achieve results than Alkibiades' methods at Byzantion. There, the Athenian was assisted by the conditions in the city, where hunger was already hurting all but the soldiers. It seems that Klearchos, as might be expected, had made sure that the defenders of the city had adequate rations; the civilians divided up the rest. But he had also behaved to his Byzantine supporters with the usual arrogance and disdain which was always deployed by Spartans to lesser breeds. The men who had originally asked for Spartan help were, so it would seem, the ruling oligarchy, either a group who had seized power in the city, or one which had been installed as rulers by Klearchos – and these were the men with whom he came most frequently into contact, and whom he thoughtlessly alienated. His absence from the city on the ship hunt was no doubt a considerable relief to the Byzantines, but it was also an opportunity for the anti-Spartan, or perhaps just anti-Klearchan, group to contact Alkibiades and let the Athenians into the city.

This was less easy than at Selymbria, though Alkibiades did make promises of the same gentle treatment. The garrison was larger and stronger in its anti-Athenian and pro-Spartan loyalty, and the walls were still manned by wary soldiers. The plotters could not guarantee much more than an entry, so there would be fighting once the Athenians had got inside the city. Alkibiades' fertile mind developed a ruse. He allowed a rumour to spread into the city that his forces were needed elsewhere – Ionia was mentioned for verisimilitude. One afternoon the whole Athenian fleet sailed away, out of sight, and the army packed up and marched away, though only far enough that it could not be seen from the city. It seems that no scouting was done from the city either by sea or by land to follow up the retreating enemy forces, which one might suppose Klearchos would have organized had he been present; the lack might be the result of a divided command: Sparta, Megara, Byzantion, and the rest.

The Athenian army crept back silently (probably only a part of it in fact, the assaulting groups), and the fleet noisily returned and attempted an attack on any enemy ships it could find in the harbour. Many of the troops manning the walls went to help the harbour defences, for it must have looked to the inhabitants as though, foiled at the walls, the Athenians were attempting a landing. The land defences were much weakened, and the plotters in the city summoned the returning Athenians. But there were still defenders near the walls, and it was soon obvious that the fleet would not be attempting a landing, so the attack at the gates was soon being fairly strongly resisted. Both sides reinforced the battle, the Athenians bringing up more of their troops, the Byzantines forming a more solid defence.

Alkibiades had another trick available. Somehow, perhaps in a pause in the fighting, perhaps when daylight arrived, he arranged for it to be known to the Byzantine forces what his terms were. The Byzantines, who knew of the terms at Selymbria, and the plotters who could explain them, accepted the story. Either they ceased fighting or they turned on their Peloponnesian garrison troops. Most of the foreigners in the garrison died in the fighting, but a remnant of 500 men fled to temples for protection. This in effect was a preliminary to surrender. The terms were, as at Selymbria, honoured. The city resumed its alliance with Athens, paid its tribute; the Athenians refrained from appointing a governor and withdrew their forces. After all, the Byzantines had shown their political attitude well enough by changing sides, and by killing so many of their former allies they had spoiled any possible return to the Spartan alliance. The prisoners were disarmed and sent off to Athens.[18]

The new regime, probably democratic, lasted only a year. In 406 BC Athens' last fleet was defeated and destroyed at Aigospotamoi in the Hellespont. The captives were killed, by a vote of Sparta's allies present at the battle, in revenge for Athens' treatment of their people and cities over the previous thirty years. The Spartan commander, Lysander, now toured the cities of the Straits and the Propontis accepting surrenders and adjusting the city governments once more. At Byzantion a governor, or *harmost*, Sthenelaus, was installed, as was a Spartan garrison; a set of ten men of the pro-Spartan faction was detailed as the governing oligarchy, referred to as a 'dekarchy'.[19] The Athenian garrisons were told to go home to Athens, where they swelled the population and helped to consume the limited food supplies. Athens itself held out for over a year, and even then succeeded in persuading the Spartans to leave the city its autonomy, though not its democracy, nor its defensive walls; its fleet had already gone.

The new Spartan system was not popular, and it became even less liked when tribute payments were imposed.[20] It was clear to its subjects that the empire of Athens had been resurrected in an even nastier Spartan guise. And this general anti-Spartan attitude seems to have communicated itself to the Thracians, who resumed raiding their Greek neighbours, both in the Chersonese and towards Byzantion – these, at least, are the places we know of, and others may be assumed.

Klearchos the former, now disgraced, governor had been tried at Sparta for his defeat by Alkibiades, and fined heavily. He left the city and took refuge at Lampsakos, where he began to drink heavily. Meanwhile in 404 BC the Persian Great King Dareios II died; he was succeeded by his eldest son Artaxerxes. In Asia Minor a younger son of Dareios, Kyros, harboured ambitions to replace his brother, and set about collecting the necessary forces clandestinely. His method was to subcontract the collection of separate forces to noted commanders, on condition that the forces they collected could be employed in the meantime but would be available when Kyros was ready to attack his brother. Klearchos was one of these contractors; he gathered an army and campaigned against the threatening Thracians, who menaced the small cities of the Chersonese.[21]

At Byzantion the connection was made. The city had been threatened, like the Chersonese, by the local Thracians. The small oligarchy, composed of the pro-Spartan party, contacted Klearchos and invited him to return. He accepted at once – or once he had sobered up – and on his arrival staged a coup by which he made himself, in effect, a tyrant. This is not necessarily something the local oligarchs disliked, at least for the time being, since it meant that he established full control over the city, in association with them.

He did campaign against the Thracians, and Polyainos records amongst his various items and anecdotes of military exploits, several stories about his campaigning against them. At least one of these was specifically related to a campaign out of Byzantion.[22] Within the city his conduct is described in the usual way that Greek historians always describe the activities of tyrants: arbitrary executions, confiscations, expulsions, and so on. How specific to Klearchos these were is not all that clear, but by this time there had been so many tyrannies in Greek cities that a new tyrant could simply pick and choose his methods from those which were already well-known; he did not need to invent anything new. Historians could do the same in their descriptions; they were not necessarily being untruthful, just generalizing from the usual tyrannical methods: if he is a tyrant, he will have done tyrannical things.

Klearchos, by his methods, however, like earlier tyrants from Sparta, alienated even his earliest supporters, and appeals were sent to Sparta. Klearchos had taken up his post at Byzantion without Spartan authorization, and even perhaps in defiance of the Spartan governor, but he evidently claimed to be acting in that city's name. The situation was thus somewhat confused. It was resolved, at least temporarily, by Sparta ordering Klearchos to return to Sparta. It seems that the message was sufficient to force him out. His unpopularity in the city will have become clear, and if a Spartan force arrived to collect him, he may well have been murdered there and then. A new governor was sent from Sparta; the oligarchy remained in power.

If Klearchos had obeyed the order to return to Sparta it would amount to a sentence of death for him after his conduct and his earlier conviction, so he simply left the city and, by way of Selymbria, he went to Kyros, who as it happened was now ready to make his attempt to overthrow his brother. It is not recorded that Kyros had already notified him of his readiness to march, but it is clear that Klearchos very easily abandoned his Byzantine tyranny.

The new *harmost* after Klearchos was removed was Anaxibios, who was still in office when he faced the next crisis for the city, the arrival of the survivors of Kyros' expedition, now under the uneasy command of the Athenian Xenophon (Klearchos had been killed on the way). The expedition arrived in Bithynia, seeking to return somewhere or go somewhere, they did not know. Anaxibios did organize shipping for the men to cross into the city, but then he led them on by making promises which he could not fulfil.[23] When they realized they had been tricked the men returned in a fury, and it proved easy for some to get into the city by climbing along the breakwater, while others, already inside, were able to use axes to break the bar on the gate. The garrison fled to the citadel, the citizens panicked, and Anaxibios sensibly took a boat to get to the acropolis. For a short while it looked as though the city might be sacked, or seized by the army, with Xenophon imposed as tyrant. Xenophon, however, refused such a promotion, and got the army to leave, telling them they would be shamed if they sacked a Greek city, but it had been a close thing.[24]

Athens slowly revived during the 390s BC, assisted by the former allies of Sparta, who did not like its overweening pride, or the overbalanced balance of power, and a new war from 396 BC (the Corinthian War) reduced Sparta's power. The Spartans retained control of Byzantion until 389 BC, when an Athenian fleet commanded by Thrasyboulos arrived in the Hellespont. There was no Spartan resistance to this expedition, which was aimed at preventing a revival of Spartan naval power; depriving Sparta of its bases in the north would assist in that reduction. Thrasyboulos sailed to the Bosporos, where he dismantled the oligarchy in Byzantion and installed a democracy, then did the same at Kalchedon. There is no mention in Xenophon's account of any Spartan governor, or any Spartan garrison.[25]

Thrasyboulos, however, also seized control of the customs system, before overthrowing the oligarchs. He conciliated the Byzantines by farming out the collection to the Byzantines themselves.[26] How this worked is hardly clear, but it seems for the moment to have satisfied the Byzantines, along with the return to democracy; oligarchy, after its association with Sparta and Klearchos, was in eclipse. It meant that they would not have lots of Athenian tax-collectors in the city – the memory of empire clearly still hurt – and the Athenians saw that their possession of the *dekate* was confirmed; the Byzantines received a percentage, or a fee, and the Athenians the larger share. Perhaps any passing Athenian ships were exempt.

This expedition performed a service for the local cities in the Straits and the Propontis in adjusting their governmental regimes, and for Athens and its allies by dismantling the Spartan imperial system in the region. Thrasyboulos' expedition, however, can also be seen as the beginning of Athens' imperial revival, as well as the city's renewal of its naval pretensions. But it had not prevented the Spartan naval revival which it had aimed to do, and two years later it was Athens which was suffering another blockade, and hunger once more. When the Spartan diplomat Antalkidas returned from a visit to the Great King at Sousa (Kyros' and Klearchos' and Xenophon's old enemy Artaxerxes) with a treaty in the form of a Persian diktat, Sparta seized on it to justify its reduced imperial ambitions, and Athens perforce accepted it in order to be released from the blockade. For Byzantion it was a guarantee of autonomy, at least until someone else turned up to attack the city.

Chapter 3

Enemy from the West – the Macedonians

The Sieges of 340 and 318 BC

The restored balance of power in Greece resulting from the revival of Athens, the growth of the power of Thebes, and the diminishment of Sparta, lasted for about five decades, until upset once more by the sudden emergence and new power of Macedon. This renewed balance had the consequence of ensuring constant warfare, since to retain the balance required cities to ally with whichever city was convenient for the moment and without any attacks of conscience. So Athens could ally with Sparta, Thebes with Athens, everyone with Persia, always temporarily. The consequence for Byzantion was that the city enjoyed a lengthy period of peace, interrupted only occasionally by an intervention from the outside, normally from the south.

The King's Peace of 386 BC, the Peace of Antalkidas, attempted to cement in place a particular international relationship favourable to Persia and Sparta. This would have been dangerous for everyone else except that Athens was already strong enough to develop its Second Confederacy, which gave some protection for the lesser cities who were its members as well as increasing Athens' own power with regard to other great powers. This alliance system developed gradually out of Athenian alliances with individual cities, but by the time Byzantion joined as an Athenian ally in 378 BC, the number of cities involved was perhaps seventy-five, most of them small islands. The official record of the agreement notes that Byzantion would be the ally of 'Athens and the other allies'. Within the same Athenian year Athens set out the general terms of the Confederacy – its 'charter'.[1] Athens carefully included distinct limits to its own authority, which were intended to prevent the alliance moving into a new Athenian Empire, but Athens inevitably was the guiding power, and the effect was to restore the city to great power status.

Byzantion, however, was evidently less than enthusiastic about its membership. In 364 BC the Theban general Epameinondas arrived in the

Propontis with a newly built Boiotian fleet.[2] He was on a maritime tour designed to challenge Athens, which simply ignored him and his fleet – and he did not repeat the feat. One result of this cruise, however, was to persuade Byzantion to leave the Athenian alliance.[3] No doubt other cities were beguiled in the same way. This was apparently accomplished without trouble, unlike the attempt several years later by three of the larger island states, Rhodes, Kos, and Chios, who also attempted to leave the alliance; another city, the island-city Keos, had earlier attempted to resign, as did Naxos, but both were recovered by Athens, the former by means of two military campaigns.[4] Presumably, with a major crisis building in the Peloponnese in the late 360s BC, the Byzantines could be ignored by Athens. Byzantion's distance from Athens and the Aegean reduced its importance, and it may have been last in the list of those cities which it had to deal with. The war which resulted from the decision of the island cities to leave the confederacy (the 'Social' War) lasted three years. Byzantion joined the seceders, as an independent city, no doubt fearing that, if Athens won, the recovery of Byzantion would be its next aim.[5] The seceders became allied with the satrap Mausollos of Karia, and the strength of the allies was too much for Athens, which had to admit defeat by 355 BC.[6]

The attempt to run the Athenian alliance without it becoming an empire therefore proved an impossible aspiration, and by 355 BC, with the removal of Byzantion, the island cities, and a number of others, the strain on the alliance brought it to collapse. The Confederacy was reduced to Athens and a considerable number of the smaller cities which found that the alliance with Athens' seapower was a useful protection, but cannot have contributed much in the way of strength to Athens, even if they were reckoned up collectively.

The Byzantines escaped serious involvement in the war. They deployed a small naval force, and helped in raids on 'loyal' islands, though this fleet would not have been strong enough to deflect or defeat a serious Athenian attack. The rebels joined their naval forces together and raided those islands which had remained in the Athenian alliance. These included Lemnos and Imbros, islands settled by Athenian colonists which stood, in a way, as guardians of the Hellespont.[7] The Athenian generals – three of them were in joint command – now decided to attack Byzantion, presumably because of its isolation from the rest, but Byzantion's allies sent their fleets to the Hellespont to prevent the attack.[8] A great battle threatened, but was avoided by a series of accidents. First, a great storm struck the several fleets, which will have compelled a delay while repairs were undertaken. Then the Athenian generals quarrelled over their plan. Two of them were accused of treason, and the other, Chares, diverted his forces into serving the local Persian satrap in order to gain enough cash to pay his men and gather supplies. But he was aiding a Persian who was in rebellion against the Great King, and the Great King complained to Athens, with threats.[9] The combination of the Great King, Mausollos, and the rebel alliance was too great for the Athenians. (This was a typical temporary alliance in a balance of power situation.) Peace was made, leaving the rebel cities independent. Byzantion had escaped with little injury.

During the war, and quite separately, King Philip II of Macedon, who became king in 359 BC, had been consolidating his control over his kingdom, and probing Athens' position in the north Aegean. This process advanced Macedonian power eastwards, threatening both the Athenian positions and the local cities of the Aegean and Propontis coasts. In reply, Athens sent settlers to take control of the Chersonese, while Philip gained control of Thessaly and the north Aegean coast as far as Abdera.[10] Both sides made alliances with Thracian rulers, and Philip, with a view to encircling his Thracian enemy, contacted Perinthos and Byzantion (and perhaps Selymbria), and made an alliance with both states.[11] He campaigned as far as Heraion Teichos, a Thracian stronghold on the Propontis just north of the Chersonese, which he captured with unlikely ease. That is, the conflict between Macedon and Athens – between the Macedonian Empire (Macedon, Thessaly, Thrace) and the Athenian alliance (Attika, Euboia, many of the islands, the Chersonese – in effect, a new empire) – was clearly approaching Byzantion and its fellow cities on the Propontis.

From the Byzantine point of view, both of the greater powers, Philip and Athens, were approaching the city in a threatening way. Their conflict, which dipped in and out of open warfare, declared and clandestine, was unending through the 350s and 340s BC. By allying with Philip, Byzantion and Perinthos had perhaps hoped that this would keep him away, for there is no indication that they took part in any of the fighting in the 350s and 340s, but as coastal cities they were clearly vulnerable to Athenian action. A period of open conflict over the city of Olynthos was concluded by a peace agreement in 346 BC (the Peace of Philokrates), but in between the Athenian negotiations and deliberations, Philip had advanced further into Thrace. Athens meanwhile concluded an alliance with the Thracian king Kersebleptes, who was Philip's enemy, and they built a line of minor forts to defend the northern approaches to the Chersonese. These were manned by Thracians though built by the Athenians; Philip at once marched to demolish them with no trouble at all.[12]

Philip campaigned in all directions in the next years, and not infrequently he clashed with Athens or encroached on Athenian interests. And as he intervened more often in Thrace he approached Byzantion more nearly. An unpleasant Athenian commander in the Chersonese, Diopeithes, exploited a quarrel between Kardia and the Athenian cleruchs in the peninsula; he captured and tortured a Macedonian envoy; such incidents as these, and more, went to exacerbate already bad relations. Philip campaigned against the Thracian Getai, inland of Byzantion.[13] One source, indeed, claims that Philip's aim was to secure control of Byzantion.[14] Finally, Athens set out on a determined diplomatic campaign to secure allies against Philip, who had campaigned yet again in Thrace and had deposed two Thracian kings, including the Athenian ally Kersebleptes. The Athenian envoys could therefore point to the threat of Philip who was approaching ever nearer, though such a warning was probably unnecessary; they did, by their presence in the cities, raise the possibility of a wider alliance, though most Greeks were sceptical, and regarded the Athenian approach as self-serving. Philip appointed a *strategos* for Thrace, implying an increased degree of Macedonian control, and campaigned along the coast of the Black Sea north of the Bosporos, securing alliances with the Greek cities along the coast.[15]

It was at this point that the Athenian politician Demosthenes went to visit Byzantion. Whereas Athens was bothered to some degree by the new Macedonian control over the Black Sea coast, from which Athenian food supplies and raw materials were dispatched to Greece, for Byzantion the problem was more immediate, for now Philip's looming presence was in their near neighbourhood. To the Byzantines, an alliance with Philip had ceased to seem to be a protection. No alliance with Athens resulted from Demosthenes' visit any more than it had from earlier diplomatic contacts, but Philip could only see the contact with misgiving, especially when other Athenian envoys visited Byzantion's old friends from the time of the Social War, Chios and Rhodes. A revival of the Second Athenian Confederacy, in a looser form, seemed to be emerging.[16] An Athenian envoy visited the Great King, and they found they shared joint fears about Philip. The Athenians were able to secure a subsidy from Artaxerxes to finance the anti-Macedonian front they were developing.[17]

In 340 BC Philip campaigned in northern Thrace, but seems to have suddenly appreciated the extent of the coalition against him which was developing. Perhaps it was the return of the Athenian envoys from the Great King, with cash, which finally crystallized both the Athenian-led coalition and the threat it posed in Philip's mind. He had a legitimate complaint against Perinthos and Byzantion, which were technically his allies, but which were now negotiating with his enemies, but it is likely that he decided to attack before the Athenian alliance was fully formed, in the hope that it would never develop at all. But this pre-emptive strike would depend for success on a swift victory by the Macedonians. If he was stuck in a slow campaign, the coalition would have the time, and still more, the motivation to consolidate and react.

Philip began by attacking Perinthos, possibly because, as the smaller of the two cities, it was thought to be the less likely to resist. If this was Philip's calculation, he was quite mistaken, since the city was geographically difficult to attack and its population was obdurate. On the other hand, he had good reason to believe that, if seriously resisted, he had the military resources to prevail. Philip's reign saw the development, partly under his inspiration and instructions, of a suite of artillery machines which were largely new to Greek warfare. Some of these had long been known in the Assyrian wars in the Middle East, but the deadening blanket of the Persian Empire had reduced their use, and restricted any innovation. Some had been developed in Sicilian warfare, or more likely, had been developed by Carthage on Assyrian models transmitted by the Phoenicians, and had been copied by the Syracusans. Philip is thought to have been shocked by the machines his own forces suddenly faced on a campaign in Phokis in the 350s BC, where the enemy forces were mercenaries who had probably learned about such machines in service in Sicily; he then arranged for improved versions of them to be built for his own forces. He now campaigned along with a siege train, in which the machines were dismantled for transport and then reassembled for the fighting. These included catapults capable of throwing large stones (though these were probably only in development at the time of the Perinthos siege), siege towers to allow archers and slingers to clear away defenders from the enemy's walls; rams to be used against gates and walls; and powerful composite bows firing large arrows long distances.[18]

Most of these military developments had not yet been used in combination in Greece, though Philip had used rams against Amphipolis and catapults against Olynthos. Perinthos, however, was to be attacked with all the methods Philip could muster and devise. Earlier sieges had often been little more than blockades – the siege of Byzantion by Athens in 407 BC was an example – and even Philip's siege of Olynthos had taken three months. In such circumstances the access of the besieged city to supplies from outside was crucial, and it was the fact that Perinthos in this crisis had plenty of friends which allowed it to survive; it was on the coast and was a port, and could therefore be replenished with food and even be reinforced by allied soldiers or hired mercenaries with relative ease. This meant that Philip's task, despite his skills and his machines, was exceptionally difficult.

The Siege of Perinthos

The siege began in July 340 BC.[19] Philip brought up an army of 30,000 men, and deployed very high siege towers, from which slingers and archers fired at the men on the walls.[20] The slingshot were probably of lead, for he had used these at Olynthos – they were more accurate than stones, being round and all the same size (or sizes). Dominating the upper part of the walls allowed the attackers to get their forces close to the walls without too much danger, and there they could be used to dig tunnels to undermine the walls, while other men could wield rams to break into the walls for the gates. No doubt, however, the gates were the better defended, as usual in a walled city, and the towers at those gates would probably be roofed, thus nullifying the efforts of the siege towers.

Fairly quickly it became clear to the Perinthians that they were liable to lose the battle if they did not get help, but also that much of the fighting must be done by themselves. As the walls began to crumble, they built a second wall behind it. And help came. The Persians did not wish to see

Philip prosper and the Great King ordered the nearby satraps to assist the Perinthians.[21] They sent supplies and mercenary reinforcements. Byzantion, which was in effect in the same situation as Perinthos – or would be, if and when that city was taken – sent supplies and some of its own catapults.[22] The coastal position of Perinthos was here an advantage in allowing both allies to send help by sea. It seems likely that Philip, a land commander above all, had not factored in this element in the Perinthian problem.

The undermined and battered walls fell along a considerable stretch. But the Perinthians' second wall had been built, and the Byzantine catapults rather redressed the balance in artillery. And when the second wall, which had must have been of lighter construction, was also breached, the Macedonians faced a continuous battle to get into the town. Perinthos, besides being on the coast, was built on a hill, with the houses close together all the way up to the top. The invaders had to break into houses and to fight street-by-street and sometimes house-by-house to make any advance (it must have been very like an ancient version of Stalingrad); casualties were no doubt heavy.

By September, Philip decided that the fight had become too costly.[23] Firing slingshot and arrows, battering the walls with rams and undermining them with tunnels, were activities which cost the defence many more casualties than the attack, but fighting street-by-street against the citizens defending their own homes, and against regular reinforcements and well-trained mercenaries, meant that the Macedonians' casualties became steadily much greater.

The Siege of Byzantion, 340 BC

Philip was faced by defeat, but he had several possibilities available. Perinthos was being supplied by sea, so he arranged that his own, fairly small, fleet should be brought round to the Propontis, obviously as a means of interrupting those supplies. But this meant passing the Athenian-colonized Chersonese, and to do so in safety the ships would need to be guarded when they drew up onto convenient beaches for the night. This was standard practice, and the men would then cook, eat, and sleep on shore. Also this was the land of Aigospotamoi, where a much greater Athenian fleet had been destroyed by a smaller Spartan one because, having landed, it did not set an alert guard. So the fleet was to be accompanied by an army large enough to protect both it and itself against any interference by the inhabitants of the Chersonese. This would certainly annoy Athens, but that city was technically Philip's ally, and he sent an explanatory letter which sufficiently foxed the Athenians that they did not immediately react to the Macedonian army's march.[24]

The Macedonian fleet, even when in the Propontis, was not strong enough to prevent supplies reaching Perinthos, but it was available, and it stood as a menace to others. Philip's next move, which he had no doubt intended from the time when he decided to bring the fleet round, was to attack Byzantion. He left part of his forces at Perinthos, probably mainly on blockade duty, and shifted the larger part of his army to face Byzantion. He evidently left his siege machines at Perinthos, and his engineers, led by a Thessalian called Polyeidos began building new machines for use against Byzantion.

Although Philip therefore began another active siege, damaging the walls of Byzantion, he also blockaded the city's ally Selymbria, in order to safeguard his communications and supply route.[25] By now, time was pressing, since it was obvious that Athens had now been sufficiently annoyed by the passage of the Macedonian ships along the coasts of the Chersonese, and the transit of that fleet through the Hellespont, that it must be on the verge of participating actively in the war. So it would be best to get hold of Byzantion as soon as possible.

Philip's method here was even more outrageous than sending his forces through an ally's territory without a by-your-leave. In the Bosporos there was a large fleet of merchant ships, 230 of them, of which 180 were Athenian or destined for Athens. This fleet was guarded by a detachment of Athenian ships under the command of Chares. This was normal, the Athenians usually being on the lookout for pirates, so the Athenian warship detachment was not particularly large. Furthermore, they were clearly not expecting the Macedonian ships to do anything, though they cannot have been ignorant of the sieges going on at the cities on the Propontis, nor of Athenian apprehensions about their results; after all, Athens and Philip were, at least nominally, allies, and Athens was neutral in the fighting.

Chares was called away to a meeting with the nearby Persian satraps, and while he was absent – he had no doubt taken several of the Athenian warships with him to emphasize the strengths of Athens – the Macedonian fleet attacked the merchantmen. Almost all of them were captured.[26]

At a single stroke Philip had acquired plenty of food for his army, other booty as well, and the ships, whose timber could be used in building his siege machines. There was, besides food, a good supply of hides on the ships, and leather was always useful to any army. The value put on the captures is said to have been 700 talents. Only the Athenian ships were seized and kept, the fifty non-Athenian ships whose destinations were elsewhere in Greece, were released. (The numbers emphasize the domination of Athens in the seaborne trade.) In addition to gathering plentiful supplies for himself and his forces, of course, Philip had deprived Athens of all these supplies.

Athens, as Philip must have expected from the start, was predictably outraged and, despite another explanatory letter from Philip, the Assembly immediately declared war.[27] It could hardly do anything else. As usual, however, Philip had some right on his side. He accused some of the ships of aiming to resupply Selymbria, his enemy, and he could also suggest that both Byzantion and Perinthos were likely to be assisted. But he might especially have pointed out that Chares, Athens' general in the Propontis, was, even as the merchantmen were being seized, conferring with the Persian satraps, who had been aiding his enemies. Chares' conference could best be interpreted as a meeting aimed at coordinating Persian and Athenian activities in support of both Byzantion and Perinthos. Philip's pre-emptive response to these negotiations was perhaps somewhat out of proportion given the presumed offence, but it was very much in line with his similarly pre-emptive attack on Perinthos; in both cases he was sure that an attack on him was in preparation, so he moved first. It is not an unknown action in other wars.

Our sources shift their attention to Byzantion and the Bosporos, ignoring the fact that Perinthos was still besieged by part of Philip's army.[28] Who was left in charge of that siege is not known, though both Antipatros and Parmenion have been suggested, somewhat inevitably. One man who was present was a man called either Antigenes or Antigonos who is said to have lost an eye in a sortie by the defenders at Perinthos. There is confusion over the name – it may be Antigonos the later king, who was called Monophthalamos, 'the one-eyed', but the name in the record is Antigenes. Concentrating on attempting to identify the man, of course, misses the point, which is that there had been a sortie by the Perinthians, in which the eye was lost, and this must have taken place after Philip had withdrawn part of his army.[29]

Philip had now spread his army over three sieges, Perinthos, Selymbria, and Byzantion, though only the last was really active. He maintained the pressure on the city for at least two more months. His engineers took timber from the captured ships to build more siege machines, and he had an advantage in that a good part of both Byzantion's machines and its defensive capability had been shifted to assist Perinthos. Evidently Byzantion had feared an attack well before the arrival of Philip's army, but by sending an adequate force to Perinthos the Byzantians had left themselves short. The walls of Byzantion were certainly breached at least once, but a fortuitous alarm raised by barking dogs (even then the city had noisy barking dogs) alerted the defence and they repaired the breach.

Athens having at last openly joined the war, Chares and his fleet – forty ships – was able to intervene decisively. He joined with Byzantion's ships and drove the Macedonian fleet into the Bosporos, and then further on into the Black Sea.[30] Chares established fortified posts to supervise the Bosporos traffic, and the Athenians sent another fleet to supersede Chares' ships (and remove Chares from command, since he was not a popular figure). Philip sent a force to raid in the Chersonese, possibly to distract the Athenians.[31] The result of the siege of Byzantion was thus the same as that at Perinthos. Philip, with his usual diplomatic skill, arranged to take his army away safely, and with his usual military sense campaigned successfully in Thrace to restore the morale of his soldiers.[32]

Philip was defeated not just by the citizens, but by a wide coalition of states which feared him and were suspicious of his longer term aims and ambitions. This was the result both of Philip's threatening power, and of Athenian diplomacy before and during the sieges. Persia and Athens could be quite persuasive with other cities; Rhodes and Chios in particular were clearly apprehensive; both were old friends of Byzantion and depended in part on the traffic through the Bosporos. Philip's siege machines had done their work well, but they were rapidly countered by rival machines which were already available in Byzantion. His diplomacy was tricky, and many states must by this time have looked askance at any favours he offered, or any message he sent. But it was the basic resistance of the citizens of the two cities to his attacks which ensured his defeat. They had plenty of assistance, of course, from Philip himself, for his decision to divide his army between sieges at Perinthos and Byzantion (and Selymbria, and the Chersonese) clearly left all his siege forces weaker, so that at Perinthos the citizens felt emboldened to make a sortie; this was clearly another of the reasons for his defeat.

Philip, despite his defeats, went on to fight and defeat Athens and its allies at Khaironeia, and formed a new Greek league with the aim of invading the Persian Empire. Killed before he could more than start this adventure, his son Alexander pursued the same course from 334 BC onwards. Neither man paid any more attention to Byzantion. Having been defeated, Philip then ignored the city in the last four years of his life, and Alexander followed him in this. Alexander crossed into Asia at the Hellespont, as had Philip's advance forces two years before. Alexander did appoint a governor for Hellespontine Phrygia and he had left one to govern Thrace, but only the latter could have had any relations with Byzantion. Whether the city was a member of the new Hellenic League developed by Philip is not known, and is perhaps, given the circumstances of its relations with Philip, unlikely.[33]

The Siege of 318

So there is no sign of any activity by Byzantion during Alexander's reign (336–323 BC), nor for some years after. But in those years Antigonos Monophthalamos was busy gaining control of Asia Minor, first against Persian satraps, and then against rival Macedonians. In Thrace, after Alexander's death Lysimachos battled long and hard to secure control of his satrapy. Byzantion was undoubtedly busy at its own affairs, trading and so on, all this time. And as the warfare of the successors of Alexander rumbled on, the city, which had already shown in Philip's war that it was alert to the latest military development, will have continued to be alert to further threats.

In 318–317 BC the warfare of the Macedonians came close. In 318 Arrhidaios, the satrap of Hellespontine Phrygia, attacked Kyzikos, apparently without cause except that he hoped to capture a rich city. Byzantion and Antigonos both moved to assist in the defence, the city by sea, Antigonos by land, but Kyzikos had successfully repelled Arrhidaios before they arrived.[34]

In the next year, 317 BC, however, further conflict, this time between several of the successors, approached.[35] Antigonos was in western Asia Minor, where he was making sure of controlling the territory; he also gathered a fleet. In Greece Polyperchon was intermittently fighting against Kassandros, who had staked a claim to be the successor of Antipatros, his father, who had been left in command of Macedon by Alexander. Polyperchon also had a fleet, commanded by Kleitos, and he sent it to gain control of the Hellespont so as to keep Kassandros and Antigonos apart. Antigonos sent his own fleet, 130 ships commanded by Nikanor, to contest Kleitos' fleet's control of the Hellespont, and Antigonos himself brought his army by land to secure the Hellespont's Asian shore.

Kleitos retreated from the Hellespont, presumably seeking some advantage. Nikanor followed. The two fleets eventually fought near Byzantion, and Nikanor was beaten. Byzantion itself appears to have already joined Antigonos' side, and Antigonos had brought his army to the Asian shore of the Bosporos at Kalchedon and Chrysopolis. Nikanor brought his surviving ships, perhaps half of the original total, to seek refuge at Kalchedon, where they would be under Antigonos' protection. Kleitos, satisfied for the moment, took his ships to shore near Byzantion. The city was clearly his enemy, and it seems probable that he laid siege to it.[36]

The sequel followed soon, but how soon is not all that clear. The account of events in Diodoros implies that Antigonos' riposte came at once, but this seems unlikely. After a sea battle there are many things which have to be done – recovering damaged ships and marooned sailors, repairs, resting the sailors, tending the wounded, burying the dead, getting the men and ships together, imposing an administrative system and discipline, feeding the sailors. And, of course, it was necessary to find out where the enemy was and in what strength; one may assume several days at least were involved in this recovery, and it would be better to reckon on a couple of weeks. During that time Byzantion was under siege, or at least under threat and blockade.

The issue of where Kleitos had gone was perhaps the easiest to solve, since he had drawn up his ships on shore close to Byzantion, and the city communicated that fact to Antigonos, no doubt along with pleas for help. Kleitos' men were also onshore, and it may be that Antigonos knew the story of Aigospotamoi, and undoubtedly he knew of Philip's ploy of sending his small Macedonian fleet round the Chersonese guarded by a land army; the naval practice of landing every night was common knowledge. This in fact was what he had been doing so far, with his army on the Asian shore marching for the Hellespont and then to the Bosporos in support of the fleet. The situation now was similar to that of the Athenians at Aigospotamoi, with Antigonos in the role of Lysander.

Maybe Kleitos did not know of these historical parallels, but Antigonos' action implies that he understood the opportunity which Kleitos was offering him, and understood that Kleitos and his men were careless. He reorganized his forces, selecting the toughest soldiers to act as marines on the ships. He implicated the Byzantines thoroughly by getting them to send their own ships across to ferry archers and slingers across the strait. These men will have been landed in the city, perhaps without Kleitos being aware that they had done so. If the city was actually being besieged, or perhaps just blockaded, these light forces could be seen, if Kleitos realized who they were, as reinforcements for the defence. He cannot have been surprised at such a development. In this situation Antigonos was able to make all his preparations fully in view of his enemy, without alarming him; such measures were only to be expected. And Kleitos now had by far the greater fleet, having captured a considerable portion of that of Nikanor.

This must have taken some days to organize, but relatively quickly (if not quite so speedily as Diodoros implies) Antigonos was able to launch his reply. The ships sailed at dawn, or perhaps in the pre-dawn twilight, and as they reached the enemy shore where the ships were drawn up and the men were camped, the archers and slingers in the city will have opened fire. Kleitos and his men, still asleep, or perhaps preparing food, were wholly surprised. The assault was instantly successful. Soldiers, sailors, and ships were captured or killed, and Kleitos' ships themselves seized. The implication is that all the men died or were taken, but Kleitos himself escaped in a ship and no doubt others of his men scattered by running away (or surrendered and were then recruited into Antigonos' forces). Kleitos' ship was forced onshore and he escaped again, only to be intercepted by some of Lysimachos' soldiers and executed.

This was the closest the city came to suffering disaster since Philip's siege. The rulers of the city had weighed the respective strengths of the opponents and had seen that despite Nikanor's defeat, Antigonos was the more potent. The sight of his forces busy in repairs and preparations, while Kleitos' continued their desultory siege, was no doubt convincing. The same calculation had evidently set the city against Philip, for he faced not only Perinthos and Byzantion but, from the start, the Persian Empire, and likely Athens, and this coalition in 340 BC looked the more powerful. The city had, however, had a lucky escape; they had chosen Antigonos' side, and it is likely that any siege he instituted would have been pursued much more rigorously than Kleitos managed. Not that the Greeks and Macedonians were very good at sieges, as Philip himself had recently demonstrated by his failure, despite the most up-to-date equipment and a victorious army, to make any impression on three separate cities. This may well have been one of the factors involved in the clash between Kleitos and Antigonos. The city had no doubt emerged from these wars with an enhanced reputation as a place difficult to capture.

This careful calculation of power, which it is clear that Byzantion had made as the two armies came closer, was also the overall reaction to campaigning warlords by many Hellenistic cities. They identified the more powerful ruler involved in a war, and joined him as an ally. Byzantion's neighbour Kyzikos was a past master at this sort of calculated diplomacy, and the policy kept it safe and prosperous for several centuries; it certainly helped that it was capable of fighting off men such as Arrhidaios.[37] This policy did lead, in this post-Alexander period, to some sudden switches of allegiance – but then the Propontis cities had had plenty of practice at this diplomacy in the previous century. In 312 BC, just six years after Byzantion joined with Antigonos against Kleitos, he arrived once more on Byzantion's doorstep asking for an alliance, and to be provided with a means of crossing the Bosporos. By this time, however, Lysimachos in Thrace had grown to be notably powerful, and he counselled against joining Antigonos. Lysimachos was already Antigonos' active enemy, and could be expected to advise as he did, but that did not really vitiate his advice; the Byzantines could calculate the odds for themselves – not to mention that Lysimachos was solidly installed on Byzantion's side of the Bosporos, and was the city's immediate neighbour, whereas Antigonos was on the Asian side, and apparently without ships.[38]

The city's decision in this case was crucial, and Antigonos turned away to campaign elsewhere. In his final campaign, in 302–301 BC, in which

Antigonos was defeated and killed, a similar situation recurred, though much less dangerously for the city. In the winter of 302/301 BC Antigonos' son Demetrios arrived outside Kalchedon and camped there with his army for the winter.[39] He does not, however, appear to have threatened Byzantion, no matter what he did to Kalchedon. The fighting in this war was in Greece and in Asia Minor and Byzantion was unimportant in this particular case. No doubt the city's merchants took advantage of this sudden huge market and sold whatever was needed to the army.

The city had survived an extraordinary bout of warfare intact. Its peripheral position with regard to the major wars had clearly helped, since commanders normally preferred to cross at the Hellespont, which would usually involve a shorter march. But it was a prosperous city,[40] and could if it wished, control the Bosporos passageway. Chares had done so, so perhaps had Philip while besieging the city. Antigonos' request for passage implies that Byzantion had a worthwhile naval force, which would normally control the strait; any challenger would need to bring up a major fleet. It is an example of a relatively small force being capable of controlling such a passage, if it is sufficiently distant from potentially hostile power centres. But in such dangerous times it would possibly be safer simply to let ships pass without hindrance. No doubt the Byzantines collected taxes when they felt they could, but the city prospered well enough from the ships and sailors forced to wait in its harbours for a favourable wind or a slackening of the current.

Chapter 4

Enemies from the North-West and the East – The Galatians and the Seleukids

The Sieges of 277, 255/254, and 220

The Galatian Siege of 277

The death of Lysimachos, Antigonos' effective successor in Asia Minor and of Kassandros in Macedon, upset the political situation. He was followed by Seleukos I, who was soon murdered (both kings died in 281 BC). Seleukos' son Antiochos I displayed a powerful determination to enlarge his father's conquests. He clashed with Antigonos Gonatos, Antigonos Monophthalamos' grandson, but also found that a string of cities and kingdoms in the north of Asia Minor had banded together to oppose him; the group is called by modern historians the Northern League. They included Byzantion.[1] But Antiochos had too much on his plate to attack the members, individually or collectively, and soon a much more serious problem than the league beset him.

The murderer of Seleukos I was Ptolemy Keraunos, a scion of the Ptolemaic family which now ruled Egypt, and a man with an ambition to be a king. Killing Seleukos gave him the opportunity to make himself king of Macedon, but he was soon attacked there by bands of warriors, called Galatians, who came down upon Macedon and Greece from their new base in the Banat, the area of the Danube Valley around modern Belgrade. They were Celts, and like all such raiders they homed in on victims which were troubled and disturbed and so unable to defend themselves adequately. After several raids into Macedon (in one of which Keraunos was killed), and into Greece as far as Delphi, several groups of these raiders headed east to try their luck in Asia Minor.[2]

These eastward-heading Galatians split into two main groups, though in fact there were three 'tribes' within the moving horde. One group, led by Loutarios, went to the Hellespont. They contacted the governor of the

Asian shore, Antipatros, who refused them permission to cross. Their reputation, gained in Greece, for destruction and killing was sufficient to ensure a refusal, and Antipatros gathered up the ships on the European side so that no clandestine crossing was possible. The second Galatian group headed for the Bosporos and camped outside Byzantion.[3]

The Hellespont group captured Lysimacheia, a city founded by Lysimachos thirty years before at the root of the Gallipoli peninsula. This was no great feat since the city had been wrecked by an earthquake not long before, and little or no attempt had yet been made to revive it. (Such a task required a royal patron to apply a subsidy, and with Lysimachos and Seleukos dead, it was bereft of any patron.) This was dangerous territory for the Galatians, for only a year before Antigonos Gonatas had defeated another roving band of Galatians there and had massacred them. This had given him the credibility to make himself king in Macedon, and he then cunningly recruited other Galatians and had used them to clear out any remaining bands of their fellows from the kingdom. So any Galatian group within reach of Macedon might expect to be attacked.

Those bands in Thrace were clearly blocked from returning to Macedon (though others had given up the search for new lands and had returned home to the Banat). The fate of the small cities in the Chersonese is not known. It is generally assumed, when any thought is given to them, that they were captured and sacked, but we have no information, and it is not reasonable to assume destruction; an accommodation between residents and invaders is quite possible. After all, the Galatians were no good at siege warfare – even worse than the Greeks – and yet at the same time they clearly understood the niceties and procedures of Hellenistic diplomacy, so it could be that the Chersonese cities were safe so long as they established diplomatic and trading relations with the invaders and did not object too strongly to a casual ravaging of their lands. It is clear that Loutarios in his negotiations with Antipatros was playing the game the Hellenistic way, politely and courteously, making requests rather than demands. This, however, would not last.

The band which headed for the Bosporos was led by Leonnorios. He evidently met with opposition, or perhaps his men were hungry, for the lands of Byzantion were ravaged. So also, possibly, were those of Selymbria (by this time annexed by Byzantion) and Perinthos, but we do not hear of them. This band was a large group of people, men, women, children and slaves, at least 10,000 in number; they were probably not very well disciplined, they were hungry, and were eager to reach the rich lands and cities of Asia Minor. But the Byzantines evidently, like Antipatros, refused them passage. Leonnorios needed ships, and Byzantion had them; like Loutarios, Leonnorios was clearly well versed in Hellenistic diplomatic processes, and he also understood the political conditions in the land he wished to reach, Asia Minor.

There were wars in Asia. King Antiochos I was attempting to enforce his suzerainty on the members of the Northern League, while in the kingdom of Bithynia, one of those members, there was also a disputed royal succession. Once he realized the numbers and capabilities of the Galatians who were menacing his ally Byzantion, Nikomedes I of Bithynia, under severe pressure from his usurping brother, negotiated an agreement with Leonnorios. It may be presumed that Byzantion acted as the intermediary, being anxious to remove the Galatians from its doorstep and to recover control of its territory, presently occupied and unavailable, and so oblige an ally as well. The agreement was that if Leonnorios and his band were allowed to cross the Bosporos they would join Nikomedes in defeating his brother's pretensions, and then turn on Nikomedes' other enemy, Antiochos.

The Galatians made an alliance with the Bithynian kingdom in proper form. All parties were satisfied – Nikomedes saved his throne without further dispute, and saw his enemy Antiochos forced into another preoccupying defensive war, the Galatians gained access to the wealth of Asia, and eventually acquired land on which to settle, and Byzantion was relieved of their new and difficult neighbours. But this last condition proved to be only temporary.

The Galatian group under Loutarios, at the Hellespont, failed in their negotiations with the Seleukid governor across the water, though negotiations of some sort did continue. Antipatros at last sent over two triremes carrying a group of people to investigate the Galatians, presumably as part of the negotiations. But the Galatians, their diplomacy having failed, seized the ships and used them to transfer their people across to Asia. There is no record of Antipatros opposing them. Since they were crossing in just two shiploads at a time, if he had any force at all at his disposal, each landing could have been contested at the water's edge. He apparently either had no forces at his command – highly unlikely for a provincial governor – or he did not try.

They were across in Asia, therefore, at both the Bosporos and Hellespont crossings, and went on to raid Asia for the next couple of years; Antiochos eventually defeated them and settled them in central Anatolia, which became called Galatia. In their raids they attacked cities particularly in western Asia Minor from Kyzikos to Ephesos and Miletos. In not one case did they capture a city, but they were able to capture the unprotected temple of Apollo at Didyma and loot its treasures, and they could kidnap anyone who was out in the countryside when they arrived. They left a vicious reputation behind them.[4]

This must count as another siege of Byzantion, though it is not usually noticed as such, most attention being directed at the events in Macedon and Greece (where they had raided the sanctuary of Apollo at Delphi), and in Asia, where numerous cities suffered – though they were quite frequently bought off by negotiated payments. Again, it is worth emphasizing that the invaders behaved much the same as any other Hellenistic army and kingdom. Byzantion, however, had been seriously threatened by Leonnorios' forces, and like the Asian cities, found its territories ravaged. The Galatians might have been unable to capture any city, but that does not mean they did not attempt to do so; they would certainly have sacked any city which did fall to them.

Byzantion, however, was not long free of the Galatians, for a new band had reached Thrace and had settled there. Most attention in this subject is given either to the raids in Greece and Macedon and Asia Minor, or to the people who settled in Asia Minor, where the three Galatian tribes became an accepted political feature. They developed into an almost normal Hellenistic state, not quite a kingdom, not quite a republic, but certainly an oligarchy of powerful feudal lords. As a polity it was generally peaceful – though the Greeks retained unpleasant memories of their raids and ravagings.

The Thracian Galatians formed into a kingdom, the first ruler being called Kommontorios; the name given to the state is Tylis, which was the name of its political centre, though this has not been definitively located. His group seems to have arrived at much the same time as those which reached Asia, and perhaps some of the Tylis group were people who had broken away from the Asian-seekers while still in Europe. It seems also that there were other groups moving about at the time, as well as those who raided or who developed into regular states. Kommontorios' group settled in eastern Thrace, on the Black Sea coast north of Byzantion. There they developed into a predator kingdom.[5]

This is what the Greeks later always assumed all the Galatian groups were, and they even assumed that the settled Galatians in Asia Minor continued to be a menace, whereas it seems that they were not, at least not more so than any other Hellenistic state or army. But Kommontorios' kingdom did retain its original predatory habits and methods throughout its existence. Its men scoured Thrace for slaves to sell, and for food and wealth, under the leadership of a line of kings; it blackmailed, or eventually taxed, any Greek city within its boundaries (which, of course, were fluid). The king took control of the collected wealth produced by these methods, and distributed it to his subordinate chiefs, who used it to maintain a war band, and it was these war bands which went out into the neighbouring lands to secure more treasure. It was a state effectively stuck in the old ways of an Iron Age tribe, and did not advance out of these ways; by contrast, the Asian Galatians, perhaps because they faced much more powerful enemies, so that raiding was no longer possible, settled down in relative peace, though they did participate in wars when one was available.

This, at least, seems to be the pattern. The theory is developed from the information that, much later, Byzantion had been subjected to the type of extortion from the foundation of the Tylis kingdom. It was not the only Greek victim; some cities along the Pontic coast were inside the kingdom, and it seems unlikely that they would therefore have been subject to much more than normal taxation. But Byzantion was different. First it was at some distance from the kingdom and so was less amenable to constant pressure. Then also, it was a particularly wealthy city, wealthier than those on the Pontic coast, and itself operated a quasi-predatory system in its imposition of the *dekate* tax on passing ships. (This tax seems to have become more widely accepted by its victims in the third century BC, on the implicit promise of suppressing piracy; Byzantion maintained its small fleet of warships for that purpose.)

The information about the Tylis kingdom's predations comes from a single source, the historian Polybios, writing at the end of the kingdom's existence.[6] He called the payments 'tribute', and notes that they started under Kommontorios in the 270s BC at 3,000 gold pieces (at the foundation of the kingdom), and rose to 5,000, then 10,000, and eventually the demand upon the city was for 80 talents. Apart from the mere greed of the king, this may have been a result of the drying up of sources of plunder and slaves in Thrace either by depopulation or the growth of Thracian opposition, and therefore the demands were laid more fully on the Greek cities, of which Byzantion was the only one for which we have information, but which was also the wealthiest in the reach of the Tylis king.

How frequently these demands were made is unclear. It does not seem that it was an annual event, at least for some time. The first demand was from Kommontorios the founder, and the irregular increases imply that the demands also came irregularly. By the 220s, however, the payment had certainly become an annual demand, and Byzantion decided that the city could no longer afford annual tribute payments of eighty talents. It was the measures the city took as a result of this decision that lead to the publicization of the system. This then implies that the Byzantines had been perfectly willing to go on paying the smaller sums for fifty years or so.

The threat was explicit – pay up, or have the city's lands ravaged. The origin of this was, of course, in part the actions of Leonnorios' band in 276 bc as the people waited to cross into Asia and meanwhile foraged for food in Byzantion's lands, and laid siege to the city in an attempt to gain access by ship to Asia. Another origin may well have come from a Byzantine attempt to preserve its lands against that damage by paying the raiders to go away. Certainly the system is associated with the first king of Tylis, Kommontorios himself, though he was not necessarily its inventor. One must assume that the city did not necessarily give in to these demands easily, and that periodic reminders of the policy of threat were required. At times this will have meant that Galatian forces came right up to the walls of the city, though a regular siege would hardly be within the Tylis kingdom's capabilities. But it seems very much as though the city lived under a sort of intermittent quasi-siege for the fifty or sixty years after the system was developed. It was under constant threat of being attacked, even if the army was not visible, and payment of the ransom in advance would probably be cheaper. Any Byzantine who owned property outside the walls would come to expect his lands to be damaged every now and again.

The Galatian Siege of 220

The Tylis king in office in the 220s BC, Kavaros, imposed the 80-talents tribute on Byzantion in 221 or 220 BC; in 220 the Byzantines decided they could no longer pay such blackmail/tribute. The smaller sums of 5,000 and 10,000 gold pieces had evidently been payable, since the alternative was probably to see much greater damage being inflicted on their lands, but 80 talents was too much. How often such a sum had been demanded (and maybe paid) is not known, but it does seem that the demand of 220 BC may not have been the first. If the city had already had to pay such a sum more than once, a Byzantine revolt would be understandable. The other question is why Kavaros was demanding such a great sum from a single city, possibly several times. Since the kingdom he ruled collapsed soon after this crisis it would seem that the demand was possibly a final desperate effort to keep the kingdom in existence. So both halves of this exploitative relationship were in desperate straits.

Byzantion's desperation is shown by its reaction. A vote was taken, no doubt in the city's Assembly, to refuse payment, but it seems that an appeal had already gone out to the city's trading partners in the Aegean and the Black Sea, asking for help, preferably financial, to stave off Kavaros' threats. Only one city, Herakleia Pontike, a former fellow member of the Northern League, responded. So Byzantion, instead of either paying or refusing to pay, imposed a new tax, a version of the *dekate*, but paid by ships passing north through the Bosporos (the original demand had been on shipping passing southwards); perhaps this 'new tax' was simply an expansion of the old one, so that ships passing in both directions would pay. Whatever the precise decision, it provoked an uproar amongst potential payers.[7]

What Byzantion was doing, of course, was attempting to transfer Kavaros' blackmail demand from the city to the trading world of the Aegean as a whole. No doubt the king was pleased at this notion, since in future he would be able to increase his demands on Byzantion without limit, and the city would then screw up its taxation demands on everyone else. The situation was, however, quite clear to those who were to pay, and a conference at Rhodes among those who were to be most directly affected by the taxation came to the decision that the demand was unreasonable and that Rhodes should do something about it.

Rhodes demanded that the new tax be cancelled, and gathered a number of supporters for this. Byzantion refused. Rhodes then conducted a sea war, sending a fleet to blockade the Bosporos, which would prevent the tax being collected.[8] But the crisis involved many other states, starting with the cities which had appealed to Rhodes to take action. Several kings joined in, but entirely for their own purposes. Akhaios, king in Asia Minor, used the crisis as a means of getting his father released from Ptolemaic imprisonment, then did nothing for Byzantion. Once he was out of the fight, his neighbour and enemy Attalos, king at Pergamon, used this as an excuse to pull out also, citing his fear that Akhaios would attack him if his forces were involved at the Straits. Prusias I, king of Bithynia joined in, with some enthusiasm. He already had a quarrel with Byzantion and used the crisis as an excuse to attack those Byzantine possessions on the Asian side.[9]

In all this, there is no indication that Byzantion made any resistance to these blockades and attacks. This is surely suspicious. It is almost as though the Byzantines had calculated in advance what would happen. In fact, of course, the city did not have the armed strength to tackle all these enemies at once, or even any one of them. The Rhodian fleet was far stronger than that of Byzantion – and it was backed up by the ships from several of its allies; Prusias' armies were more powerful than anything Byzantion could field. Behind the city's walls and behind its water defences, the city simply sat and waited for a solution to present itself.

The actual loser in that fighting, of course, was not Byzantion, despite Prusias' conquests and despite Rhodes' blockade; instead, the one who lost out was Kavaros, whose demands could not be met by Byzantion with the perfectly accurate excuse that the city was no longer receiving the tax revenue he was relying on, and needed all its resources to fend off the attack of Rhodes, Attalos, Prusias, and the rest. And Kavaros was the first to break. He intervened, ironically, as a 'broker of peace'. This was a relatively simple decision, though he cannot have liked it, since he must have seen the impossibility of either capturing Byzantion – he was surely tempted to attack the city – or now of collecting any 'tribute'. The peace simply involved everyone giving up what was in dispute – Byzantion gave up its tax, Prusias his conquests, Rhodes its blockade (the ending of the tax had been its original demand). Kavaros clearly had also to give up the prospect of receiving any tribute. Whether the Byzantines calculated all this from the start is perhaps highly unlikely, but the city was the real beneficiary, since it now wielded a potent weapon which it could turn on when any further tribute demands were made.

The loser was Kavaros and the kingdom. He had clearly reached too far, probably not counting on the great Aegean reaction. Within a few years the Thracians who had been harried for the past fifty years rose in a war for freedom, and the Tylis kingdom collapsed.[10] It may be that some elements of the kingdom had already detached themselves, for a stray Galatian band, the Aigosages, crossed into Asia at Attalos' invitation in 217 BC. Where they came from is not stated, but the obvious source is that they had broken away from the Tylis kingdom as it was collapsing. Their behaviour was a reminder to the Greeks of that which they normally expected from Galatian bands. The city of Alexandria Troas drove them away; Attalos abandoned them; Prusias massacred them.[11] The final collapse is noted by Polybios about 212 BC, with the death of Kavaros.

This book is aimed at discussing the sieges suffered by Byzantion, and more than once a crisis has emerged in which the city was threatened, without it apparently being subject to a direct siege. The problem of definition has been clear from the first. The early submission of the city to the Persians in 513 BC was later followed in 490 BC by the flight of the citizens in the face of a vengeful Persian force approaching. Neither of these events may be called sieges (though I am seriously tempted to include the second of these), but both resulted in the capture of the city by its enemy, which is always the object of any siege. The problem of definition, in other words, is not easy, and this episode of the conflict with Tylis is the most difficult. The city was not captured in the course of 220 BC, but it was clearly continuously under threat, either from Kavaros, or from Rhodes and its allies. The threat posed was that the city's lands in Thrace would be subject to a serious ravaging by Kavaros' people, but behind that was the implicit threat that, if Byzantion refused to pay up, the city itself would be at least blockaded by land, which could hardly be distinguished from an actual siege. The main threat was that the city would be blockaded by sea, and unable to import food or carry on trade. The possibility of two blockades, by enemies of Byzantion and of each other, clearly existed. So far as can be seen the Galatians never went beyond ravaging the city's *chora* (the countryside around the city), but by paying up for fifty years, even if intermittently, the ultimate, if only implicit, threat of a siege had clearly been successful. The conflict with the Tylis kingdom may therefore be included in this account of sieges even though the city was not, so far as we can see, subjected to a direct assault and capture by the Galatians – but it was certainly as much menaced and severely restricted in its situation, and even indirectly controlled by its enemies, as it had been by the Persians in 513 BC.

Chapter 5

Enemy from the East – Antiochos II

The Seleukid Siege of 255/254 BC

The Second Syrian War took place between 260 and 253 BC, between the kings of the Seleukid and Ptolemaic dynasties, Antiochos II and Ptolemy II.[1] Only the former king actually took an active part in the fighting, but this included an expedition into Thrace in 255 BC. In this campaign he is recorded as attacking Kypsela, a town in the southern part of Thrace, having passed into Thrace through Lysimacheia in the Chersonese.[2]

There is no detailed chronology of the expedition, only fragmentary and discrete notices, of which the references to Kypsela and Lysimacheia are examples. A third fragment refers to an attack by Antiochos on Byzantion.[3] How serious this was, and whether it constituted a siege and not just a temporary threat, is difficult to decide, but it seems that it brought Ptolemy's attention to the Propontis – in diplomatic terms, that is, not personally. He posed as a friend of Byzantion and presented the city with some Ptolemaic territory on the Asian side of the Propontis, together with grain, money, and weaponry.[4] The precise location of this land is not clear, but Byzantion later had a substantial territory in the peninsula between the Gulfs of Iznik and Gemlik.

The land involved would no doubt have been welcome, but it is likely that Ptolemy gave it away because it was clearly vulnerable to annexation by Antiochos, who had also been active on the Asian side, and would soon present his divorced Queen Laodike with a large estate just to the west of Kyzikos.[5] The Byzantine acquisition was probably not far from the Seleukid estate, just east of Kyzikos' own mainland territories.

The food, money, and weaponry clearly given to the city suggest that it was in need of such resources, and this must be a strong indication that it was under actual attack. If so, the defence succeeded, and the city remained independent. It voted a temple to be built in Ptolemy's honour, and he had a cult in the city afterwards; again, the expedition is a strong indication that the crisis had been serious.[6] It may be concluded that Antiochos had put the city under siege.

It will have been noticed the Seleukid expedition into Thrace happened while the Tylis kingdom was active in that same area. There is no sign that Antiochos contacted that kingdom, either diplomatically or militarily, though by reaching Byzantion he was close to it – and could be considered by the Tylis king to be encroaching on his own prerogatives. It would therefore seem that all the kings, Antiochos, Ptolemy, and the Tylis king, were operating with great care to avoid any armed clash between their various forces. Antiochos got across the Hellespont without Ptolemaic interference but Ptolemy had naval command of the Aegean and the Tylis king stayed put; Antiochos did not provoke anyone other than the Byzantines and various Thracians; the assistance that the city acquired was essentially in materials and diplomatic support, and no Ptolemaic troops were involved. The siege was evidently a diplomatic effort as much as a military, with the Seleukid king demonstrating his prowess and perhaps provoking the Ptolemaic king to expend some of his resources in an essentially futile way.

Interlude I

Polybios on Byzantion

The account Polybios gives of the Rhodian-Byzantine 'war' in 220 BC is used by him as a peg on which to hang a discussion of the city's situation, and that itself became a peg as a way to discuss the Bosporos and its currents. He discusses the site of the city, pointing out that it had particular advantage for its seaward role, but on land the city was constantly under threat from the Thracians.[1] His account then veers off into a lengthy discussion of the currents of the Bosporos before returning to give his account of the Rhodian-Byzantine war.

Several almost chance comments in this account are worth extra consideration, as do Polybios' omissions. He is brief on the site of the city, noting its relationship to the sea, but he makes absolutely no mention of the buildings in the city, or of its fortifications, though the city wall had been held against Philip II over a century before his account was written. These must be taken for granted in his references to the threat of the Thracians, which he insists were constant, an obvious exaggeration. He remarks, however, that it was impossible to win this Thracian war since if the Byzantines marched out to fight a threatening Thracian force and won, the other Thracians who had not been involved would join in to despoil the loser and the threat would continue, an interpretation which implies that he had not investigated the situation personally, but relied on Byzantine propaganda in connection with its taxing of passing ships.[2]

The omission of any details about the city, combined with the strong suspicion that Polybios had based his account on that of Strato of Lampsakos of a century earlier, makes it similarly clear that he had not seen the city himself.[3] The same may go for a much briefer reference to the city by the geographer Strabo, who was writing a century and a half after Polybios. He was in part basing himself also on Strato and on Polybios, but his main purpose seems to have been to dispute some of Polybios' conclusions and assertions. The reason for these failures to go into detail on the city can be seen in Polybios' remark that it was rarely visited by others, and that it was 'remote', a condition clearly still obtaining in Strabo's day, though Roman attention was about to turn that around.[4]

The city's situation was, however, notably favourable for trade and for supervising the passing traffic. From the trade out of the Black Sea he lists cattle, slaves, honey, wax, and preserved fish; olive oil and 'every kind of wine' were the main items sent the other way;[5] to this may be added hides, flax, iron, and hemp from the north.[6] He also notes the traffic in corn, which responded to the needs in both directions, at times sent from the Black Sea lands towards Greece, and at others from the Mediterranean into the Black Sea cities. (Walbank points to confirmation of this in an inscription from Istros, by a Carthaginian who had brought corn to sell in that city.)[7] Polybios does not fail to point out that Byzantion itself benefits favourably from both trades, and from exporting its own produce, while accepting imports easily from the passing ships.

The threat to the city from the Thracians is not something much dealt with in other ancient sources, which perhaps suggests it was either a relatively insignificant problem when Polybios was writing in the first half of the second century (he died at some point after 118 BC), or that it was so ubiquitous that it was not worth mentioning. The enmity of the Thracians towards all the Greek colonial cities dated back to the latters' foundations in the seventh and sixth centuries, but the actual fighting was only intermittent. In the early second century BC, however, there were stronger Thracian threats, including their invasion of the Chersonese and the destruction of the city of Lysimacheia – though it had been damaged in the earthquake first.[8]

This new hostility may well be a result of the collapse of the Tylis kingdom, which had perhaps monopolized Thracian hatred from the time of the kingdom's foundation in the 270s BC, and it was Thracian hostility which finally destroyed it. The Tylis blackmail of Byzantion had also sheltered the city from Thracian enmity, since the Tylians would not wish to share the product of that blackmail. (The complete disappearance of Tylis, both the kingdom and its central place, might imply the fury of the Thracians' destruction.) The Tylis kingdom clearly relied in part on seizing and selling Thracians for slaves, and no doubt on looting anything of value the Thracian victims had possessed. The destruction of Tylis will therefore have released Thracian energies and increased their hostility towards the Greek cities – hence Polybios' remarks. Byzantion would be one of the main slave markets through which the captured Thracians were sold and exported. Tylis' involvement in the slave trade, selling Thracians on to slave traders, could also have increased Thracian hostility towards Greeks since those slave traders would very likely be Greeks. The Thracian kingdoms which emerged after Tylis' destruction proved to be durable and highly resistant to conquest – it took the Romans many decades to conquer the region. The Byzantines no doubt assisted at the destruction of the Tylis kingdom, but only after decades of supporting it by their taxes and tribute payments, and so they inherited the enmity of the Thracians, or perhaps that enmity simply revived when there was no alternative for the Thracians' target, so that 'they are engaged in a perpetual and most difficult warfare.' The city evidently resorted to buying off some of the Thracians, as if the Tylis problem had never existed, but that only produced demands from the Thracians who were not paid: 'the very fact of their making concessions to one chief raises against them enemies many times more numerous.'[9]

Polybios makes no attempt to delineate Byzantium's territory. He remarks that its land is fertile, but the crops were subject to destruction and theft by the Thracians, who arrived at harvest time to seize what they could.[10] The story looks to be a local complaint in which the richness and beauty and value of the crops were increased in repute even as the barbarians seized them. The city's wider possessions he does mention, however. On the European side the city of Selymbria was annexed and so reduced in status to that of a village. This is noted in one of Demosthenes' orations, and so it had happened by the 330s;[11] the occupation of Selymbria by Philip II in 340 BC might have been the unintended result of Byzantion's annexation, or it might have been as a result of Philip's action that the city was annexed. Along the Bosporos, the European shore had long been taken into Byzantine control, and the port of Hieron on the Asian side, originally under Kalchedonian control, was bought from a Seleukid official of either Seleukos II or Seleukos III – probably the former and perhaps in the 220s BC, when Seleukid control was being exerted in the area once more.[12] It was a place where merchant ships sheltered waiting for a favourable wind; it was also the place where Philip II had seized the great fleet. It was therefore an important place to control.

The land presented by Ptolemy II in 255 BC seems to have been on the Asian side, and a study of the dialects of the inscriptions has located the probable area involved.[13] The Byzantines maintained an oppressive regime of serf-labour in these lands, likened to that of the helots of Sparta.[14]

The city therefore had a minor empire of its own, in which, in fact, it was all in the fashion, since Kyzikos and Bithynia were also expanding in the same way, while the Chersonese and the city of Alexandria Troas at the Hellespont had also each consolidated a number of minor cities into one authority. Byzantion had clearly ceased to depend on the trade and taxation, but the combination of its own resources and the trade was what made it a particularly wealthy place.

The other thing Polybios ignores is any description of the interior of the city. It had a reputation, as might have been expected of a city of sailors and merchants, for good living, drunkenness, and the easy life. It also had the full complement of temples – to Apollo, Athena, Artemis, and Rhea, but also the Thracian deities Zeuxippos and Bendis, and, unsurprisingly given the city's louche reputation, Aphrodite and Dionysos. There was a cult of Ptolemy II, which probably later also encompassed any later Ptolemies who needed to be praised; other imports included Serapis, the invented Ptolemaic god, Isis from Egypt, and Asian Kybele – the international nature of the set of deities being propitiated is another aspect of the international mercantile nature of the population and its work.[15]

But this collection of deities was normal for any Greek city, and cannot go to undermine Polybios' comment that the city was rarely visited by others, and was remote from larger events. It was still a minor place giving no indication whatever of any destiny other than as a small but busy port, and a source of salted fish. For the other thing Polybios does not mention is that it might be a notable place as a source of empire; to him it was no more than a middling Greek city, content to keep out of the way when trouble threatened.

Chapter 6

Destruction from the West – The Romans

The Siege of AD 192–194

The information about Byzantion becomes scattered and thin after 167 BC, largely because the sources for events also fail. The city's notable but remote situation could not keep it completely out of the attentions of rulers and warriors, but it appears to have avoided any more sieges after 220 BC for the next four centuries, which in the event, given the number it had endured before 220 BC and after AD 190, was clearly a creditable achievement, even if it was the result of persistently bowing the head to every conqueror who came anywhere near.

From 129 BC onwards the conquerors were primarily Romans. In that year Roman and allied armies finally crushed an attempt to maintain the independence and existence of the Attalid kingdom in western Asia Minor. Greece and Macedon had gone the same way in the 160s and 140s BC. One major result was the extension of the Roman road system from the Adriatic coast to the eastern Mediterranean. Roman roads were deliberately intended to be military routes to guide soldiers to potential or actual trouble spots. After the final conquest of Macedonia and Greece in the 140s BC the Via Egnatia was organized. From Dyrrhachium (Greek Epidauros) on the Adriatic, the landing point for ships from Brundisium (a newly developed port on the heel of Italy, which was connected to Rome by another of these roads), the Egnatia reached almost to the Hellespont, though it stopped a little short of that destination. The Chersonese and a part of neighbouring Thrace were in the possession of the Attalids of Pergamon until 129 BC, so the road stopped at the border, the Hebros River. In effect it stopped at the town of Kypsela, the last urban centre before the river. With the conquest of the Attalid kingdom, however, the Chersonese became Roman, and a new road, the Via Aquillia, was organized diagonally across Asia Minor from the Hellespont to Side in Pamphylia. The gap at the Chersonese was then also filled by an extension of the Egnatia from Kypsela to the strait. There was thus an organized and signposted route for Roman forces from Rome as far as the border of Seleukid Syria near Side.

These roads were not 'built' by the Romans; they already existed. The Roman magistrates – Cn. Egnatius and M. Aquillius – laid out the line, presumably employing engineers to do the detailed surveys, and arranged to have the roads marked and signed on the ground with mile posts, indicating the distances to the next stopping places. These mile posts were inscribed in Latin, which few if any of the local inhabitants could understand – that is to say, the roads were intended for the convenience and guidance of the Roman armies who campaigned in both areas frequently between 135 and the age of Augustus. (Another road, the Via Domitia, linked Italy and Spain: it was thus possible to travel on Roman-organized roads from Spain as far as Syria.)

One result of the combination of Roman conquests and the existence of the roads was directly relevant to Byzantion. The process of Roman expansion eventually stopped in the east of Asia Minor, where it met, in the mountains of the east, the Parthian Empire, and the independent Armenians. The combination of all this was too much for the Romans to make any further eastward progress – though they tried repeatedly to do so. This boundary therefore became the Roman fortified frontier for the next dozen centuries, and it was therefore the frequent destination for their armies; the original roads had supposed that these armies would have headed for Syria, Mesopotamia, and Egypt in the republican period, since this was, until the size of the Parthian Empire was realized, the location of the strongest non-Roman states, in Syria (the Seleukids) and Egypt (the Ptolemies). In the face of the Parthians, and particularly once the Danube frontier had also been organized, the armies marched due east for Armenia, not southeast for Syria. It was thus easier for them to use the Bosporos crossing than the Hellespont, and roads linked the Danube with Byzantion. An extension of the Egnatia was also organized from Kypsela across the south of Thrace to Byzantion, and so the main direct route from Italy was joined there by that from the Danube. From Byzantion two distinct direct routes across northern Anatolia towards the eastern frontier were organized. Byzantion had thus ceased to be remote, and was increasingly being 'visited'.

This added another element to Byzantion's rising importance. It was still a major trading centre, and at times a naval base (there was a Roman

Black Sea fleet at times), and now it became a major land route nexus as well, with roads leading to the west for the Adriatic and Italy, north to the Danube, and beyond that to Italy, and east to Armenia, the frontier, and southeast to Syria. The Bosporos crossing became far more important than the Hellespont.

Not that the city escaped entirely into a comfortable world of increasing commerce and burgeoning tax receipts. Early in the reign of the Emperor Nero it complained of the burden of Roman taxes and the demands on it for services by the generals and the armies which passed through the city – the result of the realignment of the Roman road system, and of the recent annexation of the last Thracian kingdom in its hinterland. This is recorded in Tacitus' *Annals*, and like Polybios three centuries before he diverts a little into references to the city's position and its wealth and prosperity, which the Byzantines were now claiming had been ruined by recent wars in Thrace (the Roman annexation) and in the Crimea, which imposed heavy demands on the city for supplies and accommodation.[1] (Little did they know that a long Eastern war, imposing still greater demands, was about to develop.)

The envoys to the Senate who were transmitting the complaint dated the city's membership of the empire from the Roman reaction to a minor incident in 151 bc. A pretender to the Macedonian throne, Andriskos, visited the city and received a moderately enthusiastic welcome. Rome had conquered Macedon in a series of three difficult wars during the previous half-century, and the appearance of a pretender was bad news, particularly since he went on to overthrow the Roman settlement, rule for several months as king, defeat a Roman army, and kill a Roman praetor. He was, of course, then driven out, betrayed, and displayed in a triumphal procession in Rome; a new settlement was made by turning Macedon into the formal Roman province of Macedonia.[2]

For the Byzantines there was a treaty of subordination as a punishment for the city's welcome to the pretender, and this altered its status from a completely independent city-state into a city which was directly subject to Roman authority. Eventually it was transferred into the province of Pontus-and-Bithynia, and its little 'empire' on both sides of the Propontis was removed, apart presumably from its original *chora* on the Thracian side.

The envoys, however, made it clear that Byzantion had, apart from the one mistake over the pretender, always supported Rome in its wars, and listed them: against the Seleukid King Antiochos III (in 192–189 BC), against King Perseus of Macedon (in 172–167 BC), against the Attalid pretender Andronikos (in 133–129 BC), supporting M. Antonius Creticus in the Cretan War (in 100 BC), L. Cornelius Sulla and L. Licinius Lucullus in the wars against Mithridates (in the 80s and 70s BC), and Pompey the Great and Julius Caesar in Asia (in the 70s and 40s BC), and all the emperors.[3] (The list in fact was carefully edited, and omitted several occasions when the losers or enemies had gained local support.) That is, even before the arrival of the Roman roads the city was involved in plenty of wars, so it claimed, even if only as a (possibly reluctant) supporter of the Romans. In fact, of course, as the episode of Andriskos showed, it had had little choice in the matter, even if it was technically a free city-state; its support was expected and required on all occasions, all the more so once the imperial system was fully in place; its relative smallness had no doubt rendered its support barely noticeable – it sent just one ship to Creticus, for example.

The city, having accepted a remission of tribute for five years, continued through the century and more from Nero's time as a reasonably prosperous place. But, as in 150 BC with Andriskos, it was another royal dispute which brought it to a new disaster, one as complete as that suffered at Persian hands. On the last day of AD 192 the Emperor Commodus was murdered in Rome, to great and widespread relief. Finding a new emperor, on the other hand, was to be much more difficult. Pertinax lasted three months, Julianus even less. The confusion in Rome encouraged outsiders to make their plays: Clodius Albinus, the governor of Britannia with three legions at his command; Pescennius Niger from Syria with half a dozen; Septimius Severus from the Danube frontier in Pannonia with three legions of his own, and the support of other governors on the northern frontier with several more. Most crucially, Severus was the nearest of these men to Rome, and he was able to march his army through Italy and be proclaimed emperor in the city in due form – with armed soldiers scowling at the senators as they did so. He was thus able to claim a measure of legitimacy which the others could not.[4]

This success brought further support, and soon Severus held all Europe and North Africa, except Britannia, while Niger held the eastern provinces, as far as the Propontis. Niger marched his forces westwards but could gain no new support west of Byzantion. He established a precarious control over Asia Minor, gathered support from neighbouring governors – again precariously, for there were no significant armed forces outside Syria and the eastern frontier over against Parthia. He crossed the Bosporos into Thrace. Byzantion was strongly garrisoned, but was now, suddenly, a frontier city.

But there was not to be a replay of the last imperial crisis in 69, when Vespasian from the east marched to victory in Italy. Niger found that there was a Severan army commanded by L. Fabius Cilo already in Thrace. Cilo had probably arrived from his governorship of Illyricum by sea, and the two forces clashed in rival attempts to seize the city of Perinthos. According to Dio Cassius, Niger advanced towards Perinthos but then retired on the perception of unlucky omens. He does not mention the battle itself, but it is referred to in the *Historia Augusta*, and by Herodian; Niger claimed it as a victory and celebrated it on a coin issue. His commander was Asellius Aemilianus, the governor of Asia, who had perhaps crossed to Thrace before Niger arrived and had fought the battle.[5]

The arrival of further Severan forces in Thrace compelled Niger to relinquish whatever land across the Propontis he had seized, except for Byzantion; his 'victory' did not allow him to advance further west. An army of three legions under L. Marius Maximus, the governor of Moesia, laid siege to Byzantion while a second army, commanded by Claudius Candidus, crossed from Thrace into Hellespontine Phrygia, south of the Propontis. Although no historian says so, it is obvious that the army will have crossed by way of the Hellespont. Kyzikos had apparently declared for Severus so some Severan troops may have been shipped directly from Perinthos into that city. (One notes Kyzikos' canny recognition of the locus of power once again; and that Byzantion, with a strong Pescennian garrison installed, no longer had the luxury of choice.) The appearance of these Severan forces in the Troad and advancing towards Kyzikos, brought Aemilianus' army to face the invader; it had presumably been stationed in the Bithynian peninsula, in Kalchedon and other possible landing places, to provide support to the Byzantines and to block any crossing by way of the Bosporos. The cities in the area were also no doubt garrisoned. It was control of these Bithynian cities, Kalchedon, Nikomedia, Nikaia, and Prusa, along with Kyzikos, Apameia, and others, which was now the key to the campaign. Nikomedia, with Niger's army under Aemilianus on one side, and the Severan under Candidus on the other, declared for Severus and was quickly reinforced by a Severan detachment. Any Pescennian garrison was either small or had been withdrawn by Aemilianus. The city's early defection from Niger was partly the result of rivalry with Nikaia, and partly a recognition of the fragility of Niger's political position; with Nikomedia joining Severus, Nikaia therefore supported Niger.[6]

A battle of sorts was fought near Kyzikos, and another, much more serious, at the approaches to Nikaia, with archers shooting from boats in the lake, and Niger's forces occupying defences in the hills south of the city. The battle was a hard fight and Candidus had to personally intervene at one point to rally his defeated and retreating Severan troops when Niger himself arrived on the other side to inspire his own men. The fighting lasted until dark, at which point Niger's forces retreated in defeat.[7] (Candidus' victory led to Nikomedia's confirmation as the chief city of Bithynia, whereas until then Nikaia, as the wealthier of the two, had seemed the more important. Local politics was as important as any imperial succession choice in the Bithynian cities.[8])

Aemilianus was captured and executed; Niger and the survivors of the army 'fled' eastwards, though the term seems inaccurate since the army moved across Asia Minor in relatively good order and made a stand in the Taurus passes; dislodged from that position, it retreated again and gathered at Issos on the borders of Cilicia and Syria, where, after a stubborn fight, it was finally defeated.

This campaign was, in some ways, a reprise of the campaign of Alexander the Great five centuries earlier: his first victory had been in Hellespontine Phrygia, not far from Kyzikos, and the decisive victory which opened up the Persian Empire for him was at Issos; this was a function of the military geography of Asia Minor, which is bounded by the Propontis and the Straits on the northwest, and the mountain barriers of the Taurus and the Amanus on the southeast. It is clear that once a victorious army had crossed the Straits (both armies crossed over at the Hellespont) and defeated the initial defenders, the whole of Asia Minor was open to it. (One might also cite the Galatian invasions, and from the other direction, the campaign of conquest of Kyros the Great.) The Kyzikos-Nikaia fighting between Severus and Niger was the equivalent of Alexander's Granikos battle; Issos, below the Amanus Mountains, was the last place on the route east at which Syria could be defended.

The evacuation of the Syrian army did not include the forces holding Byzantion, which Niger had commanded in person until the battle near Nikaia. The siege of the city which followed went on for another two years, described with some detail by Dio Cassius and Herodian.[9] Dio's account is superficially detailed, but, given that the siege lasted two years, is no more than impressionistic. He lays emphasis on the strength of the walls, and the machines and engines used in the defence, but gives only one incident of the fighting a full description.[10] The use of engines seems especially notable. They were lined up along the walls (which had a covered passageway) and it is clear that whatever engines the Severan besiegers deployed were no match for those used by the defence. (Despite the centuries of peace as a result of the Roman conquest, it is obvious, from Dio's account, that Byzantion's walls were in good condition.)

The Byzantines had a large fleet of ships available – though Dio's claim that they had '550' is unbelievable. He describes them as having beaks – that is, they were warships – but this would seem to be an improvisation by requisitioning and converting merchant vessels. Their fleet, however constituted, was able for a time to dominate the local seas. The Bosporos was still being used by the merchants to pass ships through, but the Byzantines had ingenious ways to capture them. Divers cut anchor cables and attached hooks and ropes so that the ships could be drawn ashore. Some shipmasters steered their ships into the city, theoretically under protest, of course – the prices of food will have risen steeply once the blockade was established.

The real weapon for the Severan besiegers was therefore to impose famine on the city, and when the Severan warships were brought up and established their control of the Bosporos entry, the Byzantines apprehended that the end was near. They were reduced to destitution, though still resisted, and attempted to use the ships to evacuate the '*bouches inutiles*', but the evacuees were intercepted and their ships were sunk; the city's shores were lined with the dead and wreckage next morning – and, as usual in a siege of this sort, the walls looking out over the strait had been lined with spectators.[11]

With the evacuation a disaster, and supplies unobtainable, the city was compelled at last to surrender. It is clear from Dio's description that the Pescennian forces, commanded by Aemilianus, were well supported by the citizens. Severus therefore felt he had to punish both. The enemy armed forces were massacred. Notably influential citizens were killed, including the city magistrates, and Dio singles out the killing of a famous but unnamed boxer. Then the city itself was razed. Severus secured for future employment the engineer Priscus of Nikomedia, whose ingenuity with engines had been a substantial force for the defence.[12]

Dio, who came from Bithynia and will have been familiar with Byzantion, makes the point of describing the walls, with their engines and covered way, but also goes into some detail on the engines used by the defence (but not those used by the Severan besiegers):

> Some … hurled rocks and wooden beams on any who drew near, and others discharged stones and other missiles and spears against such as stood at a distance.[13]

He claims that this prevented a close approach by the besiegers, which, if true, would be most unusual. Such engines could only fire one missile – rock, beam, and so on – at a time, which would hardly deter a mass attack, nor dominate a close approach. But combined with the high and strong walls this was deterrent enough, it seems. The walls were built to defend those on the walkway against missile attacks, so attacking using towers was not going to succeed either.

It is evident that the city possessed a store of these siege engines even before it was attacked, and Priscus is credited with constructing new ones on the spot; it is clear also that the general capability of such machines had risen considerably since the siege under Philip II. It is likely that, as a major route nexus, and with a considerable garrison, the machines were not the city's to deploy, as they had been at the time of Philip's siege, but were part of the imperial inventory.

The city was clearly in constant apprehension of being attacked, even after its inclusion for centuries as part of the Roman Empire. In all this it is not clear how hard the besiegers had tried to capture the city, but they had failed, until the ships arrived. The implication is that both assaults and blockades were necessary to take the city, and that the inhabitants understood this. It seems also that the commanders on Severus' side did not understand this until late in the siege. It is also unclear just how committed the citizens were to Niger's cause, though Severus clearly thought they had taken Niger's part. The city had been occupied by Niger's army before it was called on to decide, so it seems probable that, in keeping with its earlier history, the city would have opted for neutrality had it had the choice. Probably the forces put in the city by Niger compelled the resistance to continue, but it seems evident that once the siege was established, and once they understood they were all being treated as Severus' enemies, the citizens resisted as strongly as the soldiers.

The soldiers and the city magistrates were killed at once – the killing of the magistrates might suggest their eager participation in the resistance – and the rest of the citizens appear to have been left alone, though probably enslaved; the boxer who was executed attacked his guards when a prisoner, probably preferring death to enslavement. The city was destroyed, at least to the extent that it was no longer physically defensible or habitable. The walls, widely admired, and correctly so judging by the length of the siege, were dismantled. The city was also destroyed in the sense of being deprived of its civic status; the ruins were awarded as a village to Perinthos.[14]

This was the first time since the Persian Empire and the Athenian Empire that the city had been captured by siege. Of course, many of the intervening sieges were less than severe, more ways of influencing the city than attempts at conquest. But it is notable that the Athenians, the Persians, and Severus all used the same methods – active siege by land, and a blockade by sea. Clearly only one of these was not enough, and only a combined operation by sea, to block off the arrival of supplies and reinforcements, and a vigorous attack from the land side, could succeed. It was a lesson which had to be learnt repeatedly in the future.

The city's demoted status was restored soon enough. The story is that Severus' son, later called Caracalla, requested this, but the work that was done implies that the emperor was fully aware of the importance of the place.[15] Severus had gone on to a Parthian war after defeating Niger and marched his army back through Byzantion when he had achieved victory and made peace. He had a soldier's eye for strategic positions, and since the might of Roman military strength was now divided between the Danube frontier (with which he was already very familiar) and the eastern frontier, the Byzantion crossing was a vital point he cannot have missed. Hence the rebuilding and the refortification. And yet the positioning of the new city was such as would lessen its power for defence; it had put up such a strong resistance from the old site on the hill that Severus' new city was placed on the lower land, below the old city, just in case defence of the place was again intended

The city was rebuilt, with a new wall, hippodrome, agora, baths and basilica, all the normal equipment of a Roman city (though the hippodrome inside the walls was an unusual extravagance). The old city was left as a ruin field on the hill, a stark reminder of the cost of defying an emperor, though the ruins were no doubt quarried for building material for the new city. The new city was on the lower ground to the west of the old. Theoretically its new walls enclosed twice the area of the former city, which was included within the walls, but since the old site was abandoned and left as a ruin the area of the city actually occupied was about the same. Two harbours were also constructed on the Golden Horn side, one for warships, one for commerce – an imitation of other cities with notable ports, notably Carthage and Alexandria. A military base and headquarters, the Strategeion, was rebuilt nearby, and warehouses were built. A colonnaded street in the latest architectural fashion was laid from the centre of the new city to a gate in the new walls, to connect with the Via Egnatia, which by now, of course, extended from Kypsela to the Bosporos.[16] This was a city owing its existence to Severus and his son, who could thus claim to be founders. It was given a new dynastic name, Augusta Antonina, though the old name continued and soon overwhelmed the new. The one monumental building of Severus' time which lasted was the Milion, from which as in all Roman roads, distances were measured. It was a standard Roman arch, of which there must have been dozens in the Empire; it became a symbol of the city's future centrality in the Empire – but not for a century and a half yet.

Chapter 7

Enemies from the North – Goths and Heruli

The Sieges of 257 and 267

For a century and more there had been a slow movement of barbarian groups south from Scandinavia, across the Baltic Sea, and across the lands which became Poland and western Russia. The best-known of these peoples were the Goths, speaking a Germanic language, numerous, splitting into shifting congeries of tribes and clans, led by temporary chieftains who held authority so long as they were successful.[1] These ethnic movements compelled other groups to move as well, and the whole region north of the Roman frontier was upset, while the frontier itself came under increasing strain.

The Goths were in fact a mixture of all the peoples who had inhabited the Ukrainian steppe and the Russian-Polish forest. Some non-Goths were absorbed into Gothic clans, some retained their individuality, with their own chiefs; some were other Germanic groups, together with some descended from earlier Skythians, Sarmatians such as the Borani[2] who had preceded the Goths in the steppes, and probably contingents of Vandals, Saxons, Kelts who had migrated eastwards in the last centuries BC, and groups from the many German tribes who had faced the Roman forces across their northern frontier for centuries.[3] The process was partly an absorption of weaker groups by the larger, who hitched onto the greater Gothic groups as they moved; partly a result of hostile confrontations, when defeat brought foreign clans into a subordinate relationship as part of the larger; and partly the division of greater groups as they took over ever larger territories; the most notable division was into East and West Goths, Visigoths and Ostrogoths.

The Goths told of the slow migration from the Pomeranian area towards the Black Sea in their songs and sagas. Archaeologists have located their origin in the Wielbark Culture in Pomerania and Masovia along the Baltic Sea coast, and identify them later as the Cherniakhov Culture in the region of Kiev (now Kyiv) in the Ukraine (an area to which Celts had moved earlier, and which is the geopolitical base from which to control the area of central Ukraine).[4] By AD 230 they were dominant in the Ukraine, and had reached the Black Sea at the Sea of Azov, the Crimea, and the mouths of the Dniestr and Dniepr Rivers. In 238 a large Gothic invasion passed the Danube mouths and hit the old Greek colonial city of Istros.[5]

In the Empire the Severan dynasty had lasted only forty years, dissolving in a morass of religious scandal, child emperors dominated by their mothers, and assassinations. (After Septimius, all the Severan emperors were murdered.) Under this semi-dissolution of central activity, from the 230s the condition of the Empire became steadily worse, and the year 238 was one in which the Roman Empire suffered yet another breakdown. There were six emperors in that year, five of whom died by violence, and the survivor of the imperial carnage was a teenage boy, Emperor Gordian III. It is probably no accident that the Gothic attack came in that year. They may not have known the precise details of the imperial crisis in Rome and Italy, but they will already have sensed the weakening of the Roman frontier defences which accompanied the crisis – the first murdered emperor of that year was Maximinus, supposedly a Thracian, who had done good work in shoring up the northern frontier, but fell out with the Senate, who did not like him. In the next years, as emperors fell and were replaced by their brief successors, and the Empire went to war with Sassanid Persia, which absorbed imperial attention and the imperial armies, other groups from the steppes and the northern shores of the Black Sea took the opportunity to raid into the rich empire.

In the 240s and 250s Goths and Carpi and Quadi raided repeatedly into the Balkans, but it was the Sarmatian Borani who were the most enterprising. They were established north of the Sea of Azov and from there took control of the Crimea, where they seized control of the ships in the ports of the Cimmerian Bosporos kingdom and took to the sea. The first attack, in 256, reached the small city of Pityus north of the Caucasus, but was then beaten off. Next year, 257, they tried again, this time successfully, and went on to raid Trapezus in Pontos and into interior Anatolia.[6] And the year after a band of Goths emulated the Borani, seized and built a fleet of ships and raided into central Anatolia.

This raid in 258 by the Goths was their most ambitious raid yet. The earliest raids had concentrated on Dacia and the Balkans, or on the eastern shores of the Black Sea. That of 257 by the Goths had a more ambitious target. These raids were not random, but were planned with some care, and detailed preparations were made.[7] They were also inspired by other raids; it seems probable that the raids of the Borani stimulated the Goths to plan their own raid, in a mood of emulation, having seen the profitable results obtained. There were plenty of rivalries between the groups – the Carpi insisted, menacingly, 'We are stronger than the Goths', when denied a payoff on a raid – and the Goths included many non-Gothic elements within their political system who had retained their original ethnic identities while also being Goths.[8]

The Goths advanced as a land army marching along the west coast of the Black Sea, accompanied by a fleet pacing the army along the shore. (The example of Philip II in the Chersonese cannot possibly have been their inspiration.) They by-passed several of the coastal cities, and reached the area to the west of Byzantion on the coast of the Istranca peninsula. A community of fishermen at Lake Terkos took refuge from them in the marshes, but when contacted by the Goths they compliantly handed over their boats, no doubt under threat. This looks rather like an opportunistic move by the Gothic commanders; they already had a fleet, but it was evidently not capacious enough to transport the army, and they could not have anticipated finding the fishermen or their boats. The army was then loaded onto the captured boats and transported past Byzantion to land on the Kalchedonian side of the Bosporos. The fleet then sailed through the Strait.

The raiders set about their main purpose, which was to seize and loot the cities of Bithynia. At Kalchedon the Roman garrison fled, and the same thing happened at Nikomedia.[9] (These garrisons were only a dozen or a score of men, and for them to resist would be suicide; it seems clear that there was no organized militia in any of these cities, and that the soldiers had no thought for the civilians they guarded – no doubt their task was to control those civilians, not defend them, not that a tiny garrison could defend a city.) Nikaia and Kios, Apameia and Prusa were sacked, as well as Nikomedia and Kalchedon. The invaders headed for Kyzikos, marching by land, but the Rhyndakos River was in flood, so they had to turn back. (Apparently they did not have the use of their fleet at this point.) Nikomedia and Nikaia were sacked a second time as they returned, and both cities were burnt.[10] Satisfied with their achievement and their loot, the invaders returned to their ships and went home; presumably the ships had been kept at or north of Kalchedon.

The conspicuous omission among the targets and victims here is Byzantion, perhaps the richest city in the area. It is clear that the raiders knew of the city, and it is clear that they menaced it, but on closer acquaintance they had decided not to attack it. The fishermen whose boats they took at Lake Terkos lived within twenty miles of the city, and they could, and no doubt did, provide information about it. The raiders could get close enough to see the fortifications, and it was visible from Kalchedon across the Bosporos, but no attempt was made on it either by land or sea; with their fleet they should have been able to cross the Strait and make a landing. It is obvious that having threatened it, they passed it by because of its strength. It probably had a much larger garrison than any of the Bithynian cities, and the Emperor Valerian sent a commander, Felix, to take control in the city, though he was unable to achieve anything – other than to defend Byzantion, of course.[11] Despite no fighting being recorded, this close encounter must count as a siege; with the raiders in the area and active by land and sea, the city was effectively under blockade, and its ships could probably not get to sea. Like the rest of the area it was wholly unprepared for this attack.

The defences of Byzantion were strong enough to deter these attackers, though the dispatch of Felix was regarded by later historians as a derisory imperial response to the crisis; his presence, however, was obviously intended to coordinate the defence, and perhaps to control the land and sea forces.[12] That the city's garrison was unusually large is implied by a mutiny which took place a few years later in 262 or 263, when the troops turned on the citizens and began a looting and murdering spree. The mutineers were defeated by troops of the Emperor Gallienus, who persuaded the rebels to let him into the city, then supervised the recovery campaign personally and ordered the killing of all the mutineers.[13] This savage response would suggest that the mutiny was perhaps more than a mere demand for pay or better conditions or supplies, but all we know of it is that it took place. The enmity between garrison and citizens was hardly a new phenomenon; one wonders if the citizens' contempt had extended to rude comments on the soldiers' inactivity when the Goths had raided.

The Goths returned for a new raid in 267 or 268; this time they operated jointly with the Heruli, who were another Germanic tribe, but who now appear in the record for the first time, probably as a sub-Gothic group. Again a large fleet of ships and boats was assembled.[14] The Heruli came from the Sea of Azov area, the Goths from the Dniestr mouth, but the raid was clearly well organized from the start. The Roman defences were strong enough to stop their first attacks on the Black Sea city of Tomis. They then sailed up the Danube to attack Marcianopolis, which was well inland, and also well and successfully defended. The raiders gave up this plan and returned to the fleet.[15]

Their secondary target now was to raid the Straits cities once more. There again they met a much more determined and organized opposition than in their first raid. The Roman fleet based at Byzantion prevented their passage through the Bosporos, and the land army was defeated by a Byzantine force. They camped at Hieron, at the Northern Bosporos entrance where the merchant ships usually waited for a safe passage and to pay their taxes.[16] (This was the place where Philip II had captured the merchant fleet.) After a reorganization, which probably means that they put men ashore to take control of the eastern shore of the Strait, the commanders sorted out the ships which were best armed and equipped for sea warfare, then tried again. This time they broke through into the Propontis.

The city of Kyzikos was by this time fully warned and prepared, and defended itself successfully. Kyzikos, however, certainly suffered in this raid, but probably only on its island; the city itself was as well defended as Byzantion, or better, and even survived a siege, according to Ammianus Marcellinus.[17] Zosimus suggested that the strong current drove the Goth and Herulian ships through the Strait too quickly for them to do more than go with the flow, but it is unlikely that he knew much about ships or the sea.[18]

The raid so far had been a catalogue of failure, but from Kyzikos they went on to the Hellespont and got through the strait into the Aegean, perhaps by their tactic of landing the army which marched along the shore paced by the fleet. From there they raided Lemnos, and then camped at Mount Athos. There the fleet split into three sections and each group raided on its own for the next year or so.

It is clear that on this occasion Byzantion itself was a target for attack. Control of the city would provide the raiders with a firm base for wide-ranging raids, and would safeguard the raiders' line of retreat – which in the event they could well have done with. Presumably a new garrison had been installed in the city after the mutiny of 263, under local commanders who clearly had some experience, and there was also a well-organized fleet available. The Roman defensive system worked well at the Bosporos and in the Propontis, as it had at the Danube and at Tomis. Evidently it was not expected that the raiders would go on to the Hellespont, which they got through without much difficulty, and the Aegean islands and cities were unprepared. In the end the Heruli encountered the Emperor Gallienus' new force of heavy-armed cavalry and were destroyed. His successor, the Emperor Claudius II, earned the title of 'Gothicus' with a victory over another of the groups, mainly Goths; altogether very few of the raiders reached their homelands once more. It took a Roman fleet from Egypt to suppress the raiders' fleets in the Aegean. Like the Galatians five centuries before, they targeted wealthy extra-mural temples, and the great temple of Artemis at Ephesos was looted and burned. The Heruli reinforced their ships with more summoned from the homeland but were gradually defeated and driven out. Some of them had to pass through the Straits more than once, and probably the fleet at the Bosporos was in action again.

This raid amounted to a serious attack on Byzantion, where the raiders were defeated by land and sea, though not severely enough to prevent them going on to make a successful raid, at least for a time. But it is clear that the Roman defence system was much better organized than in 257, and the imperial field armies arrived reasonably quickly to destroy the raiders in their separate bands. In that enterprise the defence of Byzantion was clearly a key part.

Whether these Gothic raids can be counted as sieges of Byzantion is difficult to say. The fishermen at Lake Terkos were clearly Byzantine citizens (or subjects), and the commander Felix was installed to defend the city; it was certainly attacked in the second raid, and the troops and ships were kept busy defending the Bosporos. Altogether the city was clearly a target for the raiders on both occasions, and fended off the attacks by its strength, preparedness, and determination. The episodes can thus be counted as being as near to sieges as one can find without actually counting the casualties on the walls and in the ditches.

Chapter 8

Conqueror from the West –
Constantine the Great

The Sieges of 313 and 324, and the New City

The collapse of the Roman Empire in the mid-third century was painfully repaired by the iron military fist of the Emperor Diocletian and his colleagues from the 280s. These men in effect selected solutions from the various expedients of their imperial predecessors, which had often been of only temporary use, made them permanent, and divided the government of the Empire amongst themselves. There were in Diocletian's scheme four emperors, two of them senior, called Augusti, and two junior, entitled Caesars (terms presumably intended to disguise the newness of the regime by adopting older titles). Each of these men ruled, in effect defended, a part of the whole, with responsibility for a section of the barbarian frontier. The aim was to have the Caesars step up to replace the Augusti when the latter retired or died. Automatic retirement after twenty years was the plan. Of course, what resulted when Diocletian retired – the only one to do so – was a series of disputes between the four (and Diocletian returned to active power a couple of times in his retirement). It produced, that is, repeated civil wars – though this might be said to be another of the expedients from the past they had adopted.[1]

By 311, the year in which Diocletian probably died after six years in retirement – his only successful innovation, but one which was never adopted by the rest – there were four primary contenders. The east, from the Straits to Syria and Egypt, was ruled by Maximin Daia. The Balkans was the province of Galerius. In Italy Maxentius, the son of Diocletian's old colleague, had usurped the rule. In the West was Constantine. It was Constantine above all who had been the one who systematically and repeatedly upset any solution which was arrived at collectively. From the moment in York in 306 that his father died and he usurped the throne, he had worked to expand his territory, and in 312 he suppressed Maxentius so that by that year he held all the West, Italy, Africa, Spain, Gaul and Britain.[2] Galerius died in 311, and was succeeded in the Balkans by Licinius, while Maximin Daia emerged from Syria to take over Galerius' rule in Asia Minor.

Complicating the conflict between the emperors was the rise in importance of Christianity. Diocletian had seen it as an insidious subversive force and had instituted a persecution to drive it out. In this practice he was followed by Maximin Daia, with considerable zeal, and, with no enthusiasm at all, by Licinius. This policy was opposed by Constantine, who first established toleration of the religion in his territories, and then graduated to acceptance, and finally claimed himself to be a Christian. This, as was no doubt his main intention, gave him support from Christians throughout the Empire – and it was in Maximin Daia's realm that they were the most numerous. Constantine may well have been serious in his claim of conversion to Christianity but his basic motivation all through his career was personal ambition, and his main and permanent intention was to secure control over the whole of the Empire; he was, above all, a successful political and military man, cunning, intelligent, militarily very capable and highly ambitious.

After his victory in 312 Constantine occupied Rome, only to discover – though he must have known of it already – that the city was both the home of a senior Christian bishop, who wielded authority because he was bishop in the imperial capital, and that the city was the staunchest stronghold of paganism in the Empire, with the ruling aristocracy almost entirely pagan.[3] They argued that it was under the divine authority and encouragement of the pagan gods and goddesses, notably the trio of Jupiter, Juno, and Minerva, that the Empire had been acquired, and that to abandon such divine support was to court destruction. As always with such religious predictions it was irrelevant, and yet was both right and wrong.

In the face of Constantine's success in Italy, Licinius and Maximin Daia patched up a truce, meeting on a boat in the water on the Bosporos.[4] Then Constantine's religious policy, and his conquest of Italy in 312, brought about the next stage in the ongoing but intermittent civil war. He made an ally of Licinius, his neighbour in the Balkans, while his toleration of

Christianity and his effective encouragement of it, provoked Maximin Daia to open opposition – he could not fail to see that Constantine's religious policy was a threat to his own position; no doubt Constantine saw it that way as well.

War recommenced in 313 with a crossing of the Bosporos by Maximin Daia to invade Licinius' territory. The first task of the invader was to secure his rear, which required a siege of Byzantion.[5] (The two men had only the year before concluded their truce by a handshake at the meeting on the Bosporos; it will be seen that Byzantion and the Bosporos were central elements in the unfolding crisis over the next dozen years.)

Maximin Daia claimed the surrender of Byzantion after a siege of just eleven days – more or less the time it would have taken to negotiate the city's surrender. His army then advanced by the Via Egnatia along the north Propontis coast towards Heraklea (formerly Perinthos). He clearly believed he had plenty of time, though it will have taken some time to transport his large army across the Bosporos, and to conduct the siege of Byzantion (though these operations could have been conducted simultaneously). Licinius had learnt of the invasion while in Milan at a meeting with Constantine – it was Maximin Daia's suspicion of what was being agreed at this meeting which provoked him to launch his attack on Licinius.

Licinius then moved at great speed, bringing his field army, together probably with those parts of Galerius' old army he had inherited, and traversed the whole of the Balkans while Maximin Daia was getting his army across the Bosporos, besieging Byzantion and advancing on Heraklea. The two armies met a short distance west of that city. The battle was, after all this preparation, most suitably won by the more vigorous Licinius, even though he had the smaller army. He was clearly the more capable of the two emperors in generalship.[6] Daia's army, what was left of it, retreated and crossed to Asia again.

The brief siege of Byzantion by Daia suggests that the city's garrison was small or that Maximin Daia's siege methods were effective, perhaps by the use of siege machines, if not merely by negotiation. The late Roman army had not advanced in its siege methods much beyond those used by Philip II, but the city wall of Byzantion, which was that built by Severus a century before, may well have been in less than robust condition. The city, after all, had been deliberately relocated onto the lower land by

Severus, in order that its defence would be more difficult; it had defied the Goths and Heruli, but they had not had siege machines; it could not defy an emperor and his professional Roman army.

Daia apparently made no attempt to hold the city after his defeat. He retired to the Asian side, but, as ever in Asia Minor, he could not stop in his retreat before the Taurus Mountains barrier; perhaps short of men by the time he reached the mountains, his attempt to hold that line failed. He was also clearly ill, for he died soon after at Tarsus, possibly by suicide; the Christian historians and chroniclers give gloating accounts of his suffering, which were probably invented for propaganda purposes.

The Empire was now divided between just two men, Constantine holding Italy and the western provinces, Licinius everything east of the Adriatic. Inevitably they quarrelled, and within a few months fell to fighting. Licinius this time had the larger force, but once more the smaller army, under Constantine, was more efficient and under the better general and won this battle. Licinius retreated as far as Thrace, where they fought again. The decision of the battle was unclear, but Licinius manoeuvred his force in order to threaten Constantine's communications, and perhaps his supply line, while Constantine marched eastwards towards Byzantion, believing that he was pursuing a defeated enemy. Both had time to consider the precarious situations they had arrived at, and when Licinius sent an envoy, Constantine was willing to make peace. He had, after all, gained most of the Balkans; Licinius kept the east and Thrace. Byzantion was now a frontier town.[7]

The peace lasted eight years, but the disputes continued, and in the end, in 324, the accumulation of grievances led to a resumption of war. Constantine, as had been his practice ever since succeeding his father at York in 306, was constantly probing for advantage, needling his opponent so as to bring him to the point of war and to make his opponent start the war, so being able to proclaim his own innocence. In fact, in the end, they went to war over a misunderstanding, when Constantine trespassed into Licinius' territory while involved in a war on the Danube frontier, but it was such a trivial matter – an apology would normally have been sufficient, and perhaps payment of compensation – that the fact that it brought about a war illustrates the degree of tension and distrust which existed between the emperors.[8]

The anti-barbarian campaign by Constantine had certainly brought his main field army into the southern Balkans, and he was also busy in Thessalonica supervising the building of an imperial palace and an expanded harbour for his fleet. Such preparations might be subject to varying interpretations, but the obvious one is that Constantine was preparing to attack Licinius. This has, of course, stimulated theories of a plot by him to provoke Licinius, all the way back to the campaign against the barbarians. Whatever the interpretation, Constantine was certainly ready for war when Licinius reacted. This building process at Thessalonica might seem as though this was to be the city he might use as an imperial capital, besides the several other cities which, back as far as the Rhineland, he had used in the past two decades. This, and the presence of Constantine's army, and Constantine himself, so close to their mutual boundary, combined with Constantine's transgression into Licinius' territory, inspired the latter to bring his own field army into Thrace, where he camped at Hadrianopolis. Their mutual proximity was a material threat.

Constantine's war fleet was gathered in that new Thessalonican harbour, and Constantine's eldest and highly capable son Crispus was summoned from the Rhine frontier to command it. His first task was to meet a transport fleet at Peiraios, bringing supplies from the West for the army. With the arrival of the joint fleet at Thessalonica Constantine was ready for another war. He invaded Licinius' territory from the west along the Via Egnatia; Licinius placed his army in a strong position in the hills near Hadrianapolis. The two armies are said to have numbered 300,000 men between them, which will be the usual ancient exaggeration in numbers, but it is certain that they were unusually large. Constantine once again proved his superior generalship in the battle, but Licinius executed a competent retreat with most of his army after the battle, and put a powerful garrison into Byzantion, no doubt recalling the delay such a garrison had caused Maximin Daia when moving the other way, or even Severus over a century before. Having appointed Martinianus as his subordinate emperor, Licinius sent him across the Propontis to Lampsakos to gather another army. Constantine summoned Crispus and the fleet, said to be 200 strong. Licinius' fleet is said to have numbered 350 triremes; it was commanded by Abantus, who had gathered it in the Propontis.

Byzantion was besieged again, but Constantine's siege was perhaps more of a blockade than a case of violent assault, at least for the moment. The decision of the war would come at sea. Crispus sailed his fleet into the Hellespont and was met by Abantus' massed ships off Kallipolis, just above the Narrows. Abantus' fleet outnumbered Crispus' warships by a considerable margin, though the latter had a large fleet of transports with him. Neither commander had any idea of how to fight a sea battle. (There had been few in the centuries since the end of the Republic.)

Fighting in the narrow strait meant that only some of the ships could be engaged. This nullified Abantus' advantage in numbers, and Crispus used just eighty of his ships, called 'triaconters', smaller than the triremes of Abantus. Abantus used 200 ships, and attacked in poor order, with the result that Crispus' better-ordered fleet was less crowded in the narrow strait and under more effective command. The fight was indecisive for the first day, though Abantus' fleet suffered serious losses. The two fleets separated for the night, Crispus' force harbouring at Elaious on the southern tip of the Chersonese, while Abantus went to a harbour on the Asian side. Next day, Abantus found that the enemy had been reinforced, and the weather took a hand. A strong north wind began the day, which would drive Abantus' fleet towards the enemy, but it then swung round in the afternoon to the south, reversing the situations of the fleets and driving Abantus' fleet onto the Asian shore; he is said to have lost 130 of his ships in the wreckage, and several thousands of his men. With just four ships left under his immediate control, he surrendered. Crispus was able to then pass the strait and head for Byzantion.[9]

Licinius swiftly left Byzantion for the Asian side once the sea battle's result was known, first going to Kalchedon, then to the old customs post at Chrysopolis. Constantine meanwhile laid siege to Byzantion. He faced a well-fortified town with a large garrison, which included part of Licinius' field army. A blockade would probably have succeeded in the end, due to the necessarily large consumption of supplies, but when he began the siege Licinius still had ships in the Bosporos which could transport supplies to the city. A determined assault was required. Constantine brought up, or constructed, the same sort of artillery as Philip II – towers to dominate the exposed wall walkway so that his troops could approach the wall closely, and rams to batter the wall.

It seems that Licinius did not trust all of his men. As the siege made progress, probably by a gradual wrecking of the wall, he removed the most trustworthy and loyal troops, and himself, over to Kalchedon, while his colleague, the newly promoted Martinianus, was recruiting that new army at Lampsakos. Constantine, perhaps understanding the nature of the division of Licinius' army into loyal and doubtful groups, put a force across to the Asian side, where he landed at the Sacred Promontory (presumably the old taxation position at Hieron). Since Licinius had been able to evacuate his troops in safety, the fact that Constantine could now cross over to the Asian side suggests that by this time Crispus had won his sea battle and had established control over the Bosporos and the Propontis. Constantine moved enough men across to have an army there powerful enough to defeat Licinius' force at Chrysopolis. Licinius retreated to Nikomedia. His forces in Byzantion could see what was happening across the strait and they surrendered the city soon after Constantine's victory.

Constantine marched into the surrendered city of Byzantion and held celebratory games to honour Crispus and the fleet, as was only right, since Crispus' victory signalled his own final victory. It was, like that of Severus in the end, the result of the combination of land assault and sea blockade. At Nikomedia, Licinius' wife Constantia (Constantine's half-sister) persuaded him to give up the fight and surrender, and got her brother to give a guarantee of her husband's life. He honoured this guarantee for a whole year.

Constantine had thereby seized undisputed control of the whole Roman Empire, the first emperor to do so for almost a century. It was worth another celebration, and it seems that he was intent on doing so by means of a traditional imperial gesture: he would found a new city.

Constantine founded his new city in the year of his victory, which is unlikely to be a coincidence – it was his version of Crispus' victory games. The problem was, in a world of cities, deciding where he should put it. The previous fifteen years had repeatedly brought Byzantion to his attention – the meeting on the Bosporos of Licinius and Maximin Daia, the two sieges, both of which were successful for the besieger, a factor which did not argue for a new city on that site, and his own capture of the city after his battle with Licinius. And yet Byzantion was still only one possible choice among many, and Constantine had a wide variety of cities to consider. He had used cities all over the Empire as his temporary seats of government in the previous two decades, so that he had presumably gained some idea what he required.

He was not doing anything new. It was a long tradition among rulers in the Greek and Roman world to found a city, and a notable victory was quite often seen as a good reason for a new foundation. Alexander had the reputation of having founded dozens, though in fact he only founded four or five, Alexandria-by-Egypt being the most notable; his father Philip II had founded at least two cities in Thrace; Seleukos had founded two dozen in Syria and Babylonia, Ptolemy was a second founder of Alexandria and had others to his own name; Lysimachos had founded Lysimacheia on the Chersonese, though it had been all too easily captured and destroyed. Roman emperors had followed the pattern; some of them chose to elevate their home village to the status of a city, as did Philip the Arab and Galerius; even Roman Republican magistrates had founded cities. So, after his great victory – his succession of victories spread over two decades – it was no surprise that Constantine should emulate these predecessors, and given his enlarged ego and his enhanced ambition, it was similarly no surprise that he should have founded an unusually large city.

He already had a series of palaces inserted into existing cities, in Gaul, in Rome, at Milan and Serdica, at Thessalonica (just built), and probably at other places. As the heir of Licinius and Maximin Daia and Diocletian he had inherited a well-established palace, and a functioning imperial administration, at Nikomedia; other imperial palaces existed at Antioch-in-Syria and Alexandria-by-Egypt. Constantine, however, from the start aimed at something greater. It was suggested to him that a suitable site for a new city would be at Troy, a major site of profound historical significance for the empire he now ruled, where he could impose new buildings – another palace – and claim the rights of founder, *ktistes*. It was close to a city supposedly founded by Alexander – Alexandria Troas – though a modicum of historical research would reveal that its real founder was Antigonos, and much of the founding work was done by Lysimachos – but these were two kings who had been defeated and killed in battle, another poor omen. Troy itself was also only a small city, and therefore had plenty of space for new building, though the temple there would need to be removed, or perhaps replaced by a church; it was also depressingly short of a good water supply. Across the water was

Lysimacheia, or at least the ruins of Lysimacheia, founded by Antigonos' contemporary and conqueror, though captured and destroyed more than once by Thracian attacks. In the face of the historical significance of these cities, Nikomedia, founded by a Bithynian king and adopted as the imperial capital by a pagan persecutor, was of no actual significance.

Constantine at least visited Troy and inspected the site, during which he will have seen the site of Lysimacheia; he had also spent his early years at Nikomedia. Even as he went to Troy, he probably knew that it clearly would not do. He owed his recent victories, in Italy, and the Balkans, in part to his support of Christianity, and from Christians. There had been the vision of victory at the Milvian Bridge fight outside Rome, and in each battle since the significance of his adoption of Christianity had been noted and had increased. The lands he had now come to rule, in Asia and Syria and Egypt, were the lands which were already very strongly Christian. To choose a pagan site, like Troy, or any city of more than usual pagan importance, or one founded by pagan kings like Alexander or Lysimachos, or one promoted by the aggressively pagan Diocletian, was to insult the Christians of the east who had just emerged from major persecutions instituted by Diocletian and Maximin Daia. So in religious terms, his new capital had to be a site capable of being made into a distinctively Christian city.

With that decided, he could look at the likely centres for his city in political and military terms, and here Byzantion stood out. It was both maritime (he owed his victory to Crispus' fleet) and fortifiable. It had more than once survived siege by its situation on the coast, where supplies could be landed. It was a city of no particular pagan significance, despite hosting the usual set of temples and gods; Constantine was reported to have ordered the destruction of these temples, but this was another myth, invented by Christian propagandists, who had little regard for the truth. It was of little historical significance either, having played only minor parts in a few greater events, though it had fought for almost three years against Severus, when it was apparently a well-fortified and clearly defendable city. It was militarily weak, at least in the face of an imperial army, as the two easy captures in the recent past had shown, and it was quite evidently undefendable in its current state; Constantine had seen it damaged by his own siege. There was therefore great scope for imperial architectural innovation and supervision, and so the possibility of a yet further enhancement of the emperor's reputation – city founding was a guarantee of post-mortem fame. All it would take to make it memorable, strong, and Christian, was money and work, and he had plenty of the first, and access to large numbers of experienced workmen for the second. Byzantion was his choice, a place with less negative counts against it than any other, the least bad option.

Constantine supervised the early work personally. There is a story that he was leading a group of courtiers and architects along his planned main street. They reached the Severan wall, which was supposed to be their destination, but then he went on walking. The transgression was pointed out, but the emperor claimed to be following the man in front, though no one was in view; it was, it turned out, an angel, and it led them to the point at which the new wall would cross the line of the street they were on.[10] It was both a typical story told by citizens later, and a typical gesture by Constantine to claim divine guidance. (He had, he said, been deterred from choosing Troy by a dream – a divine revelation, of course; clearly a man of powerful imagination, able to summon exactly the story to convince his subjects.)[11]

In fact, there was already in existence at the site the basis of the plan for the new city. The street he was walking along – there seems no reason to doubt that Constantine was actually involved in the planning himself, for it was part of the traditional ruler's work – was the main street of the Severan city, which split into two roads leading out of the city in different directions about a mile from the site chosen for the imperial palace. One branch led northwest, towards Hadrianopolis in central Thrace, and then north to the Danube frontier; the other became the Via Egnatia once it was out of the city, and led to Thessalonica, the Adriatic, and Italy. (The Hadrianopolis road is now the Meze, one of the great streets of the world.) That is, a good deal of the layout of the city was clearly already in place. This included, apart from these main streets, the requisite buildings of the Greek city, to which Constantine could decree the establishment of a new palace and a Senate House, barracks for the soldiers, new harbours, churches, and all the necessary buildings of an ancient city. The old (original) city on the slightly elevated headland, which Severus had knocked down, could be revived as a living site overlooking the Bosporos entrance, if it had not already been re-colonized during the previous century. And a later wall would be built on the line the angel had indicated.

It was hardly on the best line, from the defensive point of view, so perhaps the angel was not really militarily-minded; it had, of course, been Constantine's own decision. It was overlooked by both the headland (which would become the acropolis, and is now the site of the Ottoman imperial palace, the Topkapi) and by the hills further inland. It was soon seen to be a poor line, but for the present the construction of the other buildings within the new city took priority, among them the imperial palace, and the churches to make it clearly a Christian city. Enough had been done, however, by 330 for a ceremony of consecration – a Christian ceremony, in effect a baptism of the city – to be conducted so that the city could be declared to be in existence.

Interlude II

The Five Walls of the City

Constantinople has had five defensive walls, plus some internal stockades, the latter more for privacy than defence, though they were used as such in the Ottoman capture. The first wall was that of the original Greek city, built to surround a large part of the hilly headland and enclose the earlier city. This was the wall which did not withstand the Persians or the Athenians, but did resist Philip II successfully. It was about 1.5 kilometres long (a little less than a mile), and was placed at the change of slope of the rise from the lower part of the peninsula to the summit of the hill which formed the headland. It is the obvious line for a wall for a small city, and was probably unchanged from the earliest settlement until Severus' conquest. It is followed now mostly by the wall enclosing the Ottoman Palace.

Clearly a wall which fell with no difficulty to the Persians and Greeks was not the same as that which Philip II deployed his siege machines to attack. Polybios describes the city as vulnerable from the land side, but the city had a collection of artillery pieces with which the Macedonian attacks were kept at a distance.[1] The wall at one point was battered to destruction, allowing the Macedonians to make an entry.[2] But a single narrow breach is rarely enough to cause the fall of a city and the attackers were driven out, and the wall repaired. This was clearly sufficiently strong to do its job. Herodian says the wall was a 'huge, strong wall of millstones' and 'appeared to be a single block of stone' so carefully was it built;[3] Dio Cassius comments on its seven towers.[4] Both are describing the wall which Severus' army had to attack, vainly. It was, that is, very similar, indeed perhaps the same, as that which had been damaged by Philip. It is clear at least that the old wall had been fully maintained, and even strengthened, possibly under the influence of the Roman forces who marched through the city on the way between the Danube and Armenian frontiers.

This was the wall, strengthened, maintained, and repaired, which stood against the Roman assaults in the siege by Severus' forces in

AD 193–6, and clearly it was again successful. The city was taken by blockade and starvation, not assault, despite the enemy's deployment of siege machines;[5] Severus required that, once it was captured, the wall was to be dismantled. Of course, he was still uneasy on his new throne, and Byzantion's and Niger's defence had been a major danger point which might have encouraged others to resist him in his new position. But Severus was also a malignant enemy, and defiance always called out his savagery. The site of the city had clearly impressed him, and when Caracalla suggested that the city be re-founded, he agreed, though it was to be on his terms and on a different site.

The site had been largely depopulated by 196, by casualties, by flight, by evacuations, and by massacres, and other buildings besides the walls had been destroyed. It was, after its conquest, only thinly peopled and largely a ruin field when Caracalla's suggestion of a re-foundation was accepted. Severus and Caracalla had, in effect, an empty space on which to build. The city's centre was now to be located below the hill which had been the original site, and the new wall was built in front of this area. It stretched, so it is believed, from the Neorion Harbour on the Golden Horn directly south to the Propontis shore. Exactly what line was followed is not known, and in particular the southern, Propontis terminus is suggested to have been at several different places. It was about the same length as the original wall, but about 700 metres to the west. The space between the ruins of the old city on its hill and the new wall of Severus became the new city.[6]

These walls resisted Constantine's attacks for up to three months in 324, though the city had fallen in eleven days in 313. The difference was no doubt the size and morale of the garrisons, but it is obvious that the wall was adequate to its purpose; Constantine also deployed siege machines, and the wall was badly damaged. Ammianus has a digression in which he discusses the artillery available to besiegers at this time – towers, rams ('onagers'), stone throwers ('scorpiones'), and arrow shooters ('ballistae'); these are not really different from those available to Philip II six centuries earlier, though perhaps more numerous and larger.[7] Indeed Constantine did not actually take the city until his fleet had secured control of the Straits and he had defeated Licinius' army across the Bosporos at Chrysopolis; it may be that much of the three months of the siege was a mere blockade. In the end Byzantion surrendered rather than wait to be taken by assault by the victorious army.

The strength of the city was, of course, not unusual, since even with the latest of siege machines (Constantine also had an earthen ramp built to reach the top of the wall) the walls of cities were often strong enough to defeat a siege – so long as outside help was available.[8] Perhaps its strength nevertheless did impress Constantine, but he had other reasons for choosing to locate his new city at Byzantion.

Constantine's city, to go with the size of his ego, was much larger than Severus'. The wall he marked out, or which was marked out for him (by the angel, by his intuition, or, more probably, by his architect and surveyors), is not known with any precision, but it was probably built in a long curve from the Golden Horn to the Propontis, but almost three kilometres further west than Severus' wall. The Golden Horn end was just west of an inlet called Zeugma ('bridge', or perhaps in this case, referring to a ferry point); the Propontis end of the wall was at no special place. If the wall did form a neat curve, it could have been simply drawn that way in the plans, without serious consideration of the shape of the land; if so, it will have shown weaknesses; it was on a poor line militarily. It did not last long, no more than a long generation. It enclosed two more of the seven hills which the city site eventually is said to have included, and the area within the new walls was increased by four or five times, to about 600 hectares, double the size of Republican Rome, and therefore it was now a city of equivalent size to Antioch, though still smaller than Alexandria, and only half the size of Rome as walled by Aurelian in the 270s AD.[9]

This wall has also vanished, dismantled when the area of the city was enlarged yet again, and its course is now no more than a guess. The city grew into the expanded area by being frequently the residence of the current emperor, and, more permanently, by hosting the imperial government, its officials, clerks, slaves, families, and guards. An allocation of the dole of food and wine, which was originally intended for Rome, will have helped to attract some new population, but its intra-mural area was never full.

The threat from the Goths and their allies in 378 and 395, and then the Gothic threat to old Rome and their campaigns throughout Italy, will have directed imperial attention to Constantinople's defences. The city's survival in the face of the Gothic threat had been satisfying, but the prospect of a much longer blockade – such as that by Constantine in 324, together with an increase in the population, raised the threat prospect higher. The vulnerability of the Balkan provinces to barbarian invasions was now well understood, and when the Danubian frontier was broken, there was only the Haemos Mountain range (the Balkan Mountains today) as a natural barrier between the invaders and the Aegean coast – this was where Valens placed his first defence in 376 after the Danubian line was penetrated. Refugees had no doubt poured into Constantinople in the face of the repeated Gothic campaigns in the Balkans, and the arrival of the Goths directly in front of the city will have increased the pressure on the city's resources. The withdrawal of the Goths was due in 378 to their shock at the sight of the defence, and to a shortage of supplies, and in 395 to adept diplomacy by the praetorian prefect Rufinus. That is, a cool and detailed consideration of the city's position and its defences quickly revealed that it was as vulnerable to a more determined enemy as the Danube frontier was to a barbarian attack. Constantine's wall was seen to be as badly sited and vulnerable to a serious attack as Severus' had been.

The enlarged city, even under Constantine, was in need of reliable food and water supplies. As for food, when there was a sufficiently large population, it would be brought in by merchants, and such supplies would supplement the dole. The water supply was another matter. Hadrian, two centuries before Constantine, had financed the building of an aqueduct, and there was the intermittent stream, the Lykos, which flowed into Constantine's city (incidentally forming a weak point in the main Theodosian Wall). Valens repaired this aqueduct, but since it started many miles inland, to the west of any of the city's walls, cutting it was liable to be one of the first things any besieger did. As the city grew in the fourth century therefore a concerted effort was made to provide cisterns inside the city to hold a reserve supply. The aqueduct started at Bizye in the Istranja hills, and was about 120 kilometres long. A large cistern, called 'of Modestos', was built in the 360s, and more constructed later.[10]

Once the food and water situation had been partly dealt with, the size and defences of the city could also be addressed. By the end of the fourth century there was presumed to be a need for yet another wall. The threat of waves of barbarian invaders was bad enough, and even during the fourth century it must have been obvious that Constantine's wall was inadequate. It was also apparent that food other than a corn dole was needed. Vegetables and fruits could be brought in by merchants, like any other food in peacetime, but such perishable goods would hardly be imported in wartime when they might have to wait weeks for the chance.

The new walls were therefore designed first for defence, and second to enclose a wide area where provisions could be grown during a siege. Animals were also pastured there. The purpose was not to enclose the land occupied by the population. By 408 the praetorian prefect of the eastern part of the Empire, Anthemius, had begun the new walls.[11] They took fifteen years or so to build, and were named for the emperor under whom they were built, Theodosios II, rather than their apparent inspirer, or their architect. It may be that Constantine's wall was demolished and its stones used in the new wall, but the danger of removing one defensive line before the new one was ready might have prevented that. The actual building was of stone, alternating with layers of red bricks, the usual Roman building method of the time. The stone was locally quarried limestone, the bricks manufactured in the city; the whole was bound with locally-made lime mortar. (This style of building can still be seen throughout the lands of the Roman Empire, in surviving constructions from Syria to Hadrian's Wall.)

The wall itself was from 30 to 40 feet high, with a castellated wall facing the enemy side, and a narrow walkway on the inner side, sheltered by the wall itself. It was 15 feet thick at its base, narrowing to 13 feet 6 inches. On the enemy, western, side regularly spaced towers projected from the wall; narrow shooting windows faced outwards, and others faced along the wall; there were ninety-six of these towers. Time suggested that further improvements were needed. In 447, a series of earthquakes brought down over half of the wall and its towers. The danger was acute, since the Huns were campaigning in the Balkans at the time. A great concerted effort saw to the repairs within two months, and the officer in charge, probably called Kyros, also improved the whole system by building an additional advanced wall in front of the main one, and excavated a wide moat still further in front. So the sequence as it emerged after about half a century of building was, from the outside, first a wide moat, then an outer wall ten feet high, and then the main wall, even higher. The spaces between these lines were flat, designed to trap the enemy between the almost impassable elements before and behind.

The still spectacular main wall inevitably draws attention, but there are other elements to the city's defences without which the city wall would still be vulnerable. The longest border of the city, and the most easily attacked, was the shore, along the Golden Horn and along the Propontis. (The hill of the headland was relatively easy to defend.) The wall of Theodosios in fact included the sea walls, built along both of the shores. They were not so elaborately constructed as the great land wall, but they did not need to be, since any attackers would be standing on unstable ships. (Nevertheless in 1204 it was through these walls that the conquerors penetrated.) The sea walls were built therefore to a sufficient height to prevent attack, but were usually only a single wall, not the elaborate sequence of the land wall. They were supplemented by a chain to block access to the Golden Horn, but this required to be defended at both ends, particularly on the Galata end, where a small fort was built to defend it.[12]

These walls were Constantinople's main defence until the Ottoman conquest, and even longer. Long sections are now in ruins, but much is still more or less intact, and is one of the great sights of the ancient world. At the same time, more cisterns were built, and the new wall, built a further 800 metres beyond Constantine's wall, enclosed a much-expanded civic territory, more or less doubling the size of the city. This, along with the land inside Constantine's wall, was a further resource for the population, an area for horticulture and fruit growing, and for pasturing meat animals before slaughter, and for the rich to site their villas.

This is not quite all, however. There had been four walls so far in attempts to make the city safe – the original wall of the Greek colony city, Severus' wall and Constantine's on the low land, and now Theodosios' land and sea walls. Yet another, a fifth wall, was built, called the Long Wall of Thrace. It was built about 65 kilometres west of the Theodosian Wall, at a point where the Istranja peninsula begins to widen out decisively. It was 45 kilometres long from the Black Sea coast to that of the Sea of Marmara, and was built as a less powerful version of the Theodosian wall, with a moat, an outer wall, and the main wall. It is largely ruinous now, and in parts has disappeared, but in some areas the main wall is still three metres high. It was fitted out with a series of towers, and with a number of forts attached to it on the inner side. Its plan is very reminiscent of that of Hadrian's Wall in Britain, but on a larger, more monumental scale,[13] and like that wall, which had already been abandoned when the Long Wall and Theodosios' Wall were built, it has been used as a quarry of ready-made stones for later building. The technical accomplishment of these Constantinopolitan walls makes it clear that it was not a failure of technology which brought down the Roman Empire.

It is unclear when this Long Wall was built, but at some time in the late fifth century is the usual conclusion, possibly after the Kutrighur Hun attacks. Its purpose and efficacy were not always appreciated, and it was pointed out even soon afterwards that it was impossible to man such a long wall adequately.[14] But, of course, the wall was not intended to be lined with soldiers, but to have small well-armed groups at vulnerable points, in the towers and the forts. It appears that the wall did succeed in deterring some further advances for several centuries – wandering groups of barbarians would not be able to get through with any ease, nor could cavalry. The wall – any wall – was, of course, vulnerable and a sign of Roman weakness, but by the fifth century this was hardly a surprise; it was, however, a clear sign of the Roman determination to endure.[15]

Part II

Constantinople

Chapter 9

Enemy from the North-West – the Goths

The Siege of 378

The new imperial city was slowly built up from 324, when Constantine's decision on the choice of site was made. A new city requires a new name, but Constantine was constrained by his position and his purpose, and he opted for 'New Rome', a thoroughly unimaginative choice, perhaps chosen simply to be a contrast with 'Old Rome', which was now portrayed to be antiquated and out of date – that is, pagan, not Christian. But the new name was only an official choice. The popular name, inevitably, was Constantinopolis. The city was protected quickly with a defensive wall, positioned as the emperor (or his invisible agent) directed. The first test of this came fifty years after the city's foundation

In August 376 a Gothic army confronted the Roman field army of the eastern part of the Empire not far from Hadrianopolis – the place where Constantine had attacked Licinius before capturing Byzantion. The commander on the Roman side was the Emperor Valens; on the Gothic side the war leader Fritigern commanded. Valens, the emperor who ordered the reconstruction of the aqueduct that supplied Constantinople with water, believed he faced only a part of the likely Gothic army, the Tervingi Goths, so he moved to attack. As the fighting began, Fritigern unexpectedly received reinforcements, the Greuthungi Goths. This doubled the size of his army, which now outnumbered that of Valens. The result was the destruction of the Roman army, the death of Valens, and the creation of a major crisis for the Roman Empire. It was one of the great Roman defeats, but, as with so many major battles regarded as decisive by historians and politicians in hindsight, it was not seen as such at the time.[1]

The victorious Goths slowly moved towards the city of Constantinople. They attacked Hadrianopolis and Perinthos/Heraklea, and failed each time. Fritigern had difficulty in controlling his men, since the Gothic army, as in the Gothic raids over a century before, was composed of an accumulation of separate parts, each with its chief, and in each section there were argumentative dissident individuals. Fritigern's own policy was to avoid assaults on walled cities, and the heavy casualties the army incurred in the attack on Hadrianopolis was for him a clear justification for his caution. But the reason for attacking that city was that Valens' surviving officials and senior officers, and his treasury, were all in the city. The treasury would fund the Goths for further ventures, the officials might be killed or ransomed, and in any case would be rendered impotent. The same cupidity operated as the army approached Constantinople.[2]

The army carried Fritigern, clearly only nominally in command, along with it. The Via Egnatia once again witnessed an army marching along it. Inside the city there had been confusion when it was learned that the army was defeated and the emperor was dead – made even worse by the fact that he was at the beginning thought to be no more than missing. Valens was not much missed or mourned; he was an Arian Christian, so the Orthodox Christians celebrated, deciding that he had died by fire (an invention) because it was to the fires of hell that he was destined.[3]

Fritigern attracted to his forces contingents of Huns and Alans, so increasing both the size and the heterogeneity of his army. The inducement was the wealth of Constantinople, of course, but it may also be that the senior Gothic leaders knew that the city would require to be assaulted, and they were perfectly willing for the new allies to bear the brunt of the casualties.

The defence of the city was entrusted at first to a unit of Arabs, sent to Constantinople by Queen Mavia of the Ghassanids of Syria. This is distinctly odd, since the Gothic army was certainly up to 20,000 men strong, especially given the arrival of the Hun and Alan reinforcements. The Arabs cannot have numbered anywhere near so many, perhaps no more than 1,000 or so. But the Gothic army had been carefully marshalled into blocks of troops marching in squares, fearing to encounter another Roman army. What they encountered therefore in their tightly packed phalanxes, was a group of guerrilla fighters, who attacked in small bands, harrying any attacking square to a halt, but not staying around long enough to be attacked in return. It seems quite likely that the Arabs were sent out to fight first because they were regarded as expendable (just as

Fritigern would use the Alans and Huns); instead they proved to be more than usually successful.

As if this was not cunning enough the individual tactics of some of the Arabs were very unsettling. One man, apparently called Nazir, who killed a Goth, having plunged into a crowd of them, then sucked the blood flowing from his severed neck. Such tactics and behaviour had a disproportionate effect on the enemy soldiers.[4]

The Arabs, however, no matter how momentarily effective their tactics might be, could hardly stop the advance of the whole army which outnumbered them twenty-to-one, even if its morale was damaged. The sight of the city and its defences, as it did so often to attackers who were intent on seizing the wealth without realizing the effort which would be involved, completed the Gothic army's demoralization. Fritigern's unwillingness to fight walls was once again vindicated. There was some fighting in front of the walls, perhaps as much by the Arabs as by anyone else, but the Gothic army collectively had no intention of assaulting the walls, or of staying around to wait for the city to surrender. They had had a splendid time since the great battle at Hadrianopolis in ravaging the countryside and sacking villages and undefended towns. They had no doubt collected a considerable quantity of loot, but they now inhabited a desert. The land around them was so damaged by their ravages that it could produce no food. So, despite their possession of siege machines, and despite beginning to manufacture the necessary weaponry in their 'manufactories', a lack of food soon drove the Gothic army away, leaving behind 'greater losses than they had inflicted'.[5]

They are said to have spent just two days before the city, but the effort to capture it had clearly lasted a good deal longer than that, if the vigorous approach to conflict with the guerillas may be included. The Goths' intentions were clearly originally to assault the city wall with their siege machines – rams, towers, and so on presumably – and the fact that they gave up so easily can be ascribed to the general demoralization the soldiers had suffered, both at the nature of the guerilla tactics of the Arabs and the daunting task of conquest they saw before them when they actually arrived before the city. This had been a real siege, if only a brief one.

The Gothic army disintegrated, sections separating off from the main body to continue wandering and ravaging, or to go home with their loot.

These groups could often be intercepted by Roman forces and either destroyed or recruited. Fritigern is not heard of again after about 380, only two years after the siege. In 382 a peace was agreed, whereby the Goths, such of them as were left to agree to a treaty, were given the right to settle down in designated areas in the Balkans. It was not the end of the wars, but it did end that particular conflict, which had begun in 376.[6] The Gothic failure before Hadrianopolis, Perinthos and Constantinople certainly brought them to a less ambitious frame of mind. The victory of the Romans at Constantinople redressed the balance upset by the defeat at Hadrianopolis and made a peace possible.

Another Gothic siege threatened in 395, when a reconstituted Gothic army under the command of Alaric marched towards the city. The trigger had been the death of the Emperor Theodosios I in January of that year, which ended the treaty of 382. Alaric and his followers do not seem to have been all that keen on mounting an attack, for many of them had probably been part of the foiled attack of seventeen years before. Rufinus, the new Emperor Arcadius' regent, met Alaric and made a new agreement. Rufinus came out of the city alone, dressed in Gothic costume to honour his interlocutors – he clearly understood the temper of this army, and the aims of its leader – and the agreement came quickly. Alaric and his men marched off to Greece to take up the lands allocated by the imperial government (and eventually into Italy and the sack of Rome). The Goths spent no longer at the city than in 378 but rather more profitably.[7]

Chapter 10

An Enemy from Within – Vitalian

The Sieges of 514 and 515

The main internal conflict in the Roman Empire after Constantine's acceptance of Christianity was over which version of Christianity was to be recognized as the most legitimate. The several versions competed above all for imperial support for their cause, which all too often involved violence directed at their rivals. The main conflict by AD 500 was between Orthodox Christianity and Monophysitism, a rivalry which needless to say also involved other issues, social and political and military. The precise points in dispute are too tedious and obscure and pointless to detail, for the point here is that the competition for imperial favour actually meant seeking the favour of the emperor himself, and the emperors had their own preferences, which could bring them into conflict with their subjects.

In the early 500s, the religious conflict brought the Emperor Anastasios I (491–518) to favour Monophysitism. The arguments were as usual intense, to the extent that the commander of the imperial forces in Thrace, Vitalian, who was perhaps the *comes foederatorum* (commander of allied forces), and certainly commanded an army made up of units of barbarians, went into rebellion.[1] He eventually claimed that he was acting in defence of the Orthodox Church, which Anastasios was condemning and seemed to be destroying. Vitalian's actions do seem to support that to some extent, but this was not how he began his rebellion, nor how he ended it.[2]

Vitalian was on campaign in the Balkans, recruiting forces, including Huns, Goths, and others when he came out in rebellion. He is described as a Goth, or at times as a Thracian, or as a half-Goth, but clearly he was part-barbarian in origin. In 513 he advanced close to Constantinople, outside the great walls, but was there persuaded to return to his duties when promised supplies for his troops. That is, his first complaint was of a lack of logistical support. That promise of support, however, was not fulfilled; instead, Emperor Anastasios sent out a commander called Cyril with an army to suppress the errant general.

They fought a battle, which neither could claim to have won. Cyril then moved into the city of Odessos on the Balkan Black Sea coast, while Vitalian retired in a different direction, both commanders presumably aiming to recover and see to their casualties. Vitalian was the more cunning. He bribed some of Cyril's troops to let him into the city, and there his officers killed his enemy. If he had not been an active rebel when he was seeking supplies, he was certainly one now. His programme expanded from asking for food to complaints about the emperor's Monophysite leanings, and he demanded that a Church Council be convened to decide religious policy. That is, having become a rebel because of the emperor's miserly reaction to his request for support, he picked up on the emperor's vulnerability in religious matters, and sought support amongst his enemies.

Anastasios sent out two more commanders, Hypatios (his own nephew) and Alathar, with, no doubt, another army; they were defeated, and Hypatios was captured. A ransom was demanded for his release, which was presumably to be devoted to paying Vitalian's forces, or to buying supplies for them. There was a long delay in paying this ransom, and Vitalian brought his forces close to Constantinople once more. The ransom was now paid, and Vitalian again moved away from the city. But Anastasios' promise to hold a Church Council on Monophysitism versus Orthodoxy was evaded by changing the agenda. Clearly he was unwilling to accede to the demands of a rebel, but was equally unwilling to be dictated to by a council which he probably expected to be hostile. By this time he was playing for time; Vitalian appears to have had control of all the European provinces.

The emperor had also shown that, after Vitalian's success, he was likely to submit to a close threat. So Anastasios' delays brought Vitalian and his army to Constantinople's neighbourhood for the third time. The earlier visits were not perhaps technically sieges, more in the nature of blockades, and had been aimed at the emperor, not the city. This third approach was different. It seems evident that by now Vitalian's aim was less to enforce his religious demands than to remove the exasperating emperor. Whether Vitalian saw himself as the next ruler – as a Goth or part-Goth he was hardly going to be a popular choice – or he had some other candidate in view is not clear. Anastasios himself had no direct heirs, so that post was apparently open. The issue by this time was no longer military supplies, nor even imperial religious policy, but the future of Anastasios as emperor.

Vitalian brought his army to Sykai, a suburb on the north side of the Golden Horn, where Galata later developed. It is not clear if this area was fortified at this time. In enemy hands it would threaten the entrance to the harbour area, and so give access to the city proper across the Golden Horn. It is probable that there was a wall of some sort around the harbour if not the whole suburb; this was the anchoring place for the chain which could block the harbour entrance, but that is not recorded before about 700; if the chain existed, the suburb would certainly need to be fortified. If it was not walled when Vitalian occupied the area, it would soon be, such was the potency of the threat his forces posed for the city.

Getting an army across into the city would be relatively easy from there. Vitalian gathered a fleet, presumably ships he collected from the ports in the Black Sea he controlled. Anastasios also had ships, possibly having increased his fleet recently in view of Vitalian's activities. The emperor gave the command of the ships to Marinus of Apameia, an active and successful governor of Syria. The battle was fought between Sykai and the city, at the entrance to the Golden Horn. Marinus is said by one (unreliable) source to have had a new and unexpected weapon at his disposal, which later was called Greek fire. When fired at the enemy ships it set them, and any seaman or soldier in the way, alight, and the fire was almost unquenchable. This is only reported by the historian John Malalas, writing much later; he may have been making an assumption based on the events of later sea battles.[3] But Vitalian was completely defeated.

This broke the siege, such as it was, and Vitalian retired from the fray, living at Anchialos in the Black Sea coast, but still commanding his army and remaining in control of the European region. (Coincidentally this place was close to Mesambria, to which earlier Byzantines had fled when defeated.) He was not disturbed there. In fact, he had won the religious argument, even if he had been defeated in battle. (It is not clear if he received pay for his men or supplies, but in control of much of the Balkans he could no doubt collect his own.) Anastasios seems to have halted his move towards Monophysitism, assisted by clever diplomacy by him and by the Roman Pope Hormisdas, and died only three years later, in 518. His successor was Justin (518–27), Vitalian's colleague in earlier wars, and supposedly one of Anastasios' commanders in the sea battle. His enthronement meant a decisive victory for Orthodoxy, and Vitalian came out of his hibernation to assist with its implementation. He was made *magister militari* in 518 and consul in 520, but he was seen as too great a rival by Justin's nephew, the formidable, unscrupulous, and ambitious Justinian, who expected to be the heir. This was a factor hardly surprising in the circumstances, for no one in the imperial government could seriously trust a successful rebel. Vitalian was murdered mysteriously in the palace in 520, at a time when Justinian was there also.[4]

This was a curious siege, or set of sieges. The city was not the object for which Vitalian was fighting, and he made no attempt to break into it. Instead his aim, after being denied the promised supplies for his soldiers, was to change the mind of the emperor. Three times he brought his army to the walls of the city, but each time for a different purpose; the third time, at Sykai, he was apparently quite determined to overthrow the emperor himself, having failed to persuade him. This was politics in the style of the East Roman Empire. In the absence of any consultative machinery which could overrule the imperial wilfulness, resort was had to a blockade of the city, and this became the usual response of disaffected generals and aristocrats. Also to Vitalian we may attribute the first experience of defeat by the use of chemical weapons, if the historian Malalas is correct. Greek fire was as unpleasant a weapon as could be invented, in effect the mediaeval version of napalm. It was, of course, just the sort of incendiary weapon for Christians to use against dissident Christians, since they expected their religious enemies to go to the fires of hell.

But there was more to this crisis than the possible use of a new and decisive weapon. The threat to the city was never really serious until the third of Vitalian's approaches, in 515, and even then the battle was ordered by the emperor – as it had been when he sent out Cyril and then Hypatios to attack Vitalian's forces. But these events set up a pattern which was followed with minor variations during the next nine centuries; for a rebel, or pretender, a recognized political procedure had been invented: the emperor's enemy should bring his army close to the city, but not actively to threaten to storm the walls, which was not a prospect agreeable to any army in any case. Then he would aim to negotiate, either to persuade the emperor to retire, or with some of the inhabitants or some of the guards, to let him into the city. This, until the last minute and the battle, was Vitalian's method, a political process which he had revealed. Since he would be said to have gained his main point, his religious one, it was to be later followed by other dissidents.

Chapter 11

Enemy from the North – the Kutrighur Huns

The Siege of 559

The main assault by the Huns, a formidable nation of nomads, on the Roman Empire had been broken by successive defeats in the 450s, but fragments of the people had survived, particularly in the Ukrainian steppelands. The Emperor Justinian I (518–65) played diplomatic games with them, repeatedly setting one group against another until he found that none of them trusted him. In 558, one section of the Huns, the Kútrighurs, invaded his empire.

There had been several incursions over the previous two decades. A major Hun invasion in 539 reached as far as Greece, though Thermopylae was successfully defended, and the Thracian Chersonese (passing the defensive wall at the root of the peninsula).[1] In 544 and again in 549 there were other invasions, though the second of these was mounted mainly by Sclaveni (Slavs), who came in great numbers.[2] None of these approached Constantinople, but the Huns in 539 had come close to the city. Several important cities, however, did fall to the invaders, and many smaller towns also. Procopios described the damage caused in the Balkans by all these invasions, suggesting extensive depopulation.

Justinian's diplomatic juggling was necessitated because the Empire's military resources were extremely stretched, and it is probably no coincidence that the invasions tended to coincide with the Empire's overseas expeditions, and with its frontier wars, when its armies were sent out to distant frontiers to conduct wars, often lengthy and aimed at reconquering lost regions – Africa and a Persian attack in Syria in 539, a long Italian campaign in the 540s.

The immediate reason for this sustained and repeated series of invasions, after several decades with much less trouble of this sort, seems to be that there was a drought on the steppe lands, a condition which afflicted many other regions at the time,[3] combined with the desire by the nomads to partake of the good life – subsidised food from the emperor, wine, hot baths, soft clothes, and so on, all of which were detailed in a letter from a Hun chieftain to Justinian.[4]

Apart from the widespread drought and famine (which affected Belisarios' Italian campaigns in particular) the year 542 was a plague year, in which the bubonic plague reached the Empire, with the usual horrific casualties. Up to a half of the population died in the city, though the death rate was probably less in the countryside. (But the plague seems to have scarcely affected military and political affairs, other than to make them more difficult.)[5]

The Kutrighurs lived in the western bay of the steppe, west of the Dniepr River. They found a war leader in a man called Zabergan, and he conducted the new raid in 558, bringing with him large numbers of Sclaveni. Having broken through the Danube line by crossing the river when it was frozen he was free to reach much of the Balkans. This was an unusually large force and Zabergan spread them out, possibly because they needed to be in smaller groups in order to find supplies. He divided his forces into three bands. (This had been done also in 267 by the Gothic-Herulian sea expedition which reached the Aegean; it is a sign in both cases that the defence was inadequate and the invaders felt able to divide their forces.) One of the groups followed the route of the 539 raiders into Greece, the second was directed against the Thracian Chersonese, and the third, under Zabergan himself, was directed at Constantinople.[6]

The invaders camped at Melantias, a village on the Propontis coast, well within the line of the Long Wall, which was probably built as a result of this invasion, but several miles short of the Theodosian Wall. It is obvious that they were intending either an attack on the city, or a blockade, which was probably aimed to result in the receipt of a payment to go away. Since the invaders, though 7,000 strong (an unusually large barbarian force), were entirely cavalry, the likelihood of their succeeding in breaking into the city was small, but a blockade might work; certainly the land would be ravaged. There was, it seems, a panic in the city, and the valuables from the churches and private houses were evacuated across the Bosporos.[7] All this suggests that confidence in the walls was not high, and the city was itself largely undefended.

Justinian called his general Belisarios out of retirement. With just 300 well-armed infantrymen of the hoplite type, and several hundred peltasts, he set out, selected a defensible position, and settled down. A ditch around the position was dug by the local peasants, who had been rounded up for the occasion, and he disposed his 300 (presumably this number is a deliberate memory of the Spartans at Thermopylae, and so probably an invention of the historians), while the peltasts, armed with missile weapons, were ranged on the approach to the main position, but hidden in the nearby woods. The peasants gathered behind. After some time the Huns realized they had a victim lying ready to be attacked, but when they did so Belisarios' plan operated perfectly – the attackers were confined in the narrow approach between the woods and were crowded together, and on their approach they were bombarded by the peltasts, and then stopped by the hoplites. Substantial numbers of the Huns were killed, and the Roman numbers were exaggerated, and their intentions suggested, by the shouts of the (unarmed) peasants they thought were supporting the hoplites, and who would pursue them in their retreat. The Huns withdrew, not having expected such treatment. There was, by Justinian's sensible order, no pursuit; once out in the open the Romans would be very vulnerable.[8] The other raids by the Huns were similarly less than productive, though they left large areas of Thrace and Macedonia in the usual ruin, as Procopios noted.

The approach of the invaders towards the city did not actually result in an assault, but Belisarios' victory certainly persuaded them to go away. The city was saved from danger, and from having to pay a ransom. And, of course, it was particularly helpful for the future that the raiders did not net any serious wealth. That, and their nasty defeat, were discouragement enough.

Chapter 12

Enemies from the Northwest, the East, and from Within – Avars, Persians and Greeks

The Sieges of 610 and 626

The Avars

The Kutrighurs became subsumed into the newly arrived Avars, who had been driven westwards out of Central Asia by the Turks, until they were able to occupy the Hungarian plain, a steppe territory suited to their nomad lifestyle. They were aggressive in the same way as the Huns and earlier nomad groups, and settled down to raid all their neighbours. They were in some ways unlike those predecessors who established only a precarious control over a wide variety of other peoples, including the Kutrighurs and the Slavs. The Avars had a strong ruler, the khagan, and they could mount well-organized attacks and conduct campaigns stretching over several years; the groups such as the Kutrighurs and the Goths had usually been able to raid for no more than part of a year. They were well armed with a variety of siege weapons, some, such as trebuchets, new to Europe, which had been inherited from contact with the Chinese military in Central Asia. (The Romans are known to have been using trebuchets by the 580s, having adopted them from the Avars.) The result of the activities of the Avars and the Slavs, who were migrating steadily into the Balkans, often directed by the Avars, was the progressive devastation of much of the Balkans as far south as Greece, which was still depopulated since the Kutrighur ravaging. The way was open for the gradual settlement in the damaged region of the infiltrating Slavs, especially in the 580s. These peoples might or might not acknowledge the authority of the khagan.[1]

One reason for the difficulty the Romans had in combating these raids and infiltrations was that they were also, from 572 to 590, at war with the Sassanid Persian Empire on their eastern frontier. In effect, while holding on in the east, the Romans lost the Balkans. When the east was peaceful, they could make attempts to recover the lost Balkan lands, but by the 590s the Avar Khaganate was well established in the Hungarian plain and astride the Danube, and the Slav peasant communities were well entrenched in the central and southern areas.

The Sassanid Empire

The Sassanids were the Roman Empire's most consistent, powerful, and dangerous enemy. They were the successors of the Parthians, whose kingdom had been in a similar position for several centuries before the Sassanids replaced them – but the Sassanids were more powerful and better organized than the Parthians had ever been. By the beginning of the sixth century the Sassanid Empire was prepared to attack the remnant of the Roman Empire in the east; from 600 onwards it made a serious effort to conquer at least its eastern provinces, and in 626 made another attempt to take Asia Minor – to do this it was necessary to capture Constantinople, and here was the first major test of the city's defences.

The two empires, Roman and Sassanid, had fought each other repeatedly in the seventh century, and between these wars they intrigued in various ways to secure advantage. The Sassanids had made serious efforts to secure control of southern Arabia and to make an alliance with the Ethiopian kingdom; the Romans had made the same sort of effort to secure an alliance with the Turks in the Central Asian steppe.[2] In 591 the Sassanid Khan, Khosro II, had been deposed by a distant cousin, and had been returned to his throne by an alliance of his supporters, the Armenians, and the Roman Emperor Maurice (582–602).[3] As a result the two emperors had a bond of alliance and friendship, and this condition of peace in the east was the basis of Maurice's ability to campaign in the Balkans. But in 602 the usurper Phokas, complaining of the lack of logistic support provided to the army, overthrew and murdered Maurice and his whole family.[4] Khosro took this personally. The arrival of Phokas' ambassadors at the Sassanid court to announce his accession to the throne was therefore seen by Khosro as an insult, and his reply was to issue a declaration of war.[5] No doubt Khosro had faced internal pressures to profit from Roman preoccupation with the Balkans; that is, he and his generals saw a splendid opportunity to profit from the new Roman crisis.

Phokas and his Enemies

The Emperor Phokas (602–10) therefore faced wars in both the Balkans and the east, together with a serious unpopularity at home and several plots against him within his own empire. His murdered predecessor had made progress in recovering the Balkans, but his murder encouraged the Avars and Slavs to return to the attack. To maintain control at home Phokas became very free at killing enemies and suspected enemies.[6]

The Sassanids proceeded step-by-step to conquer the Roman eastern provinces. The first step was to break through the Roman frontier line in Mesopotamia, a series of formidable fortresses; this was achieved by 605 and they were then able to campaign into Asia Minor. These campaigns tended to be slow because the cities they encountered were well fortified and had to be besieged. The opposition the Romans could put up was sapped by the need to block the Avar and Slav raids in the European provinces, together with a strong dislike amongst many in the Empire for Phokas and his regime. By 608, however, the Sassanids were in control of Cappadocia and central Asia Minor, and the Avars had begun to break into the Balkans.

The Avars and Slavs were mixtures of peoples. As the Avars occupied territory any inhabitants still there became their subjects, or perhaps their allies. Among the Avars, as usual with the nomad groups, these peoples remained distinct from the conquerors and from other subject groups, and had their own chiefs or kings. The Slavs, with a village-based political organization, proved to be very difficult either to conquer or to control, though they were usually willing to join in campaigns led by either a Roman commander or an Avar khagan, with the aim of gaining loot or land. The khagan operated a fairly primitive political economy, which required large quantities of treasure being acquired from his victims, and then distributed amongst his warriors; examples of this have been found discovered in Avar graves in Hungary and Romania.[7] (The Galatian Tylis kingdom, which had blackmailed Byzantion eight centuries before, had pursued this policy also.)

Of course, the prime source of this gold was the Roman Empire, as payment either for the raiders to go away, or not to raid in the first place. The demands began at the tens of thousands of *solidi* (gold Roman coins) and then grew (shades of Tylis again). In the 570s the Khagan Bayan (the only khagan whose personal name is known to us), demanded and got an annual payment of 80,000 solidi. With the Emperor Maurice this payment ceased or was much reduced, but that only stimulated attacks, and after Maurice was murdered Phokas was in no position to do other than pay the blackmail. The general situation was the more difficult in that even when the Avars were deterred from raiding, as they had been in the 590s by Maurice's military abilities, the Slavs continued their infiltration and raiding in smaller groups, even on at least one occasion, in 585, raiding right up to the walls of Constantinople.[8]

The Siege of 610

Phokas, at war with the Avars and the Sassanids at the same time, had much less success than the emperor he had assassinated, and his troubles increased when the exarch (governor) of Africa, Heraklios, moved to take the Empire from him. Heraklios remained in Africa, but dispatched his son, also named Heraklios, on a cautious campaign which slowly increased the pressure on Phokas and his regime. Heraklios' cousin Niketas was dispatched to secure control of Egypt, though it took until 610 to be accomplished.[9] This automatically cut off the supply of grain for Constantinople; thus, added to the shortage of coin caused by the demands of the Avars, there was a shortage of food in the city, all of which increased Phokas' unpopularity. Heraklios brought his fleet into the Aegean and then, having captured Abydos, came through the Hellespont into the Propontis. He landed first at Heraklea (the former Perinthos, though one source claims it was at Kyzikos) and there for the first time he assumed the title of emperor, wore the crown, and donned imperial robes.[10] Then he waited, seeking to gather support from the Empire's inhabitants and elite, some of whom did desert to Heraklios. So yet another pressure was being exerted on the city and on Phokas and his regime.

Heraklios' main target was the population of the city of Constantinople. Phokas' defence measures were ineffectual. He had not attempted to block Heraklios' naval intrusion through the Hellespont, and when he did bring out his ships, Heraklios' fleet defeated them in a battle at Sofia, near the city.[11] Heraklios' delaying tactics probably had the object of testing the support Phokas had, exerting pressure on both him and his supporters, and conducting intrigues to secure support for himself from inside the city. By lying in wait he was forcing individuals and groups to make decisions and assess their loyalties, and he must have hoped for some sort of declaration or uprising in the city, which would allow him to simply march in without too much violence.

If so, this calculation was unsuccessful. Heraklios increased pressure on the rulers of the city (Phokas and his party) by landing troops at the 'circular fort', outside the walls, a move which Phokas had not expected. The city was therefore now under siege by Heraklios' forces who were occupying the space between the Long Wall and the Theodosian Wall, while his ships in the Propontis and the Bosporos controlled the maritime approaches. Heraklios had, that is, reached the decisive point for any besieger, by isolating and surrounding the city. This seems to have been the point at which Phokas began to lose control in the city. The green faction, an organized sports group addicted to violence and rioting, came out in Heraklios' support, and brought – rescued – his mother and his fiancee from their monastic imprisonment. Bonosos, one of Phokas' most prominent generals and supporters, attempted to flee and was murdered with the savagery which illustrates the hatred generated by Phokas' regime. Sections of the city were burnt down, either by accident in the confusion or by design, by one or other of the combatants. Finally, Phokas was arrested in his palace and taken as a prisoner to Heraklios, who was still on board his own ship. There the emperor was savagely mutilated, executed, and his bodily parts distributed through the city.[12]

Heraklios landed in the city on 5 October 610, was crowned (officially this time), and was married to his fiancee, who was then also crowned as empress, all on that same day.[13] This established Heraklios as the legitimate ruler, but hardly did more than rid the Empire of Phokas. Some of the latter's principal supporters were killed, including his brother, but others remained to become, or pretend to be, Heraklios' men, and had to be cleared out later. Above all, the violence in the city had shown up the tensions in the population – between the factions of the hippodrome (green versus blue), which had been exploited by Heraklios, and which led to much communal violence. This sort of violence had also occurred between the political factions, and these two sources of violence had coalesced in the revolution. The violence tends to be blamed on the example of Phokas' methods, but it was clearly of a deeper origin than that.

These events in the city can be characterized as a coup d'état, or a revolution, or a civil war, but it certainly included Heraklios laying siege for several days to the city, after conducting a land and sea blockade which had lasted for several months. The siege would clearly have been longer if the support for Phokas inside the city had not suddenly collapsed. It was, of course, a prime lesson in siege warfare, that the best way to capture the city is to do so from within.

The Siege of 626

Heraklios inherited the imperial problems which had beset Phokas and Maurice. He was not going to be recognized as a friendly presence by Khosro, to whom he did not send the customary notice of his enthronement, and no doubt the Avars would seize the opportunity to exert pressure on his government. It was, however, the Slavs who moved in first. The Avars did send raids, but it was the Slavs who seized the land. Heraklios made a strategic decision to concentrate on opposing the Persian advance, who soon shifted their attention to campaigning in Syria. Heraklios probably transferred some forces from the Balkans to the eastern front in response. This had no obvious effect. The great cities of Syria fell one by one: Antioch in 611, Tarsus in Cilicia in 613, Jerusalem in 614.

A joint Avar-Persian attempt on Constantinople in 615/616 was of no avail, but a Persian force reached and besieged Kalchedon. Diplomatic contact was made across the Bosporos, and the Persian commander Shahin seemed accommodating, but when a three-man Roman delegation went to discuss terms with the Sassanid government, they were detained and then murdered.[14] The Persian forces withdrew from Kalchedon. An Avar threat to Constantinople at about the same time may have been by coincidence, and was probably not serious, but it set a precedent for future joint action by the two enemies of Heraklios.

Egypt was invaded and conquered by the Persians in 619–20. Along with the domination of much of Asia Minor, the Sassanids had now achieved most of what seems to have been their ultimate aim, to reconstitute the boundaries of the earliest Persian Empire, that of the Akhaimenids. But there was one essential difference between the sixth century BC and the seventh century AD: the existence of the great fortress-city of Constantinople. It was now seen to be essential that this city be captured, if all the conquests by Avars and Persians were to be secure. This began to be appreciated by all sides in the decade after Heraklios' seizure of power, that is, by Heraklios himself, by the Avar khagan, and by the Persian commanders, who had conquered so much of the Roman state, and yet could not be sure of keeping any of it unless the Roman imperial system was destroyed – and that meant capturing Constantinople.

The conquest of Egypt brought the Sassanids to the end of all the relatively easy and possible conquests. One result was the suspension of the corn dole in Constantinople, which had depended upon the acquisition of harvested grain from the Egyptian peasantry; it had been restored after Heraklios' conquest of the city in 610, but now was suspended again, which caused a strike by soldiers in the city, for this had been part of their salary, but this turned out not to be too serious.

By about 620 the Avars had raided widely for the last twenty years in the Balkans, and perhaps had acquired all the possible treasure they could find, while the Slavs had penetrated as far south as Greece, though they had failed three times in joint sieges of Thessalonica with the Avars. In 623 Heraklios had attempted to meet the khagan, and came out of Constantinople to head for Herakleia for a great ceremonial meeting. But the khagan instead attempted an ambush at Selymbria, having got through the Long Walls. Heraklios had to flee, carrying his crown – the capture of either of these, emperor or crown, if not both, would have been a major propaganda coup.[15]

The Avars then ravaged the area between the Long Wall and the Theodosian Wall, and carried off such treasure from the churches in that area as they could find, and took captive many of the inhabitants. But they made no serious attempt on the city itself, though they took a good look at the walls and understood the problem they posed. Despite the ambush and its failure, Heraklios and the khagan did make contact, and Heraklios bought a peace with a payment of 200,000 solidi, the biggest payment yet.[16] The khagan did keep the peace, mostly, for a few years, which was long enough for Heraklios to be able to shift some of the European forces across to Asia, and then to go himself to conduct an audacious campaign to attempt to gain a peace with Persia. He cannot have expected the Avar peace to last, but if he could force or persuade the

Persians to accept a peace, he could then turn back to deal with the Avars. This was a sort of diplomacy Maurice had conducted. Heraklios knew that the Avars could be beaten, and if they were, their ramshackle empire of peoples could well collapse. There was the example in that same year of the Moravians in the northern part of the Avar dominions – Bohemia and Moravia – who were inspired by Samo, a Frankish merchant, to rebel, and succeeded in maintaining their independence.[17] It may be assumed that Heraklios was, at least diplomatically, involved in this. He was certainly involved in continuing anti-Avar intrigues in the northwestern Balkans,[18] and was in contact with the Lombards, who had just removed themselves from proximity to the Avars and were invading Italy.

Heraklios used the respite from Avar pressure to launch a great, unexpected campaign in 624, taking his army through north Anatolia and Armenia to invade western Iran. Next year, having over-wintered in Albania in the Caucasus area, he did much the same, but using the southern Anatolian route. This temporarily reduced the Sassanid control of large parts of Asia Minor, but, spectacular though the campaigns were, the Sassanids were not beaten, though they were certainly hurt; one of Heraklios' target was Takht-i Suleiman, a powerful fortified town guarding an important Zoroastrian fire temple; taking it was a powerful humiliation for Khosro.[19] The Sassanid reply was to revitalize their contacts with the Avars and coordinate a joint attack on Constantinople, this time probably with more than a suggested itinerary, but an agreed date to institute the siege. The agreement appears to have included a proposed division of the Roman territories, with the Black Sea–Straits– Aegean Sea as the separation zone, so that the Persians would take all of Asia and Egypt, and the Avars the Balkans, including the city of Constantinople.[20]

The war had at last reached its decisive moment. The Romans now saw how both of their enemies could be defeated – the Avars by promoting the collapse of their domination of their subject peoples, as they had already begun to do with the Moravians and the Serbs and Croats, and the Sassanids by exploiting their military and political over-extension, by attacking them in their heartland, where the Shahanshah Khosro could be further humiliated. Similarly, the Avars and the Persians could at last both appreciate that to defeat the Roman Empire it was primarily necessary to capture Constantinople. With the Roman forces largely stationed in eastern Asia Minor and Armenia, the possibility existed for a joint attack on the city.

In the spring or early summer of 626, the Persians, in two armies, moved west through Asia Minor. Their main force was composed of experienced soldiers commanded by the general Shahrbaraz; the second force, commanded by the general Shahin (who had been the commander of the forces which had reached Kalchedon in 615, and had negotiated with Heraklios), was partly made up of experienced troops and partly of recent recruits, perhaps conscripts, possibly an indication that the Sassanid over-extension was hurting. Heraklios remained behind Shahrbaraz geographically, but not far from Shahin on his southern flank.[21]

Heraklios detached a force of cavalry to ride to the city as reinforcements, and to get there before Shahrbaraz; this was a sign that, though he might not be with the people in the city, he had them in mind. It was a propaganda exercise, for cavalry would be of little use in the siege. They outpaced Shahrbaraz and crossed into the city before he arrived.[22] One possibility had been that the two Persian armies might catch Heraklios' army at Sebasteia between them in a pincer movement. He had already upset any plan they had concocted by sending reinforcements to the city; now he destroyed any possibility of that pincer movement, even if that had not been intended, by suddenly sending his army under his brother Theodore to intercept Shahin's army on the northern road and destroy it. The battle took place not far from the old Roman legionary base at Satala.[23]

Meanwhile, the Avars advanced south through the Balkans, bringing a very large army, in large part composed of Slavs, and said to be 80,000 strong, a figure supposed to have been calculated by their Roman enemies; no doubt a considerable exaggeration.[24] The khagan waited for a month at Hadrianopolis to collect his forces, bring up his supplies, and adequately prepare. In July he advanced to the attack. The Long Wall did not detain him, but the Theodosian Wall was fully prepared. The advanced force of the Avars encamped before the wall on 29 June 626.[25]

On Heraklios' written instructions careful and detailed preparations had been made in the city; food had been stockpiled (probably, since Egypt was unavailable, imported from his old province of Africa); ships had been prepared and more built, armed and manned, defensive siege machines had been built, and, of course, men were conscripted. There had been a major parade of the cavalry forces in the city, including those sent by Heraklios, an exhibition designed to boost city morale.[26] When the Avar forces reached the city wall, the city was therefore fully manned and well defended. The Persians under Shahrbaraz arrived at Kalchedon but stayed across the water.

The siege proper began on 29 July with the arrival of the main body of the Avars and their installation of a palisade to isolate the city. During the next ten or eleven days the Avars tried on several occasions to break through the wall. They used siege towers higher than the walls; they used trebuchets throwing large stones; they mounted direct assaults. Their evident expertise in siege warfare was not sufficient, and they contacted the Persians, asking for help; Persian troops, a force of either 1,000 or 3,000, was ferried across. The Roman fleet seems to have been unable to prevent these contacts and movements.

The Slav allies/subjects of the Avars tried an assault across the Golden Horn in canoes and log boats they had brought along with them. Siege machines were constructed on the spot both from disassembled kits the Avars had brought with them, or built from materials found in their camping area.[27] Nor was diplomacy and propaganda neglected: at least two meetings were held between the rival commanders between the walls. In one a money offer was made to the Avars to go away.[28] In another the negotiations descended into insults from a Persian delegation which was attending with the khagan (who possibly attended deliberately to sabotage any possible agreement).[29] This display of unity did not faze the city defenders in the slightest. The Persian envoys were intercepted on their return to Kalchedon, and two of them were killed; the third, minus his hands, was returned to the khagan.[30] The Persians managed to gather a fleet of ships which was equipped for war, and was engaged by the Roman fleet in the Bosporos; who won this sea battle is unclear, but since the Persians were never able to land sufficient men on the west side to make any difference, whatever was the precise result of the naval battle, strategically the Romans had succeeded.[31]

As before, the issue was not so much the fighting as the staunchness of the walls, the determination of the citizens, and – above all, for the Avars – the problem of supplies. If it had taken the khagan a month to gather sufficient supplies to begin the siege, an eleven-day-long assault will have used up those supplies quickly. On 8 August, the Avars began burning their siege machines, and the soldiers began to withdraw.[32] The Persians probably withdrew soon after – there was no point in their staying on if the Avars could not take the city, for there was Heraklios and his Roman army still in eastern Asia Minor, victorious against their fellow army under Shahin.

This army was still capable of conducting, as it proved later, a devastating campaign. Heraklios led it into Mesopotamia and Iraq, which involved a marginal defeat for the Persian army at Nineveh. This was the third defeat for the Persians in a year, after Shahin's defeat and the failure at Constantinople, and support for the regime of Khosro II faded. In February 628, Khosro was deposed by a group of generals angered by the king's refusal to consider negotiations with Heraklios. They put his son Khavad II on the throne. He negotiated a peace of mutual withdrawal with Heraklios, though Heraklios did insist on his forces occupying a stretch of Mesopotamia for a number of years in recompense for the damage caused to two Roman territories.[33] This treaty – in effect a recognition of defeat – was followed by the collapse of the Sassanid regime, with ten rulers (including a usurpation by Shahrbazar, and two ruling queens, each for a very short reign) over the next five years (628–33). Meanwhile Heraklios' forces reoccupied Syria and Egypt. But then both Persia and the Roman forces had a new enemy as the Muslim Arabs invaded both empires.

The victory of the Constantinopolitans was the final making of the city. The minor sieges of the previous two or three centuries had been of little moment, and most – except for that of Heraklios – had not threatened the city severely. But the Avar attack, accompanied by the looming presence of the Persians across the Bosporos, had been a serious and menacing attempt to capture the city. In the peace terms suggested at one point by the khagan in one of the episodes of negotiations which punctuated the siege, he proposed that the whole population should be driven out, each person with only a single item of clothing as covering. The threat to the existence of the city was therefore quite serious, and can only have stiffened the citizens' resistance further. (If they knew their history – and some will have drawn the parallel, for they read their Herodotos – their predecessors' fates, also at Persian hands, eleven centuries before, will have been recalled.)

Beyond security and the survival of the Empire, this was the victory of a self-consciously Christian city and community and regime against a joint pagan and Zoroastrian assault. The people believed that they were commanded and protected by the Virgin Mother of God, whose image in a vision was seen at least once by some of the overwrought defenders. They were, that is, living in a city which was under their god's and his mother's special protection, and this ideology was to sustain them over the next centuries. They believed they lived in a special place, and the memory, no doubt enhanced in the telling, of this great siege and their victory was invoked repeatedly when danger threatened in the future.

As to the siege itself, there is no doubt that, unlike the attempts by the Kutrighurs and others, including earlier Avar threats, which had been essentially blackmailing attempts, this time the attackers were seriously attempting to seize and hold the city for themselves. It was to be depopulated if captured, and probably, if the Avars got it, it would be destroyed, since they knew they could not hold it if it was unpopulated. (It would not have remained empty, since the site was now regarded as particularly valuable, but would probably have reverted to the size of the original Greek town.) The Avars had brought to the siege a vast army, including the full range of the latest siege machines of the contemporary military world, and they had failed. The walls and the citizens had proved to be strong enough.

Chapter 13

Enemies from the East – Muslim Arabs

The Sieges of 674–8 and 717–18

The enhancement of Constantinople's self-identification as the pre-eminent Christian city, which came with the successful defence against the attacks by the pagan Avars and the Zoroastrian Sassanids in 626, proved to be highly useful in the succeeding generations-long crisis of the assaults by the Muslim Arabs. This was to prove a never-ending war, from the moment the first Arab forces penetrated into southern Palestine from Arabia. It has not ended yet, and the eventual conquest of Constantinople proved to be the high point of Muslim success. But that did not happen for another eight centuries, and in that time the city was the essential Christian defence.

The Arab onslaught included two great sieges of the city, in 674–8 and 717–18. The Avar-Sassanid siege in 626 lasted a month and a half (taking in the preliminary naval blockade along with the actual attacks) and was essentially a land attack by a fairly well-organized Avar army; the Arab attacks lasted much longer, in one case at least four years (plus a preliminary naval blockade) and in the second case for over a year, including major naval battles. Not only that but the city was the scene between these sieges of the enthronement and expulsion of seven emperors, and two threats which did not reach the stage of a siege, though one of them lasted for six months. All of these imperial changes involved the capture of the city, but without siege. These conflicts are all interlinked and will be dealt with here as a group.

The initial conquests of the Muslim Arabs stripped the Roman Empire of its eastern provinces within a few years – Palestine, then Syria, then Egypt.[1] These conquests permitted the caliphs to take to the sea, since all these countries were vigorous trading lands, their coasts lined with ports, and had a long exposure to naval warfare. The Persians had, with less determination, also taken to the sea and had raided Rhodes and conquered Cyprus by using a fleet, probably using the captured Roman ships from Egypt. The Arabs tended to use Syrians – ships and men – and won an extraordinary battle, the 'Battle of the Masts', against the main Roman fleet in 655 off the coast of Lykia.[2] This ability to adapt themselves to sea warfare was the key to their near successes in the attacks on Constantinople. It was, of course, as earlier sieges had shown, only by a combination of land and sea attacks, and preferably land attacks from both Europe and Asia, that the city could be captured.

The Caliph Muawiya (661–80), who had forced his way to the caliphal throne in a civil war, evidently felt the need to campaign against the Christian empire as a proclamation of his legitimacy (just as Severus had attacked the Parthians, and other conquerors before and since). At first he avoided a direct attack on the Byzantine Empire in Asia for some time, but did send attacks against its position in Africa.[3] Raids against the Byzantine territories in Asia, and along the Asian south coast, were mounted. Then the assassination of the Emperor Constans in 668 at Syracuse, while attempting to combat the Muslim campaign in Africa, probably counted as a useful pretext for mounting an attack on the Byzantine position in Asia Minor, in the hope that this revealed a weakness in its government. There were certainly internal problems, before the new Emperor Constantine IV (668–85) was fully in control. In 670 an Arab land force advanced straight across Anatolia to Kalchedon, but it was unable to achieve anything against Constantinople itself. It was commanded by Fadalah ibn Ubayd when it began and was supported by extra forces brought up by the caliph's son, Yazid. Legends quickly developed around the events, but in fact it seems that the Arabs did not get across the water to attack the city.[4]

The Siege of 674 – 678

This failure compelled a reconsideration. Naval forces were needed if the city was to be attacked with effect, for it would be necessary to get a land army across to the European side. The Caliph Muawiya, when governor of Syria, had been the moving force behind the fleet which won the Battle of the Masts, so it is no surprise that Muslim fleets were dispatched once he was free of the civil war. The first stage was the occupation of Rhodes, which had been raided more than once in the previous generation. Kos, well inside the Aegean, was occupied, and in 674 a fleet penetrated into the Propontis and based itself for the winter at Kyzikos. Smyrna, on the Asian Aegean coast, was another place seized as a base. All these places were apparently occupied on a temporary basis at first, but are significantly placed as stepping stones to the main target, which was Constantinople; the bases along the sea route from Syria were necessary for replenishing the ships and resting the crews on their long voyage. Kyzikos, however, was taken as a more permanent base.[5]

While this preparatory series of moves was taking place, the land armies were raiding from Syria into Anatolia. The chronicler Theophanes records raids, not always in a geographically specific form, in 661 and 662, and annually from 664 to 669. The land army took control of Kyzikos across from the city and camped there in 670/671, and this became the base for the fleet in 674. Constantinople was attacked from that base during the summer of 674, the troops landing on the Propontis coast close to the Golden Gate, which is the gate in the Theodosian Wall closest to the Propontis. This seems to have been the Muslims' main target in the fighting, but they made no progress. The concentration on a single part of the wall, and the singular lack of success of the attackers, would suggest that they were only a relatively small force.[6] There is little or no information, not even the usual exaggeration, about Muslim numbers in this time, but this is regarded as a 'major' campaign; it had no effect on the enemy.[7]

The base at Kyzikos was maintained for the next three fighting seasons. The Muslim fleet withdrew to it for the winter, though it was based in Crete for one winter.[8] When it emerged from its winter quarters there was usually a sea battle, which did not stop the Muslims asserting their maritime superiority – unless the Romans decided to let them attack, being confident that they would fail. A landing was then made near the city wall, as before. In these years no decision was reached, again presumably because of lack of numbers on the Muslim side. In 678, however, the Romans unveiled their new weapon, Greek Fire, said to have been invented by a Greek called Kallinikos who came from Heliopolis (Baalbek) in Syria, and moved, with his invention, to Constantinople during these fighting years.[9]

Theophanes explains, under the year 674, that Greek Fire equipment was being installed in Roman ships in the Proklianesian harbour. This was a small harbour on the Golden Horn side of the peninsula. He instances two-storeyed warships equipped with Greek fire, and siphon-equipped warships – the weapon used to shoot the liquid fire by means of an air pump – and he seems to distinguish between the two types of ship. This was done by the order of the Emperor Constantine IV. However, it appears that it was not until the last year of this series of conflicts that the weapon was actually used. Presumably Theophanes entered these details under the earlier year because that was the year Kallinikos arrived in the city. (Alternatively he had arrived much earlier and it had taken until 678 to perfect the weapon – a research and development effort over only four years would be remarkable for such an unusual and difficult weapon, whose method of discharge had to be invented, as did the correct mixture of chemicals.) The whole process of development was clearly kept secret, and when it was used for the first time it came as a major fighting surprise.[10]

The usual assault by the Arabs from Kyzikos was launched in the summer of 678, and the usual sea battle took place. This time the giant two-storeyed ships and the siphon-equipped warships were deployed by the Byzantines, both firing Greek Fire at the Muslims. This broke up the attack and contributed substantially to the victory. However, it might bring victory in a battle, but it was not a war-winning weapon – there is no indication that it was used against the Muslim land forces, for example. Nevertheless, peace talks began soon after, suggesting Arab exhaustion after four years of fighting. Maintaining a fleet and an army at such a distance from Syria must have been increasingly difficult.

When the two sides settled down to a long negotiation in Syria later in the year – presumably at the caliphal capital at Damascus – the issues were Roman support for a major rebellion by Mandaite Christians in the Lebanon, which had attracted much support from runaway slaves and prisoners. (They were called 'bandits', of course, by the caliphs.) No doubt the existence of Muslim bases in the Aegean and the Propontis was also a matter on the table to be discussed, together with the Roman desire to stop the raids by land into Anatolia. It may be noted that Kallinikos came from Heliopolis, a city in the Lebanon; his flight may well be part of the Mandaite problem; certainly many of the sailors in the Muslim fleet were Lebanese; they were possibly becoming restless.

Muawiya had initiated the peace talks, and had invited the emperor to send a delegation to Syria, even offering an annual tribute as a sweetener, so the Byzantines were able to press for good terms. A written treaty was made, with Muawiya promising a regular annual tribute of 3,000 *nomismata*, together with fifty prisoners to be released, and fifty stallions.[11] Mutual raiding across the Asian frontier would obviously cease, as would support from the emperor for the Mandaites. In the end large numbers of those Mandaites were transferred to Roman territory. The peace was to last for thirty years. In fact Muawiya died only two years after the peace was signed. His son Yazid, who succeeded him, had presumably been associated with him in signing the treaty, and the next two Caliphs, Muawiya II and Marwan, lasted only a short time; when Abd-el Malik succeeded in 685 – the fifth caliph in five years since Muawiya I's death– he requested a renewal of the treaty and did the same again next year when Constantine IV died, but at much reduced terms.[12] In other words proper diplomatic protocols were being followed, for a treaty died when one of its participants died, and it was then up to the two sides to negotiate a new agreement.

The information for this siege is, as may well have been noted in the above account, thin; probably in parts it is inaccurate, which largely accounts for the minimal discussions in modern accounts. The best source, Theophanes, lived and wrote well over a hundred years later, and was primarily concerned with chronology; his historical notices are occasional, not necessarily always accurate, and he omits items one would expect to be included. The Islamic sources are notoriously bad. The sources collectively are so poor, in fact, that at least one historian has denied that there was anything like a siege of Constantinople at all at this time.[13] This dismissal seems to be going too far, since it was clear that the city really was under considerable pressure in the 670s, and on at least three occasions major battles were fought, one of them at the very gate of the city. It seems best to conclude that the city was actively under threat, but the Arab armies were not strong enough in numbers to succeed – it was, for example, clearly impossible to maintain even a small army at Kyzikos for four years at such a distance, so we may perhaps assume that the soldiers were actually marines and sailors.

The appearance of Greek Fire is another issue; it had been supposed by John Malalas that it had been used in an earlier battle, but this is the result of an interpolation into his text and the assumption that the earlier Roman victory was due to the use of this battle-winning material. The issue, of course, was, for the Byzantines, a matter of a state secret; they made a serious attempt to keep the formula for the weapon secret, and managed to do so for about fifty years.[14]

Byzantine Conspiracies

The Byzantine Empire after the peace of 678 went through a generation of confusion and usurpations. There were seven emperors between 685 (the death of Constantine IV) and 715, all serving increasingly short reigns, and each one giving way to another usurper. The last but one of these brief rulers was a bureaucrat who took the throne name of Anastasios II.

Not surprisingly the confusion in Constantinople attracted the predatory attentions of the Empire's neighbours. The Bulgar Khan Tervel took exception to the removal of one emperor with whom he had made a treaty and began raiding through Thrace. On the eastern frontier the Muslims also began to raid and captured a series of cities so that by 715 the frontier line of defence was broken through. In fact, it had been the loss of yet another city in the east which had provoked the army of the Opsikian theme (military region) to put Anastasios on the throne.[15]

It had become clear, so clear that not even bureaucrats in Constantinople such as Anastasios could ignore it, that the Muslims were gearing up for another major attack into Asia Minor, probably aimed at Constantinople. They had gained control of enough cities on the frontier to allow them an unfettered march through Anatolia. Anastasios (713–15) was a competent emperor. Having gained power in a conspiracy his first act was to blind two of the three generals who had organized the coup against his predecessor lest they be tempted to repeat the feat. In religion he returned to Orthodoxy, after a brief episode of Monotheletism, which was a popular move. He contacted Tervel of the Bulgars with a view to making peace, no doubt pointing out that he had now avenged Tervel's imperial friend. He sent an envoy into Syria to suggest a peace treaty to the Caliph al-Walid (705–15), but also to investigate how far the caliph had progressed in his preparations for the great expedition. He organized the city for war, repairing ships, maintaining the wall, gathering supplies, and planned an expedition by sea against Phoenicia.[16]

It was not enough to secure his position. Perhaps annoyed at the blinding and exile of their commander, and suspicious of being sent on a naval expedition while a major land threat was apprehended, the Opsikian soldiers mutinied again. They were at Rhodes at the time, on the way to Syria. They murdered their commander and the whole expedition broke up. The Opsikians turned back for Constantinople. Moving by land, but with some ships pacing them along the coast, they collected support as they went. At Adramyttion they found a suitable candidate for emperor, a man called Theodosios, a tax collector, 'a good, quiet, easy man'. Theodosios ran away at once when he found out what the soldiers intended for him and did his best to evade them in the hills, but he was caught and compelled to accept the position of emperor ('Theodosius III').[17] Presumably such a man was chosen so that, unlike Anastasios, the soldiers thought he could be controlled by the mutineers' leaders.

They marched to Constantinople, and camped on the Asian side at Chrysopolis, but were unable for some time to cross the Bosporos because the fleet in the city remained loyal to Anastasios. The stand-off lasted for several months. The mutineers gathered ships, and they and the naval forces from the city skirmished repeatedly. When the defending fleet was moved to a new base, however, the attackers managed to get across. The Blakhernai sector proved vulnerable to intrigue and/or bribery, and the mutineers got into the city.[18]

Anastasios left the defence of the city to his generals and moved to Nikaia, in the midst of the Opsikians' territory – he presumably had support from non-mutinous members of that theme. His generals in the city were captured by the new invaders and they and the patriarch were taken across to Nikaia. At this Anastasios gave up, probably thankfully, and agreed to become a monk; he was sent to Thessalonica.

Over the two decades to the capitulation of Anastasios II (695–715) the city of Constantinople was seized by insurgent pretenders six times; on only two of these occasions can it be said that the city came under any sort of siege; one of these 'sieges' lasted only three days (in 705); the other 'siege' was more a threat from across the Bosporos than an active assault, though it lasted several months (in 715). And there was to be one more coup to come.

The city was captured with ease on these various occasions because the approaching forces had supporters inside the walls. Hence there was no need for a serious siege. And yet, there were also weak spots which allowed the pretenders to get through the great wall of Theodosios I. Justinian II entered by way of a through-wall water pipe, two of the pretenders got in at the Blakhernai Palace where the wall was much thinner, one entered at the Golden Gate (which must have been opened for him); and the other two captures came from the sea, with landings from ships. None of these were the results of assaults; the city depended on its population to be loyal, not on its wall – though the walls surely helped to build up that popular confidence.

The final act in this two-decade series of coups d'etat came in 717. It was launched from the eastern frontier by two men, Artavasdos the *strategos* of the Armeniac theme and Leo the *strategos* of the Anatolic theme, the two major military commanders in the front line against the Arab attacks. (The Opsikian theme was in the Anatolian interior, not on the frontier.) They clearly knew what was coming from the Muslims, and equally clearly did not believe that the government in Constantinople was in any condition to respond effectively, distracted as it was by the fighting among the soldiers of the Opsikian theme, and by the conflict between two emperors, neither of whom had any military knowledge or experience – one a bureaucrat, the other a provincial tax inspector. Leo claimed at first to be acting on behalf of the Emperor Anastasios, who had appointed him to his command, but by the time he reached the western part of Anatolia, Anastasios had gone. Leo's forces captured Theodosios' family at Nikomedia, at which Theodosios abdicated into a monastery. In March 717 Leo was in the city and was crowned at Hagia Sofia.[19]

The Siege of 717–18

Leo had had to race Arab armies from the eastern frontier to reach the city first. He had managed to distract the Arab commander, Suleiman, into attempting a siege of the fortress of Amorion, while he moved his own army westwards, but even so, Suleiman reached Sardis and Pergamon, which he captured, during late 716, while Leo, who clearly hoped to avoid an assault or a siege, was arguing his way into Constantinople and into power. The Muslim army was accompanied by a large fleet but with the winter arriving the army went into winter quarters in Sardis and Pergamon, and the fleet was withdrawn to winter in Cilicia.[20]

The overall commander of the Arab forces was Maslama, a brother of the Caliph Suleiman. The next year, when the weather was settled, he brought the fleet forward from Cilicia to the Hellespont and used it to shift a large part of the army across into Europe by way of the crossing at Abydos.[21] The army established its siege of the city on the landward side on 15 August 717, first building a palisade to cut all land communications between the city and inland Thrace. A deep ditch was excavated and a makeshift wall was built to reinforce that palisade line.[22] The fleet, said to number 1,800 ships, came into the Bosporos, and anchored in detachments off Sykai (Galata) and off the city peninsula. More of the army lay on the Asian side. For the first time in any siege the city was properly surrounded from the start, on both sides of the Bosporos, and in the Propontis. Part of the fleet, composed of large supply ships, had to be left some distance away, and part of the army had to be used to deal with garrisoned forts in Thrace. The Arab forces had therefore to be spread over a considerable area, obviously thereby weakening the power of their attack.[23] But the fortifications they had constructed facing the Theodosian Wall indicated quite clearly that they intended to blockade the city by land rather than mount assaults, which were expensive in manpower, against the wall.

The Arab commanders already knew that they were up against a cunning enemy. Leo had foxed them the year before over the issue of Amorion, which allowed him to get to the city first, and he was about to do the same at Constantinople. He had an advantage in that he had a long experience of fighting against odds, and against the Arab armies, which had developed his skills at deception; he was also blessed with a sense of timing, which enabled him to seize the correct moments for action. His predecessors Anastasios and Theodosios had both done good administrative work in preparing the city for the siege, with stocks of food laid in, repairs made to the wall, and a serviceable fleet commissioned, and Theodosios had also made a treaty with Tervel of the Bulgars, ceding some territory to Tervel, which established a clear boundary that Leo evidently recognized and accepted.[24] This kept the Bulgars out of the fight at the city until late in the siege.

Part of the Arab fleet moved into the Golden Horn with the intention of attacking the city's sea wall, a notoriously weak section of the defences, but before the attack could be launched it was attacked by Roman ships coming down the Horn and using Greek Fire. Most of the Arab ships were destroyed, and the rest driven away. Leo later lowered the chain which blocked access to the Golden Horn (the first time this is mentioned), but the Arabs did not fall into what they clearly saw as a trap; instead, they withdrew their ships to a harbour halfway up the Bosporos, probably at Hieron, the usual anchorage for waiting ships. This may well have achieved what Leo had intended without any further fighting.[25]

The Caliph Suleiman died early in October 717, but his successor, his cousin Umar, ordered the war to continue. The winter of 717/18 was unnaturally harsh at Constantinople, with snow lying on the ground for three months, and the Arab forces, with only makeshift shelter, suffered severely. Lack of fodder, combined with the cold, killed many of their transport and cavalry animals, donkeys, horses and camels.[26] In the spring the caliph sent two large supply convoys, 400 ships from Egypt, 260 from Africa, but the captains of the ships had heard horrifying stories of the effects of Greek Fire and anchored well clear of the city. The convoy which had come up from Egypt was manned mainly by Christians; some of these men deserted in the ships' boats to get to the city. There Leo interviewed them and discovered the locations of the new fleets; his ships went out and destroyed both fleets.[27]

A relief army coming from Syria was ambushed in the mountain passes of the Taurus and cut up by a Roman force, so none of these supplies or reinforcements reached the army at Constantinople. The naval victories cleared the nearby seas of Arab ships, and this allowed the fishermen in the city to operate again, while further supplies could be brought across into the city from Asia.[28] The balance of supply was therefore reversed, and the citizens were feeding better than their besiegers, who also, after a year in their camp, began to suffer from the usual diseases which always afflicted medieval sieges.[29]

At last, the caliph ordered the expedition to return to Syria. But this took time, and it was late in the season when the pull-out began (Theophanes says it started on 15 August, the anniversary of the opening of the siege the year before and the day of the Assumption of the Virgin for Christians, the protector of the city), but it would take some time to get clear, especially as the Bulgars joined in at last and attacked the Arabs from inland. The season was late enough for the evacuation fleet to be hit twice by storms, once in the Propontis, and again in the Mediterranean. The Arab accounts suggest that their casualties amounted to 150,000 men, no doubt the usual exaggerated guess, but in effect the whole expedition, fleets and armies, was destroyed.[30]

The caliph, clearly in fear of the effects of such a major Christian victory on his Christian subjects (the Egyptian Christians had shown what they might do, and the Mandaites in Lebanon similarly), turned on the Christians of Syria, forcing them to convert to Islam, denied them the wine needed for their ceremony and reduced their legal status. This was also, in its way, another victory for Leo's cunning, reminding the caliph of the unstable nature of his control in Syria. What was more, the caliph wrote to Leo to try to persuade him also to convert to Islam – one wonders exactly what stories Leo had been spreading for the caliph even to consider that such a conversion was possible.[31]

The Romans' victory was sufficiently destructive of the Arab armies that attacks on the city were not to be repeated by either the remaining Ummayad caliphs or their Abbasid successors. As a military event, of course, it was of particular interest in that it was in the main a series of naval encounters. The Arab army before the city was left alone, apart no doubt from raids mounted from inland, until it rotted in its own filth. So it was that the strongest part of the attacking force was ignored, and by targeting the supply fleets the besiegers were progressively destroyed from within by hunger and privation. The real danger was that the Arab fleet would be able to break into the city by a landing, for example, through the sea walls, but the horrifying effects of Greek Fire on the ships and sailors was sufficient to stop naval attacks after the first one, and then to force the later fleets to keep their distance (until they also could be destroyed).

The Emperor Leo, of course, was lucky as well as cunning and skilful – the Egyptian deserters could give him exact information as to the location of the supply convoys, an item of information he could not seriously have expected to receive. He immediately understood the information's importance, and that the destruction of those ships would further isolate the enemy forces on land and debilitate them. One wonders also if it was Leo's persuasiveness which brought the Bulgars into the attack, or if it was Bulgar opportunism when they saw the wasting away of the Arab forces – or possibly a combination of these. The sheer strength of the city, behind its wall, was demonstrated once again, but it was also necessary that it be defended by the ships and the citizens, by the chain, and above all by the cunning of its imperial commander, for it to survive the greatest attack in the first thirteen centuries of its existence.

Chapter 14

Two Civil Wars: Artabasdas versus Constantine V, Thomas the Slav versus Michael II

The Sieges of 741–3 and 821–3

Artabasdas and Constantine V – the Siege of 741–3

It may have been a straw in the wind when one of the ephemeral emperors in the early eighth century, Philippikos (711–13), worked to establish the version of Christianity called Monotheletism as the established version. He failed rapidly, but after the siege of 717–18 another religious dispute developed. Leo III had won the battle at Constantinople, but in the field, his armies suffered a series of defeats in the years which followed. He came to the conclusion that the 'worship' of images and icons which was prevalent was displeasing to God, who was punishing the Christian Empire by allowing its enemies to win battles. Leo was originally a Christian from Germaniceia (Marash), in northern Syria, and was fluent in Arabic as well as Greek; he will have seen the more faithful Muslims' hostility to any images of living beings. Perhaps this was the source of Muslim energy. His solution was to advocate the removal of images from the churches in the Christian Empire – iconoclasm.

This embroiled the Empire in internal disputes repeatedly for a century. It may be seen as a Muslim revenge for the defeat in the great siege, but the persecution of Syrian Christians by the caliph can also be seen as his revenge.

Being a cunning, cautious man, Leo did not go very far in the direction of abolition, but when he died he was succeeded by his son Constantine V (741–75), who had become a fervent iconoclast under his father's tuition. He was opposed by his brother-in-law, Artabasdas, who had been Leo's colleague in the military coup d'état which unseated Theodosius III in 717. Both men were very capable. Artabasdas was an experienced commander and administrator, whom Leo had clearly kept onside in the matter of images (he came out as an iconodule soon after Leo's death, and may be assumed to have held that belief under Leo). Constantine was more impetuous, and a generation younger, but proved himself to be a most capable general and a vigorous ruler. Artabasdas managed, early in the dispute, to seize control of Constantinople; he had a good deal of popular support and restored the images Leo and Constantine had already taken down.

Constantine had the support of the army of the Anatolic theme, after appealing to them in person, and he also gained the support of the men of the Thrakesian theme, under their commander Sisinnos. Artabasdas gained the support of the Opsikians and later the Armeniacs. Constantine was actually with the Opsikians when the trouble broke out, but when Artabasdas made his *pronunciamento* he escaped to the Anatolic theme having seen through a ruse designed to trap him. This was crucial, since Constantine was the legitimate emperor by inheritance; had Artabasdas captured him at the beginning of the civil war he might well have been able to make good his coup. In Constantinople, it was announced that Constantine had died and that the troops had proclaimed Artabasdas. A purge took place of Constantine's supporters.

Constantine spent some time gathering support, which, since his religious policy was not popular, was not easy. He camped for a time at Chrysopolis, across the Bosporos from the city, which was in Opsikian territory, and when he withdrew, Artabasdas broke out and raided into Asia for supplies. The two emperors met in battle. Artabasdas' forces were defeated but he was able to get back to the city by way of Kyzikos and a handy trireme. Disorder spread, as the supporters of both men turned on neighbours and enemies.

In September 743, Constantine's two thematic armies executed a joint move: the emperor himself marched to Kalchedon and from there got across the Bosporos – perhaps further north than Crysopolis at a crossing not visible from the city – and Sisinnos with the Thrakesian troops crossed the Hellespont at Abydos. The two armies then joined together and laid siege to the city. Constantine rode along the walls to show himself to the besieged, but there was no response. The supplies in the city, which Artabasdas had shown by his raid into Asia were already low, began to dwindle further, prices started to rise, and starvation began amongst the poor. Artabasdas sent a fleet of ships to gather supplies in southern Asia Minor, but Constantine's fleet from the Kibyrrhaiot theme (a naval theme on the south coast) met it at Abydos and captured many of Artabasdas' ships. This took place on the ships' return after they had collected their supplies; Constantine seized the supplies they had collected and distributed them among his own men.

After this there was only one direction for Artabasdas, and his measures became steadily more desperate. He attempted a sortie in strength against the besieging army but was defeated. His remaining ships put in an attack on the Kibyrrhaiot ships using Greek Fire, but this failed also. An attempt at relief by an army gathered in Asia on Artabasdas' behalf by his son, Niketas, approached as far as Chrysopolis, but was then intercepted and defeated by Constantine.

The end came on 2 November 743. Constantine suddenly advanced his army to the city wall and broke into the city, though it is not clear if this was a successful assault, or if he had made contact with supporters in the city who opened one or more gates for him. There followed another round of executions and blindings.

The actual siege had lasted about two months, whereas the Civil War had lasted almost two years. It is a mark of the intensity of the iconoclastic dispute that this was the first siege of the city involving two sides in a civil war. There had been captures of the city, by usurpers or excluded emperors, notably in the early 700s, which usually was the result of a party inside the city opening a gate; this was the first occasion when such a siege, resulting from an internal dispute, lasted longer than a few days. Both commanders had shown considerable ingenuity in the war, but also much ruthlessness. The big battalions, however, had won, helped by Constantine's rather greater military skill and imagination.[1]

Thomas the Slav and Michael II – the Siege of 821–823

The issue of iconoclasm convulsed the Empire repeatedly from the early 700s to the later 800s, and tended to emerge as a conflict when the Empire was distracted for some other reason. In the reign of Leo V (813–20) the dispute revived, largely from within the army, which revered the memory of Constantine V. Leo made a strong attempt to remove icons but found considerable opposition. In particular, two of his former colleagues-in-arms, Michael the Amorian and Thomas the Slav, turned against him. In 820 a plot involving Michael resulted in Leo's assassination at the altar of Hagia Sofia on 25 December.

Michael was made emperor, being carried directly from the prison cell to which Leo had sent him, still wearing the shackles, to his coronation. He was a fairly unsuitable emperor, being barely literate and speaking with a stammer. Also, having become emperor in such unpleasant circumstances he immediately faced strong opposition. Already before Leo's assassination their former colleague, Thomas the Slav, had allied with the Caliph Mamun and had received Muslim help in staging a rebellion (in exchange for a promise of Roman territory on the frontier). When Michael became emperor, therefore, he already had to cope with this rebellion.

As with the civil war of 741–3, the several military themes took different sides. Thomas had been commander of the Anatolic theme but the Armeniac and Opsikian themes supported Michael; the naval themes of Kibyrrhaiot, Peloponnesos, and Kephalonia supported Thomas, and an imperial coronation was organized for him in Antioch-in-Syria with the local patriarch presiding. As a result of the support he collected, Thomas was able to confine Michael to Constantinople. Thomas had a large number of ethnic units in his forces: Slavs, Persians, Armenians, various Caucasian groups, as well as the Arabs loaned to him by the caliph. An announcement that he was an iconophile turned public opinion to his favour, though this was only passive support.

This rebellion was therefore something more than a dispute over images. The nature of Thomas' support from a variety of groups who had grievances against the central Roman government indicates that for many of the participants the rebellion was aimed at righting their own grievances, the religious problem being of little importance to them. There are also records of a number of social disturbances, risings of slaves against their masters, for example. Thomas was leading a rebellion of the excluded. It is highly suitable therefore that the majority of Thomas' support came from outside the city, and that the rebellion developed into a siege of Constantinople, the source of Roman authority.

The siege was formed once Thomas' fleets had secured control of the Aegean Sea, though not of the waters around the city. He crossed to

Europe with the aid of his fleets, and there he was supported by Slavs and Macedonians from Europe in laying the siege. There was still fighting in various parts of Asia, however, which prevented Thomas from bringing his full force against the city; this may well have been a blessing in disguise in that it was, as usual, not numbers which would determine the result of the siege, and to gather too many people in the siege would simply put enormous and disabling pressure on the logistics.

The siege lasted for a year. It was broken by two coordinated events. The first, and the necessary preliminary, was a naval victory for the forces loyal to the Emperor Michael, which drove back the ships of Thomas' fleet. It was not necessary, of course, to destroy all the enemy vessels, only to secure control of the Propontis and the Straits, for that would allow Michael to transfer troops in and out of the city and collect supplies. The second intervention came from the Bulgars. They were wary of the participation of the Slavs of the southern Balkans, on Thomas' side. This was an area which the Bulgars had been eyeing for some time as a potential area for their own expansion. The victory of their potential victims was not something they would welcome, and by helping the emperor they could well gain helpful political influence. The Khagan Omurtag intervened, broke the siege, and drove the besieging forces away from the city.

Thomas had to flee, and was caught and killed in 823. So for the second time the iconoclastic dispute had so enraged the partisans on both sides as to bring the state to a condition of civil war, and to a siege of the city. And in this case, even though much of the Empire outside the city had supported the opposition, it was the emperor who held the city who had won. The Constantinopolitans tended, somewhat complacently and selectively, to ascribe their victory first to God, of course, but also pointed out that he who held the city ruled 'the world', or at least the Roman Empire.[2]

Interlude III

Conversions

Between 610 and 941 (331 years, eleven generations) Constantinople was attacked by besiegers ten times, an attack on average every 31 years; that is, no generation escaped such an attack. (This is not counting other menaces, which were probably as many or more, which did not culminate in a siege.) These attacks came from the east, the north, the Balkans, and from within the Empire, and some arrived without any warning. This is an extraordinary record, which no other city anywhere on earth can match. It meant that the Byzantine government and the Constantinopolitan citizenry knew that they were liable to be attacked, sometimes without notice, from almost any direction at almost any time. Life was wholly precarious. And yet, it also meant everyone knew what to do in the emergency of the siege, the defence was organized, and the city provisioned, just in case; even inadequate emperors such as Anastasios the bureaucrat and Theodosios the tax inspector knew what to do.

On the other hand, the array of greedy enemies surrounding the city was, in a curious way, a compliment. What other city was so desired by so many that it had to stand guard constantly, and fought so often to survive? Constantinople had emerged, by the seventh century, when the Roman Empire in the west and south and east had been stolen or had rebelled or was sunk into barbarism, as the ultimate citadel of Christian civilization; its defiance sheltered all Europe, while at the same time irradiating its neighbours with its culture.

The city had repelled, above all, the Persian, Muslim, and Avar attacks, and at the same time it was claiming for Christianity the whole of the Balkans and Russia, an area larger than the lands ever subject to Rome. All these regions, in effect, were converted from the single city. The only competent competitor in this was Rome, which by this time was corrupt, unorganized, and always powerless.

By the ninth and tenth centuries Constantinople's pagan neighbours had come to appreciate the advantages to be gained with a monotheistic religion. The Bulgars could see that this was one of the mainstays of the city's power, and the stories of its god's assistance in the defence no doubt lost nothing in the telling. The many prisoners taken by Krum and his successors were active in persuading the Bulgar khan's subjects to adopt the Christian faith. It was always more attractive, given its promises of salvation and life after death, in times of misery than in times of peace. The Bulgar khans could also, eventually, see the advantages for their own power in adopting Christianity; Orthodoxy in particular devoted itself in part to supporting and enhancing royal power – in exchange for wealth, of course.

The Khazars advanced to monotheism in a somewhat different way. The Khazar khanate occupied part of the steppe north of the Caspian Sea, and from there they were in contact with both the Muslim and the Christian empires. The khagan took a cool look at both of these and sent out investigators to discover the nature of their religions. The result was a debate in which the three available monotheistic faiths – Christianity, Judaism, and Islam – were discussed, with the curious result that Judaism was chosen as the official faith of the khanate. This decision was arrived at because this was not the faith of either of his great neighbours, and so neither neighbour could use its seniority in the faith to exert undue influence. In fact, the new faith was not exclusive, and a degree of toleration was demanded, not just for other monotheisms, but for paganism and atheism also. But the khagan's decision implicitly recognized that these monotheistic systems were inherently imperialist, and their aspirations also involved the likely subjugation of a new convert to the old powers.

The Rus similarly investigated the competitive religious situation. The choice this time was between Islam and Eastern Orthodox or Western Catholic Christianity, while at the same time as this debate went on the Russian Grand Prince Vladimir (subsequently called 'the great' in part for his decision in this matter) boosted the observance of paganism – in effect thereby offering a fourth choice. The debate at Kiev was influenced strongly by the power of the Byzantine Empire. No doubt the Rus remembered the effect Orthodoxy had in the Bulgar khanate, where fellow Slavs had converted to Orthodoxy, as had Serbs and others. Islam was rejected, as was Western Christianity. Islam had been adopted by the Rus' eastern neighbours, the Volga Bulgars, who were also an enemy;

the Khazars' choice of Judaism was regarded as eccentric. Western Christianity was certainly considered, but was rejected, probably in part because it had been adopted by the Poles, who were also enemies of the Rus; this was a time when the papacy had sunk to a depth of corruption and ineptitude: there was nothing for a king there. The national conversions which took place – Iceland in 1000, Norway by 1030, Denmark in the tenth century, Poland in the 960s – had taken place owing nothing to any papal initiative.

The Orthodox Christians, on the other hand, dazzled the investigators with their music, their ceremony, the splendour of the imperial palace, the gorgeousness of their imperial robes, and the curious machinery by which they raised the emperor up on his throne mechanically. It was also the faith of the great city, which the Rus called Miklagarth, to which no other city on earth could compare, not even Baghdad; it had defended itself so well and so often, always proclaiming its attachment to its religion, and so successfully from the past attacks that it stood as a living proclamation of Christian supremacy. The Rus had tested the city themselves, twice, and could testify to its power, constancy, and attachment to its faith.

Grand Prince Vladimir of Kiev was subject to some homely pressures, in that Olga his mother had become Christian years before he had to make his decision. However, it seems likely that it was much wider issues, particularly political considerations, which he brought to his choice. And it took him some time to reach a decision, so it was hardly a result of either motherly pressure or the dazzlement of the Byzantine ceremonial which was decisive. In the end, in the late 980s, he chose Orthodoxy. The pagan idols he had so recently promoted as more powerful than Christianity were overthrown and burnt; he was baptized, taking the name Basil from the contemporary, and very powerful, Byzantine Emperor Basil II (976–1025), and he accepted a Greek bishop sent from Constantinople. But he also insisted that he also be sent a Byzantine princess to be his wife; he was clearly aiming at enhancing his legitimacy, and in founding a major dynasty.

The choice was, in fact, as in all these cases, based more on the distribution of power in his neighbourhood than on the attractions of Christianity itself, or any other religion. No one could accept Christianity by a theological argument, since to conduct a theological discussion depends on belief first. Individual conversions might result from a religion's promises of salvation, but kings and emperors and princes decide such things in a different context. A display of Byzantine power, the prospect of an alliance, political and marital, the manifest strength of the city of Constantinople, were all powerful and persuasive arguments, which could sway a ruler far more than any system of belief. Once the religion had been accepted the theology could follow.

Chapter 15

Enemy from the Northwest – The Bulgars

The Sieges of 813 and 913–24

The Siege of 813

The Bulgars acquired a new khagan, called Krum, about 803. He was the ruler of a group in the nation which occupied territories to the north, in the former Roman province of Pannonia. He had made his name some time earlier by taking on and destroying the remnants of the Avars – though they had been severely damaged already in the defeat by Charlemagne. By some means Krum became the ruler of the main force of the Bulgars along the two sides of the lower Danube River, probably by a species of election.[1] His predecessors in the southern country had all been war leaders, like Krum himself, and had emerged in the same way – by achieving military victories; Krum, however, succeeded in founding a ruling dynasty.

His accession greatly increased the power of the Bulgar kingdom, partly by uniting the several fragments of the Bulgars, and partly by his own ability. This seriously disturbed the Byzantines. By 809 the two states were at war, with Krum suffering several defeats, including the loss of his capital city at Pliska, which was captured and destroyed. This was in reply to Krum's capture and dismantlement of the fortress at Serdika, and it called for his own reply. He attacked Mesambria, now a powerful well-fortified city on the Black Sea coast. He had the assistance in his siege of Eumathios, an Arab who had joined the Byzantines as an engineer until insulted and denied his pay by the Emperor Nikephoros I, a notorious miser.[2] Mesambria fell, and Nikephoros felt the need to return to the offensive. This time, having captured and burnt Pliska once again, he followed up the fleeing population into the hills, only to be trapped in a gorge by the Bulgar army, whose men built substantial stockades at both ends and trapped the entire imperial army. They then burst in and massacred almost the whole of the army, including the emperor; his son Staurakios became emperor, but had suffered serious wounds, from which he died a few months later.[3] For only the second time in its history the Empire suffered the killing of an emperor in battle – actually two emperors, since Staurakios was killed, in effect, in the battle.

Krum came with his army against Constantinople. He had specialized, when capturing a city, as at Serdika and Mesambria, in dismantling its walls after capture and deporting its surviving population into his own kingdom; he probably aimed to do the same with Constantinople. The walls of Serdika and Mesambria, however, were as nothing compared with those of Constantinople. He and his army were daunted by the very sight, not the first army to suffer so. They constructed a fortified camp nearby, then set about burning and looting, destroying whatever existed in the area. They enacted grisly sacrifices, human and animal, before the gaze of the watching citizens; this essentially psychological approach did not have any effect, other than to steel the resistance. Then Krum tried negotiations, but the new emperor, Leo V, refused his offered terms. More destruction produced a proposal for a meeting of the two rulers, unarmed and accompanied only by unarmed attendants. Krum agreed, in his arrogance, and Leo played him false. But Leo also made a basic mistake. He attempted to either capture or kill the Bulgar leader. The plan worked, except that one of the Bulgars escaped – Krum himself.[4]

Krum was wounded and enraged. But his judgment was not overwhelmed. It had been clear from the start that he would be unable, even with Eumathios' siege engines, to capture the city. His destructiveness earlier had been in place of an assault which he could see would inevitably fail. To withdraw without really fighting would be a humiliating defeat, but now he could use his affronted rage to get out of the hopeless siege and at the same time gather loot. He turned his army into a destructive machine, destroying an imperial palace, all the suburbs outside the wall, killing and enslaving all the population he could catch, and burning villages and towns. He also carefully selected some architectural items to decorate his own new palace. Appeals from Leo for peace were ignored or rejected.[5]

After capturing one more city, Hadrianopolis (the population was deported *en masse* and settled as a group north of the Danube), Krum and his army retired into Bulgaria for the winter. Leo came out with an army and succeeded in defeating a minor Bulgar detachment. Krum was still unwilling to discuss peace terms, and rumours reached the city that he was determined this time to destroy it; the stories spread of numerous siege machines he was building – as did no doubt the rumours of the number of actual machines. But the city was saved. Before he could mount his new attack, Krum died.[6]

Krum can be credited with several military victories, and with beginning the process of turning Bulgaria into a modern ninth-century state. He might have fought the Empire with the ferocity of hatred, but he used it, welcomed its deserters, and captured its skilled manpower, using them to build up his kingdom with a working administration. He captured tens of thousands of imperial subjects and transported them into his kingdom. And there lay the worm in the bud. In some cases, as with the Hadrianopolitans they were settled as a coherent group, and so existed as a foreign and disloyal element; in other cases they were distributed throughout the kingdom, and, with their superior culture and their arrogant sense of being Byzantine Christians, they had a powerful cultural – and religious – effect.[7] Krum and his people were still pagans, whereas the captives were Christians with a heightened fanaticism brought about by the iconoclastic controversy, and were able to begin to convert the Bulgars' Slav subjects and captives, though the Bulgars themselves, being the successful rulers, were more resistant (in the same way that the aristocrats in Rome had long resisted conversion). In the next half-century, several of Krum's royal descendants persecuted the converts in attempts to suppress this Christianity; they failed, and, of course, eventually they themselves succumbed. This changed the kingdom even more than Krum's victories and reforms. In many ways, at least in religious policy and social matters, the Empire won this longest battle.

The city was also victorious. The survival at the siege, which had been an unusually serious attempt at capture, was a further sign to the citizens that they were a chosen city. (And this would justify such atrocities as attempting to murder the Bulgar king in the course of negotiations, and even the use of Greek Fire.) The Bulgars had already had several successes in capturing fortified cities, and Constantinople was, in essence, just another, if an unusually well-fortified place. Having managed to ravage the suburbs however, as with other besiegers, Krum had himself run out of provisions and time.

A Siege Campaign, 913–24

After a century of intermittent and inconclusive warfare, a new Byzantine-Bulgarian War was fought for eleven years between 913 and 924. The prime cause was the ambition of Symeon of Bulgaria (893–927), the son and second successor of Boris I (852–89), who had been the first Bulgar king to be entitled tsar, by concession of the emperor. The war consisted of annual campaigns conducted reciprocally. They usually, though not always, resulted in Byzantine defeats, and the subsequent captures of Byzantine cities, including Hadrianopolis once more. The Romans were commanded first by the Empress Zoe, the widow of Leo VI (886–912), and then by her successor and supplanter Romanos IV Lekapenos (912–44); they were both acting in the name of Zoe's and Leo VI's son, Constantine VI Porphyrogenitos (who reigned, if he did not rule, 912–59).

The Bulgars' successes on the battlefield were repeatedly succeeded by armed approaches as far as the wall of Constantinople. When the war began in 913 (in part as a result of insults directed at Symeon's envoys by the drunken Emperor Alexander, who soon died), Symeon brought his army first into Thrace and then directly to the wall of Constantinople.[8] Once more the wall exerted its structural magic on an invader: Symeon, and presumably his army, was thoroughly impressed, and Symeon was so daunted by the sight that he made no attempt to mount an assault.[9] For the next three years, he took his army elsewhere and captured several places along the Byzantine borders in the west.

In 917, however, a Byzantine army came out to contest the advance of Symeon's forces. It was beaten, in fact destroyed (the Battle of the River Acheloos), and the Bulgars arrived once more at the city's wall. The assumption must have been that the defeat in the field, which was very destructive of the Byzantine forces, would have affected the will of the Empress Zoe and her advisors, and that an actual siege or assault would not be necessary to secure victory. The Bulgars advanced to the city wall, and were met by a Roman army at Katasyrtai, close to the city. That army was also defeated. It was the last available force at the Empress's command – except the wall, which still proved to be too much for the Bulgars. A Byzantine capitulation, therefore, did not happen, though some fruitless negotiations did take place. Symeon's object now was to gain access to the imperial throne by marriage or by adoptive inheritance.[10] In a way his alteration of purpose was a recognition of the impossibility of taking the city by force.

Symeon and his army came to attack the city again in 919, a year in which the regime of Empress Zoe was being replaced by that of Romanos in a slow, year-long coup d'état. Romanos had been an awkward and disloyal admiral in command of the main Byzantine fleet, but he had played a cunning waiting game as all his rivals for preferment to imperial power successively failed.[11] Symeon probably assumed, correctly, that the political turmoil indicated a degree of instability and weakness in Constantinople and in the Empire, but his demands now were more specific – he wanted the removal of Romanos, who was at the time only another regent for the Emperor Constantine VI, still a teenager. Symeon would then marry his daughter to the young emperor, and so give himself the position of regent for his son-in-law. (This had been one of the terms negotiated in an agreement in 913, which the Byzantine government carefully forgot; Symeon apparently did not insist on it until 919.) This proposal was now rejected out of hand by all the Byzantine factions in competition for the regency, and to add insult to the refusal Romanos was proclaimed emperor, and it was his own daughter Maria who was married to Constantine. It was, of course, Symeon's demands which pushed Romanos onto the throne. Meanwhile Byzantine intrigues persuaded the Prince of Serbia to attack the Bulgars from the north, which kept Symeon away for all of 920.[12]

He came back in 921, with the same demand, that the Emperor Romanos leave the capital and that he himself should take over. An imperial force came out and inflicted a minor defeat on Symeon's forces, at which he drew back, away from the city, relieving it of the intended siege. An offer of negotiations through the patriarch was rejected.[13] Again in 922 his army returned once more and ravaged the land beside the Bosporos north of the Golden Horn, easily defeating a scratch Roman force which was sent out to defend a favourite palace of Romanos at Pegai. The Bulgars defeated that Byzantine force and destroyed the palace. A sortie from the city produced another minor Byzantine victory, but it was not convincing enough for either side to make peace; in addition, the terms demanded by both were still mutually unacceptable.[14]

Again Symeon brought his army to Thrace in 923, but not closer than Hadrianopolis, which he besieged. The siege lasted for some time, against a stubborn garrison, until starvation forced the city's commander to surrender. Romanos had made no attempt to relieve it. The time Symeon took over this siege, of course, kept the Bulgar army away from Constantinople. One of the objects of Symeon's siege was probably to entice the Roman army out to attempt a relief. It also gave Romanos time to persuade the Serbs to make another attack from the north. This drew Symeon away once more.[15]

This repetitive set of campaigns was wearying for both sides, no doubt, and had been consistently inconclusive, if the object of the war was to regain a condition of peace. It did, however, persuade both to adopt new strategies. Romanos' refusal to assist besieged Hadrianopolis was an unpleasant betrayal of a gallant garrison, and above all of the city's commander, who suffered a very nasty death by torture, but it made sense in the wider war, and so saved Constantinople from being closely menaced yet again. Similarly, Symeon's repeated invasions of Thrace were clearly producing no results. By now he evidently fully understood the impossibility of realizing his aims, or of capturing Constantinople. The Roman strategy of calling in a distant ally – the Serbians twice, while negotiations were continuing with the Magyars, the Rus, and the Pechenegs, all neighbours of the Bulgars – was being slowly successful; Symeon tried the same strategy by allying with the Fatimid caliph in Africa, but Romanos bought him off without difficulty. (The Byzantine tradition of diplomacy was much more effective and flexible than Symeon's.) Maybe it was a realization of the likely success of Byzantine diplomacy, maybe it was an appreciation anew of the strength of the city wall, but Symeon now opened practical negotiations for peace.

Romanos had also come to the conclusion that there was no point in sending out Roman armies to be repeatedly defeated by the Bulgars. He lost towns like Hadrianopolis, and would probably lose more, abandoning other cities when they were attacked, so that the Byzantine Empire was being steadily chipped away. This was a new tactic – not fighting a war – but it could scarcely bring victory. He was also, therefore, ready to make peace before still more was lost. The negotiations were conducted face-to-face between the two rulers, on a specially built quay just outside the city wall, with a temporary wall built across it to keep the two men apart – no doubt the memory of Krum's ambush over a century before was in the minds of both men. Romanos harangued the Bulgar tsar, who appears to have taken the ticking off to heart without resentment. Romanos offered a subsidy. Symeon accepted. Peace resulted.[16]

Symeon died three years later, and his son and successor, Peter, had no conquering ambitions. Since the Bulgar kingdom was built on virtually continuous warfare, and only remained coherent under a war leader, the result of his pacific policy was a rapid decay in Bulgar power, and an equally rapid increase in the kingdom's instability; it ceased to be an immediate danger to Constantinople.

Symeon had attacked Constantinople, in the sense of bringing his army to the city wall and threatening it, at least four times during the war. It is not reasonable to count any one of these menaces as a siege, since none of them seem to have lasted more than a few days. On the other hand, Symeon's tactics had repeatedly ravaged the land in Thrace in front of the city, and his pressure for months at a time prevented Byzantine armies from taking the field without risking destruction. In effect, therefore, Symeon was subjecting the city to a continuous, but distant, menace, which more or less amounted to a siege. It was, as he discovered, no more successful than a closer contact would have been. The city wall was doing the work of the defeated and destroyed imperial armies.

Chapter 16

Enemy from the North – the Rus

The Sieges of 860 and 941

In June 860 a Viking army appeared at Constantinople. This came as a complete surprise to the city and to the Byzantine government. The emperor was away fighting the Arabs in the east, and the navy was absent also. The enemy fleet, said to be about 200 ships, appeared suddenly at the northern entrance to the Bosporos. The men landed and ravaged and looted along both coasts of the strait, then menaced the city, sailing past the sea walls waving their swords and shouting either insults or promises of an attack. In the Propontis they looted along the coasts and in the Princes' Islands before they turned back and returned whence they came. The Byzantines claimed later that the fleet was then destroyed in a storm in the Black Sea, but this may well have been their wishful thinking and their cultural invention.[1]

The Byzantines had no business to be surprised, even though the Patriarch Photios claimed that the raid came as a 'thunderbolt'. There had been smaller raids by these people at several places along the northern Anatolian coasts for twenty years, and in 838 a delegation of Rus (the name given to the Scandinavians who were in the process of founding a new state in Russia) had visited the city asking for a commercial agreement. They had not been able to return directly northwards because of trouble in the Ukrainian steppe, so the emperor sent them home by way of Western Europe, where their passage was noted by a chronicler in France, and they were questioned by the Emperor Otto II.[2] It was thus very likely that the envoys' reports of the riches of Constantinople was one of the stimulants of the raid of 860.

It is perhaps the memory of these linked events which provides the pattern for the Rus record of the events of 907 to 911, which was composed a century or more later, and was manifestly invented in parts. It is claimed that there was a great raid organized under the command of Oleg, the ruler of the Rus principality based on Kiev. The story elaborated on the riches, the valour, and the successes of the raid. The only problem with this notice is that nobody in Constantinople, the target of the raid, noticed anything. The conclusion must be that no raid took place. In 911, however, there was another visit to the city by Rus envoys, and this resulted in a commercial treaty by which Russian traders would be welcomed and accommodated and could purchase a strictly regulated quantity of goods. The supposed raid of 907 seems to have been an assumption by the chronicler, or his source, that only by force could such an agreement have been extorted from the Byzantine authorities. (He certainly had cause to think this, as later events testified.) In fact, the wording of the story of the raid also implies that an agreement had been made in 907. So we have two commercial agreements permitting the Rus to visit the city by trade, but no actual raid in 907.[3]

It is getting difficult to find a real attack on Constantinople by the Vikings of Russia which actually reached the city. The raid of 860 was just that, a raid, and no serious attack was made on the city itself, though the neighbourhood suffered badly, and it is here classified as a siege. The 'raid' of 907 probably never happened; the story was in all likelihood an elaboration of the account of an official visit, perhaps by Prince Oleg, more likely by his ambassadors, in pursuit of a peaceful commercial treaty, and this was succeeded by the negotiation of a supplementary treaty four years later. The Vikings are beginning to look disappointingly normal and reasonable.

The Russian background helps explain the situation. The Vikings out of Sweden had long been familiar with the eastern Baltic coast and its rivers, the present Estonian and Latvian and Polish coasts. By the mid-eighth century their traders were established along the rivers which flow north into the Baltic and the Gulf of Finland, notably at Staraia Lagoda on the River Lovat, along which there is a clear route to the south. A century later a principality ruled by Viking princes based on Novgorod (further up the River Lovat, that is further south) had been developed and traders and raiders had reached the strategic site of Kiev, where two other Viking leaders had established themselves as rulers. This was the base, in 860, from which those who conducted the first great raid set out. This was most likely an exuberant voyage conducted as a result of the Rus' realization of the possibilities presented by their possession of Kiev, a strategic position on the Dniepr River, on the boundary of the forest to the north and the steppe grasslands to the south. Along that river the Vikings could sail to reach the Black Sea, ringed by cities and with Constantinople as the ultimate target. (They must clearly have known where they were going; earlier information was available to them, such as the report of the envoys of 838, and of the minor raids of the 840s and 850s.) By 907/911 the principality of Kiev was fully established and organized, if in a predatory form at first, and was geographically very extensive, having taken over the Novgorod principality so that the Kiev prince ruled from the Gulf of Finland to the edge of the steppeland at Kiev. A commercial agreement with the Byzantine Empire was the next obvious step in gaining political legitimacy, and access to trading opportunities in the south. This would be a target both among the various subjugated tribes which the Viking dynasty claimed to rule over, and among the other established powers, of which the Byzantine Empire had the greatest prestige.

One result of these raids and visits was that the Rus traders made annual visits to the city under the terms of the treaties of 907/911. Another was that the Byzantine government investigated the Rus power and locality, identifying the vulnerabilities in the Rus state, and contacting Rus' enemies who could be activated if a new attack such as that of 860 was in prospect. That is, the Rus were being treated as a new manifestation of the traditional condition of the north, where there was always a major power, though the former powers had been nomad states, such as the Huns, the Kutrighurs, or the Pechenegs. The Rus was seen as a state which could usually be manipulated, as had been the earlier powers in that region.

The raid of 941 appears to have been a result of diplomatic manipulations, but one in which the Byzantines were the victims. It had been suggested to the Kievan prince, Igor, after a defeat he suffered at the hands of the Khazar khan, that he should attack the Empire instead – the suggestion was the khan's. When Igor did so, however, it was all rather tentative. No direct attack was made on the city, but the many boats the Rus used spent several months raiding along the Bosporos and the North Anatolic coast. Their activities constituted as close to a siege as they could develop without actually camping close to the city. The citizens were, of course, terrified, and were unable to leave the city. Eventually the emperor deployed his fleet of Greek Fire-shooting vessels to drive the raiders away.[4]

That is, the attempt to capture the city in 941 was probably no more serious than in 860 or 907, nor was there any obvious intention of an attempt to do so. The raid had been aimed from the first at securing another commercial treaty, if the result of this affair is taken into account. The result three years later was a new treaty, which repeated much of the older agreement, but also included revisions of some articles aimed at solving some of the problems which had arisen with that old treaty. This would suggest that, apart from being goaded into the attack by the Khazar khan, whose motives were surely transparent to Igor, the aim of the raid was always to persuade the emperor to renew the old treaty.[5] (It could be that the original treaty was to last for thirty years. This was the sort of time scale included in other Byzantine treaties of the period.)

This assumption follows also from the campaign which Igor's successor, Svyatoslav, conducted against the Bulgarian kingdom in the 960s. His activities were watched carefully by the successive emperors Nikephoros II Phokas (963–69) and John Tzimiskes (969–76). When it seemed that Svyatoslav was becoming too successful, a message went to the nomad Pechenegs, who occupied part of the Ukrainian steppe. This brought an attack by them on Kiev, so that Svyatoslav had to break off his operations in the Balkans and return to defend the city. But he then returned once more to his conquests in the Balkans, and this time had to face the Byzantine army, which he evidently did not wish to fight; eventually he agreed to withdraw his forces from the Bulgar kingdom; the agreement embodied a reaffirmation of the commercial treaty of 941 – and once again there had been a space of thirty years between the two treaties. Svyatoslav was attacked on the way home to Kiev by the Pechenegs; it is not recorded that they were persuaded to do so by the emperor, but one would not be surprised if they had been; then again they may have simply developed a taste for ambushing enemies.[6]

The relations of Rus and Byzantines were therefore essentially commercial from the beginning. The raids were as much aimed at promoting trading connections as they were intended to collect loot, a factor which seems to have been only incidental to their activities. None of the attacks was aimed at capturing Constantinople, though if they had spotted an opportunity the raiders of 860 and 941 would no doubt have gone for it.

It is difficult, not for the first time, to classify these conflicts as sieges, though that is how the original sources, Rus and Byzantine, do portray them. The suggestion of an attack in 907 may be dismissed, as may the operations of Svyatoslav, who did not even approach the city walls. (It is often assumed that any army operating in the Balkans was aiming at Constantinople, though the city's reputation for defence would only deter those attacks.) The raid of 860 was a hunt for loot above all, but the city was undoubtedly menaced, and its immediate hinterland was severely damaged. The attack of 941 did not come very close to the city, but it was under threat for a long time by the series of raids and by a serious blockade which was mounted from the sea; the raiders had to be driven off in the end by a full-scale naval battle. These two events may thus be classified as sieges of a distant sort; certainly the attackers terrified the Constantinopolitans.

Two Conquerors

Septimius Severus, Roman Emperor (193–211); siege of 194–96.

Mehmet II, Ottoman Emperor (1451–81); siege of 1453.

Two Defenders

Alexios I, Byzantine Emperor (1081–1118);
siege of 1097, the First Crusade.

Mustafa Kemal 'Atatürk', Ottoman
general at Gallipoli, and Turkish
President (1924–38); siege of
1914–23. (*Australian War Memorial,
PO4261.002*)

Two Attackers

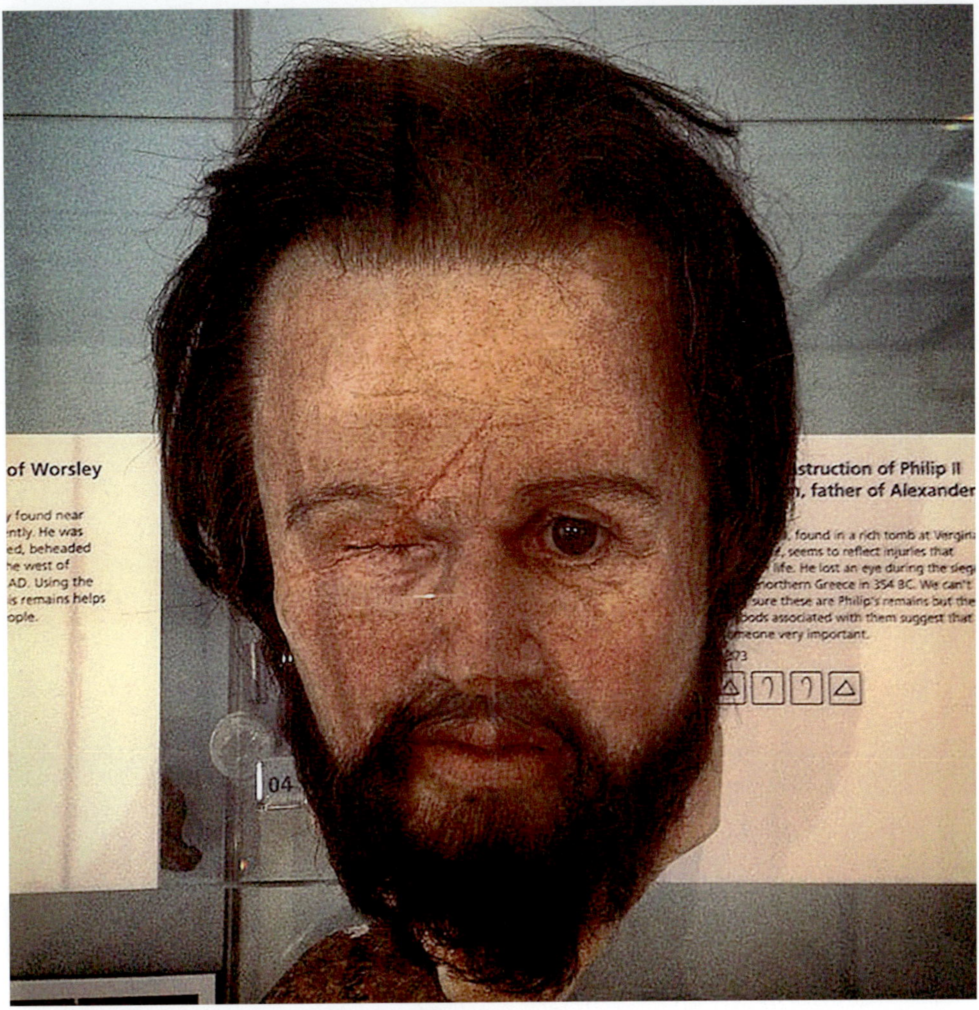

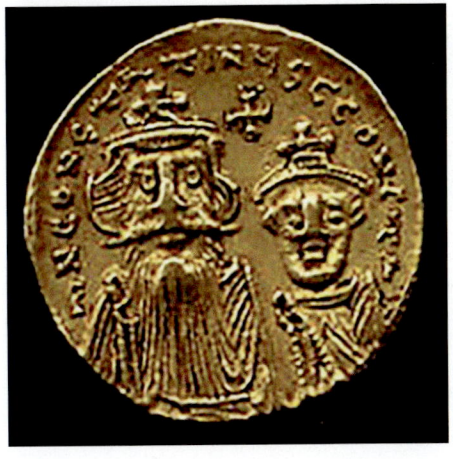

Philip II, King of Macedon (359–336 BC); siege of 340 BC.

Heraklios, Byzantine Emperor (610–41); sieges of 610 (as captor) and 626 (as defender).

The wall of Theodosius; built in the early fifth century. (*Bigdaddy1204 via Wikimedia*)

The fortress of Rumeli Hissar, built to control the Bosporos, 1452. (*Dennis Jarvis/Flickr*)

City Gates

There were a dozen gates into the city but none were ever breached by an attacker.

The Sublime Porte, the main entrance to the Ottoman Palace. (*A. Savin, WikiCommons*)

Weapons

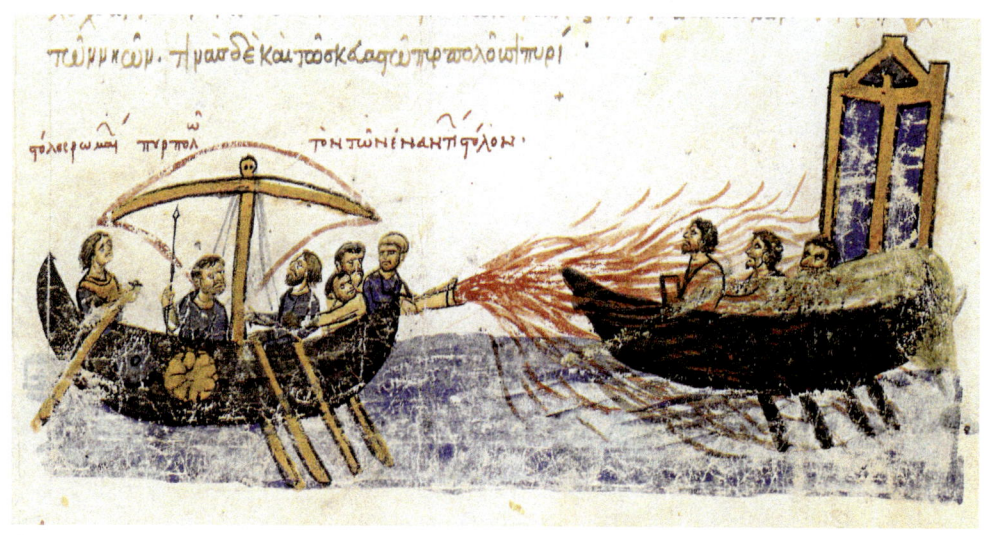

Greek fire; siege of 674, useful for fifty years, before the city's enemies learned to use it.

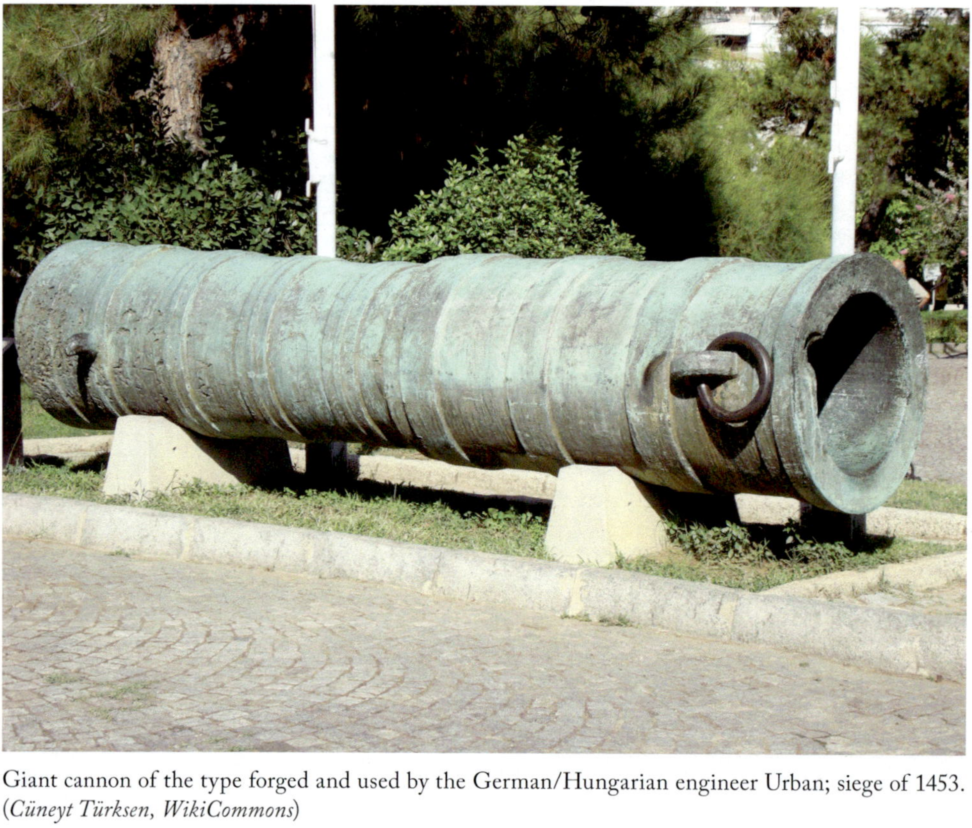

Giant cannon of the type forged and used by the German/Hungarian engineer Urban; siege of 1453. (*Cüneyt Türksen, WikiCommons*)

Two Successful Sieges

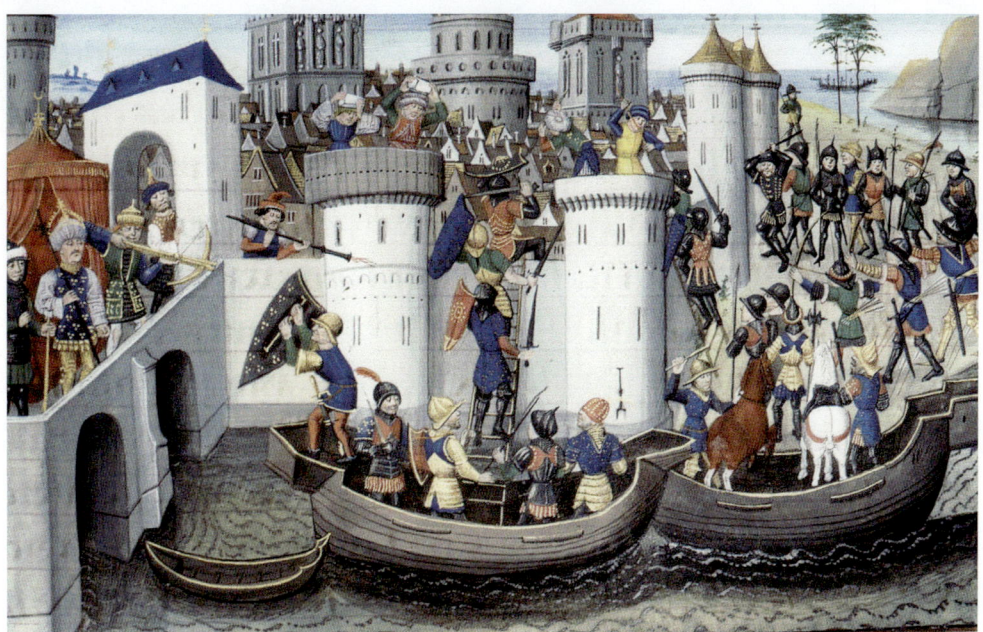

Greek fire; siege of 674, useful for fifty years, before the city's enemies learned to use it.

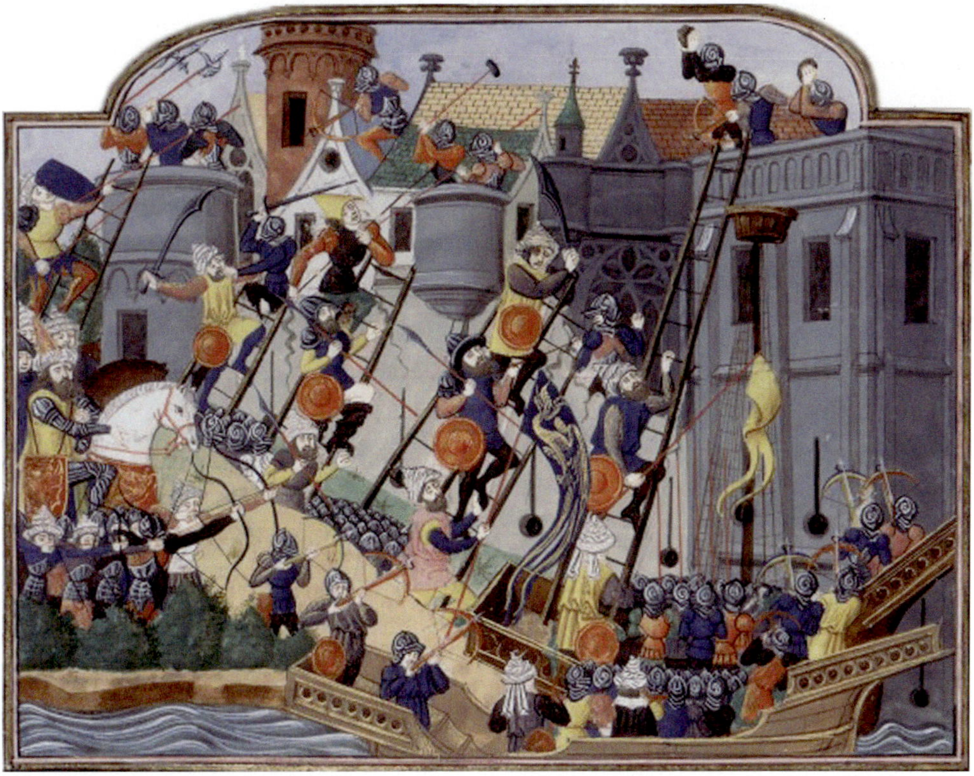

Giant cannon of the type forged and used by the German/Hungarian engineer Urban; siege of 1453. (*Cüneyt Türksen, WikiCommons*)

The City

Constantine, Roman emperor (306–37), the founder of Constantinople on the ruins of Byzantion; siege of 324. (*Jean-Christophe Benoist, WikiCommons*)

Constantinople in the fifteenth century; the great city was besieged forty times and captured by assault six times: 513 BC, AD 196, 324, 1204, 1453 and 1918.

Chapter 17

Enemies from the West – the First Crusade

The Siege of 1097

Byzantine history after the Rus raid in 941 entered a particularly expansionist period. The Bulgars were first deprived of the eastern half of their kingdom then, in a series of brutal conquests by the Emperor Basil II, the kingdom was completely subdued. This looks good on the map, bringing the Byzantine European frontier to the Danube and the northwest Balkans, but the conquered land had been extensively depopulated in the process, and did not recover easily. On the eastern frontier there were other advances, but at the cost of even more frequent wars than before, and of the abandonment of a well-organized frontier. The absence of a single authority in Syria, while it may have fragmented and weakened Muslim power, made it difficult to maintain any sort of peace.

Initially after Basil's death the Empire entered a period of decay, with over-mighty landlords resisting taxation and reducing the peasantry, who had formed the basis of the Byzantine army, to serfdom, and there was constant instability in the imperial government.[1] The Byzantines' enemies were therefore much assisted, not only by imperial military weakness after the death of Basil II in 1025, but by the continual imperial disputes. There were fifteen emperors and ruling empresses in the half-century or so from 1028, but dynastic succession failed – between 1028 and 1081 only one adult son succeeded his father as emperor.

In all this time Constantinople was not subjected to any new siege, though there were raids, especially from the north, by the Pechenegs or Cumans from the steppes and, though they came into Thrace, they did not menace the city. There was a Rus raid in 1043 but again the city escaped.[2] The city was, however, disturbed repeatedly by the internal disputes over who should be emperor.

The nearest the city came to a siege in this period was in 1047, when the rebel Leo Tornikios was only deterred from a direct attack on the city by a scratch defence force of prisoners released from jail and commanded by the emperor Constantine IX. The description of the crisis by Michael Psellos mentions occasional bouts of fighting, though more energy was put by the two sides into shouting insults at each other. He remarks that Tornikios had brought up siege machines, but does not say that they were used. Leo had expected support from within the city and when this did not happen he was at a loss, clearly not prepared to lay siege to the city, or even to mount a quick attack. His rebellion faded away.[3]

Internal conspiracies could succeed, however, as in 1057 when Isaac Komnenos was installed as emperor after his forces had defeated those of the Emperor Michael VI in battle at Nikomedia.[4] Two years later, it was a plot in which Psellos himself was involved that persuaded Isaac, ill and without support, to nominate Constantine X Doukas in his place.[5] In such years it was possession of the city which was the ticket to success. Pretenders without control of the city were usually losing. No sieges occurred because pretenders could usually count on support from inside the city. And yet, while the players were concentrating on holding the city and defying their internal enemies, the rest of the Empire was disintegrating.

Settlements of Pechenegs and Cumans in the Balkans, while helping the repopulation of the region, also encouraged the slow degradation of imperial power in favour of local autonomy; in Asia the Roman frontier was broken by the great defeat of the Emperor Romanus IV Diogenes in 1071 at Manzikert; this was not repaired and the Byzantine forces were unable to prevent large migrations of Turks into the interior in the years which followed.[6] Several Byzantine armies watched each other jealously and intrigued for their commanders to seize the throne. By the time a new and capable emperor, Alexios Komnenos, nephew of the brief Emperor Isaac, took the throne in 1081, most of Asia had been lost and imperial control of the Balkans had become extremely precarious. The Turkish ruler in Smyrna organized a fleet which came close to dominating the Aegean.[7]

Alexios proved to be the first competent emperor for some time – also the only one since Basil II to hold power for over thirty years. He managed to destroy the near-autonomous Cumans and Pechenegs in the

Balkans, and then recruited the surviving Pechenegs into his own army as light cavalry.[8] This was long the normal practice by the Romans and Byzantines, of course (as of course it is for all imperial powers), and it was the foundation for Alexios' next political move towards the salvation of his empire. He appealed to the Pope in Rome for help, expecting to receive contingents of mercenaries whom he could control.[9] (The papal authority had recently been much enhanced, and when Urban II (1088–99) was pushed out of Rome, he was able to go on a tour of France preaching the new venture, the First Crusade.) Alexios already had a contingent of western mercenaries in his Varangian Guard; this force had originally been composed of Vikings and Franks and Normans (one of its most famous members had been Harald Hardraada, who went home to Norway rich enough to make himself king); by this time the soldiers were mainly Anglo-Saxons who had been displaced from their homeland by their Norman conquerors, and had taken service in Byzantium as mercenaries. The Pechenegs, of course, were also mercenaries, and he had contingents of Turks as well. The Byzantine army was by now mainly composed of non-Greeks.

The Empire, beset on all sides, had therefore suffered the usual fate of states which expand suddenly; it was over-stretched, and did not have the military strength to properly defend its enlarged territory and lengthened frontiers. Just one defeat, at Manzikert, led to the collapse. Nor, too frequently in the mid-eleventh century, did its imperial rulers have the military ability or the political capability to govern and defend it properly, being far too concerned to simply maintain their own position – several were too old or were female, and none of them had any politico-military experience, except sometimes as bureaucrats. The extended frontier lines bequeathed by Basil II had proved to be untenable. The Turks had conquered Anatolia as far as Nikaia in Bithynia by the 1090s, and the depopulated Balkans, after centuries of invasions and damaging raids, could not supply the military manpower needed to recover those territories. Western Europe teemed with skilled military manpower, of which Alexios had met a sample in his Guard, and other soldiers in his wars, including a force of 500 Flemish knights loaned to him by the Count of Flanders. Hence Alexios' appeal to the West, asking for Christian help for the Christian Empire.

What he got was not anticipated by anyone.[10] The Pope, also beset by his own problems in Italy, took the opportunity of Alexios' message, and the news of Jerusalem being under threat from more Muslim occupiers and from fighting in Palestine, to escape his own troubles in Rome into his preaching tour of France (he was a Frenchman) and persuaded large numbers of men to join forces to go east. This was not to assist survival of the Byzantine Empire, however, but to rescue – as they would have thought – the Holy Land from its enemies. By this they meant Palestine and, above all, Jerusalem.[11] The Byzantines in Constantinople, by contrast, would have claimed that they inhabited the Holy City, and that its survival was more worthwhile than recovering control of Jerusalem. This initial confusion, or obfuscation, lay at the root of many later problems.

So Alexios, in place of the contingents of mercenary soldiers which he had hoped to recruit, and which he could then use as he could direct to recover his lost lands in Asia, found that he was due to receive several large armies of Western soldiers under their own independent commanders, intent on passing through his lands to get to Palestine. Messages came from the leaders of these contingents warning him of their approach, so at least he had some time to prepare.[12] But there were also the less organized groups, bands of townsmen and peasants who were really no more than hungry wandering pilgrims, often called the 'People's Crusade', who had been inspired to travel east by the mass delusion instigated by the Pope's preaching.[13]

The first to set off for the East were these poorly organized groups, who gathered particularly in the Rhineland. They were undisciplined, hungry, and poorly led. One large group reached Hungary where it was destroyed by the royal army because of its evil behaviour. The second group, led by Peter the Hermit and Walter Sans-Avoir, did eventually reach Constantinople, having collected the survivors of the first group on the way, but they were so unpleasant that Alexios shipped them rapidly across into Asia. They had conducted massacres, mainly of Jews, in their Rhineland homeland, and had fought against the Byzantine troops, who were defending towns and villages against their depredations, several times on their journey; at Constantinople, they camped outside city walls and were extremely destructive of the suburbs. Incorrigible thieves, the crusaders then looted and destroyed their way from Kalchedon as far as

Nikomedia, which was in ruins after a Turkish capture, and then to a new camp at a place called Cibotos, which they called Civetot.[14]

At this point their organization, such as it was, finally broke down. They divided along national lines, Germans and Italians against French. All were subject to populist leaders, or agitators, and were apparently unable to accept any real professional leadership. The Germans went ahead and occupied an unused castle, only to be besieged by the Turks; when they surrendered they were killed or enslaved. The French eventually burst out of Civetot, intent on attacking Nikaia, where it was thought the surviving Germans were dividing up captured treasure, but they were also ambushed and destroyed after going only three miles. The emperor's fleet rescued those who survived and took them to Constantinople, carefully allowing them to camp only outside the city.[15]

The more-organized and better-commanded groups arrived, after all this, more or less in sequence, between January 1096 and May 1097. Warned by the behaviour of the earlier groups, the emperor laid on supplies to prevent them from foraging and stealing, and contingents of Pecheneg mercenaries were present to marshal and control them along the road. It was fortunate that the several contingents all arrived separately, so Alexios could deal with them and their leaders one at a time. Most of these groups, often commanded by leaders whom they knew, acted sensibly, though they were liable to break out over some grievance; the Pecheneg mercenaries were very efficient in controlling them.

The first of the crusading leaders to arrive was Godfrey de Bouillon, leading the Lorrainers. This was also the most difficult group. Godfrey was required by Alexios to make a pledge of allegiance. The emperor's aim was to ensure that they did as he wished; Godfrey made difficulties. He had a point, in that he had already pledged allegiance to the German Emperor, and the two allegiances might well conflict, though the emperors were well separated, geographically. In reply to Godfrey's obduracy Alexios reduced the supplies for the whole group. They in turn replied to this by ravaging the suburbs – in effect replicating the disorderly behaviour of their peasant predecessors. This eventually developed into a regular siege of the city, concentrating on the area of the Blakhernai Palace, where the wall was weaker than elsewhere. After several attempts at negotiation made by Alexios were ignored, he sent in the imperial army, which made short work of the ravagers. Godfrey, thus abruptly brought to his senses, now quickly agreed that his men should be moved across to Asia, that they would accept supplies, and there they would wait for the other contingents to arrive.[16]

The people in the city had been convinced that the siege had been aimed at seizing the city and making Godfrey emperor.[17] They were probably wrong at that moment, but had the crusaders broken into the city, it would first of all have been brutally looted – the crusaders' earlier behaviour in the suburbs had shown their temper and their greed – and then Godfrey may well have succumbed to imperial temptation. (He eventually became king in Jerusalem, supposedly against his will, choosing to be called the 'Advocate of the Holy Sepulchre'; his brother was less scrupulous and became king.) The wealth of the city had impressed all crusaders who saw it – they were allowed to enter the city only in small, supervised groups of tourists – and it had stimulated their greed still further.

The later groups to arrive were the Provencals under Raymond of Toulouse; then the Normans and French from northern France under Robert of Normandy and Stephen of Blois; then the Normans from southern Italy under the Bohemond of Taranto; many smaller and independent groups from France and Italy tended to join up with the others speaking the same language. They were reasonably well organized and under competent leaders. All of these contingents arrived one after the other, having come by several different routes, and all of them faced and caused difficulties along the way.[18] They were carefully and quickly moved across into Asia by Alexios' smooth organization.[19] There, they faced well-armed enemies in the Turks, but these were the competent and professional military element of the crusade at last, and operated in a sensible way to make for Palestine and Jerusalem, which, to general surprise, including their own, they reached and captured in 1099. As they fought their way across Asia Minor, they were followed by a Byzantine army which took control of the conquered land, pushing the Byzantine frontier well to the east; Alexios had contrived to use the Western soldiery for his advantage after all.

This series of events, from the defeat at Manzikert in 1071 to the capture of Jerusalem in 1099, materially altered the political and military forces at work in the lands around the eastern Mediterranean. For Constantinople, it had been proved to be a taste of the future, in that more and more Westerners would now be visiting their city in the next centuries. For

Alexios, he was able to do a good deal to recover large areas of Asia in the wake of the crusaders' march and victories in Asia Minor. The Byzantine Empire gained a new lease of life, but mainly by the weakening of its enemies, and without regaining its real strength.

It is, of course, necessary to justify classifying the events at Constantinople in 1097 as a siege. The Lorrainers' attacks lasted only a few days, but this had been the final blow in relations between the Byzantines and the crusaders; earlier, there had been constant clashes with the 'People's Crusade', which had badly damaged and looted the suburbs of the city, so that no citizen was able to go out of the city while the thieves and looters were present; and certainly the Lorrainers' first move before instituting their formal siege had been to destroy the suburbs once again, having looted anything left by the 'People'. This whole episode therefore clearly lasted several weeks, and confined the citizens inside the city, no doubt reducing their supplies; it was clearly a siege, even if it was intermittent, and even if that name is not usually attached to it; it was ended by a regular battle, when Alexios sent his own army out.

This encounter of the First Crusade, particularly the men commanded by Godfrey de Bouillon, with the Empire of Alexios I, had been difficult, but it was also typical of later encounters between Byzantines and Westerners during the next century, if just a little more violent than most. In 1147 two more crusader armies – the Second Crusade – marched through the Balkans intent on fighting the Muslims in Palestine, but they had first to get past the Greek Orthodox Christians in the Balkans and then above all past or through the city of Constantinople. The suspicion with which the first crusaders were regarded in Constantinople, together with the brief siege they subjected the city to, set the mode and the political scene for these later arrivals.

The Byzantine government and the people of the city had the same strong suspicions that one or other of these new armies were in fact intent on attacking the city itself and capturing it before, or instead of, going on to Palestine.[20] They continued to hold these suspicions at the time of the Third Crusade in 1188, and, of course, were eventually proved right in their suspicions at the time of the Fourth Crusade fifteen years later.

The armies of the Second Crusade in 1147 were led not by the spontaneously enthusiastic Western nobles of the second rank, as had been the case in the First, but by the Emperor-elect Conrad III and King

Louis VII of France, the premier rulers in Western Europe. The Germans of Conrad III arrived at Constantinople first. They had experienced a difficult time in the Balkans, having had to fight local peasants and Byzantine armies, and had not infrequently had to forage for their supplies when those promised by the Emperor Manuel did not turn up. Manuel suggested that the best crossing to Asia would be at the Hellespont, but Conrad disregarded this. When he was near Constantinople there was a clash between some of his Germans and units of the Byzantine army. The Byzantine chroniclers' claimed that this was a win by the Byzantines, but the Germans kept on moving through.[21]

This in fact was the only serious clash, and the German crusaders were moved across into Asia without more ado, if at the Bosporos and not, as suggested, at the Hellespont. Louis VII did not have anything like the problems of Conrad, and his men were well supplied in their march across the Balkans. In Constantinople he was more-or-less welcomed and had a tour of the city conducted by the emperor in person, and then he moved on quickly in Conrad's wake into Asia.[22] Forty years later Conrad's successor, Emperor Frederick I Barbarossa, took the same route, but faced a much less skilled or resolute emperor than Manuel in Isaac II. But Isaac and the population of Constantinople were as fearful of a possible threat to the city as Manuel had been, especially when Frederick halted at, and occupied, the city of Hadrianopolis for the winter.[23] In the end, with no more than a few scuffles, Frederick was persuaded to do what Conrad had refused to do, and crossed into Asia at the Hellespont.[24] He and his men thus stayed well clear of the city, and the city could breathe again for a few more years.

Chapter 18

Enemies from the West – the Fourth Crusade

The Sieges of 1203 and 1204

For ninety years after the passage of the First Crusade through Constantinople the Roman emperors of the dynasty of Alexios I Comnenos had had to cope with that crusade's consequences. They also had to cope with the fact that the crusade itself was one of the consequences of the arrival in Anatolia of the Turks. The crusaders had been summoned by Alexios I to assist Constantinople, but they had gone on to Palestine. It took half a century for the new situation in the region which emerged as a result to settle down into some sort of peace and stability but, thanks in part to Byzantine realism, it did so. By the time of the death of the Emperor Manuel I Komnenos, Alexios' grandson, in 1180, the Turks, under the Seljuk Turkish dynasty, had sorted themselves out into a more-or-less stable Sultanate, centred at the city of Konya in central Asia Minor, which controlled eastern and part of central and southern Anatolia, while Manuel's Empire controlled the west and north, together with the Balkans. Not only that, but good relations, even an alliance, existed between the two rulers, Emperor Manuel (1143–80) and Sultan Kilij Arslan II (1156–92), assisted by the fact that both rulers were long-lived and held power for decades, and followed predecessors equally long-lived.[1]

On the other hand, the population of the emperor's main city had been changing during the Comnenos dynasty. The ships of the Italian merchant cities – Venice, Genoa, Pisa – were in effective control of the eastern Mediterranean, having bases in Italy and in Palestine. They traded heavily at wealthy Constantinople and throughout the Byzantine Empire, and their merchants settled in the city. Above all, the Venetians were ever present in the city and the empire. Venice was technically part of the Empire, the last piece of Italy remaining from Justinian's reconquest in the sixth century. This gave their merchants a degree of preference and tax exemption as imperial citizens, and by an old treaty which benefited them a great deal. Others, Pisans and Genoese especially, were also present in considerable numbers. These Italian groups were also constant rivals. The Venetians and the Pisans had joined in sacking the Genoese factory in Galata in 1162, and the Venetians did so again in 1170; in 1171 Emperor Manuel arrested all the Venetians in the city.[2] In both cases negotiations followed, and reparations were made – because the Venetians were in effect as powerful as the emperor. The relations of the Italians with each other, and with the Byzantines, especially the population of Constantinople, were fractious.

The Empire kept matters generally quiet under the Emperors John I Komnenos (1118–43) and Manuel I, but internal tensions in the city were gradually rising. In 1180 Manuel died, and there followed a dispute about the succession, so that matters soon became unpleasant. Existing disputatious issues were exacerbated by the weaknesses of the reigning emperors, none of whom lasted long. The new emperor was Alexios II Komnenos, young and inexperienced. His uncle Andronikos, who had often disagreed with Manuel I's policies, was brought to court as an experienced and able man, summoned from a semi-exile in Paphlagonia, which had been imposed by Manuel. He proved to be both ambitious and unscrupulous. In the next years he brought about a massacre of the Italians in the city, the deaths of Alexios II and his mother and stepfather, and numerous other opponents, and usurped the throne for himself. Andronikos I was sole emperor from 1183, but dislike of his person and of his political methods increased and caused constant disputation, rebellion in the Empire, and a progressive loss of support amongst those whom he had used to exert his control in the capital.[3]

In 1185 Andronikos was killed and a new dynasty was installed in the person of Isaac II Angelos. Politics calmed down somewhat, but a new set of problems soon developed, in particular a rebellion in the Balkans which by 1190 had re-established an independent Bulgar kingdom. In 1187 the defeat of the crusader king's forces at Hattin in Palestine, and the recovery of Jerusalem by the Muslims, called up another crusade, the Third, from the West, which was less than wholly successful but did re-establish a viable crusader kingdom in Palestine based on the town of Acre. This Third Crusade's lack of success in recovering Jerusalem led to yet another set of expeditions, collectively called the Fourth Crusade.

This was proclaimed by Pope Innocent III (1198–1216), one of the ablest of the mediaeval popes, and he had, thanks to a civil war in Germany, perforce addressed his plea above all to France; the crusaders came overwhelmingly from northern France and Flanders, which was also the source of many of the First and Second Crusaders; they were to be transported east in hired Venetian ships.[4] The main leaders were Baldwin, count of Flanders, and Boniface, marquis of Montferrat, together with several notable French and Flemish nobles and knights; these formed a committee which exercised command over the crusaders, though with some difficulty.

The Venetians were determined to make a tidy profit out of the task. The commitment for transporting the crusaders required the use of almost all of Venice's ships, and organization and command were in the hands of the Doge Enrico Dandolo, who was partially blind, but was politically highly astute, and a notable commander.[5] The crusader chiefs, however, had overestimated their ability to find the necessary resources, and when they could not produce the full passage money, the Venetians persuaded them to take on a variety of different targets. First, Zara in Dalmatia, which the Venetians claimed was in rebellion against them, was captured, scandalizing Christians who felt that crusaders attacking other Christians was wrong. Then they were to invade Egypt, which was the political base for the main Muslim power, the Ayyubids, who controlled Jerusalem. This would be a sensible strategic move, but then the crusaders were joined by Alexios Angelos, the son of the Emperor Alexios III.[6]

The Emperor Isaac's troubles had overwhelmed him in 1195 when a Norman invasion from Sicily captured Thessalonica, which news enraged the Constantinopolitans. The mob in the city broke into riot, and the emperor's brother Alexios seized power, as Emperor Alexios III, by the simple means of annexing Isaac's imperial vestments which he had left in his tent while on a hunt; the bureaucrats and the guard were already on-side; Alexios secured power, Isaac was blinded and kept in prison in the palace.[7] As emperor, however, Alexios III proved to be even less capable of controlling matters that his brother; his nephew Alexios, Isaac's son, escaped from his prison in the palace and was taken in a Pisan vessel to refuge with his brother-in-law, Philip of Swabia, one of the candidates for the Western imperial throne.[8] When the Fourth Crusade was at

Zara, Alexios arrived at the camp. Backed up by messages from Philip, he persuaded the Venetians and the crusade leaders that they could earn their passage money by helping him to seize the throne at Constantinople, for which he could pay from the imperial treasure he assumed existed at the city. Lavish with promises, Alexios carried the day.[9] In June 1203, four years after it had been originally proclaimed, the crusade arrived at the Bosporos, still nowhere near either Jerusalem or Egypt, and intent on interfering with yet another Christian state.

The empire into which the crusaders had now intruded was disintegrating. Much of the Balkans – Serbia and Bulgaria – had shifted into independence in the past decade, and the original imperial boundary had retreated from the Danube to the line of the Balkan Mountains.[10] The Seljuk Turks were going through their own succession dispute, which distracted them enough to prevent them from taking advantage of the Byzantine problems, but by disintegrating it let loose groups of eager Muslims keen to seize new lands.[11] The Byzantine army was much reduced in size and efficiency after fifteen years of expensive imperial disputation and was now composed very largely of foreign mercenaries. The Byzantine fleet had not been maintained and was reduced to no more than a score of rotten ships, plus a few hired privateers.[12] The cause, above all, of this decline was the repeatedly disputed imperial successions and the accompanying disintegration of the imperial government. Every emperor since 1180 had seized power in a coup d'état; two of them had been murdered; one had been blinded; a pretender had escaped with ease from jail in the palace; and the current holder of the imperial office was incompetent. The emperor's nephew and pretender, Alexios, was now leading the great Western fleet and army against him, and so was plotting another coup. The alliances which had sustained Manuel I had disintegrated just as had his highly competent army, fleet and empire.

The pretender did not command the crusaders' fleet and army. The Venetians were controlled by their Doge Enrico Dandolo. He was said to bear a grudge against Constantinople from earlier visits but, even if this was true, he was not the man to let it distract him from what he believed was politically or militarily advantageous to his city.[13] The crusader leaders, Boniface of Montferrat and Baldwin of Flanders, commanded as much by consent as by birth, and always consulted at crucial points with an assembly of nobles, and at times with the whole army; authority in the aristocrat-led army was thus more diffuse than amongst the mercantile Venetians.

The plan, if there really was one, was to persuade the Emperor Alexios to admit his nephew to the city and to a share of power. Only if the pretender could get some sort of a grip on power in the city would he be able to honour his promises to pay the fee of 200,000 marks to which he had agreed at Zara, and only when they had this necessary finance would the Venetians agree to take the crusaders on to Palestine. The emperor was hardly willing to accede to such a demand, either to admit his nephew to the city or to consider paying for his nephew's promises, but he was also wholly unprepared for what had happened.

The Siege of 1203

The crusaders landed on the Asian side of the Bosporos, first at Kalchedon, where the leaders lodged themselves in an imperial palace, then they moved to Chrysopolis, to another palace. This was menacing enough but the Venetian ships now controlled the Bosporos mouth and the seas around the city. In both places the crusaders found stores of grain and other provisions from the recent harvest, and this they appropriated.[14] It was supposed that Constantinople would soon go short, though it was always the crusaders who went hungry; the city was well stocked. It would nevertheless have been an elementary preparation to move these supplies into the city; that they were not moved is a mark of how unprepared Alexios' government was.

But occupying the Asian coast was not enough to compel a surrender by the emperor. It turned out that the pretender had no basis of support in the city – or indeed in the wider Empire – but it was the city which, as usual under such circumstances, was the more important. He was displayed to the citizens in a ship which sailed around the city, but this evinced neither support nor interest.[15] The Emperor Alexios offered to give the crusaders supplies if that was all they needed to go to Palestine, but by this time the crusaders and the Venetians had locked themselves into a policy of compelling the city to accept the man who had made promises to them, and whom they had promised to make emperor. When he was shown to have no support, he would have to be installed by force.

The first attack took place on 5 July. The city itself was clearly too well defended to be directly attacked from the Asian side, but it was thought that the sea wall along the Golden Horn was vulnerable – there were plenty of men in the Venetian fleet, starting with Dandolo, who were familiar with the city's defences. So the first priority was to gain access to the Golden Horn, which meant getting past the great chain which blocked access, and that in turn meant first of all capturing Galata on the north side, where the chain was anchored. The whole fleet sailed across the Bosporos mouth, the warships towing the hired merchant ships, which were filled with the soldiers, so ensuring that they were not driven away downstream by the current. The landing was successful, especially when drawbridges were lowered from some of the ships and fully armed and horsed knights rode out, directly from the ships on to the land. These formed up quickly and prepared to charge against the Byzantine forces which had formed up to contest the landing. But the very sight caused the opposing infantry to panic, a testimony to the powerful effect of such a charge, especially since many of these fleeing soldiers had not yet faced one. The rest of the army landed without interruption or difficulty.

The chain was fastened at the Galata end in a powerfully fortified circular tower. But like all such forts it had a door. Next day the Byzantine garrison attacked the crusaders by a sortie from the tower while a simultaneous landing force came in barges from the city side. Both attacks were defeated, and in trying to get back into the tower some of the garrison became mixed with some of the crusaders, who prevented the door from being closed. One of the biggest of the Venetian ships broke the chain. Whether it had already been unfastened at the tower is not clear, but it seems likely – it would have been a priority for the crusaders. The whole crusader fleet, mainly Venetian vessels, came into the Horn – two hundred ships. The city's vulnerable side could now come under attack.[16]

The crusaders and the Venetians conferred on what to do next. Both had their own preferences in how to go about the fighting, the Venetians by sea, the crusaders on land, and they came to a compromise decision whereby the crusaders would attack the wall on the land side while the Venetians would move their ships close enough to the sea wall in order to launch their own attack. It took several days to make preparations, in particular the Venetian ships had to be equipped with bridges which could allow their soldiers to cross from the ships' masts to the top of the wall. On 11 July the crusaders marched west along the north side of the Golden Horn to a broken bridge which the emperor had ordered demolished. It had been done minimally, it appears, for the crusaders were able to reconvert it into a useful bridge again within a day. They crossed and camped at the nearest point of the wall to the Golden Horn, facing the Blakhernai Palace. This was in theory an area where the wall was weakest, not being composed of the usual several parallel walls and ditches, but it was still fifty feet high, and, of course, the crusaders only had enough men for an attack on a short stretch of the wall. The Byzantines could therefore also concentrate their own forces in opposition.

Several more days were then occupied in preparing and fortifying the crusader camp, all the time being harassed by raids from the city; the defenders could come out from any one of several other gates which were well away from the crusaders' camp. Meanwhile they were constructing assault ladders, and their machines were pounding the wall. By 17 July the Venetians in their ships were also ready and a joint attack was mounted. The crusaders, attacking by land from the west, made minimal progress. The few men who got onto the wall by means of their scaling ladders were immediately thrown off by a detachment of the Varangian Guard wielding their battle-axes. Most were wounded in being repulsed, or in falling off the ladders. The Venetians had rather more success, in part because the wall they faced was a good deal lower than that on the land side. On the other hand, those who got inside over a considerable length of the wall, were then counterattacked by some more of the Varangian Guard amongst others. In the fighting some of the Venetians set fire to the buildings inside the wall as a defensive measure; about 120 acres of the city were burnt, mainly small houses and shops. It certainly blocked the counterattack, as had been intended, but it also prevented any exploitation of their initial success.[17]

The Emperor Alexios had so far deployed his forces with some intelligence (or he had been well advised) but he had stayed in his palace and was being accused of cowardice and incompetence, both qualities which were expected, of course, from an unpopular ruler. He was not trained to arms after an adolescence spent as a prisoner or in travelling through Western Europe seeking support. He felt that the Venetians had been stopped and so now he called up the whole of his army and lead it out of the city through a gate in the wall some distance from the crusaders' camp. They turned to march along the wall with the apparent intention of capturing the camp and driving the invaders into the Golden Horn. The crusaders replied by marshalling their forces, and advancing towards the Byzantines in turn, but they were daunted by the sheer size of the Byzantine army. There was some confusion on the crusader side when the main commander, Baldwin of Flanders, was advised that he had marched too far from the camp and signalled that they should turn back; this annoyed many of his knights, while those not in his contingent indicated that they would charge anyway. There was a widespread feeling that he was showing cowardice and defeatism rather than good generalship. He changed his mind and advanced once more, until the two armies faced each other across the shallow valley of the small Lykos River. At that point the emperor decided that he did not want to fight and turned his army back. The crusaders, who had been frightened by the great number of the Byzantine army, were greatly relieved.[18]

Emperor Alexios had himself been thoroughly frightened by the prospects of fighting, defeat, and death. That night he gathered together a bag full of treasure, collected his favourite daughter Irene (but not his wife Euphrosyne) and a group of his closest associates, and stole out of the palace and out of the city to find refuge elsewhere.[19] Needless to say consternation followed within the city when the news spread, but a group of bureaucrats showed uncommon good sense and organized the restoration of the blinded Emperor Isaac, meanwhile collecting all members of the now ex-Emperor Alexios' family, including his abandoned wife, and locking them up just in case they might stage a reverse coup d'état to restore the family to power.[20]

This was a clever move. Isaac was the father of the pretender Alexios, and this connection enabled a diplomatic solution to be suggested to end the siege, especially since it was clearly in a stalemated condition. Alexios the pretender was contacted in the crusaders' camp and everyone there was happy with the thought that they would have access to a friendly emperor. Isaac and his son agreed that the agreement made between Alexios and the crusaders at the beginning of their association back in the Adriatic should stand, and that the crusaders would be paid the silver that was owed to them. Alexios became joint emperor with his father and was crowned in the usual ceremony as Alexios IV – and since Isaac was blinded, it was Alexios who became the effective emperor.[21]

Of course it did not work. Alexios, all too clearly the puppet of the crusaders until he could satisfy their demands, was therefore thoroughly unpopular with the city's population. He found it impossible to raise the money the crusaders expected and required, though he could supply them with food, of which they had become rather short. The crusaders at least moved their camp away from the city and back to Galata, which relieved the pressure on the city and the new emperor. In return they decided that a section of the city wall would be demolished – 300 feet is said to have been taken down – so as to give the crusaders a sense of safety. The idea was presumably to make both sides – the city and the hungry crusaders – feel vulnerable.

Alexios IV went on a tour of the local area outside the city, in the normal way of new emperors, showing himself to his new subjects, though without eliciting any vociferous approval. Eventually he had to explain that he was unable to raise the money he owed, and the crusaders agreed to wait around for a time until he could do so. And yet he still could not. Trade was reduced, expenses had increased, and taxes did not come in, either through the inability of the people to pay, or their refusal to support yet another usurper, and the extent of the Empire was reduced. The crusaders became increasingly impatient.

Disputes and fighting broke out between the crusaders and the Constantinopolitan population. In August one of these disputes produced another great fire, which burned through 400 acres of the city, to add to the 100 or so already burnt out during the fighting.[22] By December fighting between crusaders and Byzantine forces was becoming more frequent; it was still intermittent and on a small scale, but it did include a two-day ravaging expedition by the crusaders through the territory outside the walls, aimed at collecting supplies, and another fire-boat attack on the Venetian fleet. The gap in the wall was rebuilt. The emperors became increasingly isolated from the population, and also steadily more hostile to each other. They were faced with the importunate demands of the crusaders on one side, and the growing hostility of the population of the city – partly due to their attempts to meet those demands – on the other.

The city's defences had held out reasonably well under the assaults by French knights and Venetian seamen, but the sea wall had proved to be vulnerable. Of the military and naval peoples of Western Europe these two groups were probably the most skilful at their several methods of warfare, so the Byzantine defensive achievement was considerable. The diplomatic defences of the city, despite the general incompetence of Alexios III and the naivety of Alexios IV, had also worked satisfactorily. The city had been besieged, had been assaulted, and part of its defences had been breached, but the attackers by land had been repelled, and those from the sea had in the end failed, despite gaining an entry.

Yet, as anyone familiar with the methods of a siege would know, the basic weakness in the city lay, not in the walls, but in the persons of the successive emperors who commanded inside the city and in the powers Alexios III, Isaac II, and Alexios IV wielded so hesitantly. These rulers had been in general supported by the population when they confronted or defied the crusaders, if perhaps less than enthusiastically. That included the mercenaries of the army, and the Varangian Guard. The Pisans and Genoese (and a few Venetians) who were living in the city had also turned out to fight in its defence. The reaction of the army of the besiegers to the deployment and advance of the main Byzantine army, even under Alexios III's hesitant command, had been highly instructive. If the encounter had come to a fight, there is no predicting the result, other than that there would have been a large number of casualties on both sides, which may well have been to the great advantage of the citizens – the besiegers could not afford too many casualties, outnumbered as they were. There was no basic reason for the city to be defeated, except for half-heartedness and incompetence at the centre.

Dissatisfaction with Alexios IV was now widespread. He and Isaac had made serious efforts to collect the fee for the Venetians, as being the best way of getting rid of the crusaders. They had little success in compelling the citizens to cough up, but the churches and the wealthy proved to be easier targets. The whole process was inefficient, extremely unpopular with all sections of the population, and still did not gather enough. It also brought forth an opponent of both the emperors and the process, in Alexios Doukas, called Murtzouphlos, who spotted an opportunity to gain popularity; his personal aim was to seize the throne through this crisis.

Popular hostility to Alexios and Isaac led to the summoning of a meeting, held in Hagia Sofia, where the Senate and the chiefs of the church were compelled by a large gathering of angry citizens to consider candidates to replace the emperors. Noble after noble was offered the imperial crown, and all refused, until at last a young man called Nicholas Kannavos was induced to accept it.[23] Alexios reacted to this by asking for help from his crusader colleagues, who were to drive Kannavos from the Palace. At this Murtzouphlos contacted the power centres in the city, the hierarchy of the church (threatened by a promise made by Alexios IV to work for a union of the Greek and Roman churches) and the Varangian Guard, a slightly different selection of the elite than that which had supervised the choice of Nicholas Kannavos.

With these groups on his side, Murtzouphlos could act, especially as he already had popular support because of his anti-crusader opinions and agitation. He thereupon kidnapped the Emperor Alexios IV from his bedroom, put him in the palace prison – again – and proclaimed himself emperor as Alexios V Ducas.[24]

In the face of Alexios V's widespread support none of his competitors had a chance. Alexios III had fled, Alexios IV was now in prison, Isaac II was blind and ill and almost without any support, and soon died, of fright some thought but most assumed he had been murdered; Nicholas Kannavos was soon arrested and executed. Given the existence of so many emperors all at once, the deaths of at least three of them (one was in exile and for the moment unavailable) was quite inevitable. Alexios IV was, of course, alive still, largely because of his strong connections with the crusaders; imprisoning him in effect made him a hostage; he had been the one to make the promises to the crusaders, so killing him would compel them to attack.

The new emperor had made a name for himself as a leader of the anti-crusader faction in the imperial government; he had been Alexios III's *protovestiarios*, or chamberlain, and so he had some knowledge of government, which Alexios IV had not. It was therefore clear that this coup d'état was directed as much against the crusaders as against Alexios IV, and the government in the city might become more effective. It scarcely helped the stability of the Byzantine government, however, for it amounted to yet another usurpation; by this time all sense of legitimacy in the imperial power had vanished. The new emperor made several serious attempts to harass the crusader forces, by ambushing a large food convoy, and by another fire attack on the ships, but he was regularly defeated.[25] He tried negotiation with Dandolo, who only restated the original terms of the agreement with the imprisoned Alexios; this transparent attempt to divide the crusader leadership by separate negotiation only compelled Dandolo to be even more intransigent than usual.[26] This marked the end for Alexios IV, the crusaders' candidate; his value as a hostage had ended, and he was murdered in his jail cell, some said by Murtzouphlos personally.[27] With Alexios IV dead, there was now no possibility of reaching any agreement with the crusader leaders. Any agreement Murtzouphlos made with the crusaders would likely result in his own overthrow and death at the hands of the citizens. So the armed conflict would have to be finally renewed, and this time neither side could afford to yield.

The Siege of 1204

With the death of Alexios IV the crusaders knew that the only way they could move on was by capturing the city. They were now very short of supplies – Murtzouphlos had, of course, stopped the deliveries his predecessors had made. They were now even shorter of money, and they still owed the Venetians for their passage. They could not move on to Palestine because of this lack of supplies, not until they paid the Venetians' fee, nor could they return home for the same reason. They had no hope of securing anything from the city except by breaking in and taking it.

The prospect was equally clear to the citizens. At least they now had an emperor in Alexios V who had some determination and some fighting skill, even if he had been bested so far whenever he had set out to fight the crusaders. But he commanded a much greater population than the crusader army, which was about 20,000 strong; the population of the city was perhaps four or five times that, though the number of men of fighting age was probably not much greater than their enemies. He also had a well-trained set of mercenaries from Western Europe, above all the Varangian Guard – and he controlled the well-fortified city. One measure he took, perhaps overdue, was to expel from the city all the Westerners who were still present, except the soldiers; these people had been loyal to their hosts so far, but Murtzouphlos was hardly the best liked of emperors, and their basic protection had always been Alexios IV's relationship with the crusader army; now they had to go (and, of course, they took with them information about the city and about the morale of the inhabitants).[28]

Murtzouphlos' energy and the skills of the craftsmen of the city did produce innovations which increased still further the defensive capabilities of the city. It was obvious that the success of the Venetians in breaking into the city in the first siege would inspire them to try the same methods again. So high wooden towers were built to increase the height of the walls by several storeys, which would allow the defence to fire at the approaching ships, from higher than the ships and above the wall, and to counter the wooden bridges which the Venetians had extended from the masts of their ships. Both sides prepared defences against fire – both had Greek Fire to use – in the form of vinegar-soaked leather sheets which could be counted on to at least slow the spread of any fire.

The crusaders and the Venetians once again divided the task of the attack on the city between a land attack against the wall by the crusaders and a seaborne attack against the sea wall by the Venetians, but this time they operated much closer together; the crusaders in particular were to concentrate on a section of the wall close to the Blakhernai Palace, while the Venetians were to attack the sea wall next door to the Palace further along the Horn. Artillery was prepared by both sides, on the ships, in the attack on the wall – mining, rams, stone throwers, pots filled with Greek fire – and by the defenders. This was a siege which would be conducted by the latest scientific methods as known in the early thirteenth century. The forces involved were so equal that the result was wholly unpredictable.[29]

The crusaders made careful plans for exploiting their anticipated success, knowing full well that this was necessary to avoid disputes afterwards. They were no doubt quite certain that such disputes would arise, even with a plan made in advance, but if they had agreed on such measures this would at least put one side in the wrong, and public opinion amongst the crusaders could be potent in such a case. They were confident after their earlier victories in the smaller fights; by contrast, the people of the city were somewhat despondent.

There were two further problems the crusaders anticipated. If – when – they won, the crusaders would have at their disposal both the city and the empire of which it was the ruler. They therefore would need to provide for its government, and a plan was laid out in advance for this as well. A committee of six, three crusaders and three Venetians, would choose a new emperor; a second committee, of twenty men, similarly half crusaders, half Venetians, would divide the Empire into fiefs to be held of the new emperor. The second issue was loot. Rules were laid out to limit the damage the looters would cause, and to protect the inhabitants, notably the women and children and the clergy, and more rules were laid down for the division of the loot, which was supposed to be collected in an orderly fashion and then to be distributed. The Venetians were to get their pay first and the rest then would be divided equally between Venetians and crusaders. It is unlikely that anyone believed that these looting rules would be observed once the army was victorious; too much antipathy had been built up between crusaders and the citizens for anyone to believe that a set of theoretical rules would restrain victorious, hungry, and greedy soldiers in the richest city in the world.[30]

The attack began on the morning of Friday, 9 April, and it was a failure. The crusaders concentrated their assault on their section of the wall by the Blakhernai, mining and ramming, but made no progress at all. The Venetian attacks were hindered by a wind which blew from the city, and which prevented their ships from getting close to the wall so that the bridges which were hung from the masts could not reach the opposing towers which had been built up on the wall, and which were their first targets. Meanwhile, the men on these bridges who were to storm ashore were very vulnerable to missiles fired from the wall and from the towers – arrows, crossbow bolts, stones, Greek fire.

The fighting went on all morning, but by mid-afternoon the assault had clearly failed, and the attackers were probably exhausted. They drew back, chased away by a great cheer from the defenders.[31] Crusader morale slumped; that of the citizens improved. This was the time when leadership from those in charge of the crusaders was at a premium. Many men were talking of leaving to go to Palestine even without ships, perhaps increasingly conscious that they were failing to fulfil their original vow, and fearful that they were committing a further sin by fighting and killing fellow Christians.

In response to this crisis of morale the clergy amongst them set to work with a will to persuade the men that they were doing the right thing, confessed their sins, and blessed them. Prostitutes were driven out of the camp.[32] The secular leaders got to work supervising the repair and improvement of their weapons. The Venetians had seen that their ships had failed, and now they developed an improved version by fastening ships together in pairs; they planned to create a double assault, with a heavy joint vessel for the attack, which was to be made on both sides of a tower with both bridges at once, the men then being landed on either side of it simultaneously – if the sailors could get the ships close enough.

The men were thus spiritually and psychologically fortified, and the new tactics were also available. The assault was renewed on Monday, 12 April, principally against the sea wall, with many of the crusaders being brought to join the fight on the Venetian ships. Again the assault was failing for a time, but then the wind which developed was this time favourable, and pushed one of the double ships right up to the wall. Three men were on the first bridge which reached the enemy tower. The first man across, a Venetian, was at once attacked and killed, but the second, Andrew of Dureboise, though beaten to his knees by his attackers, was better armoured and hardly hurt by the attack. As the defenders drew back, presumably believing that he was dead, he stood up and moved to the attack. This resurrection horrified the enemy soldiers, who included some of the Varangian Guard, not men usually fearful in battle, and they fell back. More men followed him across the bridge, and the tower they were attacking fell to them. This seems to have been the first breach in the defence.

Further along the wall another attack also succeeded, and the crusaders, commanded by Peter of Bracieux, the lord of Amiens, got down to ground level inside the wall. They broke through a bricked-up postern which allowed access into the city. Again the first man through, Aleaumes, a priest and the brother of the later chronicler Robert of Clari, was sufficiently well armed and equipped to frighten the defenders, and to hold them off long enough for more of his companions to crowd through the hole. (The priestly involvement was not just in providing spiritual encouragement – apart from Aleaumes, the first two ships to reach the wall with Andrew of Dureboise, were those of the bishops of Soissons and Troyes, called *Paradise* and *Fair Pilgrim*.)[33]

These penetrations began the process of conquest. As more and more armed men broke into the city, the citizens panicked. A gate was opened by the invaders, and the horse transports could discharge their armed and horsed knights again, directly into the city, as at Galata earlier. They grouped together and headed directly for the emperor's tents, dyed purple and pitched conspicuously on a hill. As they approached they drove the guards away, and Murtzouphlos himself had to flee for his life. Large numbers of the inhabitants were killed during this immediate assault, in what was in effect a dispersed and fairly localized massacre, though many more broke out through gates in the main wall (which had been bricked-up to prevent crusaders from entering) and fled into the surrounding countryside. They were not pursued, partly because the soldiers were too busy in the city, and partly because their leaders were worried that their men might scatter and become vulnerable to a counterattack.[34]

The crusader soldiers were kept under control and in their units during the night, no doubt fearing that very counterattack. The Venetians in particular could recall that in the first siege they had broken into the city in much the same place, but had then been driven out, saving themselves only by burning down a large part of the city. And indeed, during the night, some of the crusaders thought they were about to be attacked and resorted to the same deterrent: another section of the city was destroyed.[35]

The Emperor Alexios V Doukas Murtzouphlos attempted to organize an army to either resist the crusaders or to counterattack them. He failed; his career had hardly given anyone any reason to trust him, and now he had been defeated yet again. When he saw the reaction, or non-reaction, he faded from sight, collected a set of treasure and the remaining royal family, including Alexios III's abandoned wife Euphrosyne and her daughters, found a boat and left.[36] The crusader leaders meanwhile organized themselves for another battle in the morning, choosing to move their army to an open space which would suit their methods of fighting and would avoid having to fight through the city street-by-street.

The flight of Murtzouphlos compelled the surviving hierarchy of church and bureaucracy in the city to find yet another emperor. It is interesting that this was their priority, whereas finding a competent military commander might have been better use of their time. This time there were two volunteers, Constantine Laskaris and Constantine Doukas; they drew lots to decide between them, and it fell to Laskaris; this was hardly a sensible way to find an emperor who had to conduct a desperate last-minute defence of the city. He, like his predecessor, then found that he had no men he could command, and the Varangian Guard began bargaining for a pay rise if they were to go on fighting. During the night, Laskaris, like his predecessor once more, abandoned his people and fled from the city, the third Byzantine emperor to desert the city in a year.[37]

So in the morning the crusaders were drawn up in battle array waiting to be attacked. This, they might reasonably assume, was what a properly organized city population would now do. But no attack came; instead, there arrived a deputation of churchmen intent on organizing, even negotiating, an orderly surrender. Surrender was quite acceptable to the crusaders, but negotiating terms of any sort was not. As soon as the surrender was taken, the crusader soldiers set out to loot the city.[38]

The subsequent parade of theft, rape, murder, and destruction lasted for several days. Churches were stripped of anything valuable, including the precious metal covering of the high altar in Hagia Sofia; houses were invaded and anything worth stealing was taken; rich fabrics were looted to decorate drunken, bloodstained soldiers and their horses. And so on, all the usual sickeningly abandoned behaviour typical of siege victors from the time of Sargon of Akkad to the modern Islamic jihadists. As much was destroyed as was stolen. Boniface of Montferrat took a group of his men directly to secure the imperial palace on the headland, the Boukoleon; Henry of Flanders, Count Baldwin's brother, similarly took possession of the Blakhernai Palace; both were stuffed with treasures, and both were guarded more or less successfully against the rest of the looters.

There was later an attempt to gather up the treasures so as to value them and then divide them up as agreed beforehand, but undoubtedly a good deal of it escaped this collection. There was, even so, enough to be distributed, give the Venetians their fee, and more for the French as a crusader group; the ordinary soldiers were allocated a pittance each, but still according to rank. Those who had hidden their stolen treasures clearly did a lot better than that.[39]

This was the first time in the city's history that Constantinople – as opposed to its earlier incarnation as Byzantion – had been taken by force of arms. It had occasionally fallen by deceit and/or treachery, but never until 1204 by conquest. And yet there is not really so much difference between these non-conquest captures and the crusader version. The basic cause of the result of this second crusader siege was the incompetence and weakness of the imperial rulers during the decade before the siege. By the time Constantine Laskaris had fled in the night of 12/13 April, there had been eight emperors in the previous twenty years, none of whom had any pretensions to military prowess, except perhaps Alexios V Doukas. All these emperors had either been usurpers, had run away under pressure, or had been murdered. It was as sorry a record as any state anywhere could count.

The main wall had not been breached; the sea wall had been broken twice, but on the first occasion only briefly. Militarily it was the capture of the Galata Tower and the breaking of the chain which was crucial; if the Venetian ships had been kept out of the Golden Horn, the sea wall of the main city would never have been attacked and broken. And, of course, there was the fighting prowess of the Westerners, both Venetians and crusaders, which had repeatedly defeated attempts at resistance by the imperial troops and the citizens, though if the wall had been held, the Westerners' military superiority would have been of no avail.

And if the city had been scoured in a sensible and cooperative manner for the money which the crusaders had demanded, with the citizens, above all the rich, giving up a proportion of their wealth to save the city, there would have been a good chance that the crusaders would have sailed on to Palestine to accomplish their vows. The sack, even including the theft and destruction of treasure, gathered up enough to pay the Venetians, with plenty over for the looters. And so the citizens would not have lost everything, including their city. The fault, again, lay with the emperors.

The Latin Empire

The sack degenerated, if such a word can be used for something which was already dire, into pure destruction, and while this continued the decisions on the future government of the conquest were going on. A meeting of as many crusaders as chose to attend debated on who should become the next emperor, and the choice was seen to be between Baldwin of Flanders and Boniface of Montferrat, who had been the leading commanders of the crusade from the start. The choice of delegates in the planned electoral colleges was then made, with much politicking among the various groups to get their own men into the group. The choice made by the Venetian delegates was much more orderly, being based on the methods used at home; the selection was, in effect, under Doge Dandolo's effective control.[1]

It is likely that Dandolo played a crucial role in the eventual choice of rulers, given that he effectively controlled the Venetian electors and the rest were divided. He had no wish for an Italian ruler; Boniface was already powerful in northern Italy, and if he was to be established also in Constantinople, which Venice intended to exploit, this would restrict Venice's activities too much, both in Italy and in the East.[2] There was also the possibility that whoever lost in the choice would be so aggrieved that he would resort to violence. To attempt to prevent this the two men agreed that the loser would be compensated with a large appanage.

The crusaders on the committee were mainly churchmen, such men being, it was perhaps thought, less amenable to bribery and nepotism than the secular men, though several were clearly adherents of one or other of the candidates. The overall form of the election process was, it may be noted, not essentially different from that by which Nicholas Kannavos and Constantine Laskaris had been chosen in the earlier part of the year – a mass meeting, consideration of the candidates, and churchmen dominating the decision in the end. The crucial difference was, however, that between a settled organized state, and the choice of a ruler for a conquered city reeking of fire and destruction. Neither selection process had much to commend it.

The result of the discussions was that Baldwin was to be emperor. He was crowned in a ceremony in Hagia Sofia on 16 May, six weeks after the conquest.[3] The looting was in fact still going on, if in a less mindless way. The new emperor had an extremely difficult task. He ruled the city, but not the Empire, and that city was badly damaged by the fires and the looting, its monuments were still being removed or destroyed, or at least damaged, and many of its buildings were in ruins, burnt or wrecked; more important, large parts of its original population were dead, or had fled to seek refuge in the Empire outside the city. And Baldwin had no money, nor any means of getting any.

Apart from all these problems in the city, Baldwin had to pacify Boniface. After some negotiation the latter was awarded Thessalonica and the title of king, with the possibility of conquering large areas of the former Empire in Greece. He married Margaret of Hungary, the widow of the Emperor Isaac II, which would give him some credibility with the Greek-speaking population.[4] The entente between the two men did not last very long, however, and soon they were in dispute.

In addition, the empire which Baldwin now presumed to rule was surrounded by predators who were as greedy for fragments of the old empire as were Baldwin and Boniface and the looters. Tsar Kaloyan of the Bulgars developed a claim to the whole Empire as the heir of the old tsars; independent principalities were set up by nobles from the old empire in various parts of the imperial territory – Theodore Laskaris in Asia, based at Nikaia (and usually referred to as the 'Empire of Nikaia'); Michael Doukas, based at Arta in Epeiros, constructed the state usually called the Despotate of Epeiros; David and Alexios Komnenos had already, even before the conquest of Constantinople, seized control of the distant province of Trebizond. All these men had some claim to inheritance from various earlier emperors and Byzantine aristocrats, and all of them claimed the imperial title. Theodore was the brother of the brief Emperor Constantine Laskaris and son-in-law of Alexios III; the two Komneni at Trebizond were grandsons of the Emperor Andronikos I; Michael Doukas was a grandson of Alexios I, and a cousin of Isaac II and Alexios III. All three called themselves emperors and went through coronation ceremonies, but Laskaris had the marginally better claim since he was crowned by the (exiled) Patriarch of Constantinople; the Epeirote men were never recognized as emperors – hence the title of despot – but the Komneni in Trebizond were.[5]

The rest of Greece gradually fell to various Latin adventurers, French or Italian, and was parcelled out into principalities ruled by men with titles such as Prince of Akhaia, Duke of Athens, and so on. These held their lands in theory in vassalage to the Latin emperor and/or the king in Thessalonica, though, from sheer distance if nothing else, they were usually effectively independent. And all were weak. The southern princes in Athens and the Peloponnese lasted longest. Thessalonica fell to Epeiros within twenty years, and Constantinople itself to the Nikaians within little over fifty years.[6]

Baldwin campaigned along the Asian coast of the Propontis and the Hellespont to gain control of a series of places from the Turks, but they could not be held, and he had to fight at least two battles against local forces in the process.[7] He gained control of little more than Thrace, and he soon fell into dispute – not surprisingly – not only with Boniface in Thessalonica, but with the Bulgar Tsar Kaloyan. In a battle with the Bulgars at Hadrianopolis, Baldwin was captured, and many of his knights were killed, decisively reducing the Latin Empire's military potency. The defeat was due mainly to Latin over-confidence, and to their consequent indiscipline.[8] It was an early signal, along with the divisions imposed on the former empire by granting out large feudal lordships, and the secession and the delegation of other lands, that the Latin Empire of the East was highly unlikely to last for very long.

The city of Constantinople itself had suffered serious injury. Partly burnt, widely looted, its buildings wrecked, its churches defiled, it had also now lost control of the empire which had sustained it. The depopulation caused by the Latin conquerors' murderousness and vandalism and the consequent flight of survivors, was never recovered, at least not until after the next violent conquest in 1453. There was only one really competent Latin emperor during the Latin regime – Baldwin's brother, Henry of Flanders (1206–16) – but the family then dissolved into distant inheritances, unexpected rulers, husbands of princesses, and brief reigns, as complex and disruptive a series of inheritances as had affected the preceding Byzantine imperial regime. The last emperor, Baldwin II, did last for over two decades, but he spent much of his reign travelling around Western Europe seeking help, financial or military, and not receiving very much. He eventually transferred his claim to King Charles I of Anjou and Naples, which gave Charles and his heirs a good excuse to raid Greece, but hardly assisted the Latin Empire to recover or indeed to survive.[9] Western Europe, having thought about it, was in effect, ashamed of what had been done.

The city had been the essential heart of the Byzantine Empire, and the destruction and humiliation it received in 1204 weakened it decisively, a weakness which was mirrored in the weakness of the Latin Empire. The lack of population meant a lack of economic activity and wealth, and the result was military weakness. The failure of the west to support the Latin Empire only continued its weakness.

The Venetians' share in the division of the conquest was successfully tailored to the city's home interests. Doge Dandolo had claimed the unpaid part of the transport fee as the first charge on the official division of the loot, and he was also allowed to pick and choose the territories Venice wanted. These turned out not to be large sections of the imperial mainland, which would be expensive to defend and control, but a string of port-towns along the Adriatic and Aegean coasts which could be used as naval bases and commercial centres, and as ports at which ships could call and refresh and shelter on their voyages. Several islands in the Aegean were taken over, including the Cyclades and the large islands of Crete and Euboia, though the former took a long time to be conquered, thereby proving the good sense of Dandolo's choices. In Constantinople Venice claimed an enlarged section of the city as its factory, while the Genoese and Pisan bases were driven out. Clearly Venice thought there was wealth enough still in the region for its merchants to exploit. But this wealth did not benefit the emperors in the diminished Empire; thus the exploitation of the city and the Empire continued, without providing much in return to support supposed conquerors.[10]

The great city continued to decay. The Latin patriarch closed the Greek Orthodox churches in 1213, driving out the clergy and forcing the Greek Orthodox population out of neutrality and into political opposition and disloyalty. The emperors, short of cash, continued to dismantle and destroy, and sell, anything of value, including lead from the roofs of churches and even the palaces, ancient Greek sculptures and statues, and relics which had been preserved in the Orthodox churches.[11] The looting at the time of the siege, therefore, simply continued as an official imperial policy, impoverishing the city both materially and culturally, as well as financially, in religious terms and most decisively in loss of population. Constantinople as a Christian city, the 'Queen of Cities' as it was called, had been hollowed out; it never recovered.

Chapter 19

Recovery from the East –
The Empire of Nikaia

The Sieges of 1234–35 and 1260–61

S urrounded by greedy enemies, the Latin emperors in Constantinople were in effect under a sort of siege for the years they survived. At the same time, such was the political fragmentation of the lands of the former Roman Empire, many of those enemies were also under pressure from all sides as well. In the next centuries many of these Balkan and Asian polities were involved in Constantinople's history and troubles.

The capture of Constantinople by the crusaders had fragmented the former Empire; the power of its various successor states was reduced so that the whole region from the Adriatic to the Taurus Mountains was composed of minor states. As is the way of such political groupings this meant that the whole region was politically unstable, with individual states emerging briefly into prominence and then fading away again, temporary alliances being made, and frequent wars being fought. It was a condition of international affairs which was radically different from that which had preceded it, when the Byzantine Empire, even in its worst days, had clearly been at the centre of events. This change makes it necessary to consider, first of all, this new political condition before looking at the individual fate of Constantinople.

At the joint centre of the international political system which emerged were the two rival empires: the Latin Empire, in control of Constantinople and mainly holding territories in Thrace, and the Byzantine Empire centred at Nikaia, in control of part of northwest Asia Minor. These two – twin states, in a sense – existed within a larger group of states which surrounded them, and had close relations with them, and these in turn were encircled by another ring of states. Constantinople and its fate was still at the centre, despite its ragged condition.

It will be convenient to look at these surrounding states by moving anti-clockwise around the small area subject to them. To the north and northwest was the revived Bulgarian kingdom, under its third king, Kaloyan (1197–1207), referred to by the crusaders as Johanitza. This was a relatively small state, sandwiched between the Danube in the north and the Balkan mountain range to the south, but it had the vigour of newness, and was able to tap into the military manpower resources of the Ukrainian steppes – it was a largely Cuman mercenary army which had defeated and captured Baldwin I in 1205. To the west, centred in the Pindos Mountains and reaching the Adriatic coast, was the Despotate of Epeiros, developing from 1204 under Michael I Doukas.[1] This state was as hungry as the Nikaian Empire to reclaim its Byzantine heritage at the great city. For the moment it was under some threat from Venetian posts which were being established in the coastal cities of the Adriatic, and from the kingdom of Thessalonica, which was expanding over Macedon and Thessaly under its first ruler, Boniface of Montferrat; Thessalonica can be counted as yet another competitor for the city, and occupied much the same geographical space as the old Macedonian kingdom. To the south of the Thessalonican kingdom were the new states established by crusaders at Boniface's instigation in central Greece and the Peloponnese: the Duchy of Athens, the Principality of Achaia, the lordship of Thebes, and others. Technically these were vassals of Boniface and then of Baldwin, but they were in fact independent of both. In the Aegean the Venetian domination grew steadily greater as more and more of the islands were seized, notably Euboia (Negroponte), the Kyklades, and Lesbos, and eventually Crete and Cyprus.[2]

This development and rearrangement took time to work out; it was not, for instance, until 1211 that the Venetians made any attempt to gain control of Crete. In the meantime most of the rulers of the several states were fully preoccupied with establishing their administrations, gathering taxes, subduing their unwilling new subjects, and looking over their shoulders at what their neighbours were doing. By about 1210 or 1211, however, the new situation had emerged into existence. It was unstable, dangerous, and liable to change very quickly, but its components were now recognizable.

In Asia, by contrast with this European complexity, there were just two powers. The empire which had been founded by Theodore I Laskaris based on Nikaia, which controlled a considerable territory along the northern and western parts of Anatolia. It had gained control of the temporary conquests of Henry of Flanders along the Propontis coast, and so it faced the Latin Empire in Thrace across that sea. An attempt by the Komnenos brothers in Trebizond to advance westwards had been rebuffed. The boundary between the two rival empires fluctuated, and for the present the Latin Empire still controlled Bithynia. Like the Epeiros Despotate, the Empire of Nikaia aimed, as an ideological imperative, to recover control of Constantinople, but for the moment it concentrated on securing its Asian territories.

The second Asian power was its neighbour and competitor, which controlled the southern and eastern parts of Anatolia. This was the Sultanate of the Seljuk Turks, whose capital was at Iconium (Konya) and which, rather surprisingly, had not become involved in the collapse of the Empire, partly because it was suffering through its own succession crisis at the time, and partly because it felt threatened by powers further east.

Beyond this group of closely related and neighbouring states, which occupied the former imperial territories, there were others, more distant from Constantinople, and often larger in area and more powerful militarily than any of the system's core of states in the Balkans and Asia Minor; any and all might intervene in events in those areas. In the Ukrainian steppe the Cumans were the currently dominant group, but they were soon, in 1237–42, to be replaced by the Mongol Empire, the most terrible of the nomad states since the Avars. The arrival of the Mongols largely eclipsed the nascent power of the Russian states, where the original Kievan principality had broken up among numerous inheritors; these were too numerous, divided, and weak to put up any serious resistance to the Mongol khans for the next three centuries. The Mongols had penetrated as far as Hungary, but internal problems forced a withdrawal, and the Balkans; the Seljuks, however, suffered from Mongol attention out of Iran.

North of the Balkans was Hungary, interested in the fate of Constantinople from the start, in part because Boniface of Montferrat and Thessalonica had married Margaret, the daughter of the Hungarian king and the widow of Emperor Isaac II; she eventually left to take refuge with her relatives in Hungary. Venice at the head of the Adriatic had taken the opportunity of the destruction of the Roman Empire to expand from a merchant state into a developing maritime empire with positions – ports, towns, islands – in the Adriatic and the Aegean, and had, as noted, done so by seizing former territories of that empire; characteristically, given the political flexibility which Venice long displayed, the city was therefore both one of the distant states and one which was directly involved in Constantinopolitan and Aegean affairs. By taking for itself a large part of Constantinople as its trading factory, the city had also made itself the main supporter of the Latin Empire, a burden which would only grow with time.

In southern Italy the main powers were the Pope, though his power was less military than exhortative, and the kingdom of the Two Sicilies, whose kings for the past century and a half had maintained a powerful interest in the southern Balkans, and maintained an ambition to expand into the former Empire, in 1266 it fell to a French adventurer Charles of Anjou, gained a new lease of strength and menaced all its neighbours. This was expressed in raids, invasions, claims, and disruptive diplomacy; the transfer of Baldwin II's imperial claims to King Charles I of that kingdom in 1267 was another indication of that kingdom's continuing predatory interest, as was the later Emperor Peter de Courteney's invasion, launched from Apulia.[3]

Across the Mediterranean was the powerful Ayyubid Sultanate, Saladin's political and military base, having Egypt as its centre; it became the Mamluk Sultanate in 1250, controlled by the military slaves who chose the sultans from amongst themselves. The state then consisted not only of Egypt but also of Muslim Syria; its priority was to take out the surviving crusader states in Syria, a task which took another half-century to complete, and which involved the deliberate physical destruction of every crusader city, and of many of the castles they had built, in order to prevent any new crusader invasion gaining a foothold. The Mamluk Sultanate was the most formidable military state in the region, and also the most stable state, certainly in terms of longevity, since it lasted until the early nineteenth century.[4] (In this it was to be rivalled by the eventual successor of the Byzantine Empire.)

In many ways the future of Constantinople – or rather the contest for the control of the city – was one of the central elements in the foreign policies of all these states. It was still a large city, if now partly wrecked and badly depopulated; it had dominated its surroundings from the Taurus

Mountains to the Adriatic Sea for a millennium before its next conquest; its useful geographical position for trade was reinforced by its formidable walls and its intermittently effective navy. All this dictated that any state which aspired to greater power in the region must aspire also in the end – or even from the start – to gain control of the city. The Latin Empire had therefore begun well, having started with that control, but the removal of many of its fighters to perform their vows to go to Palestine, or to go home, weakened the new state. Then the deaths of many others who had remained in the city in the fight against the Bulgars in 1205, a battle which resulted in the capture, disappearance, and ultimate death of the Latin Emperor Baldwin I as early as 1205 meant that the new empire hardly was founded before it was grievously wounded. And some of the more effective subjects spread throughout Greece and the Balkans in other new states, which again fatefully weakened the Latin Empire as a state.

The major threat to Constantinople in the short term after the establishment of the Latin Empire was the Empire of Nikaia. The first ruler there, Theodore I Laskaris (1204–22), had to fight the Seljuks, the Komneni in Trebizond, and the Latin Empire to bring his state into existence, and then he faced competition from the last surviving former emperor of the years of disaster, Alexios III, who, having disposed of Alexios V Murtzouphlos by blinding him and then handing him over to the Latins for execution, had taken refuge with the Seljuk Sultan Ghiyath al-Din Kay Khusrau I (1192–96, 1204–10). The two men had known each other while the latter was a refugee in Constantinople at the time of the conquest.[5] He sponsored Alexios' return by attacking Theodore's principality, but was defeated. Alexios fell into Theodore's control, and was put into a monastery, a more comfortable fate than any of his rivals and competitors had suffered – Theodore was, of course, Alexios' cousin and son-in-law.[6] This, in fact, disposed of Seljuk hostility for the present, especially when Theodore acquired a treaty defining the boundaries between the Latin Empire and the Nikaian Empire in 1214, leaving Theodore free, if he wished, to campaign elsewhere. The Seljuks subsided into peace and their internal disputes.[7]

Theodore's successor, John III Vatatzes (1222–56), his eastern frontier more or less guaranteed, could then turn to reviving the Empire. By the time he died John had cleared away the Latins from Asia, except from the Bithynian peninsula, and had taken over some of the Aegean islands which had originally been assigned to Venice. He was able to gain control of the Hellespont by seizing Kallipolis on the Chersonesan side by a partition agreement with the Bulgarian King John Asen II (1218–41). He had already indicated his hostility to Venice, which was emerging as the main support of the Latin Empire, and the control of the Hellespont passage was an obvious means of squeezing both of these enemies.

The Epeirote Despotate was similarly successful in recovering part of the imperial territories. Michael I Doukas (1204–15) proved to be a skilful diplomatic performer, attracting and discarding alliances in turn with Boniface, Baldwin, and the Venetians. By 1212 he recovered control of Thessaly; his successor, his brother Theodore I Doukas (1215–30), defeated an attempt by the new Latin Emperor, Peter de Courtenay, to march through his territories from the west. Peter was captured and not seen again; his army disintegrated and vanished.[8] (This was the second time a Latin Emperor had been captured by an enemy and had then simply vanished.) In 1222 Boniface's successor in Thessalonica, Demetrios I, desperate for help, went to Italy to seek assistance, vainly; two years later Theodore captured Thessalonica itself. It was then set up as a separate state under his younger brother, a move which could not assist any political consolidation in the region.[9]

Given all these varied distractions and manoeuvres, it is therefore hardly surprising that any attack on Constantinople aimed at recovering it, by any of the aspirants, was delayed for thirty years. It was in no one's interest, of course, that any other state should succeed in taking the city; this was perhaps the most effective defence for the Latin Empire, the fact that it was in the midst of a competition to extinguish it. It was only in 1234 that a siege was finally attempted.

John III Vatatzes conducted a campaign in Thrace in the 1230s which reduced the Latin Empire's territory to a small area near Constantinople, plus part of Bithynia. He allied with King John Asen II of Bulgaria for a joint expedition against the city under the Treaty of Kallipolis, where the partition of Thrace was agreed. The expedition turned out to face major difficulties. Vatatzes sent his fleet to blockade the city, while he and the Bulgarians attacked by land – such a combination was the only method ever to succeed against the city – but the Venetians replied with a fleet which broke through his blockade. The allies tried again, in the spring of

1236, but again failed to make an impression on the walls. On land it was soon clear that, since both rulers aimed to seize the city for themselves, their cooperation was not going to last. The siege was more a blockade by land and sea than an active siege, but it had clearly been aimed at conquest, and just as clearly it had failed.[10]

Emperor John Vatatzes, however, did succeed in conquering Thessalonica, which had been set up as a separate state after the conquest by the Epeirotes, and as such became another target for all its neighbours, the Bulgars as well as the Epeirotes and the Latin Empire. Vatatzes' conquest set up a future conflict between the two Greek claimants for the imperial inheritance, which was won by the Nikaians in 1246, as well as another conflict between the Nikaians and the Bulgars. The Despotate survived in its Epeirote hills in the west, though diminished in size and power, and the principalities in Greece south of Thessaly also continued. John Vatatzes seized a part of Bulgaria, so that at the end of his reign he had almost reconstituted the Empire as it had been in 1200, though it had been done by fighting all his neighbours – a necessary consequence of the regional political disintegration. The only major piece missing from the Nikaian reunification was Constantinople, which was the essential piece.

The successor states all claimed to be the heirs of the Byzantine Empire which had been destroyed by the Latin conquest, and their succession systems were continuations of the old imperial system. In Nikaia the succession was as complex and undesigned as it had been throughout the preceding millennium in Constantinople, a mixture of heredity, assassination, usurpation, and secret murder. John III Vatatzes was the son-in-law of Theodore I and he was succeeded by his own son Theodore II. So far so hereditary, in a way, but Theodore II died at the age of only 34 in 1258, leaving the throne to his seven-year-old son John IV. This, in a militaristic polity, was always a dangerous event, and John was put aside by an ambitious commander, Michael Palaiologos, who first made himself joint emperor and then soon contrived the death of his young colleague; Michael never escaped the stain of usurpation and child murder, but no one would have assumed any other outcome.

Among the Doukas family, the Despot Michael I had been succeeded by his brother, Theodore I, then their younger brother took Thessalonica as his portion, where he was succeeded by two of his nephews; in Epeiros Michael was therefore followed by his son, grandson, and great-grandson, a most unusual direct succession through four generations, but which went no further. The succession in the Latin Empire was to become even worse, going from Baldwin I to his brother Henry, then to his sister Yolanda's husband, Peter de Courtenay (who vanished), then to Yolanda as regent, and on to her son, with John de Brienne – quite unconnected to the family – as co-emperor for the child Baldwin II, who was emperor from 1228 to 1261, overlapping John de Brienne's reign (1231–1237). Such irregular successions always contributed very much to the political instability of all these states.

After all the campaigning efforts by John Vatatzes, the city of Constantinople eventually fell to the Nikaian Empire by apparent accident, though it was hardly accidental that it was the Nikaians who succeeded in achieving the ambition shared with everybody else.[11] In particular, there had been a preliminary conflict in which a coalition of the Despot Michael II of Epeiros, Prince William II of Achaia, and King Manfred of the Two Sicilies was formed when it became clear that Michael Palaiologos was successful in reaching the Nikaian throne – Michael was already well known as an accomplished commander and diplomat, and was therefore feared by his neighbours. The coalition was designed to cut Michael down to size before he became properly established. The joint army of the allies met that of Nikaia in battle at Pelagonia in Macedon in 1259 and was comprehensively defeated by Michael's brother John; the Prince of Achaia was captured, and 400 of Manfred's knights were killed in the fight.[12] This was the battle which in effect sealed the fate of the Latin Empire and of Constantinople. There was now no power in the region capable of preventing the Nikaian Empire seizing the city.

The political and strategic logic of a group of minor states who constantly fought each other had emerged once more: there was only one winner in such a contest as the players were steadily eliminated. But the weakness of all of them was demonstrated when it was clear that the Nikaian Empire was not capable of finishing off its competitors – both the Despotate and the Achaian Principality continued in existence after Pelagonia, decreased in power and prestige, but without much loss of territory or independence.

Michael was a clever, disputatious, and devious man, and so a highly successful diplomat. He was also lucky, first in his brother's victory, and then in seeing the capture of Constantinople, two achievements which made him secure on his unsteady throne for the rest of his life. He also constructed a more successful system of alliances than his opponents. He gathered support among the nobles of the old Constantinopolitan families who had emigrated to take refuge in Nikaia, awarding them prestigious offices. It was the support he could command from these families which was the eventual basis of his decision to kill off his ward, John IV, in 1261.

In 1260 he contacted a disaffected Frank who had access to Constantinople. A Nikaian army approached the city, but the Frank, probably Anseau of Cahieu, failed to open the gate as agreed, though Michael's army was attacking Galata, across the Golden Horn from the city, at the time. The emperor also contacted the Genoese, sworn rivals and enemies of the Venetians, and who had been largely locked out of the trade at Constantinople for the last fifty years. By in effect promising by the Treaty of Nymphaion in March 1261 to replace the Venetian concession in the city with one for Genoa and Pisa, and permitting Genoa to establish factories also in Smyrna, Chios and Lesbos, Michael thereby organized a helpful alliance with a naval power which was capable of contesting Venice's power at sea.[13]

An army, possibly that which had been at Galata the year before, approached the city more directly in July. The town of Selymbria was captured, along with much of the area nearby where the farmers grew crops to supply Constantinople. This would put the city under yet more pressure, though no doubt the reduced population and the concomitant increase in available horticultural land inside the wall made supplies less difficult than in earlier crises. The city, even with a larger population, had noticeably maintained adequate food supplies during the Crusader sieges, even at times supplying its enemies. It was unlikely to be starved out at any time.[14] The army, commanded by an imaginative general, Alexios Strategopoulos, was to demonstrate before the city wall on its way to march about in Thrace as a martial demonstration to maintain Michael's control, and to ensure that the new sole emperor did not face rebellions. That is, Strategopoulos was not tasked with an attack on the city directly but was to be on the lookout for any opportunity which may come his way. The failure of the plot with Anseau the year before did mean that there was likely to be other possible means of entering the city by betrayal.

The army marched into view of the wall of the city, as instructed by the emperor. Sure enough an opportunity arose. It became known that the Latin Emperor Baldwin II had sent most of his forces on a campaign against an island in the Propontis, so the city was effectively disarmed. One of the farmers from Selymbria, no doubt interrogated by Strategopoulos, knew of a tunnel under the wall connecting two parts of a monastery, and in the night a small party got into the city through that tunnel and opened the Golden Gate.[15] Through the gate and over the wall using scaling ladders, the army entered the city in force, greeted with cheers by the population. The Emperor Baldwin had to flee; the Emperor Michael was soon crowned as the official emperor in Hagia Sofia.

No violent siege had been required, nor any heroics, just intrigue, preparation, and alertness. As often enough before, the city had fallen because of internal dissidence. As the Emperor Baldwin II would have put it, he had been betrayed; or, as Michael would say, it was reunited to its rightful imperial successor. On the other hand, it is clear that the city had been under severe and regular pressure for at least a year before its capture by Alexios' army, beginning with the plot of Anseau de Cahieu and the attack on Galata. In the circumstances it was a clear derogation of duty for Baldwin to allow his forces to leave the city unprotected. He clearly deserved to be evicted, and Michael's combination of a diplomatic and a military campaign was clever and deservedly successful.

The capture of the city and the elimination of the Latin Empire caused a similar shock in Western Europe as the earlier loss of Jerusalem, and the later loss of Acre. Many of the successor states also suffered in the same way, but it was hardly a surprise to any of them, especially after the battle of Pelagonia two years before, and the Nikaian alliance with Genoa. The Nikaian Empire had proved that it was the most potent of those successors.

Chapter 20

Enemies within – Civil Wars

The Sieges of 1376, 1379, and 1390

The area subject to Constantinople and its emperor shrank in the century after the successful reign of Michael VIII (1259–82). The reason was the repeated indulgence of royalty and the aristocracy in civil warfare. There were civil wars in 1321–22 and 1327–28 between Andronikos II and Andronikos III; in 1341–7 between John V Palaiologos and John VI Kantakouzenos; and again between the same men between 1352 and 1357.[1] The inevitable result was that the enemies of the Empire could seize opportunities to snatch lands from it (the Turks in Asia, the Bulgars and Serbs in Europe, Venice and Genoa by sea) so that the civil wars generally also involved one or more of these external enemies.

In addition, in 1347–8 the city and its empire were struck by the Black Death, brought in by a Genoese ship arriving from the Crimea. The city was the first place in Europe to be seriously affected, apart from the Crimea. (The disease had travelled from China where the outbreak began in the 1320s, facilitated by the increased traffic in goods and people resulting from the Mongol conquests and the subsequent ease of travel.) This outbreak reduced the urban population by between a third and a half, and similarly damaged the rural population, so that wealth declined, production declined, and agriculture declined.[2] One of the major results, at least in terms of political affairs, was that the armies which were fielded by these disputing emperors and pretenders contained no more than a few hundred men.[3]

The nearest any of the civil wars came to a siege of Constantinople was in the gap between the second and third wars, in 1347–9, when Genoa and Venice fought each other in the waters around the city. Both cities expected, or asked for, help from the emperor (currently John VI, 1347–54), which was not forthcoming.[4] At one point, when Venice withdrew after a sea battle which was mostly a draw, the Genoese turned on Constantinople and attacked the city, though rather half-heartedly, annoyed at the lack of support; a naval reply from the emperor ended in a humiliating fiasco, when the newly built Byzantine ships, manned by completely inexperienced sailors, were all captured by the Genoese. Having seen the back of the Venetians, however, the Genoese then decided against further action, an equally humiliating decision for the Empire, which was apparently not worth attacking.[5]

Of course, these Venetian-Genoese wars resumed and extended, but for neither was control of the city a worthwhile prize, in contrast to the Galata suburb to the north of the Golden Horn, which is where the Genoese factory was based, and which therefore became a Venetian target. Certainly an attack on the city would absorb far more manpower, and cost so much, that Genoa was unable to effect it. This war of the Italians took place while the Black Death was raging in the city, a curious reaction to the worst plague in European history.

The result by the 1370s was that the Empire – still so-called, despite its fearsome, extended, and continuing territorial losses – consisted of no more than the land close to Constantinople up to a distance of up to 30 miles from the wall; the isolated city of Thessalonica, which had as little country attached; part of the Peloponnese (the Morea), and several towns along the Propontis and the western Black Sea coasts; plus the city of Philadelphia, another wholly isolated inland city in western Asia Minor.

By that date also there had emerged in northwestern Asia Minor a new power. The Seljuk Sultanate collapsed in the 1260s and 1270s, and had been replaced by a set of several small Turkish emirates, of which the most vigorous was that founded by Osman in about 1300, located in the northwest of the peninsula, in the hinterland of the former Nikaian Empire – its first centre, Sogut, was only a hundred miles from Nikaia. Renamed by its enemies as the Ottoman Sultanate, this was proving to be a formidable warrior state, based on the jihadist practice of fighting the nearest Christian power, which honed the warrior skills of its men and its rulers. The Sultan Orkhan (1326–59), Osman's son, established garrisons in several places in the Gallipoli Peninsula, taking advantage of a series of earthquakes which had forced the evacuation of several of the towns.[6] This was the manoeuvre of John Vatatzes a century earlier, which was the preliminary to the Nikaian conquest of Thrace. Orkhan had already pushed his power to the Asian coasts of the Bosporos, the Propontis, and the Hellespont – the area in the ancient world called Hellespontine Phrygia, Bithynia, and the Troad. Turkish troops had been hired by, or loaned to, all the various contenders in the Byzantine civil wars for the past half-century, so the permanent establishment of a Turkish force in Europe was hardly a surprising development. But here was a very potent new participant in those civil wars, and the Balkans was a region where several weak kingdoms were available for conquering, or who would happily ally with the Ottomans in pursuit of their own purposes. The next Ottoman Sultan, Murad I, gained control of Hadrianopolis in the 1360s; it became the Sultanate's European capital for the next century.

From the recapture of Constantinople by Michael VIII in 1261 until the renewal of the civil wars in the Empire in 1376, therefore, Constantinople itself rarely came under active threat; the Genoese menace in 1350 had hardly been severe. On the other hand, it was not unusual for the city to have its limited territory ravaged by an enemy force, or by a force under an imperial pretender. Yet no siege took place in that century and more, despite the several civil wars. Badly damaged during the Latin Empire period, the city could recover somewhat, its population could revive – until cut down again by the recurrent plagues – and its trading system was rich, even when much of the trading was done by the Italians. When that century-long lull ended, however, in 1376, there began a series of sieges, seven of them in the next eighty years, which ended in another conquest of the city.

In 1376 the Emperor John V was overthrown by his son Andronikos, who had escaped from prison with the aid of some Genoese; in turn they were concerned that John was about to conclude an advantageous deal with Venice. This was also, however, in part a case of sibling rivalry, in that John V had begun to favour his younger son Manuel for the succession – John had been on the throne since 1354 and might be expected to die at any time – and he had cut Andronikos out of the order of succession, such as it was. Andronikos had attempted once already to challenge his father for the throne, whence his imprisonment. Now, with Genoese assistance, he laid siege to Constantinople. John had no allied support, and the Ottoman Sultan Murad I gave at least nominal support to Andronikos. The siege lasted a month, and at the end John and Manuel capitulated. They were then jailed in the Tower of Anemas, part of the old Blakhernai Palace which had been made into a political prison.[7]

John V might well feel aggrieved at the support given by Sultan Murad to his usurping son, now the Emperor Andronikos IV, since for several years he had been acting as Murad's vassal and military captain. But Murad had seized on the dispute between father and son to support Andronikos in exchange for a choice piece of territory, the port town of Kallipolis, which was the keystone of the Turkish position in the Gallipoli Peninsula; it was the European end of the ferry between Asia and Europe; control of it by an Asian power gave it also control of the Hellespont, and the ability to prevent traffic through it. They had held it briefly in the 1350s, but John had recovered it. Now in 1377 Murad gained control of it definitively and used it to move his army across into Europe; it meant that the foothold he held inside Thrace was more secure, and from there most of the Balkan lands were soon conquered. He also controlled the Hellespont and soon developed Kallipolis as a naval port. With that as a port where they could land at any time, and with their military expertise, the Ottomans had become immovable. They had thus found a way, as had John Vatatzes, to expand their power into Europe without having to take Constantinople.[8]

John V and Manuel escaped from their tower prison in 1379, and, once more gaining the support of Murad, who was presumably really interested in weakening the Byzantine power, they returned to besiege Andronikos IV in Constantinople. This conflict lasted much longer than the siege in 1376. Andronikos eventually left the city and moved across to Galata where he had Genoese help, and the civil war was ended in negotiation in 1381. So reduced was the Byzantine Empire in strength, in power and in prestige, by this time that John and Manuel commanded a Turkish army loaned to them by Murad in their attack, while Venetian ships carried them across into Europe, and in the siege of Andronikos in Galata, which lasted a year, the fighting was done on Andronikos' side by a Genoese force. No imperial soldiers seem to have been involved on either side, certainly a curious Civil War.[9] The terms John had agreed to in exchange for Murad's help reduced the Byzantine Empire to a tribute-paying vassal of the Ottoman Sultanate. Such was the cost of fraternal conflict.

The quarrelling was not yet finished. Andronikos IV died in 1385, and his son John inherited his position as heir (and he had been crowned as co-emperor – John VII – while Andronikos was in power). In 1390 John arrived at the city with an army of Turks supplied by the new Sultan

Bayazid and the Genoese. They began a siege, but then got into the city and demanded that the people acclaim John as their new emperor, but he had so little support that they had to threaten the bystanders – it was night time and most of them were in their night clothes – with their weapons to achieve any supporting salutes. John V, however, had taken refuge in the fortified Golden Gate, while Manuel escaped and collected ships from several allies, including help from the Knights of St John at Rhodes. These, and some soldiers, sufficed to drive John VII out – they caught John's soldiers at lunch. The fighting was Lilliputian – Manuel had collected only five galleys and some small ships for his counterattack, and these and a small contingent of soldiers were sufficient to do the job.[10]

John V died the next year, after what must be called a very troubled reign. Manuel was now emperor, but John VII was located close by at Selymbria. The new Sultan, Bayazid 'Yilderim' ('Thunderbolt') had demanded as the price for his assistance that he provide a force of soldiers to campaign with the Ottoman army. The contribution from the Byzantine Empire was limited to 100 soldiers, which may have been all that John could provide, or it may have been simply intended to be a token of John's vassalage. Bayazid, in other words, demanded the contribution as a public mark of John's vassal status. At least Bayazid took John VII with him in his campaign and so kept him from attempting another coup d'état.

While the Palaiologoi emperors were conducting their little family arguments at the expense of the remains of the Byzantine Empire, the Ottoman power had been growing. Having secured Kallipolis first in 1366, and then finally and permanently in 1377, the way was clear for Ottoman conquests in the Balkans among the several weak and unstable kingdoms between the Hellespont and the Danube. At the same time, the sultans were able to reduce the rival Turkish emirates in Anatolia to vassal status – though some of them had their territories wholly annexed. This established the eastern boundary of the Ottoman Sultanate at the Taurus Mountains. Then in Europe the Bulgars were defeated and reduced to vassalage in 1371, the Serb power was destroyed (at the Battle of Kosovo in 1389, where Sultan Murad I died), and the rump of the Bulgarian kingdom was finally annexed in 1396. By then the Ottoman northwestern boundary was on the Danube. Bayazid had done most of this annexation, but only after a century of battles and defeats of his rivals and enemies by his predecessors. The Ottoman Sultanate was now more or less the size, and had very similar boundaries, to the Byzantine Empire as it had been after the Arab conquest in the seventh century, and again after the conquests of Basil II.[11]

The Ottoman military method was the normal one for empire builders. The sultans had a core force of Turkish soldiers, well-trained, loyal, and well rewarded. They supported them by conscripting manpower from the conquered lands, and with contingents often under the command of their own rulers who had been reduced to vassalage – as with John V and John VII. Many of the Christian rulers of the Balkans were not averse to this, since they in effect received Ottoman support for their unsteady thrones in exchange – again as with the Byzantine emperors. And yet, the continued existence of these subordinated kingdoms marked the Sultanate as unstable. Bayazid's annexations were in part a recognition of this basic weakness.

But the one place not yet taken, and the one place necessary to crown these conquests and acquisitions, and to make them more secure, was Constantinople. With interruptions, this was to be the next place on the Ottoman agenda, but they can scarcely have expected it to take more than half a century.

Chapter 21

An Encircling Enemy – The Ottoman Turks

The Sieges of 1394–1402, 1411–13, 1422, and 1442

The Ottoman Sultanate was a combination of two types of empire, the Islamic *jihad* state, and the warrior empire. The two are similar, of course, but not wholly identical. A *jihad* state tends to be disorganized internally and to break down fairly easily into warfare between factions, often over differing emphases in religious matters; relying on its warriors' interpretation of Islam, its people became discouraged quickly enough if regularly defeated. The warrior state, by contrast, is one which is organized for regular warfare and which lives off its conquests. The Arab Empire of the early conquests in the seventh century is an example of a *jihad* state, and the early Ottoman state of the fourteenth century is very like it, as would later be, for example, the Sokoto caliphate in West Africa, and the Mahdist state in the Sudan, both in the nineteenth century, and the brief Islamic *jihad* state in Mesopotamia in the early twenty-first century. The prize example of the warrior state would be Republican Rome, and, to some extent, that of Alexander the Great. The United States in its western expansion, was similarly a warrior state, as was the British conquest in India.

When these two types combine they begin as *jihad* states – *gazi* is the Ottoman term – and if they last long enough they tend to evolve into warrior states, with their religious origins being their justification for their conquests; the Arab Caliphate is the prime example. Their victims tend to be non-Islamic, such as the Ottoman campaigns against the Christian states of Eastern Europe, but also heretical Islamic societies, such as Shi'a Iran after the Safavid takeover. By their evolution they tend to become very bureaucratic – indeed, if any empire is to last, a stable bureaucracy is essential – with the tax revenues spent increasingly on war and little else. They are very good at conquests, but as with all conquest states they eventually reach their geographical limits, and at that point the bureaucracy and the military ossify, glorifying past victories and content above all to hold what has been won. This marks the beginning of decline.

By the late fourteenth century the Ottoman Sultanate was on the cusp of shifting from a jihadist state, as it had been since its origin, into a bureaucratic warrior empire. At that point it turned its hungry gaze to Constantinople; and during the first half of the fifteenth century, in four sieges of the city the Ottoman sultans attempted its conquest.

The Siege-Blockade of 1394–1402

The evolution of the Ottoman Sultanate from *gazi* status to a bureaucratic empire was typified by the reign of Sultan Bayazid I (1389–1402). He crushed rebellions and converted several disaffected provinces and many vassal states into governable provinces, many inhabited by Christians, who were not compelled to convert to Islam. One of the measures he took was to make the first move in a campaign to gain control of Constantinople, especially when the new Emperor Manuel II (1391–1425) began to refuse tribute payments. In 1394, the city's Thracian hinterland was taken over and a line of forts was built to contain its population and enforce a land blockade.[1] There was, therefore, in sequence, the city wall, which consisted of two walls and two ditches, then a space – a 'no man's land' – and then the line of the Ottoman forts. The city was under a blockade which approximated to a siege. From 1394 Ottoman armies turned up repeatedly in the following years, but their assaults were thwarted, even though their destruction of the nearby countryside beyond the wall was distressingly thorough. This siege-blockade went on for eight years, and conditions in the city were bad, though never bad enough to force a surrender.[2]

Bayazid campaigned in Europe at the same time, reducing Bulgaria to a vassal state, and subduing Serbia; he set up frontier marches facing the unconquered areas in Bosnia and across the Danube in Wallachia, whose lords raided their Christian neighbours repeatedly, in true *jihad* fashion. The sultanate was thus both a bureaucratic entity and had a *jihad* frontier. In Asia, Bayazid converted much of the region which still remained under vassal rule into a super province, Anadolu. The surviving Turkish vassals in Asia subsided but looked to the east for succour (just as Constantinople's Emperor Manuel II would be appealing to Western powers for help, against the very same Turkish power). In Central Asia and Iran the latest conqueror from the steppes, Timur the Lame, was rampaging as an Islamic champion. In 1396 he conquered Iran and was then ready to move into Iraq and Mesopotamia, with Ottoman Anatolia clearly his next target. (All of his victims were in fact Muslims.) Bayazid organized a defensive alliance with the Mamluks of Egypt and an Armenian king, but then Timur turned away to deal with a problem in Central Asia and to invade India.[3]

The blockade of Constantinople from 1394 was interrupted by occasional assaults, all of which failed, and by reverse raids by the inhabitants, none of which was decisive in relieving the pressure.[4] The city was quickly reduced to near-famine conditions. Occasional shipments were sent by Venice – three annual shiploads of 300–400 tons of grain (though they may not have got through) – and more came from Trebizond and a number of Black Sea ports. Other attempts at relief came from outside. In 1395 Bayazid had to withdraw most of his forces to fight enemies in the north; next year he faced a great crusading army led by the king of Hungary which he defeated at Nicopolis on the Danube. In 1399 Marshal Boucicaut, who had been captured at Nicopolis and had visited Constantinople on his way home to France after being ransomed, returned to the East, bringing a force of about 1,000 soldiers to reinforce the city's defences. This force helped the garrison to be active on the walls and in raids, including the capture of Riva, one of Bayazid's forts on the Bosporos shore.[5]

The Turkish ships at sea – which Bayazid had taken over with the annexed emirates on the Aegean coast – attempted to enforce the blockade but they could not seal off the city completely. There are records of individual Constantinopolitan merchants sending out ships to buy supplies in parts of the Aegean and getting them back into the city, landing at Pera (i.e. Galata) where the Genoese still operated; from Pera it was always possible to get across the Golden Horn into the city, since the entrance had been blockaded by a boom (which had replaced the old chain). The monasteries of Mount Athos were instructed to supply grain to the city from their lands on the island of Lesbos, and they must have been able to get the shipments through to the city.

Inside the city the advantage lay with the rich, who could afford the inflated prices now being paid for food, or who could send out a ship to buy and import supplies, as did John Goudeles, a member of a noble family in the city, who was already rich and who sold his imports at the maximum price recorded during the siege. The price for housing fell as desperate inhabitants sold their dwellings or businesses for money to buy the expensive food; equally the price of agricultural land inside the wall rose as profits from the food produced there rose. In other words, Constantinople was going through the same processes of immiseration, impoverishment, and the unequal distribution of food and wealth as every other city which was ever laid under siege.

The Emperor Manuel II was persuaded by Marshal Boucicaut that the one recourse left was for him to appeal directly for possible help to the powers in Western Europe. This meant essentially the Pope, the King of France, and the German Emperor, though Manuel also went on to London. To facilitate this Boucicaut arranged a reconciliation between Manuel and John VII.[6] Manuel and Boucicaut sailed away in 1399, leaving John VII in control of the city, but the help gained was very scarce, if there was any at all.[7]

On the other hand, the several threats to Bayazid's territories from outside – such as the wars of 1395 and 1396 on the Danube – had forced him to loosen the blockade during the various emergencies, while Bayazid's impatience with the slow siege led him to go off on other ventures. However, neither Venetian nor Genoese ships were apparently interfered with by the Turkish vessels in their trading voyages, which could clearly be to the advantage of the city. Presumably Bayazid did not wish to make them into active enemies. In the east the threat from Timur, which had faded once, returned in force in 1400.

Timur's statesmanship was minimal. His army was highly efficient in winning victories and conquering cities, and in massacring defeated populations, but his political imagination went no further than victory in the field and the destruction of his enemies; replacing that destruction with something stable seems to have been beyond him. As a statesman, on the other hand, Bayazid had been demonstrating his ability to begin the construction of a viable and long-lasting imperial power; this work had been just beginning, and had been interrupted at times by a certain degree of paranoia on his part, but it was a more useful exercise than anything Timur did. In 1402 the armies of these two men clashed at Ankara, and Bayazid's army was destroyed; the sultan himself was captured (he died next year). But all that Timur could do with his victory was to reinstate the recently conquered Muslim emirates, without further damaging the Ottoman Sultanate. The Ottoman power survived in Europe, and soon returned to resume control of much of Anatolia; the reinstated emirates were too weak to survive for long.[8] Timur's invasion was a temporary thing, which set back the Ottoman Sultanate's progress by a generation. It was not deflected.

For Constantinople the Timurid victory was the city's salvation – but only temporarily, as with the rest of the region. Bayazid withdrew his troops to face Timur, and they did not return; Christian survivors of the battle were helped back across the Bosporos in imperial ships. Bayazid's absence left the sultanate in a state of collapse, and for the next decade and more there was a complex dispute over the succession in the Ottoman state, leaving it unable to conduct any sort of coherent foreign policy.[9]

The Siege of 1411–13

Bayazid left four brothers, and gave no indication of his choice for successor. The only means of deciding the matter was for them to fight each other. This left an opportunity for their enemies to take advantage. John VII secured a treaty at a meeting at Kallipolis with one of Bayazid's sons, Suleiman, who aimed to control the European provinces, and recovered some territories near the city. The Ottoman fighting in Anatolia pitted another son, Mehmet, who was established in northeast Asia Minor at Bursa, against some of Timur's governors, and he extended his control from Bursa along the northern part of Anatolia. Meanwhile his brothers Isa and Musa fought each other elsewhere in Anatolia. In Europe Suleiman established himself in control from Hadrianopolis, but unsteadily; several of the Christian vassal states were less than enthusiastic at their renewed subordination.

Manuel II was in Europe when all this happened. When he got back he learnt that his nephew, John VII, had negotiated a new treaty with Suleiman, by which several areas, in the Morea, along the Propontis coast, along the Black Sea coast, and in Thrace near the city, together with the city of Thessalonica, had been recovered; the tribute which had been paid to Bayazid was cancelled. This was a fairly good outcome for the Empire, even though its recovered lands were scattered and so were very vulnerable to an Ottoman revival. Suleiman, in a subsequent confirmatory treaty with Manuel when he returned, accepted the emperor as his feudal superior.[10] It all suggests that Suleiman felt that he was in a desperate situation, and was buying off potential or actual Byzantine hostility.

This was an unexpected reversal of relationships, but Manuel did not expect it to last, and he juggled his support for the several Ottoman brothers over the next several years. Not long after the treaty with Suleiman, Musa crossed into Europe and challenged Suleiman. In Asia Mehmet gained control, extending his territory throughout Anatolia after Timur's death in 1405. So the Ottoman state was split in two, between the European and Anatolian sections, and Manuel probably hoped that this division would continue, or at least that their mutual fighting might go on, particularly as the Christian population of the Balkans might be rallied into independence by the Byzantine emperor.

The fighting in Europe between Suleiman and Musa lasted until 1411, when Musa was at last victorious.[11] Ominously for Manuel, Musa appealed to the *gazi* element in the Ottoman population, whereas Suleiman had appealed for Christian support, and as Musa's victory implied, he was the less vigorous. At one point he was supported by troops sent to Hadrianopolis by Manuel. When Musa came out victorious, therefore, one of his first acts was to turn on the emperor, and he established a new siege of Constantinople in February 1411. The land in Thrace which Suleiman had allocated to the Empire was burned and looted. Musa placed his army under the city's wall, and much of the land which had been returned to the Empire were retaken.[12] Isolated Thessalonica was attacked.

Manuel had, however, used the respite since Bayazid's death to good purpose. He had built up stocks of food and weapons, repaired the wall (which John VII had tried to do earlier, but had been ordered to stop by Bayazid) and had developed a naval force which was sufficient to take on the Turkish ships, if not those of Venice and Genoa. And he had the great advantage of the city wall. The Turks apparently did not have much in the way of artillery, being a more mobile army, largely of light infantry and fast cavalry. They were certainly able to capture some cities, but not easily, and the wall of Constantinople was an obstacle much greater than anything they faced elsewhere. Musa's army accordingly made no impression, and his ships were driven off by Manuel's new fleet.[13]

Manuel now exercised his diplomatic cunning. He contacted Mehmet in Asia and agreed to transport Mehmet's army across to Europe. So, while Musa was besieging Constantinople, Mehmet attempted to disrupt that siege with his Asian army, or perhaps he aimed to catch the besieging army in its camp. Manuel was thus defending the city with his own forces with some success. It was a variation on the usual Byzantine tactic of calling in a distant ally – Venice, Genoa, Hungary, crusaders, steppe nomads – at times of major stress and emergency; the difference this time being that the relief came from an Ottoman prince. In fact Mehmet had to make three attempts before his army was landed in Europe; he then met and defeated Musa's forces. And with Musa defeated and dead, the siege, which had lasted for two years (1411–13) was lifted. Mehmet, a man of honour, as was Manuel, restored the concessions given by Suleiman in 1403, in a new treaty agreed in 1413.[14] The Empire lived again, having survived yet another period of siege and anxiety.

The Siege of 1422

Sultan Mehmet I died in 1421, and was succeeded by his eldest son, Murad II. In Constantinople there was a dispute over policy towards the new sultan between Emperor Manuel II and his son John VIII. Manuel was old and weary, and suffered from poor health. He had already handed over detailed government work to John, and now he let him take hold of policy towards the Ottoman succession. Once again, there had been several Ottoman heirs, three sons of Mehmet, plus a pretender, Mustafa, who claimed to be another son of Bayazid, and who was in Manuel's custody after a failed coup some years before. He had fled to Thessalonica and had been passed on to Manuel, who agreed with Mehmet to keep him in custody for the rest of his life. The actual power in the Ottoman state went to Murad II; the two younger sons of Mehmet were too young to rule; one of them was soon killed by Murad.

John VIII decided that the pretender Mustafa was a good weapon to be used against Murad. This was probably a mistake, since recognition of Murad would probably have led to a renewal of the 1403 and 1413 treaties, whereas the pretender could not be trusted.[15] Further, Murad was a tough customer, who bore grudges and remembered slights. The pretender was loosed into the Ottoman lands in Europe, and had some success, but Murad quickly returned from Anatolia, and dealt with him. Anger at the role played by the Byzantine emperor in the matter brought him and his army against the city in 1422. So another siege began; for once, a contemporary account by an eyewitness exists, by John Kananos.[16]

Murad began by ordering the digging of a ditch before the wall and the piling up of a rampart. How much of the wall was thus confronted is not certain, but if it was placed before the few gates it seems it would certainly block any sorties from the city. The Ottoman camp was inhabited also by slave dealers, loot merchants, and provision sellers; this is an aspect of sieges which is rarely mentioned in those mounted against Constantinople, but only those which were seriously seen as having a good chance of success were attended by such a civilian camp. And this one was a serious and sustained attempt at conquest. Murad also had firearms amongst his forces. Such weapons had been used by Bayazid in the long siege-blockade in the 1390s, though, like Murad's firearms, they were, for the moment, ineffective when used against the city wall. This was a lesson the Ottomans learned.[17]

Inspired by an Islamic holy man's predictions, a major assault was made on 24 August but, after desperate fighting by both sides, it was thrown back. Murad is said to have brought an army of 10,000 men to the siege – a more-than-usually acceptable figure – but sheer numbers were not what was actually needed. Any assault on any city wall had to be conducted by a relatively small party of soldiers – later referred to as the 'forlorn hope' – and only when that party could get inside, or on top of the wall, and could hold the penetration open long enough for their comrades to reinforce them, would a larger number be needed. The model would be the Fourth Crusade's eventual success against only a short part of the sea wall. But Murad had to attack the land wall, a much greater and more formidable obstacle, since his ships were insufficient for an attack from the sea, and the boom prevented their entry into the Golden Horn.

The relief, as so often, came as a result of cleverness and cunning. Manuel may have been old and weary, and more-or-less retired from active government, but he still retained his diplomatic skills and penchant for intrigues. Murad had eliminated the threat from the pretender Mustafa, and had killed one of his younger brothers, but there was still a second brother, also called Mustafa. Manuel contacted the boy's tutor at Bursa. The boy's name had already been used among Murad's enemies in Anatolia, notably among the surviving vassals and the independent emirs, who felt themselves threatened. Manuel let it be known that he would support Mustafa's claim to the Ottoman throne if he was to make it. This was enough to spark a rebellion in Anatolia, and to distract Murad and his army from Constantinople, so the siege was lifted. This was the second time the Empire had been able to play on the internal family politics of the Sultanate to save the city.[18]

There were two other obvious consequences to this failed siege, apart from the continuing existence of the Byzantine Empire. The child Mustafa suffered the same death as his brother, strangulation at the sultan's command. This had been the means of other sultans ridding themselves of awkward relatives who were felt to be dangerous or ambitious, but from now on it became the custom for each new sultan to inflict that punishment on all his male siblings at the time of his accession – punishment for existing, in other words. This was a dangerous practice, only made possible by the Muslim practice of polygamy, which generally provided a multiple supply of male children, and so providing sultans with a wide choice of possible successors. (The poisonous atmosphere of the harem might cull these possible successors even before the sultan was given a choice.) Normally in a monogamous system the practice of pre-emptive execution would ensure the extinction of the dynasty within only a few generations. As it happened, the Ottoman dynasty had a direct succession from Osman in the thirteenth century to the late nineteenth, despite the killings on each accession; on the few occasions when more than one male heir existed when a sultan died, the result was usually a civil war; so it could be said that the custom was justified. It was enacted as a law by Mehmet the Conqueror, though this law was later discarded; not so the custom.[19]

The second consequence more directly affected the surviving fragments of the Byzantine Empire. Manuel was also involved in negotiating the new treaty which followed. The success against the siege army had not modified Murad's terms, except that the city remained under a Byzantine emperor. Otherwise, the cities and lands gained in the treaties of 1403 and 1413 were lost, and the tribute was reimposed at a much higher figure. Murad was, reasonably enough, clearly vindictive.[20] He then vented his anger at the failure of the siege by campaigning to suppress many of the rest of Manuel's territories, which had not been assigned to him in the 1424 treaty. For the siege of Constantinople had been a very serious attempt to take the city, and its failure clearly angered the sultan. Some earlier sieges had been little more than gestures, blockades mounted with a few token attacks, in the hope that something would give, or a traitor might open a gate. Sometimes, indeed, these sieges worked, though invariably it was in a civil war that attackers were admitted by treason – foreign attackers were not welcomed in that way. The Muslim practice of massacring or enslaving defeated non-Muslims rather discouraged treasonous behaviour by the besieged civilians.

So Murad moved away from the city and aimed to eliminate other parts of the imperial fragments. Thessalonica was one such, and the threat was potent enough for its governor, a son of Manuel II, to sell the city to Venice, on the assumption that it might well be better defended. Murad spent some time suppressing some of the Anatolian emirates, especially those which had supported his brother Mustafa's rebellion, then turned once again to Europe. Thessalonica was besieged, and eventually captured – it had not been as profitable as Venice had expected so no great effort was made to defend it. Having rejected terms of surrender earlier, the population suffered a massacre.[21] The Turkish forces then reduced the remains of the Epeirote despotate to submission, and marched into the Latin and Greek states in the south of Greece, breaking through the Hexamilion, the wall recently built across the Isthmus of Corinth, using cannons to destroy a section of it. So it was penetrated with disappointing ease, and the lesson of gunpowder artillery was learned. The Morea was badly ravaged and some of its imperial territories were annexed; thus in the process of Murad's revenge the Byzantine Empire was effectively reduced to Constantinople, a few nearby places, and a part of the Peloponnese.[22]

The Siege of 1442

One of the long-standing issues in the relationship between the surviving Byzantine Empire and its contemporaries in Western Europe lay in the differing traditions of Christianity they espoused. They disagreed on several points, both doctrinal and procedural, and the supremacy of the Pope in Rome over the whole Church was always a fundamental issue as well. Whenever Constantinople was under threat from the eleventh century onwards, an appeal for military help went to the Pope as the only supra-national authority in the West who could exert moral pressure on its rulers and populations. Through him their fellow Christians in the West might respond. But invariably the reply was essentially with the condition that the two Churches, Catholic and Orthodox, or perhaps more explicitly Roman Catholic and Greek Orthodox, should be 're-united'. This was a situation in which the doctrinal and procedural authority would lie with the Pope. Every time the issue was raised it led to lengthy discussions, as a result of which, to get that military help, the Byzantine emperor in Constantinople agreed to a union, only to be opposed and thwarted by his own Church and his people, to most of whom the idea was abhorrent.

This happened once more in the 1430s. The decisive reduction of Byzantine imperial territory after the siege of 1422 left the city virtually alone in the Empire except for the Morea and a few isolated places elsewhere. When John VIII asked for help, since the likelihood of a new Ottoman attack in the relatively near future was clear, the condition was that he and his chief churchmen should participate in a Council at Florence in Italy to hammer out the conditions for Church union. This process took several years to come to a conclusion, and John and many of his churchmen signed the subsequent agreement.[23] This lasted only until they were back home, and gradually many of the churchmen repudiated their agreement. John VIII stood by his word, however, and the imperial regime dissolved into bitter disputations. Those of the signatories who kept their word tended to stay in, or go to, Italy, where they were honoured and admired, but more for their learning than for anything else. This was one of the essential elements of the developing Italian Renaissance, since the Greek learning of these religious refugees was valued above all else.

At Constantinople John VIII's attempt to promote the union generally failed, though the Pope was slowly organizing a new crusade, taking his time because he was waiting to see how the union project was received and implemented in the Empire. One of the commanders for the crusaders, John Hunyadi of Transylvania, was proving to be adept at defeating Ottoman detachments, but before the crusade could be mobilized (and it did not arrive until 1444, then to be defeated at Varna on the Bulgarian coast by Murad II), the continuing Byzantine religious crisis broke into internal violence.

John VIII had several brothers, who were employed as governors of detached parts of his empire. In the Morea, for example, Theodore was the governor of that province (using the town of Mistra above Sparta as the capital of his province[24]), with a second brother, Constantine, to assist; Constantine had married the Lady Maddalena Tocco of the family which ruled at Arta in the despotate; she died after only a few months of marriage, but Constantine had accepted a dowry, which he used to expand his control over the rest of the Morea not already ruled by Theodore – that is, the areas still under Latin lords, until Constantine cleared them out; the Peloponnese was thus built into a substantial Byzantine province. Constantine was proving himself to be the most capable of the several brothers.[25]

Another brother, Demetrios, had been made governor of Mesambria on the Black Sea coast. He was a restless, ambitious man, and the internal religious dispute in the Empire appealed to him as a means of gratifying his own ambitions, which were to become emperor. He contacted Sultan Murad, who was increasingly concerned at the possibility of a coalition between the Empire, the men in the Morea, the surviving fragments of the despotate, and the approaching crusaders; the majority of the population of the European provinces were Christian, and a Christian victory might produce a collapse of the Ottoman regime. Demetrios had attended the Council of Florence, but had left before the end, and had not signed the resulting document. As the agreement unravelled when the participants returned to Greece, Demetrios and Murad saw their chance. Demetrios collected a contingent of Turkish troops from Murad and laid siege to Constantinople (summer 1442).[26]

John and the city were almost disarmed. The Emperor had a garrison of mercenaries in the city, but could not necessarily rely on support from the citizens in view of their disagreement over Church Union, and the fact that Demetrios was proclaiming himself the leader of the rejectionist party. And yet the prospect of a Turkish occupation, which would automatically mean Murad displacing John in the city, and the extinction of the Byzantine Empire, was sufficient to prevent any gate-opening by traitors. The Emperor's brother Constantine was summoned from the Morea with his own soldiers. The Turks were also perhaps not too keen on mounting any vigorous assaults on behalf of Demetrios, while Murad himself was not interested in anything for the moment other than continuing the Byzantine divisions; if they continued the Byzantines were powerless, if either side won he could impose a new subordination on the winner. Constantine's arrival brought victory for John, and Demetrios was captured.

The siege presumably took some time, perhaps a month, since Constantine had to be summoned, collect his forces, and sail across the Aegean with them. The end was a reconciliation amongst the brothers. Constantine's assistance had emphasized his worth and John was clearly now considering him as his heir to the Empire; this did not please Theodore, but he died the next year. Demetrios was forgiven, but transferred to rule at Selymbria, close to Constantinople, where he could be more carefully watched.[27]

For half a century it had been clear that one of the major objectives of the Ottoman Sultanate was to gain control of Constantinople, which they would attempt given any excuse. Three successive sultans had made violent attempts to capture the city, only to be distracted by crises elsewhere in their empire. But persistence will pay; the sultans' repeated attempts would surely succeed in the end. After all, the contest was between an empire which stretched from the Danube to the Taurus, and a single city.

Chapter 22

Success for the Ottoman Turks

The Great Siege, 1453

Sultan Murad II was one of the main founders of the Ottoman Empire, along with his grandfather Bayazid I and his son Mehmet II. He took up the work of Bayazid in eliminating several vassal states in Anatolia and the Balkans and thereby he instituted a well-organized administration. He established the Ottoman variation of the Muslim institution of a slave army by extending the *devshirme* system of taking a selection of Christian male children to train as Muslim janissaries, and doing it so well that even those who retained a connection with their birth families became fanatical Muslims;[1] the Mamluks in Egypt and Syria had a similar system, but this involved buying children from outside their kingdom and importing them; the Caucasus and Africa were the main sources. While they lasted both systems provided the two states with powerful, well-trained armies, though in neither case were they always as obedient to their sultans as the latter might have expected when dealing with slaves.

The Ottoman system was well in place by 1444 when Murad attempted to retire, handing power to his son Mehmet II. In fact, he tried twice to retire but had to return each time when Mehmet got into political trouble. The first time Mehmet was only twelve years old. Eventually Mehmet was exiled for two years to Manisa in Anatolia, where he had his own court, and meanwhile Murad had to deal with the Crusade of Varna in 1444, and a simultaneous offensive by the Despot Constantine out of the Morea. So when Murad finally died in 1451, Mehmet was nineteen years old, and had already had two brief periods of power. Clearly, in his semi-exile, he had thought out what he wanted and intended to do.[2]

His first priority was to rearrange the personnel at the head of his government, the second was to reassure all his neighbours, and the third was to capture Constantinople. In fact, in his own mind this last was his main priority, and the others were the necessary preparation for that.

There had also been changes in Constantinople. The Emperor John VIII died in 1448. There was a brief struggle over who was to succeed him. Three of his sons were still alive, and all three aimed to gain the throne. First on the scene was Demetrios, who came up from Selymbria, and claimed the throne; Thomas arrived soon after; he had spent his life working with, and subordinate to, Constantine. Constantine himself was in the Morea.

It was, however, not a potential emperor's presence in the city which was decisive, but the authority of the Dowager Empress Helena, the widow of the Emperor Manuel II, who had died back in 1425; Demetrios clearly did not have the necessary determination to ignore or defy her. She knew what John's intentions had been and insisted on proclaiming Constantine as the new emperor, and she was given vocal support by much of the population of the city. Demetrios, more-or-less alone in his ambition, had not enough strength to defy her and her supporters, nor the gall to turn to force. When Constantine arrived in the city two months later, in January 1449, he was fully accepted.[3]

Constantine had been crowned at Mistra before he left for Constantinople. The crowning ceremony was conducted by the local metropolitan, and the new emperor did not repeat it when he got to Constantinople, where it would normally be performed at Hagia Sofia by the patriarch. The patriarch, however, was politically isolated from the rest of the clergy over the dispute about Church Union. John had accepted this and Constantine's decision to be crowned in Mistra was a neat way of evading the issue in the great city. He followed his father's policy and accepted the union, but when appointing his ministers he chose men who were from both sides of the argument, but who were not fanatical about it. He collected a loyal set as a result.[4]

His brothers were dealt with in the same way, but less successfully. Their earlier disputes had not been personal, and none of the three were at all fanatical about the religious problem, though Demetrios had tried to use it in his attempted coup in 1442. It was only too obvious that at some point, fairly soon, Sultan Mehmet would attack the city – every sultan for the last half-century had done so, and it had become a test each one of them had so far failed. By 1449 Murad was old and his erratic attempts to retire had made everyone nervous, but he would probably not launch an attack. The equally erratic behaviour of his son and heir were similarly disturbing, but he probably would attack the city. It behoved the royal family in the Byzantine Empire therefore to cleave together, in the hope of lasting in power a little longer. The two unsuccessful brothers were therefore each given responsibilities in the Peloponnese, as joint despots, Demetrios ruling the southeast from Mistra, and Thomas the northwest from Glarenza. Their harmony did not actually last longer than a few months; Constantine had to attempt to patch up their disputes. This is exactly what it had been hoped to avoid by sending them to the Morea, and by the preference for Constantine.[5]

When Mehmet became sultan, in 1451, two years after Constantine's arrival in Constantinople, he surprised many observers by his calm and sensible arrangements. He broke up the governing team which had worked well under his father, but only to redistribute the men to other, equally important, responsibilities; he retained his vizier Halil, even though they did not agree over the attack in Constantinople.[6] Apart from Constantinople, his other neighbours were quite reasonably somewhat anxious about what the new sultan would do to establish his authority, and having done so, what he would do to extend it. They were fully aware of Mehmet's earlier erratic behaviour as an adolescent, and sent embassies with the usual congratulations and presents. But he was gracious to them all, which disarmed just about every neighbour. Venice was pleased to have the peace treaty it had made with Murad renewed; John Hunyadi of Transylvania was granted a new three-year truce; Ragusa's offer of an increased annual tribute was welcomed; the Serbian ruler was allocated some towns, and his daughter, the widow of Murad, was returned to him with rich presents; embassies from the Knights Hospitaller of Rhodes, the Genoese merchant oligarchy of Chios, and the ruler of Wallachia, were all greeted pleasantly. And so was the embassy of the Emperor Constantine, who was more aware of the probability of threats from Mehmet than anyone, and was pleasantly surprised at the graciousness of the sultan's greeting. There was an Ottoman prince, Orhan, living in Constantinople as a refugee-hostage, and an increased allowance was granted to Constantine so that he would keep Orhan in the city.[7]

This unusual and unexpected diplomacy by the sultan charmed and disarmed his visitors, and their home governments sighed with relief. It was, of course, only sincere for the moment, and anyone experienced in diplomacy will have quickly understood the purpose of Mehmet's actions when taken in total. He was rearranging his government for greater effectiveness, and he was gaining time in international affairs to organize his aggressive priorities. By reviving and extending peace treaties and acting peacefully towards all his neighbours, he was doing just that. The priority he had set himself was, of course, the conquest of Constantinople, and he soon developed a set of actions which made that clear to all.

Mehmet campaigned in Anatolia late in 1451, where the emir of Karaman had been arranging a rebellion, but subsided quickly when Mehmet arrived nearby with his army. Mehmet then had trouble with his army on the return march, when some of the janissaries demanded a pay rise. In reply Mehmet diluted the rebellious regiments with other, more loyal, troops, and replaced their commander, who had been Halil's appointment. Had anyone still harboured delusions that Mehmet was lazy and easy-going, this will have resolved their doubts.[8]

This no doubt all seemed fairly normal to outsiders, the sort of problems that any sultan would face at the time of his accession, but the Karamanid emir was in fact crushed, and the army's condition rapidly improved, two major problems solved in a few weeks. Combined with his other measures, Mehmet was in fact showing steeliness, determination, and military and political capability and ambition; he had control of the empire from the start, rather more quickly perhaps than earlier sultans. And his return march also saw the beginning of his campaign against Constantinople.

In his journeys from Asia into Europe, and in the other direction, he had usually crossed at Gallipoli. Travelling from Manisa to Hadrianopolis on his accession, as he did when taking up the sultanate, the Gallipoli crossing was the quickest way. For his return from Karaman to Hadrianopolis, on the other hand, he heard that an Italian squadron was patrolling the Dardanelles, while at the same time the shortest journey would be to cross the Bosporos, and that was the way he took his army on its return. (The Great King Dareios had faced the same choice 2,000 years before, and the Romans had developed their road system for this very problem.) The Sultan Bayazid had built a castle on the Asian side, called Anadolu Hissar, which overlooked the crossing point. The traditional waiting place for ships, called Hieron in the ancient period, a comfortable bay where the ships could wait for a change in the wind, was just to the north.

It was also the place where Byzantion and Athens and others had placed their customs posts.

Bayazid had placed Anadolu Hissar just south of this bay, where it could overlook the anchorage. It had been one of Bayazid's forts for his siege-blockade of Constantinople during the siege of 1394, placed precisely at the narrowest point of the strait. Mehmet's army crossed at this place, with Mehmet probably staying in the castle. Whether it was the original purpose of the castle, which dominated that part of the Bosporos or perhaps his eye for a strategic position, Mehmet decided that there should be a companion castle built on the opposing side of the strait. Or it may be that he knew that this would annoy the emperor in Constantinople.

The chosen site was a rocky point, equivalent to Anadolu Hissar on the other side. At the end of 1451 he sent out a call for artificers and masons and unskilled labourers to gather and to build. He sent in his surveyors, a plan was made, and in the spring of 1452 building began. Local churches and monasteries were demolished to clear the site, and the stone so acquired was used in the construction of the castle. In four months the castle had been built.[9]

This was land which was technically part of the territory of Constantinople. It could not be clearer what Mehmet now intended. One of the fights during Bayazid's siege had been the capture of the fort at Riva, which Bayazid had built as one of his blockading forts, and which was not far from the site of the new castle. A series of complaints came from the city during the building, culminating in an embassy asking for an assurance that the new castle did not presage an attack on the city. This was the third or fourth set of envoys which had come from the city during the building, one of which had demanded an increase in the sultan's allowance for holding Orhan, with a muted threat to release him. At this Mehmet had had enough. The last set of envoys were imprisoned and later executed.[10] If anyone in Constantinople had not yet understood what was happening, the murder of the ambassadors made it clear; it was an action which throughout Europe was tantamount to a declaration of war. As if to make certain that his intentions were clear, Mehmet brought his army right up to the city wall and camped there for three days, spending the time leisurely inspecting the defences.

A siege being now certain in the near future, both rulers began detailed preparations. Of course, the building of Rumeli Hissar – the name of the new castle – was in effect part of Mehmet's preparations; Constantine organized the repair of the city walls, and saw to the clearing out of the moat. Within the city arms were collected, more were manufactured and bought, and they were placed where they could be accessed by the fighters. Outside the city a new diplomatic effort was made to recruit foreign assistance. Appeals went to Venice and Genoa, to the Pope, and to the king of Aragon. None of these felt able to put their own home concerns aside to help the exiguous remains of the Byzantine Empire, yet again.[11]

These were the Latin powers; the Orthodox potentates of Eastern Europe were even less forthcoming, and no help at all came from Russia, Serbia, Wallachia, Trebizond, and others; indeed both Serbia and Wallachia, Ottoman vassals, sent troops to reinforce the sultan's army.[12] It was left to foreigners in the city and soldierly volunteers from outside to offer their help. There was a considerable Venetian colony in the city, and most of the men remained in the city and fought for it; a force of 700 Genoese soldiers commanded by Giovanni Giustiniani Longo, an accomplished Genoese commander, arrived and was a welcome reinforcement.[13]

The use the Turks made of the new castle helped Venice to move from neutrality to active assistance to the city. Three great cannons were installed in the new castle near water level, and it was proclaimed that any ships sailing through the Bosporos must stop and be inspected, otherwise they would be sunk. Probably the sailors who heard of this regarded it mainly as bluff, and certainly the first two Venetian ships which passed the castle got through without damage, despite being fired on. But the third, a fortnight later, was hit, its crew were taken prisoner and executed. This, especially the execution of the sailors, swung Venetian opinion round into offering help to the city, and confirmed the decision of the Venetians there to fight in the city's defence. And yet Venice itself, despite the resolution to render assistance, found it difficult to escape its current commitments and conflicts in Italy, and anything Venice could do would not seriously assist Constantinople given the new circumstances.[14]

The Ottoman navy had been developed from ships originally belonging to the defunct seagoing emirates of Anatolia, particularly of Aydin and Mentese (the former Ionia and Karia in the southwest of Asia Minor). They had been conquered by Bayazid, revived briefly by Timur, and then conquered again by Murad. Bayazid had concentrated his naval power at Gelibolu (Kallipolis, Gallipoli) on the Dardanelles (Hellespont), where there was a fleet of forty warships by 1403 based in a naval dockyard; its aim was obviously to control the passage of the Dardanelles, just as Rumeli Hissar and Anadolu Hissar controlled the passage of the Bosporos.[15] A group of Burgundian ships heading for Constantinople and the Black Sea to assist in the crusade of Varna in 1444 were bombarded with some effect by the guns of these Ottoman vessels. So it should have been no surprise when a fully equipped Ottoman fleet of up to 200 ships came in from western Asia Minor and Gelibolu in 1452 to establish a clear Ottoman domination of the Sea of Marmara (the Propontis), together with its attendant straits.[16] Between them Venice and the Pope sent a score of warships and some merchant vessels with supplies, but in the face of the suddenly developed and deployed Ottoman strength at sea, this would not be effective.[17] The Ottoman fleet quickly established a blockade of the city.

Both sides had firearms, and cannons were crucial to the success of the siege. The main Ottoman gun foundry was at Hadrianopolis (which the Turks called Edirne) and this had supplied the big guns used at Rumeli Hissar, and presumably those at Gelibolu and on the ships. There had been an active recruitment of foreign experts, gunsmiths, gunfounders, bronzesmiths, and artillery theoreticians. Several of these were volunteers and others were discovered by seeking out prisoners with the relevant skills. These men were all well rewarded for their work. The most famous of these European gunsmiths in Ottoman employ was Master Orban, presumably a German, but certainly from Hungary (where there was a large German colony). He had first offered his services to the emperor, but Constantine could not afford his price; he went on to Mehmet, who by contrast offered him four times his asking price. He appears to have been responsible for casting the main cannons that were used in the siege, including the great monster gun which broke the wall.[18] The emperor's men also had a supply of guns, though none were comparable with the giants made in the Edirne foundry, but then they were not faced with having to blast a way through the great Theodosian Wall.

All the preparations came together in the early months of 1453. The sultan, after spending some time considering his options, finally ordered the attack to get under way in January. He persuaded his court that this was his will, and that it was both possible and necessary that Constantinople be captured. He pointed out that previous sieges had failed because the emperors had been able to call in help, but now this was no longer possible; assaults on the walls had failed because the wall was so strong and so well defended, but now he had a much stronger army, cannons, and an effective navy; the city, open to the sea, had been able to bring in supplies and so evade starvation, and this could be prevented by that same navy which formed the blockade. And yet it was clear to all the court that if Mehmet began the siege and failed, he would have wasted large resources, and both he and his sultanate would be humiliated. Some in the court, including Halil, felt that leaving the city independent but essentially powerless would be perfectly acceptable. This was to ignore the psychological effect of the capture of the city – this was a city only taken by treachery in the past, or by its Christian enemies using betrayal from within. It had been a desired Muslim target since the time of the Prophet Muhammad.

If Mehmet failed in his attack, his enemies would be greatly encouraged, and it might be that his empire would collapse in a welter of rebellions and invasions – it was, after all, surrounded by enemies, and potential enemies, and had a European population consisting mainly of Christians only recently conquered, and the Muslim emirates in Asia were even more recently deprived of their local independence. The courtiers and the officials accepted, in some cases reluctantly and with many misgivings, that the siege should go ahead. Mehmet must have known that he was wagering his own life in ordering the attack. He would be the ultimate victim – perhaps the immediate victim – in the event of failure.[19]

In January, when the court had been persuaded, and the decision had been reached to launch the attack, Mehmet, amongst all the other preparations needed, sent an advanced force under Dayi Karadja Bey, the governor of Rumeli (the European provinces), to take over the several towns and cities still under imperial control along the coasts to either side of Constantinople. There were three of these on the Black Sea coast, Mesambria, Anchialos, and Byzos, all of which surrendered at once. On the Propontis coast Selymbria and Perinthos (Herakleia) resisted; they were taken and sacked and their walls destroyed. Control of these places would have given the Emperor, if he had retained them, the opportunity for an unanticipated attack by a landing force in the rear of the besieging force; that possibility had now been removed, unless he could use his ships for that purpose.[20]

So the Ottoman fleet was brought up into the Sea of Marmara (Propontis), the army was assembled, and the satellite towns on the coasts were taken. The great guns, including Master Orban's monster, were trundled along especially straightened and levelled roads from Edirne, and over specially strengthened bridges. The janissaries, 12,000 strong, formed the core of the army, the Christian vassals sent their contributions, the available forces in the European provinces (Rumeli) and the Anatolian lands (Anadolu) were mustered, and a flock of irregular soldiers – *bashibazouks* – were added. The total Turkish force was perhaps 80,000 regular troops and perhaps 20,000 irregulars, all assisted by several thousands of camp followers, to cook and clean and otherwise service the soldiers. In effect, the whole empire was being mobilized for the task of capturing a single city.

And, of course, there were the cannoneers. Orban's masterpiece was a little over 26 feet long, the barrel was made of bronze 8 inches thick; it fired stone balls weighing 12 hundredweight. It was carried in a specially built cart, pulled by 60 oxen (and so will have travelled at no more than 2 miles an hour), and was attended by an escort of 200 men, plus the cannoneers. The journey from Edirne to Constantinople for this gun took about a month. And meanwhile the army was gathering from all over the empire.[21]

The Ottoman frontiers had to be guarded as well. The possibility of Demetrios and Thomas invading Greece from the Morea was prevented by an army at the Isthmus of Corinth under a senior general, Taruhan Bey,[22] who sent raids south into the Peloponnese. (This was a larger version of the expedition to take the coastal towns beside Constantinople.) The Danube frontier and the Taurus frontiers were watched and guarded. The numerous Venetian coastal forts and territories were strung all around the European provinces from Dalmatia to the Aegean (including Crete and Negroponte) and were largely inhabited by Orthodox Christians under Venetian governors, and they might be considered sympathetic to the Empire, so had to be watched. This was especially so once it became clear that Venice had shifted from neutrality to hostility. It will also have become clear, once it was seen that the sultan was in deadly earnest, and that his forces included a much more formidable naval power than the earlier Turkish sultans – an obvious threat to others – that his European enemies in particular could well intervene if they could muster and cooperate, and if he gave them time; an attack from his Muslim enemies was not to be ruled out either, given the heavy concentration of Mehmet's forces against the city. It was clearly urgent to take the city relatively quickly, before external forces could be brought into play; Constantinople was as much a Christian talisman as a Muslim target.

It is not known if the Ottomans had studied the previous sieges to see what went wrong in their earlier attacks. There must have been men in the army who had taken part in the siege of 1442, and there were surely old men who remembered the siege of 1422. Depending on the state of record-keeping in the Ottoman chancellery there could well have been accounts available of Bayazid's long blockade in the 1390s, and the attack by Musa in 1411–13. But the most important attack to study would be that of the Fourth Crusaders two and a half centuries before, because it had, eventually, been successful. On the other hand, to a commander's eye, the best method of conquest was all too obvious – a sea blockade, combined with a land assault. Easier conceived than enacted, of course, and Mehmet did not actually use the same method as the crusaders. What was different, in 1453, from all the earlier sieges, was Master Orban's guns.

In Constantinople the emperor, perhaps rather late in the day, and maybe assuming that what he saw in the city was less than he hoped, commissioned his secretary George Phrantzes to do a count of the men in the city capable of fighting and of bearing arms. Counting monks and foreigners, both of whom would be expected to fight, the total came to less than 7,000 men. Constantine charged his secretary to keep the number secret, though it was obvious to anyone that the defenders were hugely outnumbered. Estimates in the city of the number of Mehmet's army were anything up to double the actual total, making the comparison even worse.[23]

Mehmet left it to his commanders to march the army and bring the navy into position at the city, and arrived on 5 April to institute the siege officially. As usual, however, it had in fact been going on in a preliminary way for several months, in effect since the building of Rumeli Hissar. But now at last the assault could begin.[24]

The fleet was stationed on the Bosporos to the north of Pera, so that it could use the current and the prevailing north wind to reach the city, when necessary. It faced a difficult task. The sea walls were quite good enough to deter any assault, the currents and the reefs prevented easy access to them, and the boom across the entrance to the Golden Horn, made of large logs joined by tough cables, was strong. It could be defended by the ships which were stationed in the Golden Horn, a mixture of Imperial, Venetian, Genoese, and other ships. The Genoese garrison in Pera stood neutral, even though there were Genoese ships and soldiers defending the city, and the sympathy of the Genoese was clearly with the defenders.

On land the Ottoman army was stationed all around the walls, a force on the Pera side under Zaganos Pasha able to communicate with the main force by a pontoon bridge laid across the Golden Horn. Karadja Pasha, fresh from his conquests along the coast, had command of the European troops facing the northern end of the wall and the Blakhernai Palace. The janissaries were next, under the sultan himself, in the Lykos Valley, where it was thought the wall was most vulnerable. South of that valley, where the land sloped gradually down to the Marmara shore, was Ishak Pasha and the Anatolian troops.[25]

They all faced a mixture of Genoese, Venetian, and imperial troops, and volunteers, Greek and foreign, all manning the wall. Small detachments were also placed around the sea walls, which, because of the difficult currents, and the boom across to Galata, were less likely to be attacked. A group of Greek monks, Prince Orhan and some renegade Turks stood guard at the small harbours on the Marmara side; a group of Catalans was below the acropolis, and Cardinal Isidore, a Russian prelate who had accepted Church Union, was on the top; sailors from Venice and Genoa manned the walls on the Golden Horn side. Given the shortage of manpower in the city these detachments were all small; the main forces were, of course on the main wall.

The forces on both sides were thus an international mixture, and their commanders were often renegades. The commander of the fleet, Suleiman Baltoglu, was a Bulgarian convert to Islam; several of the Venetian commanders were from the elite of that city's merchant families – Contarini, Venier, Dandolo – and the same was the case with the Genoese, of whom the greatest asset to the defence was Giovanni Giustiniani Longo, a highly active and inspiring commander. Among the imperial commanders were two Palaiologoi relatives of the emperor, and a Kantakouzenos. This heterogeneous mixture could have been a weakness, but the emperor distributed them in small units where they would need to support each other.

When Mehmet sent in the ritual demand for surrender on 5 April, there was no response at all. The preliminary bombardment began, therefore, on 6 April. It was directed at the wall near the Charisian Gate, which was the road to Hadrianopolis, and caused some damage, but this was repaired in the night. The biggest guns had not yet arrived, so a few further preliminaries occupied the time – the fosse in front of the wall was partly filled by pioneers, indicating where the assault would be made, and a ditch-and-rampart was built to protect the Turkish camp. Two isolated strong points in front of the wall were captured; the survivors of the garrisons were publicly killed by impalement where the defenders could see them and hear their screams. The fleet attacked the Princes' Islands; there was some resistance which forced an attack to be made on a fort, and again the survivors of the garrison were killed; the civilian population of the biggest island was enslaved for allowing this resistance to take place on their island. The logic was terror, of course, not justice, or even revenge. There is no indication that these deliberate atrocities had any effect on the defenders.

The great guns were in position by 11 April, and in the next week the outer wall was largely destroyed on the Lykos Valley section, where the janissaries were stationed. A stockade of earth and wood was quickly built in its place, and some repairs to the main wall were made. A Turkish fleet attack on the boom failed, in part because the Venetians and Genoese defenders were better equipped with armour than the Turkish sailors. On 18 April the janissaries assaulted the damaged wall in the Lykos Valley, but failed, largely again because the defenders had better personal armour than the attackers.

These early attacks had all failed, and worse (from the Turkish point of view) then happened. Three Genoese galleys sent by the Pope took advantage of a rare south wind to pass through the Dardanelles, and they escorted an imperial ship carrying supplies towards the city. They were met by most of the Turkish fleet. The two forces collided close to the city, the fight being watched by many Constantinopolitans from the acropolis, and by the sultan from Galata. The four ships were stronger, higher, bigger, and the Genoese were the better armed. On the Turkish side large numbers of ships, mainly smaller and less well armed, came down the Bosporos to the attack, but only a few could mount an attack at any one time, and they were rarely able to close effectively. The four Christian ships lashed themselves together for mutual support and fought off all the attacks. In the end it was the wind which decided matters, when a north wind drove the Christian ships directly through the Turkish fleet, and after dark the boom was opened to let them in. The Turkish ships had already been withdrawn to their anchorage further up the Bosporos.[26]

Baltoghlu, who had been in command, was dismissed with ignominy by the sultan, who had been watching all the time and shouting orders which were disregarded – he had no knowledge of seamanship and his advice was valueless. It was another Turkish defeat, and he was enraged. But he was also forced to reconsider his tactics, and showed his quality by doing so. Perhaps because Mehmet had been in Galata to watch the sea fight, he took note of where the fleet was anchored and where a road had been constructed from there to the army camp of Zaganos Pasha on the top of the hill; also that another road was being constructed from there down to the other side. The new plan was to move half of the Turkish ships by land over Galata and relaunch them into the Golden Horn behind the boom. He may have got the idea from an Italian in his army, but he it was who put it into practice.

Some preparations had already been made, but the sultan's decision pushed matters rapidly forward. On 22 April the transport of the ships began. Each one was put on a wheeled cradle, which had been pushed into the water, collected a ship, then was hauled onto dry land and the road by a team of oxen, and escorted and helped by a line of men along the passage. By the end of the day seventy ships had been launched into the Golden Horn. Surprise had been complete, despite, or perhaps because of the whole affair being accompanied by a loud, never-ending concert of drums and trumpets.

The Christians thought of several replies they could make, and the emperor held conferences about it, but the plan which was implemented was that of Giacomo Coco, a captain from Trebizond. He proposed to attack by night and attempt to burn the Turkish ships, which were close together at the landing point. This was a Venetian plan, and was kept secret – but then it was delayed for a day, the Genoese heard about it and made a fuss about being excluded, so this caused yet more delay. The Turks then learned of the plan, probably from the Genoese in Pera, who were in communication with both sides. The Turks brought up more guns to the landing place. When the attack went in, therefore, it was met by heavy fire, and so failed. In the morning there was a grisly display of competitive execution; on both sides the men who had escaped from the fight to scramble ashore onto enemy land were executed – forty by the Turks, 260 by the Christians.[27]

The siege settled down to a continuous Muslim bombardment by the great guns, with Christian repairs being made to the damage caused, while the close blockade meant that the supplies in the city steadily decreased; this was one result of beginning the assault in the spring, since the gardens and the city were not producing much yet. A committee was set up to buy up all available supplies of food and to distribute them evenly. By early May the possibility of being forced to surrender by starvation existed and this threat could only get worse. Morale in the city slumped in the aftermath of the defeat in the harbour and the arrival of the Turkish fleet in the Golden Horn, and as a result there emerged quarrels and disputes, between Genoese and Venetians, between adherents to the Church Union and those opposed; it was proposed that the emperor should leave the city to seek assistance in the West, as had been done by John VIII and Manuel II in past sieges; a brief exchange of messages between emperor and sultan produced no change in the terms demanded; it is said that the emperor agreed to surrender everything except Constantinople; it is doubtful if the sultan was amused.

The Ottomans launched occasional assaults, none of which succeeded. The bombardment brought down one of the large towers, but the gap in the wall was plugged during the night. Miners attempted to undermine the walls, but were stopped by counter-mining which brought down the roofs of the mines. A great tower was brought up to shelter men who were filling in the fosse, which had proved to be a major obstacle in the assaults; in the night the defenders came out and blew up the tower with barrels of gunpowder. In one counter-mine a senior Turkish officer was captured and tortured to reveal where the other mines were; systematically they were all destroyed.[28]

Right at the start there had been hopes that Venice would send a relief fleet – the execution of the Venetian sailors had hardened the city's attitude. But the preparations moved at a glacial pace, and the fleet of galleys which was eventually organized moved slowly, and was burdened by a set of instructions which seemed to be designed to slow its progress even further. The emperor sent out a ship (with the men disguised as Turks) to find the Venetian fleet and hurry it along, but there was no sign of it. The ship returned with the bad news on 23 May. The implication was that the city was quite on its own. The city had by that time been under siege for seven weeks; no help was coming, the city faced starvation; the enemy's numbers never seemed to grow less.

It was obvious in the city that a new assault would soon come. The slow siege, lack of support, the loss of control of the Golden Horn, were all demoralizing, and the people in the city were tired and hungry. In the Turkish camp the sultan made arrangements for a new attack – the ships in the Bosporos were to move round to menace the sea wall along the Marmara coast, those in the Golden Horn to do the same against the wall along the north side; neither was expected to break in, but their menaces would preoccupy some of the defenders.

On land Zaganos Pasha in Galata was to send some of his men to reinforce the sailors on the ships in the Golden Horn, and the rest were to cross at the pontoon bridge and reinforce the army at the wall, preparing to attack the Blakhernai Palace section. Ishak Pasha would attack along the southern part of the wall, concentrating at the Third Military Gate, halfway between the Lykos Valley and the Marmara coast, and at the middle part of that section. But the main assault would be an attack in the Lykos Valley, and here the greater part of the Turkish forces were concentrated, the big guns, the janissaries, the *bashi-bazouks*, and other infantry forces, arrayed so that they were to attack in series, giving the defence no rest.

The assault was fixed for Tuesday, 29 May. The previous day the sultan had ridden through the camp, raising morale, exhorting his men, promising them the usual three days in which to sack the city; in the city the emperor did much the same, encouraging the defenders, checking on the distribution of his forces, and on the day before the assault he joined the whole population for a service of intercession in Hagia Sofia, Greeks and Italians, pro- and anti-unionists, Catholic cardinals and Orthodox bishops, all together. The preparations on the Turkish side included filling the fosse, bringing forward the guns, and a day of rest and quiet and prayer.

The attack began at 1.30 am on Tuesday. The filling of the fosse had been completed at the point of assault. The *bashi-bazouks* went in first. These were a motley collection of men of a dozen nationalities, many of them Christians, armed with whatever weapons they had been able to find or buy or steal, undisciplined and inefficient. The purpose of their attack was to wear down the defence, but no one expected these ragged troops to succeed. For two hours, in the dark, they repeated their assaults, either voluntarily, or driven to it by Mehmet's police armed with whips, lined up behind them to prevent desertions and to force them forward. At last they were withdrawn, having failed as expected, and Ishak Pasha's Anatolian soldiers came from the south to launch a new attack. This went on until dawn; when an attack paused, or was in the process of reorganization, the guns fired. The final assault went in about dawn, after the guns had broken a long section of the stockade, but it also failed. The Anatolians, like the *bashi-bazouks*, were pulled out.

Mehmet's last force were his janissaries, the best of his troops. Two great assaults had already failed; all the distractions along the sea walls had got nowhere; the attacks at the Blakhernai front and the Third Military Gate, as serious as those in the centre, had also failed to make any impression. The janissaries were Mehmed's last chance; if they failed, he would need to accept defeat; and there were plenty of men in high places who would turn on him in that event. Even a couple of days earlier Halil had stood in the council and argued that the siege should be abandoned. And this last attack made no progress at first.

Two almost simultaneous incidents turned the battle. At the Blakhernai front, a postern, called Kerkoporta, which was used by the defence to send out sorties to raid the Turks and disrupt their attacks, was left unfastened after one of those raids, and a small force of Turks seized it and got inside. On the Lykos Valley front, the Genoese commander, Giustiniani, was severely wounded and was carried off through another gate. When they saw this, the Genoese he had been commanding began to falter and some of them followed him through the gate. The sultan, who was on the spot (as was the emperor), saw the opportunity and sent the janissaries forward yet again. He picked out a giant soldier, Hasan, to lead the attack, followed by thirty janissaries, and they got through the stockade. Most of them were killed, including Hasan, but more soldiers followed them, and having reached the main wall, were able to use their ladders to reach the top. At the Kerkoporta postern the Turkish flag was raised, indicating that part of the wall had been taken. The two penetrations finally broke the defenders' resistance, and provided the Turks with the first sense of triumph. The emperor tried to lead a counterattack; he was swallowed up in the Turkish rush and was killed. His empire died with him; the city was conquered.[29]

As the word spread to both armies, the sultan systematically moved his regiments into the city, where they first took control of the wall, and opened the other gates. On the Christian side the foreigners fled to the ships in the Golden Horn, while the citizens headed for home to safeguard their families and possessions. At the sea walls, the resistance collapsed, and the sailors on both the Golden Horn and Marmara sides got into the city.

A number of ships, Venetian, Genoese, imperial, and others, perhaps twenty in all, escaped out of the Golden Horn, cutting their way through the boom. They collected as many refugees as could reach them, then took advantage of a north wind and sailed away, back to the West, spreading the news of the disaster. Other ships were trapped in the harbour and captured along with those who had taken refuge on them. The city was sacked. Murder and theft were the next activities, and the sultan saw to the execution of some of the more prominent prisoners – many senior Italians were killed, others would be redeemed at a price; a number of captured imperial officials were captured, then released, but then soon afterwards also executed.

Three weeks after the conquest, Mehmet left the city, much of it burnt and in ruins. He lamented the destruction, but in this he was hardly sincere. He had done what every Muslim soldier in the past thousand years had dreamed of doing. He was hardly saddened.

Interlude V

Islamization of the City

The city was badly damaged in the conquest, as would be expected, and Mehmet might lament the ruins he saw, but the effect of the Ottoman invasion was a good deal less serious than that of the crusaders of the Fourth Crusade. The Christians are thus rather better at destruction, if not so effective at massacres and enslavement. One reason for this was the better discipline of the Ottoman army – and that Mehmet halted the looting after only one day; he had made it clear beforehand that the buildings in the city were not for destroying, since in a conquered city they would belong to him. The other reason was that the city was already in a bad state before the conquest, buildings in some areas ruinous, and its population much reduced. The looters certainly found plenty to steal, but the fact that the looting lasted only a single day (at least officially) suggests that there was much less material of value available for them to steal. They were not interested in acquiring Christian relics, one of the main causes of damage in the 1204 sack, nor, if the Muslims were in any way devout, did they indulge in drinking themselves into a rage or into oblivion; however, many of the soldiers were Christians, and would have had fewer inhibitions.

The city therefore proved to be less wealthy than expected. Most of the loot was acquired from the churches, where plate in precious metal, jewelled crosses, and so on, were kept. There was more to be found in the richest houses, but the poorer areas of the city held little or nothing worth taking – except people. The first invaders had begun by killing everyone they found in the streets, but this did not last long, since survivors were valuable, and could be sold or ransomed. After a while only the old and infirm, and helpless children, were killed, since they had no immediate value as slaves, or as objects for sale. By the end of the first day there was probably little left to steal, since the sultan's order that the violence should stop was not complained about.[1] Much of the city's Christian veneer was therefore fairly quickly removed or tarnished, or ended up out of sight. The richest churches were stripped of anything valuable, and the Christian population was captured for ransom, enslaved, or killed.

Mehmet at once began the process of re-making it into an Islamic city. One of his first acts after riding in triumph, from the wall at the Hadrianapolis Gate (Edirne Kapi) to the acropolis, was to visit Hagia Sofia. It was cleared of its worshippers, who had been crying to their god for help; some worshippers were killed and its riches had been stolen. But the sultan also at once decided that it should be cleansed and converted into a mosque.[2] By the next Friday, the place was usable. This was one of the most famous buildings west of India, so its conversion into an Islamic place of worship would be an everlastingly visible sign of the Muslim triumph – and, of course, of the triumph of Sultan Mehmet 'Fatih' ('the Conqueror').

Other churches were similarly converted, but by no means all, because another of the necessary measures taken by Mehmet was to begin the repopulation of the city.[3] He had already taken measures to limit the destruction and looting. Several sections of the city had surrendered quickly, and had then been protected by Ottoman soldiers sent to do so by the sultan. These areas retained most of their population and much of their wealth, and so were able to ransom many of the Christian captives, their former fellow citizens, from their captors.[4]

The city was nevertheless partly emptied of its people, many slain, enslaved, or refugees. It had been thinly inhabited even before the conquest – only 7,000 soldiers to defend it including visiting foreigners, suggests a poplulation of no more than 25,000 – indeed it had never really recovered from the destruction of the Fourth Crusade. One of Mehmet's first acts therefore was to encourage the immigration of anyone willing to move in, Christian, Muslim, or Jew, Turk or Greek. Prisoners who were released were able to stay, as were those who had been ransomed; Turks were expected to arrive; captives made by the sultan in his later campaigns were moved to the city where they were freed and settled. And, of course, there was the city's name and fame; it remained a place to which people were willing to move voluntarily, because it was rumoured to be wealthy, even after the sack, or at least a place where one could gain wealth. So a wide collection of immigrants came to join the remaining citizens.[5]

Mehmet appointed the senior clerics of each faith to be the legal head of each group, or *millet* in the Turkish term, so that the patriarch officiated over the Orthodox Christians, as did the chief rabbi for the Jews, and the Gregorian patriarch for the Armenians. These officials, appointed by the sultan after a process of election in the normal way, dealt with religious issues and many legal questions within their communities, but not with criminal cases. One of the results of the system was that the issue of the union of the Greek and Latin Churches was settled; the new patriarch appointed by Mehmet (who had been found enslaved in Hadrianapolis) was Gennadios, a prominent opponent of the union. This *millet* system divided the population handily into mutually antagonistic communities, and relieved the sultan of much of the burden of administering them. He, of course, had the same position with regard to the Muslims.[6]

The city, despite its overwhelmingly Christian population when first conquered, was therefore steadily converted into a mainly Muslim place; the extensive depopulation before the siege certainly assisted in importing new, largely Muslim, inhabitants. But it was not simply the people who made the city but the buildings as well. Apart from the instant conversion of Hagia Sofia into Aya Sofya Camii, other churches were also converted into mosques, many of them by prominent members of his court or government, though this conversion took place over a fairly extended period. Mehmet also ordered the construction in the centre of the city, astride the great Meze Street, of the Fatih Camii – the Mosque of the Conqueror – demolishing the church of the Holy Apostles to free up the site. It became not only a place of Islamic worship, but a centre for education, for the distribution of charity, a market, and a burial place; it was also where Mehmet himself was buried; even more than the conversion of Hagia Sofia, it was a sign of the conquest and conversion of the city.[7]

Mehmet also organized new building. The Fatih Camii was one, but the main change was in beginning the construction of the new imperial palace. This new palace took up most of the space originally occupied by the early Greek colony city, Byzantion, on the acropolis of Constantinople. A new fort was built at the Golden Gate (Yeni Kapi), garrisoned by janissaries, and its towers used as prisons (just as the tower of Anemas at the Blakhernai Palace had been a high-status jail in the past). This was, of course, merely the beginning of the city's alteration, but there were clear indications of it continuing over a century or so after the conquest. The whole city was adapted by its conquerors to the new faith.

These invasions of Islam and of immigrants, following on the invasion of the Ottoman army, did not totally change the city, at least not at once. The process was only gradual. The Christians retained many of their old churches, indeed they continued to inhabit whole quarters of the city – the *millet* system encouraged this type of *apartheid*. Immigrants could, for a couple of centuries, find large areas of the city to move to, since its reduction over the last two or three centuries of Byzantine rule had left many open areas, quite apart from the wreckage and depopulation of the conquest. The 25,000 or so people inhabiting the city before the conquest was reduced by flight, death, and eviction, perhaps by half or more.[8] Mehmet's repopulation measures increased that to about 80,000 by 1477, when a census of households was conducted. (Of course, none of these figures can be counted as accurate to within a few thousands.)

It would seem, therefore, that between 1453 and 1477 the city's population had increased by a factor of three. The increase continued for another century and more, but reached a halt at perhaps 150,000; the area within the walls would only accommodate about 200,000 at the most (its population at the time of an early nineteenth-century census) and though there was some expansion beyond the wall, this was very limited until the nineteenth century. It is, of course, as with all capital cities, often assumed that the population was – must have been – greater, and the figure of 1,000,000 is often offered without evidence. Furthermore, the census of 1477 had, in accordance with the *millet* system, reckoned the households by religion. Of the total of over 16,000 households, about 9,500 were Muslim, and about 3,700 were Greek Orthodox. The Islamization of the city had therefore made steady progress over no more than a quarter of a century. These populations (there were over 2,000 households of other religious groups, mainly Christians of various sorts) remained more or less stable for the next four centuries. In effect, Mehmet II was the fourth founder of the city, after the first Megarians, Septimius Severus, and Constantine the Great. In terms of ancient Greek practice, he was fully entitled to have his tomb within the city's bounds.

The rise of national feeling in the nineteenth century, together with the *millet* division of the population, and the steady erosion of Ottoman power and prestige, at last began to alter the population balance. Repeated Muslim/Turkish riots targeted minorities, and the general atmosphere became hostile to Christians and Jews alike. By the end of the twentieth century, large groups of Greeks, Armenians, Kurds, and Jews had been massacred and/or driven out. Ironically, it was after the adoption in the 1920s of a Turkish constitution of a strongly secular type that the expulsion purges achieved their final successes, including a massacre of Greeks as late as 1955. In a secular Turkish Republic the capital is now almost entirely a Muslim town. And recently a Muslim revival in the republic has led to the Hagia Sofia, long secularized into a museum and tourist attraction, returning to use as a mosque in 2020.

Chapter 23

Enemy from the Balkans – the Bulgarians

Threats, and the Siege of 1912–13

After the conquest of 1453 Constantinople was free of siege for the next four centuries. It was not, however, free from the threat of being attacked. In 1624 a Cossack fleet from the Ukraine crossed the Black Sea and sailed into the Bosporos, where it raided both shores and sacked the village of Yenicoy before heading home.[1] Yenicoy was just north of Rumeli Hissar and, with Anadolu Hissar opposite, it is clear that the raiders would not be able to get past those castles. In 1656 a Venetian fleet sailed into the Dardanelles and defeated the Ottoman fleet stationed there, but then turned back and captured the islands of Tenedos and Lemnos; perhaps the twin fortified towns of Gelibolu and Canakkale on opposite sides of the Dardanelles deterred them – these forts were certainly armed with formidable guns.[2] Then in 1770 a Russian fleet which had defeated the Ottoman fleet at the Battle of Chesme off Asia Minor blockaded the Dardanelles, but not for long.[3]

The defences of Constantinople – as Ottoman enemies and many Turks (and all Christian inhabitants) still called it, though the Turks had begun to use the term Istanbul – were no longer just the city wall and the Ottoman fleet, but the forts established well in advance of the city at the narrows of the Bosporos and the Dardanelles. Theodosios' Wall, as the siege of 1453 had shown, was no longer adequate in the face of the new gunpowder weapons. The serious defences had to be at a distance, and the forts at the halfway points along the Straits were now required – and they had evidently worked in the seventeenth and eighteenth centuries against Russians and Venetians. But not in 1807. In that year, in pursuit of an attempt to make the regime of Sultan Selim III make peace with Russia, Britain sent a fleet into the Dardanelles to threaten the city.

This was an affair confusing to both parties. Britain was allied with Russia and the Ottoman Empire, but those two were at war with each other, and the Ottomans had been urged on by their French friends. The Russians also had a fleet in the Aegean at the time, and offered to join the British in their expedition. A detachment of the British Mediterranean fleet was sent under Vice-Admiral Sir John Duckworth with the aim of suggesting to Britain's ally (the Ottomans), at the point of a gun, that it would be best if Britain, Russia, and the Ottoman Empire turned their fire on the main enemy, the French Empire of Napoleon. Duckworth got his ships up the Dardanelles by a skilful piece of seamanship, despite being bombarded from the forts. But once in the Sea of Marmara, and then at anchor off the city itself, he was prevented from further action by the dithering of Arbuthnot, the British ambassador, who had fled from the city under threat and had been picked up by Duckworth's ships at the Dardanelles entrance. The delay allowed the Ottomans to prepare their ships to defend the city and to gather a formidable force, said to amount to 200,000 armed men. The strong current through and out of the Bosporos, and a failure of the south wind, also hindered any further movement forward of the British fleet. After several days Duckworth pulled his fleet out. Some of the sailors, clearly not understanding the wider political situation, wanted him to attack the city, and one has the vision of British carronades firing at the Topkapi Palace and the Blue Mosque and Aya Sofia. (And they would have done; this was the year in which a British fleet bombarded Copenhagen and destroyed half the city, and a British army in South America attacked Buenos Aires, and when defeated, seriously considered that the artillery should bombard the city to destruction.) It is very doubtful, in fact, if the British fleet in the Sea of Marmara could have done serious damage to the city. A bombardment would certainly have enraged the Ottomans, which would have driven them even further into the arms of France than the sultan already was. The real reason for Duckworth's retirement was that the purpose of his expedition was always unclear, and the longer he waited the more ridiculous it seemed. The Russian fleet took Tenedos a little later and instituted a blockade at the mouth of the Dardanelles; it defeated two attempts by the Turkish fleet to break out. The blockade lasted into 1808; the Dardanelles forts held against the Russians, though they had not against the British.[4]

The Ottomans in fact could only see that Russia was their enemy, an empire they had already fought at least six times in the previous century, and would do so at least five more times in the coming century. In such circumstances Ottoman attention was obviously directed towards the north; Duckworth's fleet was a negligible threat compared to the Russian army of invasion, as well as clearly dithering over what it was to do.

The weakness of the Ottoman Empire encouraged other countries to meddle in its affairs. In 1829, in a war in Greece in which the Ottomans fought against a large-scale Greek rebellion, the Russians intervened and a Russian army reached Edirne and sent some forces on towards Istanbul; peace came before further fighting, but the city was clearly threatened.[5] In the early 1830s the khedive of Egypt, Mehmet Ali, sent an army under his highly capable son Ibrahim into Syria and then into Anatolia. Ibrahim defeated an Ottoman army at Konya in central Asia Minor and marched on as far as Kutahya, about a hundred miles from Istanbul. By this time, the sultan had appealed to Russia, of all countries, for help, and a Russian squadron took up a position in the Bosporos, then a Russian army arrived to defend the city. This was not an Egyptian or Russian siege, but both certainly posed a threat, and those of the Russians present in the city were highly unpopular. Russian forces were all withdrawn once Ibrahim made a peace, but a subsequent Turkish-Russian treaty opened the Ottoman Empire to Russian interference.[6]

The city was by this time clearly in danger of occupation or attack by both friends and enemies. The threats for the last two centuries had come steadily closer, from the forts of the Bosporos and Dardanelles to Edirne and Kutahya, both only a hundred miles away; the Duckworth expedition came right up to the city's doorstep. The balance of military and naval power had decisively shifted against the Ottoman Empire. Ottoman diplomacy succeeded in switching alliances so that the Russians assisted in defending the city against Ibrahim Pasha, and then the British and French forced the Egyptians to retire from Syria. A dozen years later the British and French came to the assistance of the sultan once again when he fell into a new Russian war (the 'Crimean' War). The city was not in any serious danger from a Russian attack (even though the Russians had destroyed an Ottoman fleet at Sinope in northern Anatolia at the beginning of the war), but it saw itself virtually occupied by British and French soldiers in support of their joint expedition into the Crimea, and armed Christians in the city were not liked.

By the next crisis, another Russian-Turkish war in the 1870s, the Turks had recovered sufficiently to hold up the Russian invasion of the Balkans at the Danube long enough to wake up the British to what was happening. So when the Russians finally advanced after capturing the fortress at Plevna in the winter of 1877, the British had a fleet in the Aegean. It was moved forward into the Sea of Marmara, after much dithering and changing of minds in the Cabinet in London. The Russians, already more or less exhausted, were warned not to occupy Constantinople, while a new British fleet was being prepared to be sent into the Baltic, where the Russian capital St Petersburg was vulnerable, as had been seen in the Crimean War. A peace treaty was agreed at San Stefano, close to the city, which was therefore the Russians' furthest advance. But then the terms were revised heavily in Turkish favour in an international conference at Berlin which followed.[7]

This series of crises, rebellions, wars, and invasions showed that the Ottoman Empire was visibly failing throughout the nineteenth century. Its friends and enemies alike were seizing choice morsels of Ottoman territory for themselves: the British took over Egypt and Cyprus, France took Tunis and Algeria, Russia had gained the Crimea and the Black Sea coast as far as the Danube, and Greece, Romania, Serbia, Bulgaria, and Montenegro all gained their independence. In the process Ottoman friends had twice occupied Istanbul, and each Russian invasion of the Balkans had come closer to an armed attack on the city. Those with eyes to see will have understood that a direct assault on the city would soon come; the nearest enemy frontier was now, after 1879, at the line of the Balkan Mountains, no more than a hundred miles away. But it is unlikely that anyone expected the attack to come from Italy, and then from Bulgaria.

In 1911 Italy, pursuing the all-pervading European nationalist desire for an overseas empire, began a campaign to take Libya from Ottoman rule. This involved preventing reinforcements being sent from the heart of the empire, so once again the entrance to the Dardanelles was blockaded; this was countered by the Ottoman government closing the Straits to all traffic, which caused serious economic damage to Russia, whose exporters used that route. The military weakness which the Ottoman government displayed in this war encouraged the Balkan states who were the Ottomans' neighbours in Europe to pursue their own ambitions. They formed an alliance, the Balkan League, consisting of

Greece, Serbia, Montenegro, and Bulgaria, with an aim of seizing by force sections of Ottoman territory. This was, of course, no more than other European imperialists had done, but the difference was that the league essentially aimed at the destruction of the Ottoman Empire – one of the targets of Greece and Bulgaria was Constantinople. Greece would march north, Serbia south, Bulgaria south and southeast, but it was Montenegro which began the process, the First Balkan War. It was all an unexpected military success for the allies.[8]

Bulgaria aimed to seize the country between its southern boundary on the Balkan Mountains and the Aegean, and this area included the cities of Salonica (Thessalonica) and Constantinople. In neither case was it successful – Greece got to Salonica first, and the Turks put up a good defence to save Constantinople.

The Bulgars, however, did push forward into Thrace far enough to put the city under a distant siege, defeating the Turkish Eastern Army in the battles of Kirkkilesse and the Luleburgas. The Turkish retreat from the second battle was in the nature of a rout, but the Turks had organized a trench line across the peninsula, the Chatalja Lines, as a rear defence. This had been originally organized in the crisis of 1878, when the Russians had broken the Turkish defence on the Danube and were, like the Bulgars, approaching Istanbul. In the similar situation of 1912, the position had been refurbished and re-manned. It stopped the Bulgars. The line was, in fact, only a little way closer to the city than the Long Wall which had been built as the most forward fortification to defend the city back in the fifth or sixth century. This had rarely figured in any of the sieges since it had been built, but the Bulgars noted it when they camped beside it to enforce the siege. There were two archaeologists among the officers, and they made the first survey of the wall, and wrote reports on it afterwards.[9]

The position of the defence line was different from that of the Long Wall, which was a linear defence of a ditch backed by a stone wall, dotted with towers; this would be effective in stopping infantry and cavalry attacks, at least, before the development of gunpowder weapons. (This was an intractable problem, since the length of the line of the Long Wall, as the name suggests, was too great to be effectively occupied and defended. All it would take to break through was a concentration of force at one point while the defenders were spread along the line.)

The Chatalja Lines, as the new defence position was termed (Chatalja is a village located between the Long Wall and the lines), were designed for defence against the more recent types of attack, against an enemy with modern artillery and infantry armed with modern rifles which could shoot accurately over a long distance. It was a series of entrenched positions along a ridge, facing an open plain. The plain enabled any attack to be discerned even as it began several kilometres away; the ridge was high enough to stop any advance and to force the attackers into a laborious climb under fire; the entrenched positions provided the defence with shelter from the enemy artillery and from which the attackers could be beaten back as they crested the ridge.

The lines were laid out at the top of the ridge, between inlets of the Black Sea and the Sea of Marmara which reduced the 45 kilometres of the Long Wall to about 30 for the Lines; rivers flowed across the plain just in front of the ridge and where they reached the sea marshland increased the difficulty of approaching the position.[10] On the ridge top there was a series of trenched positions lining the whole distance, backed by fortified posts, some dating from 1878. They had been laid out by a German military engineer called von Blum in that year; others were more recently built of concrete, partly planned by Brialmont, a ubiquitous Belgian military engineer of the period, and other improvements had been recommended by later German engineers. The artillery was kept ready in shelter nearby, and the guns could be brought forward and likely targets in the plain had been plotted and measured and could be hit from the start of any bombardment.[11] The seaward ends of the line were dominated, when the fighting came, by Turkish warships armed with even heavier artillery than on land. It was, as the Bulgars rapidly discovered, a very strong position even from a distance, and they discovered other unpleasant factors when they got close enough to be able to begin an attack.

The defeats of the Ottoman forces in the battles to the west compelled a frantic rehabilitation of these defences. They had been allowed to decay in the previous three decades, and the guns and the garrisons had been removed to fight the recent battles. But the Bulgars, keen enough to attempt to gain at Constantinople, were distracted by the need to besiege Edirne, held for some time by the Turks; this blocked the railway which the Bulgars needed to bring up supplies. They brought up 176,000 men to the attack on the Turkish positions. The Turks had a garrison of 140,000;

more to the point they had over 300 guns and the support of warships on each flank, with good supplies of ammunition; the Bulgars had 460 guns, but were in difficulties over bringing forward the supplies to keep them firing. (These were very large battles indeed.) The Bulgarian troops were hungry and weary, and cholera and typhoid were working in their ranks. They reached their position in front of the lines in batches during the first half of November, and launched an attack on the 17th. Having crossed the plain to come within range of accurate and damaging artillery fire, they were then faced by tangles of barbed wire, machine guns, well-hidden rifleman in dug-in positions and naval gunfire enfilading their advance. The attack failed with over 20,000 casualties.[12] It was yet another rehearsal (after the American Civil War, the Boer War, and the Russo-Japanese campaign in Manchuria) for the Western Front.

The inhabitants of Istanbul could hear much of this, as the artillery boomed out, and they even learned to distinguish naval from land fire. The approach of the Bulgars had revived old antagonisms among the population, and tensions had risen between Muslims and Christians, between Turks and Greeks, and between Turks and Armenians (for there was fighting between Ottomans and Armenians in the east at this time as well).[13] A joint force of ships contributed by all the Great Powers of Europe moved into the Bosporos and the Golden Horn, with Turkish permission, aimed at providing protection for the Christian inhabitants. It included ships from the British, French, Austrian, German, and Russian navies, and arrived on 12 November, just as the Bulgarian assault was being organized. Detachments of sailors, armed with rifles and machine guns, were landed on the 18th, in effect taking control of Pera.[14]

The Bulgars' defeat at the lines lessened tensions, and an Ottoman request for an armistice, transmitted by the Russians, was agreed by the Bulgars. They had been sobered by their defeat and their casualties, and still had to continue the siege of Edirne. It went into effect on 3 December, but only at the lines; the armistice therefore did not extend to the rest of the war, and Edirne remained under siege. In Istanbul the Ottoman defeats provoked a coup d'état by some of the 'Young Turks', the group who had seized power in 1908, with Enver Pasha emerging as the new strong man – the sultan had been deprived of all power by this time. One of Enver's stated reasons for the coup was that he intended to relieve Edirne, but this changed later to recapturing it after it had been taken.[15] Occasional fighting broke out again at the Chatalja Lines until Edirne fell to the Bulgars late in March.

The armistice, which was eventually extended to other fronts, revealed numerous disputes and jealousies amongst and between the victors. Bulgaria, Serbia, and Greece disputed control of Salonica, while Bulgaria's aim of seizing Constantinople had annoyed, and been prevented by, Russia. Just as the Egyptian advance towards Constantinople eighty years before had triggered Russian jealousy, so did the Bulgars' advance; Russia's own ambition for the city precluded anyone else gaining control of it, and therefore they offered to come to the assistance of the Turks in holding it. They now proposed to send a force to act in its defence, as they had on earlier occasions. Russia's transparent hope was to gain the city, perhaps after the Bulgarians had broken through the Chatalja lines and they could come to the city's rescue. This alarmed the British, who had no wish to see a Russian fleet having an easy means of exit from the Black Sea into the Mediterranean. This was one of the triggers of the international intervention fleet in the Bosporos, since that blocked the Russian aims by recruiting them into the intervention; also, of course, all the rest of the participants were eyeing choice cuts of the Ottoman Empire for themselves.[16]

The British took the lead in organizing the peace conference. For the moment, in fact, the urgency about Constantinople was relaxed, as a number of cities still held by the Turks, including Edirne, remained besieged. Once those cities had been captured a wider armistice could be arranged, and the conference could begin. Edirne had been taken by storm, to Turkish anger and sorrow; it had been the first city in Europe the Ottomans had conquered, and had been their early capital, while the tombs of its early sultans were there.[17] Also, once it was taken, Bulgaria would be able to send even more of their troops against Constantinople, and their commanders had shown a willingness to use their peasant soldiers extravagantly, and to ignore the armistice – as indeed did the other belligerents at times.

The Turkish defence of Constantinople had so far been successful, but the first peace treaty (the Treaty of London, 9 June 1913) which separated the two belligerents left the Turks with a new political boundary only a little in front of the Chatalja Lines. They still controlled the Gallipoli Peninsula, however, and a strip of land along the Marmara coast – the formal boundary was a straight line from the Black Sea to the Aegean. But the Bulgarian forces remained, and, in effect, despite the Armistice, the city had remained under siege.

The Ottoman naval forces, and the forts at Gelibolu and Canakkale, controlled the Dardanelles, but the Ottoman ships were repeatedly defeated by the Greek fleet in attempting to sortie. The Greeks were busy capturing Aegean islands, yet at the same time they were unable to get through the Strait. So the Ottoman fleet remained in control of the Sea of Marmara and the Straits, and this enabled reinforcements to be ferried across in safety from Asia; the Turks also dominated the nearby Black Sea, which permitted the Bulgarian coast to be threatened, and supplies to be ferried to the Ottoman army. (One of the major constraints on land operations was the difficulty of moving supplies by land to the troops who were doing the fighting, hence the importance of the railway through Edirne.) The Greeks in effect blockaded the Dardanelles from the Aegean side, and were replied to by the Ottomans with their countering prohibition of entry.[18] That is, the Dardanelles were, in these wars, as they had been throughout the gunpowder centuries, the forward defence of Constantinople just as were the forts in the Bosporos and the Chatalja Lines.

Three weeks after the peace treaty was signed, the Bulgarian General Savov launched surprise attacks on the Greeks and the Serbians – these were surprises to his superiors and to the Bulgarian government, not just to his enemies. Bulgaria felt that it had grievances on all its borders, and in some cases it had a reasonable case, but its enemies formed a new Balkan League in their defence, and fought back successfully. The Bulgar army aimed to gain Salonica, but Serbia and Greece resisted; Romania, complaining that it needed 'compensation' in the face of the increased power gained by its neighbours, invaded Bulgaria and headed straight for Sofia, the capital, which was essentially undefended. And the Turks, smarting at the loss of Edirne, launched an attack from the Chatalja Lines which succeeded in retaking the city.[19]

The siege of Constantinople in 1912 had been a more severe threat to the city than anything since the Ottoman conquest in 1453. The people of the city could hear the guns all too clearly, and the Bulgars had brought up every gun they had to launch their attack at the Chatalja Lines. The need to hold the Gallipoli Peninsula had been emphasized yet again.

More widely, it would have been a useful lesson to the future belligerents if they had realized that massive bombardments, such as that launched by the Bulgarians, had much less effect on well entrenched troops than the attackers expected – but European soldiers basically discounted such lessons, despising the apparent miniature nature of the wars.

What had happened, of course, was that there had been really only one siege lasting for several months, interrupted by a lengthy truce. And in a further reprise of past encounters, the Russians at one point suggested that they send a naval force to hold the Bosporos and an army to defend the city. Yet again, this was blocked by the British, always fearful of Russian ambitions. In the next year, of course, all this would be overturned once more.

The failure of the Bulgarians to approach the city, or, in the traditional way, to attack the wall, cannot disguise the fact that the city really was under siege in these events. What had changed was the array of weapons available to both sides, in particular the distance they could fire with accurate effect. Therefore any city could be bombarded from a distance of several miles. In 1912 Constantinople's defence was no longer the wall but lay at the gates of the Straits and at the Chatalja Lines, as it had since the great guns of the siege of 1453; if the Bulgars had broken the lines, or the Greek ships had passed the Dardanelles, the city's surrender would have been actively discussed. It is doubtful if either the Bulgars or the Greeks would have restrained themselves as Admiral Duckworth had a century before.

Chapter 24

Enemies from the Sea –
The Great War Allies

The Siege of 1914–1923

After the Italian War and the two Balkan Wars (1911–13), the Ottoman Empire then fell into the Great War. One of the effects of the Balkan Wars was to bring the empire into a closer political alignment with the German Empire. German officers had been advising in several areas of fortifications, and in military training, for some years. (The British had been doing the same for the Ottoman Navy.)[1] Then, in August 1914, in the first naval action of the Great War, the Ottomans allowed two German ships, the battlecruiser *Goeben* and the cruiser *Breslau*, to shelter in Istanbul when they escaped from the British Mediterranean fleet. This 'shelter' was formalized when the ships were 'sold', or rather given, to the Ottomans; the German crews became Turkish sailors wearing the fez.[2] In reply the British established a blockade of the Dardanelles in the hope that the German ships would come out, and made it clear that they regarded the 'sale' as phoney.[3] This confirmed the Ottoman government in its political inclination towards the German side in the war, which already existed, fuelled by the German war with the Ottomans' traditional enemy Russia, and the Germans offered a subsidy in gold if the Ottomans would join in the fighting. In the end, after some Ottoman delay and dithering, the two ships went out into the Black Sea and bombarded several Russian ports.[4] It turned out that the British were all too ready for the Ottomans to join in the war, and moved directly to seize control of the mouth of the Euphrates and the Abadan oil refinery, and on 3 November bombarded the forts at the mouth of the Dardanelles.[5] This was all before war was declared, which happened on 5 November.

This, of course, effectively closed both Straits in both directions; the Russian Navy blockaded the Bosporos, and the British and French the

Dardanelles. Almost at once the idea of driving a naval force through the Dardanelles to threaten Istanbul occurred to more than one man in the Admiralty.[6] It occurred to the Turks too, and as early as 8 September, two months before the Ottomans declared war, the German engineers and sailors were manning forts in both straits; Admiral Souchon (in *Goeben*) was appointed to command the Turkish Navy, replacing the British Admiral Limpus.[7]

The bombardment of the Dardanelles entrance in early November was supposed to be a warning to Turkey of what might be expected from an Ottoman declaration of war, but it was also a clear sign that Turkey's enemies were seeking to exploit the vulnerability of the Straits. Winston Churchill, First Lord of the Admiralty, as early as 27 August ordered that, if the two German ships, which had technically been sold to Turkey, came out of the Dardanelles they should be sunk; the ships, after all, still had their German crews on board, even if they had become pseudo-Turks and were wearing fezzes.[8]

With the official declaration of war, British attention turned to more direct aggression, and the Dardanelles was an obvious target. It did not take much imagination to conceive of attempts to force the strait, and both the army and the navy were fully aware of the difficulties involved. A good deal of that imagination was needed to produce a sensible plan, but it was absent from the Admiralty planners. In retrospect, of course, it is obvious that a combined naval and military operation was required from the start, and a very large one at that. The military would gain control of the coasts and their forts, particularly in the Gallipoli Peninsula, and the naval force would drive the ships through into the Sea of Marmara. The over-confident Royal Navy felt it could do the second part without bothering the army – and the army was very busy elsewhere, of course, so much so that the war minister Lord Kitchener, who at first took part in the planning, subsequently withdrew the offer of troops. The Turkish defeats by the Italians and the Balkan states had given an erroneous impression of Turkish weakness, so that it was expected that any operation would be straightforward, and would bring on a Turkish collapse and its rapid exit from the war.[9]

The plan, when it was finally made, was for the navy to advance into the Dardanelles in overwhelming force. The Turkish forts were to be bombarded, the existing minefields were to be swept aside by minesweeping trawlers, and the great ships – eighteen battleships of various ages, mainly British but also French – would move majestically forward, at the rate of a mile a day. Kum Kale would be seized by French Marines, but only to destroy the fort there, then they would be withdrawn. The assumption was that this display of power and its inexorable advance would so demoralize the Turks that opposition could be removed without difficulty, but the Turks were consistently under-estimated throughout the naval operation, and indeed throughout the war. The existence of Turkish artillery was not ignored, and there were two divisions of troops, plus marines, available if needed. An advanced force of marines had already secured the Greek island of Lemnos, which became the allies' base. The French sent a contingent of ships and a division of troops, since they did not want the British to establish themselves immovably at the centre of the Ottoman Empire; a Russian force also participated in the Black Sea – for the Russians did not want either the French or the British to become established in control of Istanbul. The Russian force raided the northern entrance to the Bosporos on 28 March but without having any real effect.[10] The imminence of the attack on the Dardanelles could not, of course, be disguised. One only had to stand on one of the hills of the southern part of the Gallipoli Peninsula and look east or south and the whole Allied fleet would be visible, while the island of Lemnos could be inspected with field glasses or a telescope; the camps of the Allied divisions were apparent.

The attack began with several days of less-than-effective bombardments of the forts at the entrance to the strait, and unsuccessful attempts to sweep it clear of mines. The first ships to move into the strait were the minesweeping trawlers, manned by civilian volunteers; these ships proved to be instantly vulnerable to Turkish artillery, and soon they turned away and retreated when several were sunk or damaged by Turkish fire.[11] When the big ships advanced, on 18 March, they were found to be equally vulnerable. The minefields were largely located, but there was one which was not, and it claimed three battleships. The attack was called off.[12]

It was replaced a month later by an attempt to seize the Gallipoli Peninsula by an armed landing. If successful this would allow the Allies to dominate the Turkish positions on the Asian side, and so permit the ships to go through, or so went the theory. (Note that this had actually been the original suggestion, but was jettisoned in favour of the navy-only operation.) But this also failed. It was mounted too weakly, and reinforced piecemeal, and suffered from erratic and bad generalship; even more important, it also had to face the grit and valour of the Turkish defence. But the naval attack had lasted one day, and the battles on the peninsula lasted eight months.[13]

It is well to be clear what the aim of these operations was. The capture of Istanbul was perhaps hoped for, but the detailed intention of the naval operation was to mount a selective bombardment at the city, concentrating on the military and naval establishments, the dockyard and the Arsenal and any other arms dumps or factories.[14] This would hurt the Turks, but would hardly have forced them out of the war. (In 1807, Admiral Sir Sydney Smith in Duckworth's expedition had much the same idea.) It was seen in the naval attacks that land-based artillery could easily dominate and drive off the largest warship, and an allied attack at the city would certainly have resulted in a duel between the allied fleet and the Turkish guns in the city, as well as defensive operations by the Turkish navy. And it might take only a single shot to sink a warship, but the artillery, particularly the high-shooting howitzers, were much less vulnerable, and were easily and rapidly movable into hiding, or out of range. All this had become obvious during the naval attack in March. The Turkish guns could, if the city was attacked, be hidden in houses and so fire from cover. It was found at the Dardanelles that all that gunners had to do was to stop firing and take shelter; the ships would move elsewhere, then the gun could be re-manned, or moved, and could fire again; defending the city would be even easier. Naval casualties would be heavy.

The Straits at both ends were closed both by the Turks in the forts, and by the Allies who blockaded their entrances. The Russians had blocked the Bosporos by laying a minefield as soon as the war began in the Black Sea, and this was refreshed occasionally, though the Turks could get through with care. At the Dardanelles the blockade needed to be constantly revised and elaborated as Turkish and German countermeasures, notably by submarines, came into use; and the blockade became steadily more difficult and expensive to maintain. Allied submarines also got through the Dardanelles with care and so into the Sea of Marmara; there they could sink every ship they found, and by the end of the war there were very few vessels left afloat, and yet this was no more than a nuisance to the Turks, since land transport was always available, if slower than by ship.[15]

That is to say, Istanbul was once again under siege, with the forward defences at the Bosporos forts, and at the forts of the Dardanelles, a condition which had threatened the city repeatedly since the forts were built and elaborated, since 1453 in fact. The defences were effective in the Bulgar War and would still work. The inhabitants and the Turkish government could have no doubt that, if the battle at Gallipoli was lost, the city would be the next target – in fact, that it was the real target of the invaders. The besieging forces were prevented from approaching any closer to the city by sea (except below the surface) by the forts; and the only way to reach it was by land through Thrace, as in 1912 and 1913; but the city this time was also defended by Bulgarian neutrality, which then shifted into an actual Bulgar-Turk-German-Austrian alliance in late 1915. This allowed the supplies, both of food and of munitions, to be delivered from the German and Austrian factories, and after the conquest of Belgrade in 1916, these supplies would be moved by both river barge on the Danube and by rail; this supply by land was a variation on the usual theme of a close landward siege relieved by seaborne supplies. The allied effort was therefore hardly a close and rigorous siege in a military sense, and was perhaps less of a strain to the citizens than the Bulgarian sieges in 1912–13, but classification as a siege makes it clear what was at stake.

The aim of the Turks' attackers was the same as ever – to gain control of the city of Constantinople. Even though the Russians had instigated the Dardanelles campaign by appealing as early as January 1915 for an Allied expedition to distract the enemy, they still achieved a particularly favourable treaty by which, in the event of victory, they would be awarded the city, much of Turkish Thrace, and control of the Sea of Marmara and the Dardanelles. The King of Bulgaria, though he fought as a Turkish ally, had not given up hope that if Turkey collapsed, he would be able to seize the city, a completion in his eyes of the Thracian campaigns of 1912 and 1913. Greece aimed to gain the city to restore the Byzantine Empire, together with as much of Anatolia as it could seize. France had its eye on the city also, and pointed to the large French financial investments made in the region before the war; Britain had strong reservations about the Russian intentions, and indeed everybody else's; Germany, with its own investments, but in industry and railways in particular, and having provided a large military and financial subsidy to the Ottomans, was as greedy as anyone, but perhaps thought of gaining control of the whole empire, not just the city. Constantinople, even as it became the target for all these enemies, had not lost its allure, nor its ability to confuse those enemies.

The military and naval pressures, even though the besieging forces did not actually approach the city (other than by submarine), had their effect on the people there. The tensions particularly operated on the relations between Muslims and Christians, and between citizens and foreigners. In 1915, together with mass deportations and murders in eastern Anatolia, many Armenians in Istanbul were deported, and others were lynched by mobs.[16] The reduction of supplies brought hunger to many, starvation to some, fistfights in bakeries, and the occasional riot. The news of the capture of Baghdad produced mobs sacking foreign-owned buildings. The increasing presence of Germans in the city, who behaved even more arrogantly than most foreigners, produced the same reaction as the presence of 'protecting' Russians in 1831, and the British and French in the Crimean War, and led to their great unpopularity by the end of the war. Hygiene suffered and disease spread – the usual diseases of poverty and filth and sieges, such as typhoid, dysentery, cholera. Even though the enemy was still at a distance, the conditions of starvation and disease in the city were typical of any city under siege. The effect of the allied policies was, perhaps inadvertently, to impose traditional tactics of attempting to starve out the city. It was clearly an extremely unhappy time to be living in Istanbul, and of course by 1918 the city had gone through nearly eight years of this unhappiness.[17]

The city was already crowded with refugees from the recent wars and from the lost lands of Europe by the time the Great War began, and some also from Libya; others now arrived from the threatened areas of the Straits, and from the invasions of the Russians in the eastern parts of the empire; the conscription of men into the army imposed starvation in the rural areas of Anatolia, where the farming could not be done because the men were absent. In the city the citizens and the refugees were able to hear the fighting in Gallipoli, particularly with a southerly or westerly wind, and the sinking of ships in the Sea of Marmara sometimes took place within sight of the city; a second Allied army was camped at Salonica, immovably for a time, but still a threat. In 1917 a huge explosion destroyed the Haydarpasha station on the Asian side, the terminal of the

Baghdad railway; it was rumoured to be the result of sabotage by Allied agents, but it may well just have been due to carelessness in the storing of munitions.[18] The people and the government could have no doubt that the city was under constant threat, and that the Allies might break through somewhere and bring the city under a much closer siege.

That threat became a reality in October 1918, four years after the Ottoman war began. Defeats in Syria and Mesopotamia in September brought British forces close to southern Anatolia; the collapse of Bulgaria, also in September, led to that country's exit from the fighting, and severed the Ottoman lifeline to Germany; the subsequent advance of Allied forces along the Aegean coast of Thrace, from its long and moribund occupation of Salonica, convinced the Turkish government also to ask for an armistice. Terms were negotiated on the British battleship *Agamemnon* by a British admiral (who had been recently appointed to the post so as to outrank the French admiral who was also there); the French commander at Salonica pushed his forces on to reach the city first; the Allies had begun quarrelling with each other already.[19] The Russians, who had instigated the Dardanelles campaign, had already been driven out of the war, and had to watch their former Allies snatch the prize which Russia had hungered after for centuries. A British destroyer, HMS *Shark*, was sent through the Dardanelles and into the Sea of Marmara to check, by not getting sunk, if the passage was clear.[20] The collapse of Russia into revolution meant that the British and French had the place to themselves, though they made room for Italian and Greek contingents; the United States, which had not been at war with the Ottoman Empire, muscled in as well.[21]

The terms of the armistice excluded an Allied occupation of the city, but these were immediately ignored by the Allies, and the British, French, Italians and Greeks sent their forces into Istanbul, where they behaved as conquerors, occupying palaces and ordering the Turkish government and citizens about; the French general at Salonica entered the city on his white horse, almost as if he had conquered it. This, of course, only reflected the reality of Turkish defeat in the greater war, but since the city had not actually been captured and always remembered that, the occupation was the more resented.

That occupation continued for four years, as the Allied politicians quarrelled and intrigued, and the Turks increasingly came to resent the occupiers. Early signs of disorder and resistance brought a full Allied military occupation, and a military governor, General George Milne.[22] The interior of Anatolia was not occupied, though its Aegean and Mediterranean coasts and its Syrian frontage were, and it was there, in the unoccupied high land of central Anatolia, that the rehabilitation of the country began, with a republican revolution, led by one of the victorious commanders of the Gallipoli campaign, General Mustafa Kemal.

One of the sources of disorder in the city was the political dispute between the new republican regime, and the old imperial regime of the Ottomans under the sultan. The sultan, Mehmet VI (1918–22) and Abd-al-Majid II (1922–4), was by this time under complete Allied control, a factor which led eventually towards the abolition of the sultanate and later of the caliphate. Fighting therefore went on intermittently, Turks against the British, Turks against Armenians, Turks against Turks, Turks against Greeks. The French were eventually largely content with their share of Syria and soon made an unofficial truce in their area, having been defeated in attempts to move north into Anatolia; the Italian occupation of their slice of the southern coastlands scarcely began in the face of Turkish hostility, and was mirrored in their minimal presence in Istanbul. In the city tensions developed, and the British and allied troops were frequently harassed.

All this was complicated by the revolution which was simultaneously taking place in Russia (HMS *Shark* was used again to make contact with White Russians in the Crimea), and the refugees from within the Ottoman Empire were soon supplemented by Russian refugees who came across the Black Sea in their thousands from the last refuges of the 'White' Russians in the cities along the north coast.[23] At one point the British ships were fighting both the Russian Bolsheviks and the Turkish Republicans, patrolling the Straits to stop arms being ferried into Constantinople from Asia – not very successfully, it has to be admitted; it was not difficult to carry a few rifles in a row boat across the Bosporos without being stopped. The Russian refugees moved on fairly quickly to France and the United States, and the confrontation simplified into British forces (who formed the main occupying power) and the Turkish Republicans. In the Turkish interior, the Greek adventure to seize a large part of Anatolia was bloodily defeated in 1922, and this ended with the massacre and incineration of the city of Smyrna (Izmir from now on).

The final confrontation came, fittingly, when the Turkish Republicans had advanced from the interior as far as the Dardanelles and faced off against a British garrison in Canakkale, one of the forts which defended the city at a distance. The British could not afford the loss of Canakkale, which would also mean losing control of the Dardanelles. Ironically, of course, it was one of the forts which had fought off the Allied attack in 1915. The prospect of another large-scale Turkish war dismayed all sides, including the Turks. The result in Britain was the overthrow of the government of Lloyd George when it became known that the Australian and New Zealand governments would not support a new war.[24] The risk of division within the British Empire, on top of the secession of Ireland, and the determined independence of Canada, together with the prospect of fighting a Muslim state and its effects on the Muslim parts of the empire, was to be avoided: the removal of an unpopular British government was a small price to pay.

This Turkish victory over the British Empire made the name of the republican leader, Mustafa Kemal, who had already won fame in Turkey by his command of the defence at Gallipoli, by blocking a further advance by the British in Syria late in 1918, and now by his leadership of the revolutionary government.[25] At the same time the level-headedness of General Sir Charles (Tim) Harington, the British commander of the occupation forces in Istanbul, and his disobedience to the orders sent to him from London, succeeded in persuading the Republicans to agree to a truce, and so prevented any more fighting.[26]

It was clear by this time that the lack of support for the British position meant that the occupation of Istanbul would have to end soon. The Turkish victories over the Greeks (and over the French and the Italians) in Anatolia compelled a revision of the 1920 Treaty of Sevres. A new treaty was agreed at Lausanne in neutral Switzerland, and was less of a triumphal gesture than the peace treaties negotiated in Paris.[27] At that point the Allies, though by this time they were almost entirely a British force, withdrew from the city. The last sultan, now only a caliph, left soon after.

Constantinople had survived another siege, though one which is rarely described as such, but a city which is blockaded, even at a distance, attacked at the defence perimeter, starved, assaulted (by submarines and eventually by bombing from aircraft), and occupied by its enemies, can surely count itself as having been besieged. It had been threatened in the same way as in 1878, 1912, 1913, and even further back. Just as the wall of Theodosios had protected the city in all but one of the assaults directed at it before gunpowder and cannons, so the forts of the Straits – Rumeli Hissar and Anadolu Hissar, Gelibolu and Canakkale – were the fortified outworks defending the city after 1453. And this siege was perhaps the worst for the population of the city, in that the pressure was continued for eight years (1911–18), with occasional short interruptions, and was followed by over four years of occupation by foreign soldiers (1918–23), who near-universally expressed nothing but contempt for the inhabitants and their city. The Ottoman government had finally failed its citizens and subjects by being unable to protect them from such treatment. The Republicans in the end, took over the power the Ottomans had apparently discarded.

Bibliography

Alexandrescu-Dersca, M.-M, *La Campagne de Timour en Anatolie* (Bucharest, 1942).

Anaheim, M.T.W, *The Senatorial Aristocracy in the Later Roman Empire* (Oxford, 1972).

Angold, Michael, *The Byzantine Empire, 1025 – 1204, A Political History* (Harlow, Essex, 1985).

Angold, Michael, *A Byzantine Government in Exile, Government and Society under the Lascarids of Nicaea (1204–1261)* (Oxford, 1975).

Angold, Michael, *The fall of Constantinople to the Ottomans, Context and Consequences* (Harlow, Essex, 2012).

Argoston, Gabor, *Guns for the Sultan, Military Power and the Weapons Industry in the Ottoman Empire* (Cambridge, 2005).

Baladhuri, Abu-l Abbas, *Kitab Futuh al-Buldan, The Origins of the Islamic State*, translated by P.K. Hitti (New York, 1916, reprinted 2002).

Barker, John W, *Manuel II, 1391–1425, a Study in Late Byzantine Statesmanship* (New Brunswick, NJ, 1969).

Barnes, Timothy D, *Constantine and Eusebius* (Cambridge, MA, 1981).

Bartusis, Mark C, *The Late Byzantine Army, Arms and Society, 1204–1453* (Philadelphia, 1992).

Billows, Richard A, *Antigonos the One-Eyed and the Creation of the Hellenistic State* (Berkeley and Los Angeles, 1990).

Birley, Anthony, *The African Emperor, Septimius Severus* (London, 1988).

Blankenship, Khalid Yahya, *The End of the Jihad State, the Reign of Hisham ibn Abd al-Malik and the Collapse of the Umayyads* (Albany, NY, 1994).

Blois, Lukas de, *The Policy of the Emperor Gallienus* (Leiden, 1976).

Boardman, John *The Greeks Overseas* (Harmondsworth, 1975).

Bradbury, J, *The Mediaeval Siege* (Woodbridge, Suffolk, 1992).

Brauer Jr, George V, *The Age of the Soldier Emperors* (Park Ridge, NJ, 1975).

Brubaker, Leslie, and John Haldon, *Byzantium in the Iconoclastic Era (ca 680–850), The Sources, An Annotated Survey* (Birmingham, 2001).

Burn, A.R, *The Lyric Age of Greece* (London, 1967).

Burn, A.R, *Persia and the Greeks* (London, 1983).

Bury, J.B, *The History of the Later Roman Empire from the Death of Theodosius I to the Death of Justinian*, 2 vols (London, 1889, reprinted 1958).

Cahen, Claude, *The Formation of Turkey* (Harlow, Essex, 2001).

Cawkwell, George, *Philip of Macedon* (London, 1978).

Celik, Zeynep, *The Remaking of Istanbul, Portrait of an Ottoman City in the Nineteenth Century* (Berkeley and Los Angeles, 1986).

Codoner, Juan Signes, *The Emperor Theophilos and the East 829–842, Court and Frontier in Byzantium during the last Phase of Iconoclasm* (Birmingham, 2014).

Contamine, Philippe, *War in the Middle Ages* (Oxford, 1984).

Cook, J.M, *The Persian Empire* (London, 1983).

Crow, J.G, 'The Long Walls of Thrace', in Mango and Dagron (eds), *Constantinople and its Hinterland* (Aldershot, 1995) pp 109–24.

Davison, Roderic H, 'The Armenian Crisis, 1912–1914', in *Essays in Ottoman and Turkish History, 1774–1923, The Impact of the West* (Texas, 1990), pp 180–205.

Davison, Roderic H, 'Turkish Diplomacy from Mudros to Lausanne', in *Essays in Ottoman and Turkish History*, pp 203–42.

Decker, Michael J, *The Byzantine Art of War* (Yardley, PA, 2013).

Dignas, Beate,and Engelbert Winter, *Rome and Persia in Late Antiquity, Neighbours and Rivals* (Cambridge, 2007).

Dvornik, F, *The Slavs, their History and Civilisation* (Boston, MA, 1956).

Edmonds, Sir James, *The Occupation of Constantinople, 1918–1923*, Official History of the War (Uckfield, 2010).

Ellis, J.R, *Philip II and Macedonian Imperialism* (London, 1976).

Fields, Nic, *Ancient Greek Fortifications 500–300 BC* (Oxford, 2006).

Foss, C, 'Strobilos and Pylai, two ports of Bithynia', *Epigraphica Anatolica*, 28 (1997), pp 85–96.

Francopan, Peter, *The First Crusade, the Call from the East* (London, 2012).

Franklin, Simon, and Jonathan Shepard, *The Emergence of Rus 750–1200* (Harlow, Essex, 1996).

Freely, John, *Istanbul, the Imperial City* (London, 1996).

Freely, John, *The Bosphorus* (Istanbul, 1993).

Freely, John, *The Companion Guide to Istanbul* (Woodbridge, Suffolk, 2000).

Gardner, Alice, *The Lascarids of Nicaea* (London, 1912).

Gibbon, Edward, *The Decline and Fall of the Roman Empire* (London, 1788).

Grainger, John D, *Rome, Parthia, India, The Violent Emergence of a New World Order, 150–140 BC* (Barnsley, 2017).

Grainger, John D, *The Galatians* (Barnsley, 2020).

Grainger, John D, *The Syrian Wars* (Leiden, 2010).

Grainger, John D, *The Straits from Troy to Constantinople* (Barnsley, 2021).

Grainger, John D, *13 Sharks* (Barnsley, 2016).

Gregoire, H, 'Deux Champs de Bataille: "Campus Ergenus" et "Campus Ardiensis"', *Byzantion*, 18 (1938), pp 585–6.

Gul, Murat, *The Emergence of Modern Istanbul, Transformation and Modernisation of the City* (London, 2009).

Haldon, J.F, *Byzantium in the Seventh Century, the Transformation of a Culture* (Cambridge, 1997).

Halpern, Paul G, (ed), *The Royal Navy the Mediterranean, 1915–1918* (Navy Records Society, 1987).

Halpern, Paul G, *A Naval History of World War I* (London, 1994).

Hammond, Nicholas, *Philip of Macedon* (London, 1994).

Harington, Sir Charles, *Tim Harington Looks Back* (London, 1940).

Harris, Jonathan, *Constantinople, Capital of Byzantium*, 2nd ed (London, 2007).

Harris, Jonathan, *Byzantium and the Crusades* (London, 2003).

Harris, Jonathan, *The End of Byzantium* (New Haven, CT, 2012).

Hasluck, F.W, *Cyzicus* (Cambridge, 1910).

Heather, Peter, *Goths and Romans* (Oxford, 1997).

Heather, Peter, and John Matthews, *The Goths in the Fourth Century* (Liverpool, 1991).

Helliesen, J.M, 'Andriscus and the revolt of the Macedonians, 149–148 BC ', *Ancient Macedonia*, IV (Thessalonica, 1986).

Hengst, Daan den, 'Preparing the Ruler for War, Ammianus' Digression on Siege Engines', in J.W. Drijvers and David Hunt, *The Late Roman World and its Historian, Interpreting Ammianus Marcellinus* (London, 1999).

Hitti, P.K, *History of Syria*, 2 vols (London, 1951, republished 2002).

Hooton, E.R. *Prelude to the First World War, the Balkan Wars, 1912–1913* (London, 2014).

Howard-Johnson, J.D, 'The Siege of Constantinople in 626', in Mango and Dagron (eds), *Constantinople and its Hinterland* (Aldershot, 1995), pp 131–142.

Hughes, Bettany, *Istanbul, A Tale of Three Cities* (London, 2017).

Ibrahim, Raymond, *Sword and Scimitar* (New York, 2018).

Inalcik, H, 'The Rise of the Ottoman Empire', in M.A. Cook (ed), *A History of the Ottoman Empire to 1730* (Cambridge, 1976), pp 21–4.

Inalcik, H, *The Ottoman Empire, the Classical Age 1300–1600* (London, 1973).

James, Robert Rhodes, *Gallipoli* (London, 1965).

Jones, A.H.M, *Constantine and the Conversion of Europe* (London, 1948).

Kaegi, Walter E, *Heraclius, Emperor of Byzantium* (Cambridge, 2003).

Kaegi, Walter E, *Muslim Expansion and Byzantine Collapse in North Africa* (Cambridge, 2010).

Kagan, Donald D, *The Fall of the Athenian Empire* (Ithaca, NY, 1987).

Karpat, Kemal H, *Ottoman Population 1830–1914, Demographic and Social Characteristics* (Madison, WI, 1985).

Kennedy, Hugh, *The Armies of the Caliphs* (London, 2001).

Kern, Paul Bentley, *Ancient Siege Warfare* (Bloomington, IN, 1999).

Keys, David, *Catastrophe, an Investigation into the Origin of the Modern World* (London, 1999).

King, Charles, *Midnight at the Pera Palace Hotel, the Birth of Modern Istanbul* (New York, 2014).

Lambert, Andrew, *Admirals* (London, 2008).

Lane, F.C, *Venice, a Maritime Republic* (Baltimore, 1973).

Lawrence, A.W, *Greek Aims in Fortifications* (Oxford, 1979).

Lemerle, P, 'Thomas le Slave', in *Travaux et Memoires*, 1 (1965), pp 255

Little, Lester K. (ed), *Plague and the end of Antiquity, the Pandemic of 541–750* (Cambridge, 2007).

Lock, Peter, *The Franks in the Aegean, 1204–1500* (Harlow, Essex, 1995).

Lumby, E.W.R. (ed), *Policy and Operations in the Mediterranean, 1912–1914* (Navy Records Society, 1970).

McEvedy, Colin, *Cities of the Classical World* (London, 2011).

McMeekin, Sean, *The Berlin-Baghdad Express* (London, 2010).

MacMullen, Ramsay, *Roman Government's Response to Crisis, AD 235–337* (New Haven, 1976).

MacMullen, Ramsay, *Constantine* (Beckenham, Kent 1969).

Mackesy, Piers, *The War in the Mediterranean, 1803–1810* (London, 1959).

Madden, Thomas F, 'The Fires of the Fourth Crusade in Constantinople, 1203–1204, a Damage Assessment', *Byzantinische Zeitschrift*, 84/85 (1992), pp 72–83.

Madden, Thomas F, *Enrico Dandolo and the Rise of Venice* (Baltimore, 2003).

Madden, Thomas F, *Istanbul, City of Majesty at the Crossroads of the World* (New York, 2016).

Majesta, G.B, *Russian Travellers to Constantinople in the Fourteenth and Fifteenth Centuries* (Washington, DC, 1984).

Mango, Cyril, 'The Water Supply of Constantinople', in Cyril Mango and Gilbert Dagron, *Constantinople and its Hinterland* (Aldershot, Hants, 995), pp 9–18.

Mango, Cyril, and Gilbert Dagron, *Constantinople and its Hinterland* (Aldershot, Hants, 1995).

Mansel, Philip, *Constantinople, City of the World's Desire, 1453–1924* (London, 1995).

Manz, Beatrice Forbes, *The Rise and Rule of Tamerlane* (Cambridge, 1989).

Marder, Arthur J, *From the Dreadnought to Scapa Flow*, vol. II (Oxford, 1965).

Marder, Arthur J, 'The Dardanelles Revisited, Further Thoughts on the Naval Prelude', in *From the Dardanelles to Oran* (Oxford, 1974), pp 1–32.

Marsden, E.W, *Greek and Roman Artillery*, 2 vols (Oxford 1969 and 1971).

Marsot, Afaf Lutfi al-Sayyid, *Egypt in the Reign of Muhammad Ali* (Cambridge, 1984).

Matthews, John, *The Roman Empire of Ammianus* (London, 1989).

Meiggs, Russell, *The Athenian Empire* (Oxford, 1975).

Melvin, Mungo, *Sebastopol's War, Crimea from Potemkin to Putin* (Oxford, 2017).

Miller, William, *The Latins in the Levant* (Cambridge, 1908, reprinted 1964).

Mitchell, Donald W, *A History of Russian and Soviet Sea Power* (London, 1974)

Mitchell, Stephen, *A History of the Later Roman Empire, A.D. 284–641* (Oxford, 2007).

Moorhead, John, *The Roman Empire Divided, 400–700* (Harlow, Essex, 2001).

Nachtergael, G, *Les Galates en Grece et les Soteria a Delphes* (Brussels, 1997).

Necioglu, N, 'Economic Conditions in Constantinople during the Siege of Bayazit (1394–1402)', in Mango and Dakron (eds), *Constantinople and its Hinterland* (Aldershot, Hants, 1995), pp 157–170.

Nicol, Donald M, *The Despotate of Epirus, 1267–1479, a Contribution to the History of Greece in the Middle Ages* (Cambridge, 1989).

Nicol, Donald M, *The Last Centuries of Byzantium, 1261–1453*, 2nd ed (Cambridge, 1993).

Norwich, John Julius, *A History of Venice* (London, 1982).

Obolensky, D, *The Byzantine Commonwealth, Eastern Europe 500–1453* (London, 1971).

Olmstead, A.T, *History of the Persian Empire* (Chicago, 1948).

Orga, Irfan, *Phoenix Ascendant, the Rise of Modern Turkey* (London, 1958), pp 70–72.

Pares, Bernard, *A History of Russia* (London, 1955).

Peters, Edward, (ed), *The First Crusade*, 2nd ed (Philadelphia, 1998).

Phillips, Jonathan, *The Fourth Crusade and the Sack of Constantinople* (London, 2004).

Potter, David S, *The Roman Empire at Bay* (London, 2004).

Preiss, Reuven Amitai, *The Mamluk-Ilkhanid War, 1260–1281* (Cambridge, 1995).

Robert, L, 'La titulature de Nicee et de Nicomedee: la gloire et la haine', *HSCP*, 81 (1977), pp 1–39.

Rosen, William, *Justinian's Flea, Plague, Empire and the Birth of Europe* (London, 2008).

Rostovtzeff, M, *Social and Economic History of the Hellenistic World* (Oxford, 1944).

Runciman, Steven, *History of the Crusades* (Cambridge, 1951–54).

Runciman, Steven, *A History of the First Bulgarian Empire* (London, 1930, reprinted 2018).

Runciman, Steven, *The Emperor Romanus Lecapenus and his Reign* (Cambridge, 1929).

Runciman, Steven, *The Sicilian Vespers, a history of the Mediterranean world in the later thirteenth century* (London, 1958).

Runciman, Steven, *Mistra, Byzantine Capital of the Peloponnese* (London, 1980).

Runciman, Steven, *The Fall of Constantinople 1453* (Cambridge, 1965).

Runciman, Steven, *The Great Church in Captivity* (Cambridge, 1968).

Russell, Thomas, *Byzantium and the Bosporus* (Oxford, 2017).

Saltzman, Michele Renée, *The Making of a Christian Aristocracy* (Cambridge, MA, 2002).

Saul, Norman E, *Russia and the Mediterranean 1797–1807* (Chicago, 1970).

Shaw, Stanford J, *History of the Ottoman Empire and Modern Turkey*, vol 1, *Empire of the Gazis* (Cambridge, 1976).

Shepard, J, 'Why did the Russians attack Byzantium in 1043?' *Byzantinisch-neugreichischen*, 22 (1978/1979), pp 197–212.

Sherk, Robert, *America's Black Sea Fleet, the US Navy amidst War and Revolution, 1919–1923* (Annapolis, 2012).

Smith, John Holland, *Constantine the Great* (New York, 1971).

Sondhaus, Lawrence, *The Great War at Sea, a Naval History of the First World War* (Cambridge, 2014).

Still, William N, jr, *American Sea Power in the Old World, the United States Navy in European and Near Eastern Waters, 1865–1917* (Annapolis, 1980, republished 2018).

Toynbee, A.J, *Constantine Porphyrogenetus and his World* (Oxford, 1973).

Turnbull, Stephen, *The Walls of Constantinople*, (Oxford, 2004).

Vryonis, Spyros, *The Decline of Mediaeval Hellenism in Asia Minor* (Berkeley and Los Angeles, 1971).

Walbank, F.W, *A Commentary on Polybius*, vol 1 (Oxford, 1957).

Walder, David, *The Chanak Affair* (London, 1969).

Waterson, James, *The Knights of Islam, the Wars of the Mamluks* (London, 2007).

Welles, C.B, *Royal Correspondence of the Hellenistic Period* (New Haven, 1936).

Whitby, Michael, *The Emperor Maurice and his Historian* (Oxford, 1988).

Williams, Stephen, *Diocletian and the Roman Recovery* (London, 1985).

Wolfram, Herwig, *History of the Goths* (Berkeley and Los Angeles), 1988.

Notes

Introduction

1. The precise date is uncertain, but seventh-century pottery was discovered by archaeologists: John Boardman, *The Greeks Overseas* (Harmondsworth, 1975), p 236.
2. Thomas Russell, *Byzantium and the Bosporus* (Oxford, 2017), discusses the mythology in chapter 1; A.R. Burn, *The Lyric Age of Greece* (London, 1967), pp 113–14.
3. John D. Grainger, *The Straits from Troy to Constantinople* (Barnsley, 2021).
4. Outline plan in Colin McEvedy, *Cities of the Classical World* (London, 2011), pp 102–3, and in most books on the city.
5. See 'Interlude II, the Five Walls', for details.
6. Herodotus, *Histories*, 1.144.
7. Kemal H. Karpat, *Ottoman Population 1830 – 1914, Demographic and Social Characteristics* (Madison WI, 1985), suggests a population of about 360,000 in 1829 rising to 1,160,000 in 1900. All figures are estimates; the census counted 'families' and multiplied by assumed family size.
8. See 'Interlude I' on Polybios' and Strabo's take on the city.

Chapter 1

1. For the emergence of Dareios, see J.M. Cook, *The Persian Empire* (London, 1983); A.T. Olmstead, *History of the Persian Empire* (Chicago, 1948); A.R. Burn, *Persia and the Greeks* (London, 1983).
2. Herodotos, 4.96.
3. *Ibid*, 4.97.
4. *Ibid*, 4.138; Burn, *Persia*, p 136.
5. Burn, *Persia*, p 130.
6. Herodotos, 4.136–142; Burn, *Persia*, p 133 and note, for the variety of interpretations.
7. Herodotos, 4.87.
8. Burn, *Persia*, p 136.
9. Herodotos, 5.26.
10. *Ibid*, 5.105.
11. *Ibid*, 6.1–5; Burn, *Persia*, pp 207–8; Thomas Russell, *Byzantium and the Bosporus* (Oxford, 2017), pp 56–7.
12. Herodotos, 6.5, 26–30.
13. *Ibid*, 6.33.
14. The Thracian name-ending 'bria' (meaning 'town') indicates the origin of the place; sixth-century Greek pottery from the site implies Greek contact, and perhaps a small Greek settlement within the Thracian town. It was therefore not a new Greek colony: John Boardman, *The Greeks Overseas* (Harmondsworth, 1973), p 243.
15. Herodotos, 9.66.
16. Thucydides, 1.94; Plutarch, *Aristeides*, 33.
17. Plutarch, *Aristeides*, 23.
18. Thucydides, 1.95.
19. *Ibid*.
20. Diodoros, 15.28; M. N. Tod, *Greek Historical Inscriptions* (henceforth GHI), (Oxford, 1948) 2.103; Russell Meiggs, *The Athenian Empire* (Oxford, 1975), p 43.
21. Thucydides, 1.128.

22. Justin, 9.12; Thucydides, 1.128–30.
23. Thucydides 1.131; Meiggs, *Athenian Empire*, pp 73, 465–8.

Chapter 2

1. Meiggs, *Athenian Empire*, does not discuss Byzantines date of joining.
2. Russell, *Byzantium*, p 62, citing Dionysius of Byzantium, 109.
3. Tod, *GHI*, 1.49; Meiggs, *Athenian Empire*, pp 160–63.
4. Thucydides, 1.115 and 118; Nepos, *Timotheus*, 1.2; Diodoros 12.28.3–4; Meiggs, *Athenian Empire*, p 192.
5. B.D. Merritt, H.T. Wade-Grey and M.F. McGregor, *The Athenian Tribute Lists*, 4 vols (Cambridge, MA, and Princeton, 1939–55), years 449, 442–440 BC (15 talents); 432 (8); 429 (21).
6. Plutarch, *Perikles*, 20.1–2.
7. Thucydides, 8.80.
8. Xenophon, *Hellenica*, 1.1.12.
9. *Ibid*, 1.1.20.
10. *Ibid*, 1.1.21.
11. *Ibid*, 1.1.24–6.
12. *Ibid*, 1.2.12–13.
13. *Ibid*, 1.1.35–6.
14. *Ibid*, 1.2.15–17; Plutarch, *Alkibiades*, 29.2 – 3; Diodoros, 13.6 4.4; Donald D. Kagan, *The Fall of the Athenian Empire* (Ithaca NY, 1987), pp 275–6.
15. Xenophon, *Hellenica*, 1.3.1–12; Diodoros, 13.6 6.1 – 3; Plutarch, *Alkibiades*, 29.3 – 31.2; Kagan, *Fall*, pp 276–81.
16. Xenophon, *Hellenica*, 1.3.14–16; Diodoros, 13.66.4; Plutarch, *Alkibiades*, 31.2.
17. Xenophon, *Hellenica*, 1.3.17.
18. Xenophon, *Hellenica*, 1.3.14–20; Diodoros, 13.66.4–67; Plutarch, *Alkibiades*, 31.2–6; Kagan, *Fall*, pp 282–4.
19. Xenophon, *Hellenica*, 2.2.2; Diodoros, 14.10.1–8; Plutarch, *Lysander*, 13.3–5; Kagan, *Fall*, pp 396–7.
20. Diodoros, 14.10.2.
21. Diodoros, 14.12.2; Polyainos, 2.2.7.
22. Diodoros, 14.12.2–9; Polyainos, 2.2.7–10; Frontinus, 3.5.1.
23. Xenophon, *Anabasis*, 6.6.1–7.1.
24. *Ibid*, 7.1.6–10.
25. Xenophon, *Hellenica*, 4.9.25–28.
26. *Ibid*, 4.8.27.

Chapter 3

1. Tod, *GHI*, 121 and 123.
2. Diodoros, 5.79.1.
3. Diodoros, 15.7 8.4 – 79.1; Russell, *Byzantium*, p 89.
4. Tod, *GHI* 141, 142.
5. Diodoros, 15.79.1.
6. Hornblower, *Mausollos*, pp 206–14.
7. Diodoros, 16.21.2.
8. Diodoros, 16.21.3.
9. Diodoros, 16.21.3–22.2.
10. Diodoros, 16.34.3; Polyainos, 4.2.22.
11. J.R. Ellis, *Philip II and Macedonian Imperialism* (London, 1976), pp 87–9.
12. *Ibid*, p 110.
13. Athenaios, 13.557b – e; Ellis, *Philip II*, p 116 and note 37.
14. Justin, 9.1.1 – 2.
15. Arrian, *Anabasis*, 1.25.1 – 2; Ellis, *Philip II*, pp 170–71; Diodoros, 16.71.2; Justin, 9.2.1.
16. Demosthenes, 18.244 and 300; Hypereides, F5 – 6; Plutarch, *Vit. X Or.*, 850 a (Hypereides).

17. [Demosthenes] 12.6; Ellis, *Philip II*, p 173 and note 75.
18. E.W. Marsden, *Greek and Roman Artillery*, 2 vols (Oxford, 1969 and 1971).
19. The siege is described by Diodoros, 16.74.2–76.4; modern accounts include Ellis, *Philip II*, pp 174–8; George Cawkwell, *Philip of Macedon* (London, 1978), pp 135–6; Marsden, *Greek and Roman Artillery*, volume 1, pp 100–101; Paul Bentley Kern, *Ancient Siege Warfare* (Bloomington IN, 1999), pp 198–200.
20. Diodoros, 16.74.5.
21. Diodoros, 16.7 5.1–2.
22. Diodoros, 16.75.2.
23. Diodoros, 16.76.3.
24. Ellis, *Philip II*, 176–7.
25. Demosthenes, 18.76.
26. Didymos, *In Demos.*, 10.45–47; Frontinus, *Stratagems*, 1.4.13; Demosthenes, 18.139; Justin, 9.1.5–7; Ellis, *Philip II*, p 179; Nicholas Hammond, *Philip of Macedon* (London, 1994), p 132; Cawkwell, *Philip*, pp 138–40.
27. Ellis, *Philip II*, 179–80.
28. Diodoros, 16.76.3 – 4; Kern, *Ancient Siege Warfare*, pp 199–200.
29. Plutarch, *Alexander*, 70; Richard A. Billows, *Antigonos the One-Eyed and the Creation of the Hellenistic State* (Berkeley and Los Angeles, 1990), pp 27–9.
30. Plutarch, *Phokion*, 14.2–3; Dionysius of Byzantion, F41.
31. Diodoros, 18.139; Justin, 9.1.7; Frontinus, *Stratagems*, 1.4.13.
32. Hammond, *Philip*, pp 174–5; Ellis, *Philip II*, pp 183–5.
33. Tod, *GHI*, 187.
34. Diodoros, 18.51.1–7.
35. Diodoros, 18.7 2.2–4; Polyainos, 4.6.8; Billows, *Antigonos*, pp 86–7.
36. Billows, *Antigonos*, p 87, note.
37. F.W. Hasluck, *Cyzicus* (Cambridge, 1910).
38. Diodoros, 19.77.6–7.
39. Diodoros, 20.111.3.
40. M. Rostovtzeff, *Social and Economic History of the Hellenistic World* (Oxford, 1941), pp 589–91.

Chapter 4
1. Memnon, *FGrH*, 434 F9–10.
2. G. Nachtergael, *Les Galates en Grece et les Soteria a Delphes* (Brussels, 1997); John D. Grainger, *The Galatians* (Barnsley, 2020), chapters 1–3.
3. Livy, 38.1 6.1–9.
4. Grainger, *Galatians*, pp 89–100.
5. For the varying discussions on the Tylis state, its location and customs, see Grainger, *Galatians*, pp 68–72 and the notes and references on that section.
6. Polybios 4.46.3 – 4.
7. Russell, *Byzantium*, pp 95–6; Russell lists a wide range of modern studies of this war.
8. Polybios, 4.47–52.
9. Polybios, 4.51–2.
10. Polybios, 8.2 2.1.
11. Polybios, 5.111.1–7.

Chapter 5
1. J.D. Grainger, *The Syrian Wars* (Leiden, 2010).
2. Polyainos, 4.16.
3. Memnon, *FGrH*, 434 F 15.
4. Dionysios of Byzantion, 41.
5. C.B. Welles, *Royal Correspondence of the Hellenistic Period* (New Haven, 1936), pp 18–20; *OGIS*, 225.
6. Dionysios of Byzantion, 41.

Interlude I
1. Polybios, 4.38.1–13 and 43.1–44.8.
2. Polybios, 4.45.1–3.
3. F.W. Walbank, *A Commentary on Polybius*, vol. 1 (Oxford, 1957), pp 486–7.
4. Polybios, 4.38.11.
5. Polybios, 4.38.4.
6. Walbank, *Commentary*, vol. 1, p 487.
7. Polybios, 4.38.4–5; Walbank, *Commentary*, vol 1, p 487; S. Lambrino, *Dacia*, 3–4, (1927–1932), p 400f.
8. Polybios, 4.16.
9. Polybios, 4.45.3–5.
10. Polybios, 4.45.7–8.
11. Demosthenes 15.26; *I Byz*, 5.23.
12. Polybios, 4.50.3; Dionysios of Byzantion, 92–4.
13. See Chapter 5.
14. *I Apameia* (ed. T. Corsten); C. Foss, 'Strobilos and Pylai, two ports of Bithynia', *Epigraphica Anatolica* 28 (1997), pp 85–96.
15. Bettany Hughes, *Istanbul, a Tale of Three Cities* (London, 2017), ch 6, p 338, has more on this aspect of the city.

Chapter 6
1. Tacitus, *Annals*, 12.63.2.
2. J.M. Helliesen, 'Andriscus and the revolt of the Macedonians, 149–148 BC', *Ancient Macedonia* IV (Thessalonica, 1986); J.D. Grainger, *Rome, Parthia, India, The Violent Emergence of a New World Order, 150 – 140 BC* (Barnsley, 2017), chapter 3.
3. Tacitus, *Annals*, 12.63.
4. Anthony Birley, *The African Emperor, Septimius Severus* (London, 1988), pp 97–102; (in fact all three of the contenders were African); David S. Potter, *The Roman Empire at Bay* (London, 2004), pp 103–4.
5. *Historia Augusta, Severus*, 8.13; Dio Cassius, 74.6.3–6; *ILS*, 1141.
6. Herodian 3.2.9; L. Robert, 'La titulature de Nicee et de Nicomedee: la gloire et la haine', *HSCP* 81 (1977), pp 1–39.
7. Dio Cassius, 74.6.4–6.
8. Robert, '*La titulature de Nicee et de Nicomedee: la gloire et la haine*', note 6.
9. Dio Cassius, 75.10.1–14.6; Herodian, 3.6.9.
10. See Interlude II for a discussion of the walls.
11. Note the similar reaction at Syracuse in 413 BC, and at Malta in the Second World War as the battered ships of Operation Pedestal arrived.
12. Dio Cassius, 75.10.1–14.6.
13. Dio Cassius, 75.11.1
14. Dio Cassius, 75.14.1–3.
15. *SHA, Caracalla*, 1.7.
16. John Freely, *Istanbul, the Imperial City* (London, 1996), pp 27–8, quoting Dionysios of Byzantion and the *Chronicon Pasquale*.

Chapter 7
1. Herwig Wolfram, *History of the Goths* (Berkeley and Los Angeles, 1988), pp 36–42.
2. Borani may not be the name they used themselves, nor may they be Sarmatians: Peter Heather and John Matthews, *The Goths in the fourth Century* (Liverpool, 1991), p 2, notes 5 and 6.
3. Ibid, pp 42–43.
4. Ibid.
5. Jordanes, *Getica*, 91, p. 81.
6. Zosimus, 1.33.
7. As noted by Wolfram, *Goths*, repeatedly; also George V. Brauer Jr, *The Age of the Soldier Emperors* (Park Ridge, NJ, 1975), ch 12.

8. For the Carpi, see Petrus Patrinus, frag. 8 – quoted by Wolfram, *Goths*, 44.
9. Zosimus, 1.34.
10. Zosimus, 1.35.
11. Zosimus, 1.36.
12. Zosimus, 1.35; Lukas de Blois, *The Policy of the Emperor Gallienus* (Leiden, 1976), p 32, note 39, points out that Felix can be identified as the ordinary consul of 237, an experienced man 'and so perhaps an old acquaintance of Valerian'; Valerian was the father of Gallienus, an associate of the Gordians, and emperor from 253. We do not know what information the emperor had of the events at the Straits; quite probably all he knew was that Byzantion was under threat.
13. *SHA, Two Gallieni*, 7.2–3.
14. Zosimus, 1.42, claims 6,000 boats and 320,000 men!
15. Zosimus, 1.42.
16. *SHA, Two Gallieni*, 13.6–7; this source is always suspect, but the author names the two Byzantine army commanders as Cleodamus and Athenaeus, with Venianus as the admiral, who was killed in the fight; the detail tends to convince; Wolfram, *Goths*, p 53, for the camp at Hieron (no source given).
17. Ammianus Marcellinus, 31.5 and 16 and 16.8; Hasluck, *Kyzikos*, pp 190–91.
18. Zosimus, 1.40 and 43; on the chronological problems see Potter, *Roman Empire*, p 263, note 3; Brauer, *Age of the Soldier Emperors*, p 265.

Chapter 8

1. Stephen Williams, *Diocletian and the Roman Recovery* (London, 1985); Ramsay MacMullen, *Roman Government's Response to Crisis, AD 235–337* (New Haven, 1976).
2. John Holland Smith, *Constantine the Great* (New York, 1971); Timothy D. Barnes, *Constantine and Eusebius* (Cambridge MA, 1981); Ramsay MacMullen, *Constantine* (Beckenham, Kent, 1969); A.H.M. Jones, *Constantine and the Conversion of Europe* (London, 1948). There are numerous other discussions of Constantine's career.
3. M.T.W. Anaheim, *The Senatorial Aristocracy in the Later Roman Empire* (Oxford, 1972); Michele Renée Saltzman, *The Making of a Christian Aristocracy* (Cambridge, MA, 2002).
4. Lactantius, *On the Deaths of the Persecutors*, 36.2.
5. Zosimus, 2.18.
6. Lactantius, *Persecutors*, 45.2–46.12.
7. Eutropius 10.4.1; H. Gregoire, 'Deux Champs de Bataille: "Campus Ergenus" et "Campus Ardiensis"', *Byzantion* 18, 1938, pp 585–6.
8. Smith, *Constantine*, p 169, for the barbarian campaign.
9. Zosimus, 2.22–28; Barnes, *Constantine and Eusebius*, p 76.
10. Philostorgus, *Church History*, 24–6.
11. Sozomen, *Ecclesiastical History*, 2.3.

Interlude II

1. Polybios, 4.38.1; for a general account see Nic Fields, *Ancient Greek Fortifications 500–300 BC* (Oxford, 2006); A.W. Lawrence, *Greek Aims in Fortifications* (Oxford, 1979).
2. Diodoros, 16.74.4; Athenaios, 10.442c; Aelian, *Varia Historia*, 3.4; Marsden, *Greek and Roman Artillery*, pp 59–60, theorized that Philip and his engineer Polyeidos developed torsion artillery in the last years before the Persian expedition, and that Perinthos was the first target to suffer from it.
3. Herodian, 3.2.1.
4. Cassius Dio, 74.10.
5. Diodoros, 3.6.9; Dio Cassius, 74.10–14.
6. See maps 1 and 2 in Jonathan Harris, *Constantinople, Capital of Byzantium*, 2nd ed (London, 2018), pages 4 and 32, for the walls of the city; only the line of one of those shown is certain.
7. Ammianus Macellinus, 23.4.1 – 15; Daan den Hengst, 'Preparing the Ruler for War, Ammianus' Digression on Siege Engines', in J.W. Drijvers and David Hunt, *The Late*

Roman World and its Historian, Interpreting Ammianus Marcellinus (London, 1999), pp 29–39; John Matthews, *The Roman Empire of Ammianus* (London, 1989), pp 290–95.

8. For the ramp, see Zosimus 2.24–25.

9. See the outline plans in Colin MacEvedy, *Cities of the Classical World* (London, 2011), p 1 (Alexandria), p 19 (Antioch), p 100 (Constantinople), p 208 (Republican Rome).

10. C. Mango, 'The Water Supply of Constantinople', in Cyril Mango and Gilbert Dagron, *Constantinople and its Hinterland* (Aldershot, 1995), pp 9–18.

11. I rely heavily here on Stephen Turnbull, *The Walls of Constantinople, 324 – 1453* (Oxford, 2004).

12. The sea walls are rarely noticed; see Turnbull, *Walls*, pp 15–16.

13. J.G. Crow, 'The Long Walls of Thrace', in Mango and Dagron, *Constantinople/ Hinterland*, pp 109–24.

14. Procopios, *De Aedificium*, 4.9.7.

15. Edward Gibbon, *The Decline and Fall of the Roman Empire* (London, 1788), 4.250–53.

Chapter 9

1. Ammianus Marcellinus, 31.12.1–13.12; Peter Heather, *Goths and Romans* (Oxford, 1991), pp 142–7; Wolfram, *Goths*, pp 326–8.

2. Ammianus, 31.15.1–16.1.

3. Zosimus, 4.24.3.

4. Ammianus, 31.16.3–6.

5. Ammianus, 31.16.7.

6. Heather, *Goths and Romans*, pp 177–81.

7. Zosimus, 5.5.4; Claudian, *In Rufinum*, 2; Heather, *Goths and Romans*, p 201.

Chapter 10

1. *PLRE*, 1171–76 (Vitalianus 2) for his life and career.

2. Sources for this episode include John Malalas, 402–6, 411–12; Evagrius, 3.43; modern accounts are erratic and inconsistent, mainly concentrating on the religious dispute; the most coherent is J.B. Bury, *The History of the Later Roman Empire from the Death of Theodosius I to the Death of Justinian*, 2 vols (London, 1889, reprinted 1958), vol 1, pp 447–52.

3. Malalas, *Chronographia*, 411–12.

4. Procopios, *History of the Wars*, vi; Malalas, frag 43.

Chapter 11

1. Procopios, *Persian Wars*, 2.4.4–12; G. Greatrex, 'Procopius and Agathias on the Defences of the Thracian Chersonese', in Mango and Dagron, *Constantinople and its Hinterland*, pp 125–30.

2. Procopios, *Gothic Wars*, 7.11.15–16 and 29.1–3.

3. Stephen Mitchell, *A History of the Later Roman Empire, A.D. 284 – 641* (Oxford, 2007), summarizing David Keys, *Catastrophe, an Investigation into the Origin of the Modern World* (London, 1999).

4. Procopios, *Gothic Wars* 4.25.8.

5. Keys, *Catastrophe*; William Rosen, *Justinian's Flea, Plague, Empire and the Birth of Europe* (London, 2008); Lester K. Little (ed.), *Plague and the end of Antiquity, the Pandemic of 541–750* (Cambridge, 2007), especially chapters 5 and 6.

6. Bury, *Later Roman Empire*, pp 304–5.

7. Ibid; Agathias, 5.2; Theophanes, 6051.

8. Bury, *Later Roman Empire*, 305–7.

Chapter 12

1. Constantine Porphyrogenitus, *De Administrando imperii*, 28; A.J. Toynbee, *Constantine Porphyrogenetus and his World* (Oxford, 1973), pp 620–37.

2. Beate Dignas and Engelbert Winter, *Rome and Persia in Late Antiquity, Neighbours and Rivals* (Cambridge, 2007), pp 100–114; the two empires were at war for seventy-one years between 502 and 591.

3. Theophylact Simocatta, *History*, edited and translated by M. and M. Whitby (Oxford, 1986), 4.11.1–15.1; Dignas and Winter, *Rome and Persia*, pp 237–240.
4. *Chronicon Pasquale*, edited and translated by M. and M. Whitby (Liverpool, 1989), t683–4; Theophanes, *Chronicle*, translated by Harry Turtledove (Philadelphia, PA, 1982), 286.14–289.26; Theophylact, 3.10.4–15.9; Michael Whitby, *The Emperor Maurice and his Historian* (Oxford, 1988).
5. Al-Tabari, *History*, volume V: *The Sasanids, the Byzantines, the Lakmids and Yemen*, translated C.E. Bosworth (New York, 1999), pp 317–18.
6. *Chronicon Pasquale*, 695–97.
7. Noted, with an example, by John Moorhead, *The Roman Empire Divided, 400 – 700* (Harlow, Essex, 2001), p 170.
8. Theophylact, 1.7.3–6.
9. Walter A. Kaegi, *Heraclius, Emperor of Byzantium* (Cambridge, 2003), pp 44–5.
10. Theophanes, 6102; Kaegi, *Heraclius*, pp 48–9.
11. Theophanes, 6102.
12. *Chronicon Pasquale*, 151–8; John of Nikiu, *Chronicle*, 110.4–7; Kaegi, *Heraclius*, pp 49–51.
13. Kaegi, *Heraclius*, pp 50–51.
14. *Chronicon Pasquale*, 160–62; Theophanes, 6107–6108; Sebeos, *Armenian History*, trans. R.W. Thompson, 2 vols (Liverpool, 1999), pp 79–80; Kaegi, *Heraclius*, pp 83–6.
15. *Chronicon Pasquale*, 165 and 203–5 (discussion of the date).
16. *Ibid.*
17. Toynbee, *Constantine Porphyrogenitus*, 621, quoting F. Dvornik, *The Slavs, their History and Civilisation* (Boston, MA, 1956), pp 60–61.
18. Constantine Porphyrogenitus, *De Administrando*, ch 30, pp 133–4; Toynbee, *Constantine Porphyrogenitus*, 624–5.
19. Kaegi, *Heraclius*, p 127.
20. *Chronicon Pasquale*, 721, 19–21; as J.D. Howard-Johnson points out in 'The Siege of Constantinople in 626', in Mango and Dagron (eds), *Constantinople*, pp 131 – 142 (at 133), this is an inference from the *Chronicon* report of the khagan's comments, but they fit with the Persians' unwillingness to join in the siege, and their failure to bring up a naval force.
21. Kaegi, *Heraclius*, pp 132–3.
22. George of Pisidia, *Bellum Avaricum*, pp 280–81; *Chronicon Pasquale*, 718, 4–22.
23. Theophanes, 315.13–22.
24. *Chronicon Pasquale*, 717.4–5; *Bellum Avaricum*, lines 217–19; Howard-Johnson, 'Siege', p 137, note 22.
25. *Chronicon Pasquale*, 717.4–5.
26. Howard-Johnson, 'Siege', pp 135–6.
27. Kaegi, *Heraclius*, pp 136–8; Howard-Johnson, 'Siege', pp 138–41.
28. Howard-Johnson, 'Siege', p 135.
29. *Ibid*, p 139.
30. *Chronicon Pasquale*, 720.10–723.15.
31. *Ibid*, pp 724.21–726.3.
32. Howard-Johnson, 'Siege', p 141.
33. Dignas and Winter, *Rome and Persia*, pp 47 and 148–51; Kaegi, *Heraclius*, pp 174–9.

Chapter 13

1. This may now be called the 'Byzantine' Empire, though this is a much later historians' invention – the inhabitants still considered themselves Roman.
2. Theophanes, 345.
3. For this war see Walter E. Kaegi, *Muslim Expansion and Byzantine Collapse in North Africa* (Cambridge, 2010).
4. Theophanes, 352.
5. Theophanes, 353.
6. Theophanes, 353–4.
7. Hugh Kennedy, *The Armies of the Caliphs* (London, 2001), p 12.
8. Theophanes, 354.

9. Theophanes, 352; Michael J. Decker, *The Byzantine Art of War* (Yardley, PA, 2013), pp 222–3.
10. Theophanes, 353–4; Malalas, of course, had claimed it was used a century before; either he was wrong, or it was a different weapon, or this was an interpolation into his account.
11. Theophanes, 355–6; this treaty does not seem to have applied in Africa, where fighting continued.
12. Theophanes, 361, 363.
13. Khalid Yahya Blankenship, *The End of the Jihad State, the Reign of Hisham ibn Abd al-Malik and the Collapse of the Umayyads* (Albany, NY, 1994), p 26, calls it 'a great exaggeration'. Abu-l Abbas Baladhuri, *Kitab Futuh al-Buldan, The Origins of the Islamic State*, trans. P.K. Hitti (New York, 1916, reprinted 2002), does not mention it at all.
14. Toynbee, *Constantine Porphyrogenitus*, pp 327, 329–30.
15. A 'theme' was a military region; the system's origin is unclear; several are mentioned in this period of crisis; three in particular, the Opsikian, the Anatolic, and the Armeniac, were prominent and politically active.
16. Theophanes, 384.
17. Theophanes, 385.
18. Theophanes, 385–6.
19. Theophanes, 386, 395; J.F. Haldon, *Byzantium in the Seventh Century, the Transformation of a Culture* (Cambridge, 1997), pp 82–3.
20. Theophanes, 386–7, 390.
21. Theophanes, 395.
22. *Ibid.*
23. Theophanes, 395–6.
24. D. Obolensky, *The Byzantine Commonwealth, Eastern Europe 500–1453* (London, 1971), pp 65–6.
25. Theophanes, 396.
26. *Ibid.*
27. Theophanes, 396–7.
28. Theophanes, 397.
29. *Ibid.*
30. Theophanes, 397–8.
31. Theophanes, 399; elaborated by P.K. Hitti, *History of Syria*, 2 vols (London, 1951, republished 2002), vol 2, pp 487–8.

Chapter 14

1. The only source of any value for these events is Theophanes, *Chronicle*, 412–20; other sources, providing little further information, are collected in Robert Hoyland, trans. and ed., *Theophilos of Edessa's Chronicle and the Circulation of Historical Knowledge in Late Antiquity and Early Islam* (Liverpool, 2011), pp 237–44.
2. Sources for the Iconoclastic period are collected in Leslie Brubaker and John Haldon, *Byzantium in the Iconoclastic Era (ca 680 – 850), The Sources, An Annotated Survey* (Birmingham, 2001); see P. Lemerle, 'Thomas le Slave', in *Travaux et Memoires*, 1 (1965), pp 255–97; and Juan Signes Codoner, *The Emperor Theophilos and the East 829–842, Court and Frontier in Byzantium during the last Phase of Iconoclasm* (Birmingham, 2014).

Chapter 15

1. Steven Runciman, *A History of the First Bulgarian Empire* (London, 1930, reprinted 2018), pp 42–4.
2. Theophanes, *Chronographia*, pp 752–4.
3. *Ibid*, pp 751–4, 772–8; Runciman, *First Bulgarian Empire*, pp 46–52.
4. Theophanes, *Chronographia*, 785.
5. *Ibid*, 785–6; other sources are noted by Runciman, *First Bulgarian Empire*, p 55.
6. 'Scriptor Incertus', pp 346–48.

7. The Hadrianopolitians were collected *in toto* after twenty years of 'captivity', by a naval expedition from Constantinople: Runciman, *First Bulgarian Empire*, p 75; Cordonor, *Theophilus*, pp 350–51; both provide references to sources.
8. Theophanes, *Continuatus*, 378.
9. Much of the evidence in this war is in the letters of the Patriarch Nicholas, the *Epistles* (*Ep.*); the source here is in *Ep.* V, vii.
10. Theophanes *Continuatus, 383; Runciman, First Bulgarian Empire*, pp 138–40.
11. Steven Runciman, *The Emperor Romanus Lecapenus and his Reign* (Cambridge, 1929), ch 2.
12. Constantine Porphyrogennitos, *De Administrando Imperii*, 153; Nicholas, *Ep.*, xvii.
13. Nicholas, *Ep.,* xviii–xix; Theophanes, *Continuatus*, 400.
14. Theophanes, *Continuatus, 401–3; Nicholas,* Ep., xxii.
15. Theophanes, *Continuatus*, 404.
16. Runciman, *First Bulgarian Empire*, pp 150–53.

Chapter 16
1. Photios, *Homilies*, ed. C. Mango (Washington DC, 1958), pp 82, 98, 101; *Analecta Bruxelliana*, ed. F. Cumont (Ghent, 1894); Simon Franklin and Jonathan Shepard, *The Emergence of Rus 750–1200* (Harlow, Essex, 1996), pp 50–51.
2. *The Annals of St Bertin*, ed. Janet Nelson (Manchester, 1991), p 44.
3. Franklin and Shepard, *Emergence of Rus*, pp 106–8.
4. Franklin and Shepard, *Emergence of Rus*, pp 113–17.
5. *Ibid.*
6. *Ibid*, pp 150–51.

Chapter 17
1. Michael Psellos, *Fourteen Byzantine Rulers*, trans. E.R.A Sewter (Harmondsworth, 1966); Michael Angold, *The Byzantine Empire, 1025–1204, A Political History* (Harlow, Essex, 1985), ch 1, 'Basil II and his Legacy'.
2. Angold, *Byzantine Empire*, pp 12–14; J. Shepard, 'Why did the Russians attack Byzantium in 1043?', *Byzantinisch-neugreichischen Jahrbucher*, 22 (1978/1979), pp 197–212.
3. Psellos, *Fourteen Byzantine Rulers*, pp 205–219.
4. Psellos, *Fourteen Byzantine Rulers*, pp 276–302.
5. Psellos, *Fourteen Byzantine Rulers*, pp 312 – 330; he was proud of his role in these events.
6. Spyros Vryonis, *The Decline of Mediaeval Hellenism in Asia Minor* (Berkeley and Los Angeles, 1971), pp 85–113; Claude Cahen, *The Formation of Turkey* (Harlow, Essex, 2001), pp 7–10.
7. Angold, *Byzantine Empire*, p 110.
8. *Ibid*, pp 110–11.
9. *Ibid*, pp 138–40.
10. Jonathan Harris, *Byzantium and the Crusades* (London, 2003), ch 3.
11. It seems clear that it was quickly assumed in the West that Jerusalem was to be the target, not Constantinople, still less assisting the Byzantine Empire.
12. Steven Runciman, *History of the Crusades* vol. 1, *The First Crusade* (Cambridge, 1951), pp 106–120; Peter Francopan, *The First Crusade, the Call from the East* (London, 2012), ch 7; Edward Peters (ed.), *The First Crusade*, 2nd ed (Philadelphia, 1998), prints a wide selection of original materials on this subject.
13. Peters (ed.), *First Crusade*, ch 11, 'The People's Crusade'; Runciman, *First Crusade*, pp 121–33.
14. Runciman, *First Crusade*, pp 127–38.
15. Peters (ed.), *First Crusade*, pp 143–51 (four sources); Runciman, *First Crusade*, pp 128–33.
16. Peters (ed.), *First Crusade*, pp 161–70; Runciman, *First Crusade*, pp 147–51.
17. Runciman, *First Crusade*, p 151.
18. Peters (ed.), pp 152–58, but in detail only covering the journeys of Bohemond and Raymond.
19. *Ibid*, pp 159–89.

20. Voiced by John Kinnamos, *Deeds of John and Manuel Comnenos*, trans. C.M. Brand (New York, 1976), p 58, before the Crusaders had come anywhere near the city.
21. Jonathan Harris, *Byzantium and the Crusades* (London, 2003), pp 94–6.
22. *Ibid*, p 96.
23. Niketas Choniates, *Annals*, 221–22.
24. *Ibid*, 224–26; Harris, *Byzantium*, pp 132–36.

Chapter 18
1. Their predecessors were John II (1118–43), and Masud I (1116–56).
2. Angold, *Byzantine Empire*, pp 199–201.
3. *Ibid*, 263 – 271; Vasiliev, *Byzantine Empire*, vol. 2, pp 377–9 and 433–7.
4. Jonathan Phillips, *The Fourth Crusade and the Sack of Constantinople* (London, 2004), pp 1–55, for the preaching of the Crusade and preparations for departure.
5. For Venetian policy see F.C. Lane, *Venice, a Maritime Republic* (Baltimore, 1973), pp 36–7; John Julius Norwich, *A History of Venice* (London, 1982), pp 122–30; Thomas F. Madden, *Enrico Dandolo and the Rise of Venice* (Baltimore, 2003), pp 117–29.
6. Phillips, *Fourth Crusade*, chs 4 and 6.
7. *Ibid*, 92–3.
8. Vasiliev, *Byzantine Empire*, p 440.
9. Phillips, *Fourth Crusade*, ch 7.
10. Cahen, *Formation of Turkey*, pp 32–46.
11. Angold, *Byzantine Empire*, pp 272–5.
12. Phillips, *Fourth Crusade*, pp 158–9.
13. Madden, *Enrico Dandolo*, p 64.
14. Phillips, *Fourth Crusade*, pp 159–61.
15. *Ibid*, pp 163–4.
16. *Ibid*, pp 166–70; Madden, *Enrico Dandolo*, pp 158–60.
17. Phillips, *Fourth Crusade*, pp 173–6; Madden, *Enrico Dandolo*, pp 160–62.
18. Phillips, *Fourth Crusade*, pp 176–82.
19. *Ibid*, pp 182–3.
20. Niketas Choniates, *Annals*, trans. H.J. Margoulis (Detroit, 1984), pp 299–301; Phillips, *Fourth Crusade*, pp 183–4.
21. Phillips, *Fourth Crusade*, pp 185–90.
22. *Ibid*, pp 207–9.
23. Niketas Choniates, *Annals*, pp 307–8.
24. *Ibid*, pp 308–9; Phillips, *Fourth Crusade*, pp 222–35.
25. Phillips, *Fourth Crusade*, pp 227–30.
26. *Ibid*, pp 232–33; Madden, *Enrico Dandolo*, pp 166–7.
27. Phillips, *Fourth Crusade*, pp 225–6.
28. Most of these Westerners had left after the fires; Murtzouphlos expelled the last of them in March 1204: Madden, *Enrico Dandolo*, pp 164, 169 note 79.
29. Robert of Clari, 92; for the methods of mediaeval siege war see J. Bradbury, *The Mediaeval Siege* (Woodbridge, Suffolk, 1992), and Philippe Contamine, *War in the Middle Ages* (Oxford, 1984), pp 193–207, 'Artillery'.
30. Robert of Clari, 70–71; Villehardouin, sec. 237–240. Phillips, *Fourth Crusade*, pp 242–4; Madden, *Enrico Dandolo*, pp 169–71.
31. Robert of Clari, 92.
32. Phillips, Fourth Crusade, 244 – 246.
33. Phillips, Fourth Crusade, 247 – 252, a detailed and convincing account of the fighting.
34. Nicholas Choniates, *Annals*, 313.
35. Thomas F. Madden, 'The Fires of the Fourth Crusade in Constantinople, 1203 – 1204, a Damage Assessment', *Byzantinische Zeitschrift* 84/85 (1992), pp 72–83.
36. Niketas Choniates, *Annals*, 313.
37. *Ibid*, p 314.
38. *Ibid*.
39. Phillips, *Fourth Crusade*, pp 259–69.

Interlude IV
1. Phillips, *Fourth Crusade*, p 270; Madden, *Enrico Dandolo*, pp 175–6.
2. Phillips, *Fourth Crusade*, pp 270–71.
3. Nicolas Choniates, *Annals*, 357.
4. Villehardouin, *Chronicle*, 97.
5. Harris, *Byzantium*, p 165; Runciman, *History of the Crusades*, vol.3, pp 126–7.
6. Peter Lock, *The Franks in the Aegean, 1204 – 1500* (Harlow, Essex, 1995); William Miller, *The Latins in the Levant* (Cambridge, 1908, reprinted 1964).
7. Lock, *Franks*, p 51.
8. Villehardouin, *Chronicle*, 404–570; Phillips, *Fourth Crusade*, pp 289–91.
9. Lock, *Franks*, pp 66–8.
10. Madden, *Enrico Dandolo*, pp 184, 188, 191; Lock, *Franks*, ch. 6; Lane, *Venice*, pp 42–3 ('an empire of naval bases'); a beguiling tour of the Venetian territories is given by Jan Morris, *The Venetian Empire, A Sea Voyage* (London, 1980).
11. Harris, *Byzantium*, pp 169–71.

Chapter 19
1. 'Despot' did not signify a political method; it was a title which had developed in the late Empire, usually one rank below emperor; 'despot' was also a rank in the Nikaian Empire.
2. Morris, *Venetian Empire*.
3. Steven Runciman, *The Sicilian Vespers, a history of the Mediterranean world in the later thirteenth century* (London, 1958).
4. James Waterson, *The Knights of Islam, the Wars of the Mamluks* (London, 2007); Reuven Amitai Preiss, *The Mamluk-Ilkhanid War, 1260 – 1281* (Cambridge, 1995).
5. Robert of Clari, 78–9; Phillips, *Fourth Crusade*, p 191; Cahen, *Formation of Turkey* (Harlow, Essex, 2001), p 48.
6. Alice Gardner, *The Lascarids of Nicaea* (London, 1912), pp 82–3.
7. Michael Angold, *A Byzantine Government in Exile, Government and Society under the Lascarids of Nicaea (1204 – 1261)* (Oxford, 1975), p 240; Cahen, *Formation of Turkey*, pp 48–9.
8. Lock, *Franks in the Aegean*, pp 60–61.
9. Donald M. Nicol, *The Despotate of Epirus* (Oxford, 1957), continued in *The Despotate of Epirus 1267–1479* (Cambridge, 1984).
10. Gardner, *Lascarids of Nicaea*, pp 150–51; Angold, *Byzantine Empire in Exile*, pp 22–3.
11. This capture is generally described as accidental by moderns – Runciman, for example, in *Sicilian Vespers*, and in his *History of the Crusades*, vol. 3. No doubt this is due to its lack of violence. The only detailed account is by Gardner, *Lascarids of Nicaea*, pp 251–8. The reaction at the time was to see it as an accident, an 'act of God', but there was more involved than that, as Gardner's account makes clear; it was not in Michael Palaiologos' interest, of course, to have one of his generals acquiring the credit.
12. Vasiliev, *Byzantine Empire*, vol.2, p 536; Gardner, *Lascarids of Nicaea*, pp 247–50, calling it the battle of 'Castoria'.
13. As noted earlier, the best account of all this is by Gardner, *Lascarids of Nicaea* (note 8).
14. There are several essays on provisioning the city – with water, grain, vegetables, and fish – in section 1 of Mango and Dagron, (eds), *Constantinople and its Hinterland*.
15. The existence of this tunnel is extraordinary, but the troops did get into the city easily, and the gate was opened from the inside.

Chapter 20
1. Donald M. Nicol, *The Last Centuries of Byzantium, 1261–1453*, 2nd ed (Cambridge, 1993), Part III.
2. *Ibid*, pp 216–18.
3. Mark C. Bartusis, *The Late Byzantine Army, Arms and Society, 1204–1453* (Philadelphia, 1992), pp 260–69.
4. Nicol, *Last Centuries*, pp 235–7.

5. Bartusis, *Late Byzantine Army*, pp 92–9.
6. *Ibid*, p 101; Nicol, *Last Centuries*, pp 241–2.
7. Nicol, *Last Centuries*, pp 278–9; Bartusis, *Late Byzantine Army*, p 107.
8. Nicol, *Last Centuries*, p 241; Stanford J. Shaw, *History of the Ottoman Empire and Modern Turkey*, vol. 1, *Empire of the Gazis* (Cambridge, 1976), pp 16–17.
9. Nicol, *Last Centuries*, pp 281–2; Jonathan Harris, *The End of Byzantium* (New Haven, CT, 2012), pp 48–9.
10. Bartusis, *Late Byzantine Army*, pp 109–10; Nicol, *Last Centuries*, pp 291–2; G.B. Majesta, *Russian Travellers to Constantinople in the Fourteenth and Fifteenth Centuries*, Washington, DC, 1984), pp 100–105 and 408–15; Harris, *End*, pp 49–51; John W. Barker, *Manuel II, 1391–1425, a Study in Late Byzantine Statesmanship* (New Brunswick, NJ, 1969), 68–83.
11. Shaw, *Empire of the Gazis*, pp 15–22; H. Inalcik, 'The Rise of the Ottoman Empire', in M.A. Cook (ed), *A History of the Ottoman Empire to 1730* (Cambridge, 1976), pp 21–4.

Chapter 21
1. Bartusis, *Late Byzantine Army*, pp 110–11; Nicol, *Last Centuries*, pp 300–302; Harris, *End*, pp 10–12.
2. 'The Beginning and Duration of Bayazid's Siege of Constantinople', Barker, *Manuel II*, pp 479–481.
3. For Timur's career see Beatrice Forbes Manz, *The Rise and Rule of Tamerlane* (Cambridge 1989), and René Grousset, *L'Empire des Steppes* (Paris, 1965), pp 486–546; for his activities in Anatolia, see M. M. Alexandrescu-Dersca, *La Campagne de Timour en Anatolie* (Bucharest, 1942).
4. Nicol, *Last Centuries*, p 302; Shaw, *Empire of the Gazis*, pp 29 and 33–34; Bartusis, *Late Byzantine Army*, pp 110–12.
5. N. Necioglu, 'Economic Conditions in Constantinople during the Siege of Bayazit (1394–1402)', in Mango and Dakron (eds), *Constantinople and its Hinterland*, pp 157–170.
6. 'The Reconciliation of John VII and Manuel in 1399', in Barker, *Manuel II*, pp 419–93.
7. Nicol, *Last Centuries*, p 308.
8. Shaw, *Empire of the Gazis*, pp 34–35.
9. *Ibid*, pp 35–6; Nicol, *Last Centuries*, pp 314–17; Raymond Ibrahim, *Sword and Scimitar* (New York, 2018), pp 224–26.
10. Nicol, *Last Centuries*, pp 319–20; Barker, *Manuel II*, pp 251–3.
11. Shaw, *Empire of the Gazis*, pp 37–8.
12. *Ibid*, pp 38–9; Nicol, *Last Centuries*, p 326; Barker, *Manuel II*, pp 284–7.
13. Bartusis, *Late Byzantine Army*, p 113.
14. Nicol, *Last Centuries*, pp 326–7; Bartusis, *Late Byzantine Army*, pp 112–13; Barker, *Manuel II*, pp 287–8.
15. Nicol, *Last Centuries*, p 332, calls him 'shifty'.
16. Giovanni Cananos, *L'assedio di Constantinopoli*, edited and translated by E. Pinto (Messina, 1972); Vasiliev, *Byzantine Empire*, pp 639–40; Shaw, *Empire of the Gazis*, p 45; Bartusis, *Late Byzantine Army*, p 117; Barker, *Manuel II*, pp 359–67.
17. Bartusis, *Late Byzantine Army*, pp 334–8; Gabor Argoston, *Guns for the Sultan, Military Power and the Weapons Industry in the Ottoman Empire* (Cambridge, 2005), p 28, points out that it was Murad II who founded the Ottoman artillery corps, but perhaps not until after this initial crisis was over.
18. Nicol, *Last Centuries*, pp 332–3; Barker, *Manuel II*, pp 366–9.
19. Inalcik, 'Rise of the Ottoman Empire', in Cook (ed), *History*, p 44.
20. Nicol, *Last Centuries*, pp 334–35.
21. Harris, *End*, pp 123–8.
22. *Ibid*, p 126.
23. Vasiliev, *Byzantine Empire*, pp 670–74.
24. Steven Runciman, *Mistra, Byzantine Capital of the Peloponnese*, (London, 1980).
25. Donald M. Nicol, *The Despotate of Epirus, 1267–1479, a Contribution to the History of Greece in the Middle Ages* (Cambridge, 1989), pp 191–2.

26. Nicol, *Last Centuries*, p 360; Steven Runciman, *The Fall of Constantinople 1453* (Cambridge, 1965), p 49; Bartusis, *Late Byzantine Army*, p 118.
27. Runciman, *Fall*, 49.

Chapter 22
1. Shaw, *Empire of the Gazis*, pp 113–14.
2. *Ibid*, pp 52–4; Runciman, *Fall*, p 46.
3. Runciman, *Fall*, pp 48–52; Nicol, *Last Centuries*, pp 368–70.
4. Nicol, *Last Centuries*, p 371; Runciman, *Fall*, pp 53–4.
5. Runciman, *Fall*, pp 52–3; Miller, *Latins in the Levant*, pp 415, 425–6.
6. Shaw, *Empire of the Gazis*, pp 55–6; Runciman, *Fall*, p 61.
7. Runciman, *Fall*, pp 60–61; Shaw, *Empire of the Gazis*, p 56, assigns the pacific ploy to Halil.
8. Shaw, *Empire of the Gazis*, p 56.
9. Nicol, *Last Centuries*, p 375; Runciman, *Fall*, pp 65–6; Harris, *End*, pp 184–5.
10. Runciman, *Fall*, p 66; Nicol, *Last Centuries*, pp 374–6.
11. Runciman, *Fall*, pp 67–9, 80–81; Nicol, *Last Centuries*, p 376.
12. Runciman, *Fall*, p 82; Nicol, *Last Centuries*, p 373.
13. Runciman, *Fall*, pp 82–5.
14. Norwich, *History of Venice*, pp 326–7; Lane, *Venice*, p 235.
15. Agoston, *Guns for the Sultan*, pp 18, 49.
16. The number of ships is, of course, disputed, and they varied in size and purpose. The sultan deployed about 200 in 1460 in the Danube campaign; about that number would be needed against Constantinople.
17. Runciman, *Fall*, p 81.
18. Aguston, *Guns for the Sultan*, 45–8; Runciman, *Fall*, pp 77–8.
19. Runciman, *Fall*, p 74.
20. *Ibid*.
21. *Ibid*, pp 76–8.
22. *Ibid*.
23. Runciman, *Fall*, p 85; see also Bartusis, *Late Byzantine Army*, pp 130–31.
24. The sources for the siege are listed in Runciman, *Fall*, pp 236–9, and the modern accounts at 239–45. Runciman's is the best and clearest modern account, though clearly biased towards the defence. For the Turkish side there is a very brief account in Shaw, *Empire of the Gazis*, pp 56–57, partly because the Turkish sources are relatively few. See also Nicol, *Last Centuries*, pp 377–90; Bartusis, *Late Byzantine Army*, pp 121–34, Raymond Ibrahim, *Sword and Scimitar* (New York, 2018), pp 234–43; Harris, *End*, pp 197–206; all histories of the city and the Byzantine Empire have accounts of the siege, some more summary and inaccurate than others.
25. Runciman, *Fall*, p 93, a plan of the city and the stations of the troops and commanders.
26. Runciman, *Fall*, pp 101–3.
27. *Ibid*, pp 104–8.
28. *Ibid*, pp 116–20.
29. *Ibid*, pp 134–41.

Interlude V
1. Runciman, *Fall*, pp 145–8; John Freely, *Istanbul, the Imperial City* (London, 1996), p 177; the original sources for the sack usually exaggerate the looting and the danger and the killing, especially Christian sources composed at some distance from events.
2. Runciman, *Fall*, pp 148–9; Freely, *Istanbul*, pp 181–2.
3. Freely, *Istanbul*, pp 317–82, provides much information on this.
4. Runciman, *Fall*, pp 1523.
5. Shaw, *Empire of the Gazis*, pp 59–60.
6. Freely, *Istanbul*, pp 183–4; Runciman, *Fall*, pp 154–7 and appendix II; Steven Runciman, *The Great Church in Captivity* (Cambridge, 1969), pp 165–85.

7. Freely, *Istanbul*, p 185.
8. Freely, *Istanbul*, p 188; Philip Mansel, *Constantinople, City of the World's Desire, 1453–1924* (London, 1995), pp 19–20.

Chapter 23

1. Mansel, *Constantinople*, p 137.
2. *Ibid*; Lane, *Venice*, pp 407–10.
3. Shaw, *Empire of the Gazis*, pp 248–9; Donald W. Mitchell, *A History of Russian and Soviet Sea Power* (London, 1974), p 64; Bernard Pares, *A History of Russia* (London, 1955), p 307.
4. Piers Mackesy, *The War in the Mediterranean, 1803–1810* (London, 1959), pp 163–78; Norman E. Saul, *Russia and the Mediterranean 1797–1807*, pp 216–20.
5. Pares, *History of Russia*, p 370.
6. *Ibid*, pp 386–7; Afaf Lutfi al-Sayyid Marsot, *Egypt in the Reign of Muhammad Ali* (Cambridge, 1984), pp 222–30.
7. Pares, *History of Russia*, pp 430–35; for the British fleet's predicament see Andrew Lambert, *Admirals* (London, 2008), pp 269–74.
8. There are numerous accounts of these wars, but the latest and most militarily detailed is E.R. Hooton, *Prelude to the First World War, the Balkan Wars, 1912–1913* (London, 2014).
9. J.G. Crow, 'The Long Walls of Thrace', in Mango and Dagron (eds), *Constantinople and its Hinterland*, pp 109–24, at p. 109.
10. Hooton, *Prelude*, p 86, has a plan of the lines.
11. *Ibid*, p 74.
12. Figures in Hooton, *Prelude*, pp 75–77.
13. Roderic H. Davison, 'The Armenian Crisis, 1912–1914', *American Historical Review*, 53 (1948), pp 481–505, reprinted in *Essays in Ottoman and Turkish History, 1774–1923, The Impact of the West* (Texas, 1990), pp 180–205.
14. Mansel, *Constantinople*, pp 366–7.
15. Mansel, *Constantinople*, p 367.
16. *Ibid*, p 368.
17. *Ibid*.
18. Hooton, *Prelude*, pp 89–93, 137–52.
19. *Ibid*, pp 185–87.

Chapter 24

1. Mansel, *Constantinople*, pp 368, 372.
2. E.W.R. Lumby (ed), *Policy and Operations in the Mediterranean, 1912–1914* (Navy Records Society, 1970), pp 131–238 for the pursuit, 433–36 for the sale.
3. Arthur J. Marder, *From the Dreadnought to Scapa Flow*, vol. II (Oxford, 1965), p 31, and 'The Dardanelles Revisited, Further Thoughts on the Naval Prelude', in *From the Dardanelles to Oran* (Oxford, 1974), pp 1–32.
4. Mungo Melvin, *Sebastopol's War, Crimea from Potemkin to Putin*, (Oxford, 2017), pp 349–52; the German ships made the raid on instructions from the Ottomans, and had had those instructions for several weeks before they were acted on.
5. Marder, *Dreadnought*, vol. II, p 201; Lumby (ed), *Mediterranean*, pp 456–9.
6. The exploit of Duckworth in 1807 was recalled, and a brief account of his passage of the Dardanelles is in the Admiralty papers on the Dardanelles expedition; there is no sign that any useful lessons were drawn, particularly the need for speed to make the passage.
7. Lumby, *Mediterranean*, p 427.
8. *Ibid*, p 448; Lawrence Sondhaus, *The Great War at Sea, a Naval History of the First World War* (Cambridge, 2014), p 106.
9. Marder, *Dreadnought*, pp 199–228, for the planning and preparations.
10. Paul G. Halpern, *A Naval History of World War I* (London, 1994), p 113.
11. Marder, *Dreadnought*, pp 240–44; Marder, 'Dardanelles Revisited', pp 12–14.

12. Marder, *Dreadnought*, pp 245–53.
13. The Gallipoli campaign has been extensively written about: note especially, Marder, *Dreadnought*, vol. II, pp 249–58 and 308–28; and Robert Rhodes James, *Gallipoli* (London, 1965).
14. Marder, 'Dardanelles revisited', pp 28–32.
15. Halpern, *Naval History*, p 119; Mansel, *Constantinople*, p 375; Hughes, *Istanbul*, p 565.
16. Charles King, *Midnight at the Pera Palace Hotel, the Birth of Modern Istanbul* (New York, 2014), pp 165–6; Hughes, *Istanbul*, p 565; Madden, *Istanbul*, pp 347–8.
17. Mansel, *Constantinople*, pp 373–8.
18. Sean McMeekin, *The Berlin-Baghdad Express* (London, 2010), p 317; Hughes, *Istanbul*, p 570.
19. *The Royal Navy in the Mediterranean, 1915–1918* (Navy Records Society, 1987), pp 583–5.
20. John D. Grainger, *13 Sharks* (Barnsley, 2016), p 179.
21. Hughes, *Istanbul*, pp 570–74; Robert Sherk, *America's Black Sea Fleet, the US Navy amidst War and Revolution, 1919–1923* (Annapolis, 2012); the United States had a minor naval presence in the Mediterranean from 1865, but did not involve itself in wars: William N. Still jr, *American Sea Power in the Old World, the United States Navy in European and Near Eastern Waters, 1865–1917* (Annapolis, 1980, republished 2018).
22. Sir James Edmonds, *The Occupation of Constantinople, 1918–1923*, Official History of the War, (Uckfield, 2010); Mansel, *Constantinople*, pp 380–88; Irfan Orga, *Phoenix Ascendant, the Rise of Modern Turkey* (London, 1958), pp 70–72.
23. Mansel, *Constantinople*, pp 398–400; King, *Midnight*, pp 91–110.
24. David Walder, *The Chanak Affair* (London, 1969).
25. Orga, *Phoenix Ascendant*, Part I.
26. Sir Charles Harington, *Tim Harington Looks Back* (London, 1940); Mansel, *Constantinople*, pp 403–4.
27. Roderic H. Davison, 'Turkish Diplomacy from Mudros to Lausanne', in *Essays in Ottoman and Turkish History*, pp 203–42.

Index

Abadan, 239
Abantus, Roman commander, 75–6
Abd al-Majid II, Ottoman Sultan, 246
Abd al-Malik, caliph, 119
Abdera, 26
Abydos, 5, 15–16, 18, 106, 123, 127
Acheloos River, battle, 138
Adramyttion, 121
Adriatic Sea, 55, 74, 80, 162, 176, 178
Aegean Sea, 3, 45, 69, 106, 117, 129, 148, 176, 196, 205, 216, 237, 246
Africa, xi, 100, 106, 111, 116, 140, 194, 207
Aigosages, Galatian band, 47
Aigospotamoi, battle 20, 30, 36
Akhaia, principality, 175
Akhaios, King, 46
Alaric, Gothic commander, 94
Alathar, Roman commander, 96
Albania, 110
Aleaumes, priest, 169
Alexander III the Great, King of Macedon, 34–5, 60, 78, 194
Alexander, Byzantine emperor, 138
Alexandria-by-Egypt, 64, 78
Alexandria Troas, 47, 54, 78
Alexios I Comnenos, Byzantine emperor, 148–53, 155, 174
Alexios II, Byzantine emperor, 156
Alexios III, Byzantine emperor, 157, 159–62, 164, 165, 174, 182
Alexios IV, Byzantine emperor, 157–8, 162–4, 165–6
Alexios V, Byzantine emperor, 164–7, 170, 172, 182
Alexios Comnenos, emperor at Trebizond, 174
Alexios Strategopoulos, commander, 186–7
Algeria, 232
Alkibiades, 12, 15–20
Amanus Mountains, 60
Ammianus Marcellinus, historian, 69, 83
Amorion, 123
Amphipolis, 29
Anadolu Hissar, 210–11, 213, 229, 248
Anatolic theme, 122, 127, 129
Anastasios I, Emperor, 95–9
Anastasios II, Emperor, 120–1, 123, 131
Anaxibios, Spartan harmost, 22
Anchialos, 97, 214
Andrew of Dureboise, 169
Andriskos, Macedonian pretender, 57–8
Andronikos I, Byzantine Emperor, 156, 174
Andronikos II, Byzantine Emperor, 188
Andronikos III, Byzantine Emperor, 188, 190
Andronikos IV, Byzantine Emperor, 191

Anglo-Saxons, 149
Ankara, 197
Anseau of Cahieu, 186
Antalkidas, Spartan diplomat, 23–4
Antandros, 5, 15, 18
Anthemius, Praetorian Prefect, xi, 32, 35
Antigenes, Macedonian commander, 32
Antigonos I Monophthalamos, king, 22, 34–7, 39, 78
Antigonos II Gonatas, King of Macedon, 39, 40
Antioch-in-Syria, 78, 84, 108
Antiochos I, king, 39, 41
Antiochos II, king, 49–50
Antiochos III, king, 58
Antipatros, Seleukid governor, 40–1
Antonius Creticus, M., 58
Apameia, 59, 67
Apulia, 181
Aquillius, M., 56
Arab Empire, 194
Arabia, Arabs, viii, 92–3, 104, 115–24
Aragon, King of, 212
Arbuthnot, British ambassador, 230
Ariston, tyrant, 4, 6
Armenia, Armenians, 58, 110–11, 129
Armeniac theme, 127, 129
Arta, 174, 205
Artabasdas, Byzantine pretender, 122, 126–8
Artabazos, Persian commander, 7
Artaxerxes, Great King, 20, 23
Asellius Aemilianus, Roman commander, 59–60
Athens, 7, 10, 22–3, 82, 211
  empire of, 8, 11–20
  revival, 24
  Second Confederacy, 24–5
  and Philip II, 24–33, 37
  duchy, 175, 179
Athos, Mount, 196
Attalid kingdom, 55
Attalos I, King of Pergamon, 46–7
Attika, 26
Aurelian, Emperor, 84
Australia, 247
Avars, ix, 103–106, 180
Aydin, emirate, 212
Ayyubids, Muslim dynasty, 157, 181

Baghdad, 133, 245
Baldwin I, Count of Flanders, Latin Emperor, 157, 158, 162, 173–5, 179, 182, 185
Baldwin II, Latin Emperor, 175, 181, 185
Balkan League, 232–3, 237

Balkan Wars, 239
  First, 233
  Second, 237–8
Balkans, 66, 71, 103–104, 131, 158, 232
Baltic Sea, 65, 143, 232
Baltoglu, Suleiman, Ottoman commander, 217, 219
Banat, 39–40
Basil II, Byzantine emperor, 133, 147–8, 187, 193
Bayazid I, Ottoman Sultan, 192–3, 195, 197–8, 201, 207, 210–12, 216
Belgrade, 243
Belisarius, Roman commander, 101–102
Berlin, 232
Bithynia, Bithynians, 16, 22, 41, 54, 59–60, 67, 180, 183, 190
Bizye, 85
Black Sea, 3–4, 6, 11, 14, 27, 33, 43, 45, 57, 58, 65–7, 87, 97, 142, 189, 196, 198, 205, 213, 229, 234, 237, 239–40
Boiotia, 7, 18
Bohemia, 110
Bohemond of Taranto, 152
Bolsheviks, 246
Boniface of Montserrat, King of Thessalonica, 157–8, 171, 173, 179–80
Bonosos, Roman commander, 107
Borani, 65–7
Boris I, Bulgar tsar, 138
Bosnia, 195
Bosporos, ix, xi, xii, 4–5, 10, 12–13, 16, 31, 33, 36, 40, 42, 51, 67, 70, 72, 123, 127, 142, 159, 190, 192, 211–12, 219, 229–30, 236, 239, 243
  battle, 112
Boucicaut, Marshal, 196–7
Brialmont, Belgian engineer, 234
Britain, British, viii, 229–32, 236, 238–48
Britannia, Roman province, 55
Brundisium, 55
Buenos Aires, 230
Bulgaria, Bulgars, viii, 124, 132, 135–41, 147, 156, 158, 182, 184, 188, 192, 229–38, 243, 245
Burgundy, 213
Byzantion:
  founding, viii, xii
  wall, ix, 51, 64, 73, 82
  population, xiii
  and Persian Empire, 4
  tyrants of, 4–5
  and Ionian revolt, 6–7
  government of, 11–13, 20, 22
  Athenian tax assessment, 13, 211
  rebellion, 14
  and Civil War
    and Philip II, 26–33
    trade, 52
    temples, 54
    as route centre, 56–7
    Roman treaty, 57
    destruction and refoundation, 60–4
    harbours, 64
    Strategeion, 64
    Milion, 64
    see also Constantinople, Istanbul
Byzas, King, ix, xii
Byzos, 24

Canada, 247
Canakkale, 229, 237, 247–8
Cappadocia, 105
Caracalla, Emperor, 63, 83
Carpi, 66–7
Carthage, 28, 64
Caspian Sea, 132
Caucasus, 66, 110, 207
Central Asia, 3, 104, 196
Chares, Athenian commander, 29, 31–3
Charles I, King of Two Sicilies, 176, 181
Chersonese, 5, 13, 17, 20–1, 26–7, 30–1, 33–4, 36, 40, 49, 52, 55, 67, 78, 100–101
  see also Gallipoli Peninsula
Chesme, battle, 229
China, 103
Chios, 25, 27, 33, 186, 209
Christianity, 72, 79, 95
  Iconoclasm, 126
  Mandaite, 118–19, 125
  Monotheletism, 120, 126
  Monophysitism, 95–6, 98
  Orthodox, 95, 120, 132, 176, 204
  Western (Catholic), 132–3, 203
Chrysopolis, 12–13, 15–16, 35, 76, 83, 121, 127
Churchill, Winston, 240
Cibotos (Civetot), 154
Cilicia, 60, 122, 127
Cimmerian Bosporos, 66
  see also Crimea
Claudius II, Emperor, 70
Claudius Candidus, Roman commander, 59–60
Clodius Albinus, Imperial pretender, 58
Coco, Giacomo, 219
Commodus, Emperor, 58
Conrad III, German Emperor, 153–4
Constans, Emperor, 116
Constantia, wife of Licinius, 77
Constantine I the Great, Emperor, ix–x, 71–81, 83–4, 91, 95, 227
Constantine IV, Emperor, 116, 118–20
Constantine V, Emperor, 126–8
Constantine VI, Emperor, 138–9
Constantine IX, Emperor, 148
Constantine X, Emperor, 148
Constantine XI, Governor of Morea, 205–207
  Emperor, 207, 223
Constantinople (for individual sieges, see contents page):
  Empire of, viii
  founding, viii, 79–81
  Golden Horn ix, x, xii, 83, 84, 97, 112, 117–18, 122, 123, 139, 160–1, 172, 186, 189, 196, 201, 217, 219–21, 223, 235
  buildings, x, 80
  population, x, xii
  Hagia Sofia, xi, 122, 164, 171, 187, 208, 221, 225–6, 228
  aqueduct, xii, 85
  harbours, 83, 117
  Blakhernai Palace, 121, 151, 161, 167, 168, 171, 190, 217, 221–2, 226
  Boukoleon Palace, 171
  Walls:
    first (of Byzantion), ix, 64, 80, 156
    second (Severan), x–xii, 80–1, 83–4

third (Constantinian), xi–xii, 83, 85
fourth (Theodosian), 85–8, 101, 107, 109, 111, 117, 121, 123, 138, 199, 213, 229, 248
fifth (Long wall), 87–8, 101, 107, 109, 111, 233, 239
Latin Empire, 173–7
sack of, 170–2, 174, 176
Gates:
Golden, 187, 192, 226
Charisian, 218
Third Military, 221–2
Kerkoposta postern, 222–3
Hadrianapolis, 225
see also Byzantion, Istanbul
Copenhagen, 230
Corinth, Isthmus of, 203, 215
Cornelius Sulla, L., 58
Cossacks, 229
Crete, 117, 176, 179, 215
Cretan War, 58
Crimea, 57, 66, 188
Crimean War, 231, 244, 246
Crispus, Roman commander, 75–7, 79
Croats, 110
Crusades:
First, 146–55
'Peoples', 150, 153
Second, 153
Third, 153, 156
Fourth, 153, 155–72, 201, 216, 224
Cumans, 147–8, 179–80
Cyclades, 176
Cyprus, 116, 179, 232
Cyril, Roman commander, 96, 98

Dacia, 66
Dalmatia, 157, 215
Damascus, 118
Dandolo, Enrico, doge of Venice, 157–9, 166, 173, 176
Danube River, 4–5, 39, 66, 70, 101, 135, 179, 192, 195, 197, 206, 232–3
frontier on, 56, 74, 80, 147, 158, 213
Dardanelles, 210, 212, 218, 229–30, 232, 237, 239–43, 245, 247
see also Hellespont
Dareios I, Great King, 3–5, 210
David Comnenos, Emperor at Trebizond, 174
Dayi Karadja Bey, Ottoman commander, 214, 217
Dareios II, Great King, 20
Daskyleion, 8
Delian League, 8–9, 11–12
Delos, 13
Delphi, xi, 39, 42
Demetrios Poliorketes, King, 38
Demetrios I, King of Thessalonica, 183
Demetrios, governor of Mesambria, 205–206, 208–209, 215
Demosthenes, Athenian politician, 27, 53
Denmark, 133
Didyma, 42
Dio Cassius, historian, 59, 61–2, 82
Diocletian, Emperor, x, 71, 79
Diopeithes, Athenian commander, 27
Dniepr River, 66, 101, 143
Dniestr River, 66, 69

Doriskos, 4, 7
Doukas, Constantine, 170
Duckworth, Sir John, British admiral, 230–1
Dyrrhachium, 55

Edirne, 213, 215, 231, 234–6
see also Hadrianopolis
Egnatius, Cn., 55
Egypt, x, xi, 70, 108–109, 113, 115–16, 124, 157, 181, 231–2
Elaious, 76
Enver Pasha, 235
Epameinondas, Theban commander, 24–5
Epeiros, Despotate, 174–5, 179–80, 183–4, 203
Ephesos, 42, 70
Estonia, 143
Ethiopia, 104
Euboia, 26, 176, 179
see also Negroponte
Eumathios, engineer, 135
Euphrates River, 239
Euphrosyne, Empress, 162, 170

Fabius Cilo, L., Roman commander, 59
Fadalah ibn Ubayd, Muslim commander, 116
Felix, Roman commander, 68, 70
Finland, Gulf of, 143–4
Flanders, 157
Count of, 149
Florence, Council of, 204–205
France, French, viii, 157, 196–7, 230, 232, 245–6
Fritigern, Gothic commander, 91–4
Franks, 149
Frederick I, Emperor, 154

Galata, xii, 87, 97, 123, 156, 160, 162, 169, 172, 186, 187, 191, 196, 217, 219
see also Pera
Galatia, Galatians, xiii, 39–48, 70
Galerius, Emperor, 71–3, 78
Gallienus, Emperor, 68, 70
Gallipoli peninsula, 40, 189, 191, 210, 236, 240–1, 244
see also Chersonese
Gelibolu, 213, 229, 237, 248
see also Gallipoli
Gemlik, Gulf of, 49
Gennadios, Patriarch, 226
Genoa, 155–6, 164, 186–90, 192, 196, 199, 212, 217–20
Germaniceia, 126
Germany, Germans, 150–1, 154, 157, 197, 239–48
Getai, Thracian tribe, 4, 27
Ghiyath al-Din Khusrau I, sultan, 182
Glarenza, 209
Godfrey de Bouillon, 151–3
Gordian III, Emperor, 61
Goths, 65–70, 74, 84–5, 91–5, 103
Goudeles, John, 177
Granikos River, battle, 60
Great (First World) War, 239–48
Greece, Greeks, viii, xii, 4, 55, 100, 103, 109, 203, 215, 231–3, 237, 245
Greek fire, 97–8, 117–20, 123–4, 128, 137, 144, 167

Hadrian, Emperor, 8
Hadrianopolis, 75, 80, 91–4, 111, 136–8, 180, 190, 198–9, 210, 213, 218, 226
    battle, 175
    see also Edirne
Hadrian's Wall, 86–7
Halil, vizier, 209–10, 213, 222
Harington, General Sir Charles, 247
Harald Hardraada, 149
Hasan, Ottoman soldier, 222
Hattin, battle, 156
Hebros River, 55
Helena, Empress, 208
Heliopolis, 117–18
Helixos, Megarian commander, 14, 18
Hellespont, 4, 7, 14–15, 18, 22, 25, 31, 34–6, 42, 54–6, 58–9, 69, 106, 123, 154, 175, 183, 190–2
    battle, 76
    see also Dardanelles
Hellespontine Phrygia, 5, 34, 59
Henry of Flanders, Latin Emperor, 171, 175, 180, 185
Heraion Teichos, 26
Herakleia, 73, 91, 106, 109
    see also Perinthos
Herakleia Pontike, 45
Heraklios, Emperor, 106–13
Herodian, historian, 59, 61, 82
Herodotos, historian, 7
Heruli, 69, 74
Hexamilion, 203
Hieron, 53, 69, 77, 124, 210
Hippokrates, Greek commander, 16
Hormisdas, pope, 98
Hungary, 103–105, 180, 196, 200, 213
Huns, viii 93, 95, 100, 144
    Kutrigur Huns, 100–103, 144
Hypatios, Roman commander, 96, 98

Ibrahim, Egyptian commander, 231
Iceland, 133
Iconium, 180
    see also Konya
Igor, Kievan ruler, 144
Illyricum, Roman province, 59
Imbros, 5, 25
India, 3, 194, 196
Innocent III, Pope, 157
Ionia, 212
Ionian revolt, 5–7
Irene, daughter of Alexios III, 162
Isa, Ottoman pretender, 198
Isaac I, Emperor, 148, 156, 162, 174
Ishak Pasha, Ottoman commander, 217, 221
Isidore, Cardinal, 217
Issos, battle, 60
Istanbul, x
    population, xii, 227
    Üsküdar, xii
    Istranja peninsula, 67, 85
    buildings, 81–2
    Islamization, 224–8
    Edirne Kapi, 225
    repopulation, 225
    Aya Sofya Camii, 226, 230
    Fatih camii, 226

Yeni Camii, 226
Topkapi Palace, 230
Blue Mosque, 230
Chatalja Lines, 233, 236–7
riots, 244
Haydarpasha station, 244
enemy occupation, 246
    see also Byzantion, Constantinople
Istros, 52, 66
Italy, 100, 110, 232, 239, 245–6
Iznik, Gulf of, 49

Jerusalem, 108, 150, 152, 156–7, 187
John I, Emperor, 156
John III Vatatzes, Emperor, 181, 183–5, 189
John IV, Emperor, 186
John V Palaiologos, Emperor, 188, 190–2
John VI, Emperor, 188
John VII, Emperor, 191–2, 197–8
John VIII, Emperor, 200, 204–206, 208, 220
John de Brienne, Latin Emperor, 185
John Asen II, Bulgar King, 183
John Hunyadi, Prince, 204, 209
Judaism, 133
Julianus, Emperor, 58
Julius Caesar, C., 58
Justin I, Emperor, 98
Justinian II, Emperor, 121–2

Kalchedon, xi–xii, 4–5, 7, 12, 14–16, 22, 35, 38, 53, 59, 67–8, 76–7, 108, 111–12, 116, 127, 150
Kallias, Peace of, 12
Kallinikos, engineer, 117–18
Kallipolis, 76, 183, 191–2, 198
    treaty of, 183
    see also Gallipoli, Gelibolu
Kaloyan, Bulgar tsar, 174–5, 179
Kananos, John, historian, 201
Kannavos, Nicholas, 165, 173
Karaman, 210
Kardia, 27
Karia, 25, 212
Kassandros, Macedonian commander, 35, 39
Katasyrtai, battle, 138
Kavaros, king of Tylis, 45–7
Kelts, 65
Kemal, Mustafa (Ataturk), 146, 247
Keos, 25
Kephalonia theme, 129
Kersebleptes, Thracian king, 27
Khaironeia, battle 34
Khavad, Sassanid Emperor, 113
Khazars, 132–3, 144–5
Khosro II, Sassanid Emperor, 104, 108, 110, 113
Kibyrrhaiot theme, 128–9
Kiev, 66, 132, 143–4, 180
Kilij Arslan III, Sultan, 155
Kimon, Athenian commander, 9
Kios, 67
Kirkkilesse, battle, 233
Kitchener, Lord, 240
Klearchos, Spartan commander, 17–19, 20–2, 23
Kleitos, Macedonian commander, 35–7
Koiratadas, Boiotian commander, 18
Kolonai, 9
Kommontorios, Galatian commander, 42–4
Konya, 155, 180, 231

Kos, 25, 117
Krum, Bulger Khagan, 132, 135
Kum Kale, 241
Kutahya, 271
Kyklades, 179
Kypsela, 49, 55–6, 64
Kyros the Great, King, 3
Kyros, Persian pretender, 20–1
Kyzikos, 13–15, 34, 37, 42, 49, 54, 59–60, 67, 69, 106, 117–19, 127

Lakedaimon, 18
Lampsakos, 13, 20
Laodike, Seleukid queen, 49
Laskaris, Constantine, 170–1, 173
Latvia, 143
Lausanne, treaty, 247
Lebanon, 118
Lemnos, 5, 7, 25, 229, 241
Leo III, Emperor, 122–4, 126
Leo V, Emperor, 128–9, 136
Leo VI, Emperor, 138
Leo Tornikios, Byzantine rebel, 148
Lesbos, 3, 179, 186, 196
Libya, 232, 244
Licinius Lucullus, L., 58
Licinius, Emperor, ix–x, 72, 73–7, 83
Lloyd George, Prime Minister, 247
Lombards, 110
London, 232, 247
    treaty, 236
Longo, Giovanni Giustiniani, 212, 217, 222
Louis VII, King of France, 154
Loutarios, Galatian commander, 39–41
Lovat river, 143
Luleburgas, battle, 233
Lykia, battle, 116
Lykos, stream, 85, 217–18, 221
Lysander, Spartan commander, 20
Lysimacheia, 40, 49, 52, 78–9
Lysimachos, Macedonian commander, 34, 36–7, 39–40, 78

Macedon, Macedonians, viii, 4, 24, 39, 102, 179
    Roman, 55, 57
Maddalena Tocco, 205
Malalas, historian, 97–8, 119
Mamluk Sultanate, 181, 196, 207
Mamun, Caliph, 129
Mandrokles, architect, 4
Manfred, King of the Two Sicilies, 185
Manisa, 207, 210
Manuel I, Emperor, 154–6, 158
Manuel II, Emperor, 190, 195, 199–202, 220
Manzikert, battle, 148–9, 152
Marcianopolis, 69
Margaret of Hungary, 174, 180
Maria, daughter of Romanos IV, 139
Marinus of Apameia, Roman governor, 97
Marius Maximus, L., Roman commander, 99
Marwan, Caliph, 119
Maslama, Muslim commander, 122
Masovia, 65
Maurice, Emperor, 104, 106, 108, 110
Mausollos, satrap, 25–6
Mavia, Arab Queen, 92

Maxentius, Emperor, 71
Maximin Daia, Emperor, 71–5, 77, 79
Maximinus, Emperor, 66
Mediterranean Sea, x, 4, 52, 246
Megabazos, Persian commander, xi, 5
Megara, founding city of Byzantion, viii, ix, 227
Mehmet I, Ottoman Sultan, 198, 200
Mehmet II, Ottoman Sultan, 202, 207–23, 224
Mehmet VI, Ottoman Sultan, 246
Mehmet Ali, Khedive of Egypt, 231
Melantias, 101
Mentese, emirate, 212
Mesambria, 6, 8, 97, 135–6, 205, 214
Mesopotamia, 113, 194, 245
Michael II, Emperor, 128–30
Michael VI, Emperor, 148
Michael VIII, Emperor, 184–8, 190
Michael II Doukas, Despot, 174, 179, 183–5
Michael Psellos, historian, 147
Milan, 74
Miletos, 6, 14, 42
Milne, George, British general, 246
Miltiades, Athenian commander, 5
Mistra, 205, 208–209
Mithridates, Pontic king, 58
Mavia, Arab queen, 198, 203–205, 215
Mongol, 180
Montenegro, 232–3
Moravia, 110
Muawiya I, Caliph, 116, 118–19
Muawiya II, Caliph, 119
Murad I, Ottoman Sultan, 191
Murad II, Ottoman Sultan, 200–205, 207, 213
Musa, Ottoman pretender, 198–200, 216
Mustafa, Ottoman pretender, 200
Mustafa, Ottoman pretender, 201–202

Napoleon, Emperor, 230
Naxos, 25
Nazir, Arab soldier, 93
Negroponte, 215
    see also Euboia
Nero, Emperor, 17, 58
New Zealand, 247
Nicopolis, 196
Nikaia, 59–61, 67, 121, 149, 151, 178, 180, 189
Nikaia, Empire of, 174, 178–87
Nikanor, Macedonian commander, 35–6
Nikephoros I, Byzantine emperor, 135
Niketas, son of Artabasdas, 128
Niketas, Roman commander, 106
Nikomedes I, King of Bithynia, 41
Nikomedia, x, 59–60, 67, 77–9, 122, 148, 150
Nineveh, battle, 113
Normans, 149
Novgorod, 143
Nymphaion, treaty, 186

Odessos, 96
Oleg, Rus ruler, 143
Olga, Rus princess, 133
Olynthos, 27, 29
Omurtag, Bulgar khagan, 130
Opsikian theme, 120–2, 127, 129
Orban, gunsmith, 213–14, 216
Orhan, Ottoman Prince, 209, 211, 217
Orkhan, Ottoman sultan, 189

Osman, Ottoman Sultan, 189, 202
Ostrogoths, 65
Otanes, Persian governor, 5, 7
Otto II, German Emperor, 142
Ottoman Empire, 189, 192–3, 231–2
  jihad state, 194–5
  millet system, 225–7
  fleet, 229
  decline, 232–3

Palestine, 115, 150, 155–6, 168
Paphlagonia, 156
Paris, 247
Parthian Empire, 56, 59
Pausanias, Spartan commander, 7–8
  at Byzantion, 8–10, 11
Pechenegs, viii, 140, 143, 145, 147, 148–9, 151
Pegai, 139
Pelagonia, battle, 185, 187
Peloponnesos, 175, 179, 189, 203–205
  league, 14
  theme, 129
  see also Morea
Pera, 196, 217, 220, 235
  see also Galata
Pergamon, 122
Perinthos, 13–15, 26, 28–30, 32–3, 37, 59, 63, 94, 214
  see also Herakleia
Perseus, Macedonian king, 8
Persian Empire, 3, 12, 24, 29–30, 37, 82
Persians, viii, x, 10
Pertinax, emperor, 58
Pescennius Niger, imperial pretender, 58–63
Peter the Hermit, Crusader, 150
Peter de Courteney, Latin Emperor, 181, 183
Peter, Bulgar tsar, 141
Peter of Bracieux, 169
Pharnabazos, Persian satrap, 15–18
Philadelphia, 189
Philip the Arab, Emperor, 78
Philip II, King of Macedon, 28–34, 36–7, 51, 53, 62, 67, 69, 76, 82
Philip of Swabia, 157–8
Philippikos, Emperor, 126
Philokrates, Peace of, 27
Phoenicia, 120
Phokas, Emperor, 104–108
Phokis, 28
Photios, Patriarch, 112
Phrantzes, George, 216
Pindos Mountains, 179
Pisa, 155–6, 163, 166
Pityus, 66
Plataia, battle, 7–8
Plevna, 232
Pliska, 135
Poland, Poles, 65, 133, 143
Polybios, historian, xiii, 51–4, 57, 82
Polyeidos, engineer, 31
Polyperchon, Macedonian commander, 35
Pomerania, 65
Pompeius Magnus, Cn. (Pompey), 58
Pontos-and-Bithynia, province, 57
Pope, 197, 203–204, 212–13, 218
Princes' Islands, 142, 218
Priscus of Nikomedia, engineer, 62

Procopios, historian, 100, 102
Propontis, 6, 9–11, 15–16, 18, 20, 23, 25–6, 49, 69, 70, 107, 117, 123, 130, 142, 175, 198
  see also Sea of Marmara
Prusa, 59, 67
Prusias I, King of Bithynia, 46–7
Ptolemy Keraunos, King of Macedon, 39
Ptolemy I, Egyptian King, 78
Ptolemy II, Egyptian King, 49–50, 54

Quadi, 66

Ragusa, 209
Raymond of Toulouse, 152
Rhineland, 150
Rhodes, 25, 27, 33, 115, 116, 121
  war with Byzantion, 45–6, 51
  Knights of, 192, 209
Rhyndakos river, 67
Riva, fort, 196, 211
  see also Anadolu Hissar
Robert of Clari, 169
Robert of Normandy, 152
Romania, 105, 232, 237
Romanos I, Emperor, 138–41
Romanos IV, Emperor, 148
Rome, x, xi, 55, 66, 72, 78, 79, 84, 131
  and Byzantion, 55–8
  and Macedon, 57
Rufinus, imperial Regent, 94
Rumeli Hissar, 211–13, 216, 229, 248
Rus, 132–3, 140, 142–7
Russia, 65, 131, 212, 229–32, 234–6, 238–9, 243, 245–6

St Petersburg, 233
Salonika, 233, 236, 245
  see also Thessalonica
Samo, Slav leader, 110
Samos, 3, 13
San Stefano, 232
Sardinia, 78
Sardis, 5, 122
Sarmatians, 65
Sassanid Empire, 66, 103–15
Satala, 111
Savov, Bulgar general, 237
Saxons, 65
Scandinavia, 65
Sea of Azov, 66, 69
Sea of Marmara, ix, 87, 213, 215, 217, 230, 232, 234, 237, 240, 244–5
  see also Propontis
Sebasteia, 111
Seleukos I, King, 39–40, 78
Seleukos II, King, 53
Seleukos III, King, 53
Selim III, Ottoman Sultan, 229
Seljuk Turks, 155, 180, 189
Selymbria, xii, 13–14, 17–19, 22, 26, 31–2, 34, 53, 109, 186–7, 192, 206, 208, 214
Septimius Severus, Emperor, ix–x, 58–64, 66, 83, 227
Serbia, Serbs, 110, 132, 139–40, 158, 188, 192, 209, 212, 232–3, 237
Serdica, 135–6
Sestos, 5, 7

Sevres, Treaty of, 247
Shahin, Sassanid commander, 108, 111, 113
Shahrbaraz, Sassanid commander, 111–13
Ships,
    British:
        Agamemnon, 245
        Shark, 245–6
    Crusaders:
        Fair Pilgrim, 169
        Paradise, 169
    German:
        Breslau, 239
        Goeben, 239
Sicily, 14, 28, 157
Side, Pamphylia, 55
Sinope, 231
Sisinnos, Byzantine commander, 127
Skythia, Skythians, 3–4, 6, 65
Slavs, 100–101, 103–105, 107–108
Smith, Sir Sydney, British admiral, 242
Smyrna, 117, 148, 186, 246
Sofia, battle, 106
Sogut, 189
Soissons, Bishop of, 169
Souchon, German Admiral, 240
Sousa, 16–18
Spain, 56
Sparta, 8, 14–22, 24, 54, 102, 205
Staraia Lagoda, 143
Staurakios, Byzantine emperor, 136
Stephen of Blois, 152
Sthenelaus, Spartan *harmost*, 20
Strabo, geographer, 51–2
Straits, ix, 237, 240, 244
Strato of Lampsakos, 51
Sudan, 19
Suleiman, Arab commander, 122
Suleiman, Ottoman pretender, 198–9
Svyatoslav, Kievan Prince, 145–6
Sweden, 143
Sykai, 97–8, 123
Symeon, Bulgar khagan, 138–41
Syracuse, 14–15, 116
Syria, 56, 58–60, 86, 100, 108, 113, 116, 118, 120, 124, 147, 231, 245–6

Tacitus, historian, 57
Takht-i-Suleiman, 110
Tarsus, 74, 108
Taruhan Bey, Ottoman commander, 215
Taurus Mountains, 60, 74, 124, 178, 192, 206, 215
Tenedos, 229–30
Terkos, lake 67, 68, 70
Tervel, Bulgar khagan, 120, 123
Tervingi Goths, 91
Thebes, Boiotia, 24
    lordship of, 179
Theodore, governor of Morea, 204–205
Theodore I Doukas, Despot, 183–4
Theodore I Laskaris, Emperor, 174, 179, 182
Theodore II Laskaris, Emperor, 184
Theodosios I, Emperor, 94
Theodosios II, Emperor, xi, 86–7
Theodosios III, Emperor, 121–3, 126, 131
Theophanes, chronicler, 117–19, 124
Theramenes, Athenian commander, 16–17
Thessalonica, ix–x, 75, 78, 80, 109, 157, 169, 198–9, 203
    kingdom of, 174–5, 179, 183–4
    see also Salonika

Thessaly, 7, 26, 179, 184
Thomas, Byzantine pretender, 206, 209, 215
Thomas the Slav, Byzantine pretender, 128–30
Thrace, Thracians, ix, xii, 4, 7, 12–13, 17, 20–1, 26, 43–4, 51–3, 57, 59, 74–5, 95, 102, 123, 175, 178, 198, 243, 245
Thrakesian theme, 127
Thrasyboulos, Athenian commander, 12, 22–3
Thrasyllos, Athenian commander, 15–17
Thucydides, historian, 14
Timur the Lame, 196–9, 212
Tomis, 69–70
Trapezus, also Trebizond, 66, 174–5, 180, 182, 196, 212, 219
Troad, 9
Troy, x, 78, 80
Tunis, 232
Turks, viii, 103–104, 148, 192
    see also Ottoman Sultanate, Seljuk Turks
Two Sicilies, 181
Tylis, Galatian kingdom, 42–8, 50, 52–3, 105

Ukraine, 4, 65–6, 100, 179, 229
Umar, caliph, 124–5
United States, 194, 245–6
Urban II, Pope, 149–50

Valens, Emperor, x, xii
Valerian, Emperor, 68
Vandals, 65
Varangian Guard, 149, 161, 164, 166, 169
Varna, battle, 204, 207, 213
Venice, Venetians, 155, 172–3, 183, 188–9, 196, 199, 203, 209, 212–13, 217, 220–1, 229
    empire of, 176, 179–81, 215
Vespasian, Emperor, 59
Via Aquillia, 55–6
Via Domitia, 56
Via Egnatia, 55–6, 64, 73, 75, 80, 92
Vikings, viii, 142–3, 149
Visigoths, 65
Vitalian, Roman officer and rebel, 95–9
Vladimir, Russian Grand Prince, 132–3
Volga Bulgars, 132
Von Blum, German engineer, 234

al-Walid, Caliph, 120
Wallachia, 195, 209, 212
Walter Sans-Avoir, 150
William II, Prince, 185
White Russians, 246

Xenophon, Athenian commander, 22

Yazid, Caliph, 116, 119
Yenicoy, 229
Yolanda, Empress, 185
York, ix, 72, 74
Young Turks, 235

Zabergan, Hun commander, 101
Zaganos Pasha, Ottoman Sultan commander, 217, 219, 221
Zara, 157–9
Zoe, Empress, 138–9
Zoroastrian religion, 110, 115
Zosimus, historian, 69